Readings on

COLLECTIVE NEGOTIATIONS IN PUBLIC EDUCATION

Readings on

COLLECTIVE NEGOTIATIONS
IN PUBLIC EDUCATION

Stanley M. Elam
Phi Delta Kappa

Myron Lieberman
Rhode Island College

Michael H. Moskow
Temple University

Rand McNally & Company, Chicago

RAND McNALLY EDUCATION SERIES

B. Othanel Smith, *Advisory Editor*

PREFACE

Full-time formal education in the United States involves over 60,000,000 students and at least as many parents. It is of concern to 100,000,000 taxpayers, for school expenditures, after national defense, take the largest share of tax revenue—some $40,000,000,000 a year if we include college and university costs. Included in these gigantic expenditures are the salaries of more than 2,200,000 teachers, administrators, and other school employees.

It is characteristic of twentieth-century United States that occupational groups organize in order to strengthen their position. Teachers have built significant organizations to protect and advance their interests only within the past forty to fifty years, and often these organizations have subordinated salary and welfare to other professional concerns. But this is no longer the case in the Sixties. In this decade teachers have grown militant. They are making themselves felt as a pressure group in an increasingly professionalized and bureaucratized society.

The emergence of collective negotiations in the Sixties is what this book is about. Basically, collective negotiations are a set of procedures by which teachers, acting through their designated representatives, and school boards codetermine the terms and conditions of employment for teachers. Obviously, such codetermination means a revision of the power relationships that have accounted for the low status of teaching during most of the nation's history. While new and as yet still in the developmental stages in education, collective negotiations, in conjunction with certain other trends, provide a significant potential for the early maturation of teaching as a full-fledged profession, attracting its full share of competent and energetic young people as a lifetime career. At least this is the opinion of the editors of this volume, who have had a major part in organizing and conducting several national and regional institutes on collective negotiations.*

Because collective negotiations in education are such a recent development, there is a great need to discuss these issues and possibilities. There is

---

* In addition, the editors have taught courses and participated in several other programs devoted to collective negotiations in public education. Each has written extensively on various aspects of the subject.

also need to analyze some views about collective negotiations that have been encouraged by its extreme supporters as well as its extreme detractors. Nevertheless, the reader will find little unanimity of opinion among the selections in this volume. He must be alert to recognize, in some selections, the bias of vested interest or limited experience. In compiling and organizing these selections, however, the editors hope to produce a more sophisticated and knowledgeable approach to the important issues involved.

Stanley M. Elam
Myron Lieberman
Michael H. Moskow

Bloomington, Indiana
June, 1967

TABLE OF CONTENTS

I

THE BACKGROUND OF
COLLECTIVE NEGOTIATIONS
IN PUBLIC EDUCATION

"Collective negotiations" refers to a process by which employers negotiate with the duly chosen representatives of their employees concerning terms and conditions of employment, and on such other matters as the parties may agree or be required to negotiate. In public education, such negotiations are typically conducted by a school board and its administrative staff as the employer, and a teacher organization which represents the professional staff. Frequently, the school administration (school board and administrative staff) will negotiate also with representatives of the noncertified school employees, such as bus drivers, custodial personnel, school secretaries, and cafeteria employees. Although negotiations between school authorities and such employees are becoming more frequent and are an important aspect of educational administration, this book is devoted primarily to negotiations with and by professional personnel in the schools.

Such negotiations are a recent phenomenon. One indication of this is the legislative history of collective negotiations in public education. In 1960, not a single state authorized or required collective negotiations between teachers and school boards. By June, 1967, such legislation had been introduced in about half the states, and had been enacted in nine. Legislation authorizing such negotiations seems certain to be enacted in several other states in the immediate future. Meanwhile, school boards, school administrators, professional organizations, institutions of higher education, and other groups and agencies are devoting increasing attention to collective negotiations.

It is true that local, state, and national organizations of teachers have existed and communicated to school administrators and boards of education for many decades. Nevertheless, collective negotiations should not be confused with earlier and less formalized procedures for determining conditions of educational employment. Under collective negotiations, a particular teacher organization is formally recognized as the exclusive negotiating representative of the teachers. Boards of education are legally obligated to negotiate with this representative, and the latter in turn must meet certain legal requirements to enjoy the benefits of board recognition. The scope of negotiations and the procedures available to resolve an impasse are usually spelled out in the statutes. In brief, collective negotiations usually constitute a legally established, but more structured and regulated, procedure for determining conditions of educational employment than the procedures prevailing in the pre-negotiations era.

The articles in this section are intended to provide a broad perspective on collective negotiations in public education. The first article, by Secretary of Labor W. Willard Wirtz, explains why collective negotiations have become an integral part of public personnel administration. Wirtz's article is especially valuable because it deals candidly with the basic issues involved in collective negotiations for public employees. Although the article makes only incidental reference to public education, it clearly suggests that collective negotiations in public education cannot be considered in isolation from the emerging trends in public personnel administration generally.

The next three articles deal with public policy aspects of collective negotiations in public education. The first article is by Dr. George W. Taylor, an authority on employment relations in private employment who has also played a key role in the development of collective negotiations in public employment, including public education. Taylor's article is an outstanding analysis of both the similarities and the dissimilarities between collective negotiations in the private and in the public sector. His article also includes some thoughtful suggestions concerning several crucial issues pertaining to collective negotiations in public education. The intrinsic merits of Taylor's suggestions plus his tremendous experience and prestige in the field make careful study of his observations a "must" for persons seeking clarification of the important problems and issues.

The article by John H. Fischer sets forth some criteria by which to evaluate the use of collective negotiations in public education. As a former large-city superintendent who is now president of an institution of higher education actively engaged in the preparation of school administrators, Fischer's views are worthy of thoughtful consideration. The article by Morton R. Godine sets forth some of the basic public policy considerations in collective negotiations by teachers and school boards. Author of a landmark study of employment relations in public employment (The Labor Problem in the Public Service, 1951), *Godine is well qualified to analyze the issues in public education from the broader perspective of public employment generally. His article is especially valuable for its realistic assessment of employee initiative in collective negotiations and for its treatment of the resort to political action in the context of collective negotiations.*

Collective negotiations involve a readjustment of the power relation-ship between various groups directly involved in education. The article by Myron Lieberman emphasizes the fact that power does affect policy-making in education, and that educational policies should be based upon a recogni-tion of this reality instead of futile efforts to ignore or evade it.

Teachers are public employees and also professionals. The article by Ronald Corwin examines some of the sociological implications of these matters and discusses how they might be reflected in collective action by teachers. The author, an assistant professor at The Ohio State University, has done extensive research into the sociological aspects of collective action by teachers. Thus, as a whole, these six articles deal with the public, the profes-sional, and the power dimensions of the collective negotiations movement in public education. In many cases, the articles have been selected because of the questions they raise rather than the answers they give.

I-1

PUBLIC EMPLOYMENT AND PUBLIC POLICY*

W. Willard Wirtz

The nation's habit, like that of most people, is to put off facing up to hard problems, even as they get worse and worse, until something or other suddenly forces them on our attention.

This was true, until very recently, of disproportionate representation in the state legislatures, of cities rotting at the core, of decreasing fresh water supplies. We are right now facing up to the cumulative catastrophe of death on the highways; but not yet to the full implications of ignorance about birth control or to the fact of mass suicide by cigarette.

It exaggerates—but not much—to put in this category the subject of government employment policy.

It comes as a shock to most people to learn that one out of every six employees in this country is today on a *public* payroll.

It comes as an even greater shock when some group among these 10-1/2 million government employees—transit workers or welfare workers in New York, city employees in Milwaukee, teachers in Utah and Michigan—suddenly decides to use its power to do what the other five out of every six employees are recognized as entitled to do as a matter of right.

What is most astonishing of all is the growing realization that these 10-1/2 million men and women are employed today on terms dictated by dogma traceable directly to the medieval doctrine of the divine right of kings, and that employment relations in most public agencies in this country are 30 years behind those in private employment.

The significance of this situation increases with the magnitude of government employment.

Ten years ago, there were 7 million public employees.

Today there are over 10 million.

By 1975, there will be about 15 million.

Specialists in the uncovering of conspiracy will conclude from these

* Remarks made by Secretary of Labor W. Willard Wirtz before the American Federation of State, County, and Municipal Employees (AFSCME) in Washington, D. C., April 27, 1966. Published by permission.

figures that a plot is afoot to subvert American democracy, that government has now become in fact the monstrous Leviathan of Hobbes' imagination, or a Gulliver among Lilliputian citizens who grow smaller and smaller by comparison.

There are, however, some very different facts behind these figures.

First, and contrary to popular impression, little of this growth in government employment has been at a federal level.

Federal employment is today only 190,000 more than it was 10 years ago—an increase of 9%. The national population increased during this same period by 17%.

Between 1960 and 1965—and despite the initiation of broad, new public programs—the number of federal workers increased only from 2,270,000 in 1960 to 2,378,000 in 1965. There are presently fewer federal employees for every 1,000 people in the country than there were five years ago. Every large occupational grouping except farm workers has increased more in the last five years than federal employees.

The truth is that a quiet revolution has taken place in American government. Public employment has continued to grow, but almost all of this growth has been at the state and local level.

Three-quarters of the public employees today are state or local employees. Their number has increased from 4.7 million ten years ago to 7.7 million now. For every one federal worker added in the past ten years, there have been 15 state and local workers added. Most of the additional 5 million employees who will be on public payrolls by 1975 will be state and local.

What these figures reflect is that people in the states and the local communities of this country are responding with vigor, and often not a little courage, to their changing needs. One out of every two state and local employees is engaged in education. The rest, with remarkably few exceptions, can measure the purpose of their endeavor favorably against the rule laid down by James Madison nearly two centuries ago. "The real welfare of the great body of the people," he said, "is the supreme object to be pursued, and no form of government whatever has any other value than as it may be fitted for the attainment of this object."

It is right, and it is inevitable, that the shifting emphasis in this society from goods to services—including services necessarily provided through public agencies—should continue.

It is right, but it will take more determination and constructive effort to assure it, that these services should be performed in increasing degree at the state and local levels.

There are forces which work today in the other direction.

It is the federal government that has taken the initiative, for example, in the war against poverty and ignorance, in the campaign to translate equal rights into equal results, in the development of new training programs, in the campaign to rebuild America's cities, to cleanse her streams, to restore natural beauty to her face.

We are rapidly approaching a critical stage in the building of the Great Society: that point at which it is determined how—and whether—the responsibility for carrying it forward can be shifted to the states and the counties and the cities.

The war against poverty was declared by President Johnson and launched by the national Congress. But that war will not be won in Washington.

Mrs. Johnson has dedicated herself to making America beautiful in fact as well as in song, and again the Congress has started the country along this course. But this can be in itself little more than holding a mirror up to America's face so that she can see the blemishes there.

New federal Departments of Housing and Urban Development and of Transportation can be only catalysts for precipitating nationwide efforts that must center in the cities themselves.

There must be developed a "creative federalism" that will implement and carry forward the present trend toward the transfer of responsibilities to the states and the local governments.

It is essential, in this connection that substantial changes be made in the public fiscal structure, for one of the hard facts today is that state and local financing resources are depleted. State and local indebtedness has increased 123% in the past ten years, while the federal debt has increased by 16%—and is in fact lower in relationship to the gross national product than it was in 1955.

It will also be imperative that local governments develop a new independence of the status quo, a new inventiveness—that pays less attention, for example, to city lines. The reapportionment of state legislatures will make them more constructive partners in this enterprise.

Nothing could be more important to the long range future of the AFSCME than the strengthening of the forces of decentralized federalism. It isn't a matter any longer of states' rights—but a matter rather of state and local preparedness to assume larger responsibilities. The fact is that *change* is more at home today in the national capital than it is in some statehouses and some city halls. This, too, must change.

The AFSCME has a more direct role to play in this future.

It is clear—in the record of this Federation and others—that ten million government employees will not accept an employment relationship built on the proposition that their employers exercise a "sovereignty" which makes it lesé majesté to file a grievance and equates disagreement—at least organized disagreement—with disloyalty.

This doctrine is wrong in theory. What's more, it won't work. Abusing the sovereignty concept this way is only the public employment equivalent of the assertion in private labor relations of "managerial prerogatives." The authority of government in a democracy comes from below, from the people who make it up, not from above. In more practical terms, any government employer tempted to assert, "I *am* the people," will invite the proper reply: "Who do you think *we* are? And there are 10 million of us."

Without attempting to go into detail, I suggest several guidelines (if you will pardon the phrase) for developing in this country a pragmatic—instead of a dogmatic—doctrine of public employment relations.

First. It should be accepted generally, and removed from controversy, that some effective form of bi-lateral and representational labor relations is inevitable, proper, and desirable in public employment in this country.

It is a mistake to think of this as exclusively a matter of employee rights. Half the case for collective bargaining is that the enterprise operates better—in the long run and the broader view—if there is constructive employee participation in its affairs.

This is a matter of institutional government. Democracy has never boasted of either its logic or its efficiency, but only of its awkward effectiveness. The answer to authoritarianism is the same in connection with governing a government agency as in governing a country.

Second. Whatever system is developed has to be worked out jointly, by representatives of all who will be affected by it.

The weakness of present public employment policy is not just that it *operates* unilaterally, but that it has been *established* unilaterally. The attempt to set up new rules unilaterally would be inevitably self-defeating.

Third. To whatever extent the development of new doctrines of public employment relationships is focussed or permitted to center around the argument about whether there is a "right of public employees to strike," the development will be at best delayed, at worst defeated.

Labor's understandable feeling is that every time it has relied very much on "a decent respect for the opinions of mankind," mankind has responded with remarkably indecent opinions. And labor's current mood is in general that it gains more from controversy than from consensus.

The fact remains that every strike by public employees creates at least as great a crisis of public opinion as it does a crisis of transportation or education or whatever else may be involved.

Fourth. The basic principle should be to provide for maximum practicable participation of public employees in developing and in administering their employment relationship. Each of the three words, "maximum practicable participation," carries a full cargo of meaning—and some trouble.

A good deal of this meaning—and some of the trouble—can be borrowed from experience in the area of private labor relations. The interests involved are substantially the same. Where there are differences which make traditional private application of the basic principles impracticable, there should be mutual recognition of the necessity, and the sufficiency, of alternative equivalents.

These four principles become meaningful only in terms of their application to particular issues:

They dictate adequate provision by agreement, executive order or statute, for organizational and representational rights for all public employees, substantially similar to those provided in the Wagner and Taft-Hartley Acts for private employees.

This includes unqualified provision for resolution by a separate agency of any disputes regarding organization and representation which may arise, and provision, too, for union security.

It is harder to be specific about the appropriate authority and responsibility of the public employees' union in setting the basic terms of the employment relationship. This necessarily depends, as a practical matter, on the nature and the sufficiency of the legislative processes that are provided.

Wages and other money issues present the greatest difficulty. It is pointless to disregard the fact that in the usual situation the government employer, in a practical sense, is part of the executive department and that the money involved must come through another—and proudly "separate"—power within the government. But this is no legitimate excuse for the government's avoiding its responsibilities as an employer.

It is an essential element of a public employment policy that there be some table, some place, whether in the executive or legislative or some independent office, where employee representatives can sit across the table from somebody with the authority and the courage to say "I will" or "I won't" instead of "I can't."

The concept of establishing "comparability" of government wages and salaries with those paid privately in similar occupations has become an important and I think comparatively satisfactory principle of *federal* practice. Experience is showing the value of using special boards and independent committees in the administration and application of the comparability principle.

The "right to strike" question arises inevitably here.

Any answer to this question which is cast in terms of absolutes—and as though this is even a legitimate question standing alone—seems to me wrong.

The Condon-Wadlin Act is a glaring illustration of the unfairness, the absurdity, and the ineffectiveness of outlawing the strike without any provision whatsoever for alternative procedures settling the honest and legitimate issues which might cause a strike. The recent report of the New York Governor's Committee on Public Employee Relations, under the chairmanship of George W. Taylor, reflects a constructive approach to this problem.

I disagree, if it is a separate proposition, with the Federation's endorsement of the public employee's right to strike. Your support of voluntary arbitration means, however, that you face squarely and constructively the essential question of alternative procedures.

The occasional attempt to distinguish between governmental functions in terms of their "essentiality" is fruitless. Policemen and firemen are no more essential than school teachers; it is only that the costs and losses from doing without the police and fire departments are more dramatic and immediate. *Every* government function is essential in the broadest sense, or the government shouldn't be doing it. In almost every instance, the government is the only supplier of the service involved—and there is serious question about the legitimacy of any strike which deprives the public of something it needs and can't get from somebody else.

I come to the conclusion, accordingly, that the sound doctrine of public employment relations is one that assures a reasonable and fair procedure—with independent third party determination if necessary—for settling new contract disputes, and which therefore does not include the strike.

Finally, there is the question of participation by the public employees union in the *administration* of the employment relationship, with the handling of grievances as an example.

In my view of it, there should be such participation to at least as full an extent as has developed under private collective bargaining, including full provision for independent arbitration of unresolved differences regarding the application of the employment rules—whether they are the product of bargaining or of legislation.

Public employees have at least as much to offer in this process as do private employees, perhaps in some cases more.

Public employers, furthermore—many of whom are selected for other reasons than their proven or even promised managerial ability—have at least as much need of the restraint and assistance this process provides as do private employers, perhaps in some cases more.

In general, and in conclusion, I urge and predict the development of a doctrine of public employment relationships based on the strength of good sense instead of the sentimentality of "sovereignty."

It was not true that kings could do no wrong. They were not, as Mr. Justice Jackson almost said of the Supreme Court, final because they were infallible; they were deemed infallible only because they were final. This is equally true of their lineal managerial descendants—except that the assumption of infallibility was repealed and the need for finality rejected in the Magna Charta and in the Declaration of Independence.

Democracy is as sound a principle for employment as it is for government.

I-2

THE PUBLIC INTEREST IN COLLECTIVE NEGOTIATIONS IN EDUCATION*

George W. Taylor

For reasons not fully comprehended, I have frequently been called upon to be a "so-called public representative." The modifier—"so-called"—connotes a doubt, which I share, about the capacity of any individual to enunciate those interests and needs considered to be most imperative by the public in our free society. Diversity of views and of objectives are the hallmarks of this society. Spokesmen for "labor" and "management" interests, in both private and public sectors, also have some obligations to admit a similar difficulty in expressing the "views" of their free-thinking constituencies. We are not cast from a common mold.

The misgivings just confessed were intensified, earlier this year, during investigations undertaken in New York by "The Governor's Commission on Public Employee Relations." We were told about the mayor of a small municipality who adamantly refused to include, in a tight budget, provision for funds to purchase a certain snorkel for the Fire Department. This is a water tower designed to douse blazes atop a ten-story building. The tallest building in town was five stories high. Nevertheless, purchase of the snorkel was overwhelmingly approved by the voters in a referendum. We were told that parading this piece of equipment in the annual contest with other localities would virtually assure first prize for "our Fire Department." The same voters would doubtless be reluctant to approve a bond issue for improved school facilities. On second thought, such preferences should not really surprise one. As individuals, most of us, at one time or another, have provided for snorkels in our own tight personal budgets.

Divergent expressions of public interest obtain in the field of education. They are fashioned by the mores of each locality, and by each state, because

* A paper delivered on June 22, 1966 at the National Institute on Collective Negotiations in Public Education cosponsored by Phi Delta Kappa and the University of Pennsylvania, Philadelphia, Pennsylvania. A slightly different version was published in the Phi Delta Kappan, September, 1966, pp. 16-22. George W. Taylor is Harnwell Professor of Industry at the Wharton School of Finance and Commerce, University of Pennsylvania.

of the high degree of local control which exists. The "traditional wisdom" has been (1) that broad policies are made by local school boards composed of laymen who serve, often at great sacrifice and with great devotion, but who sometimes conceive their major functions to be guarding the public purse strings and preserving local autonomy; (2) that carrying out the board policies is the limited function of the professional school administrators; (3) that to a considerable extent, teachers follow instruction from above in their teaching even though their professional calling requires a high degree of intelligence and a questioning mind.

This pattern of relationship between the board and the administrators has been commonly breached. The school teachers, however, have long continued to be voiceless outside the classroom. This has emerged as an acute deficiency in recent years especially in the growing and changing urban centers. A centralization of administrative control has resulted in more government by mimeograph, in a diminution of the opportunity for teachers to participate in policy-making, and obstacles in the way of having their grievances heard. Teacher frustrations have been compounded by salaries which have been out-of-line with others—"below the earnings of truck drivers." So, the teachers are organizing themselves and the structure of the educational system gets more complex. The conflicts of interests and of functions within the system are, to say the least, quite confusing to the public.

The need for better arrangements between these several levels of educational responsibility is evident. How can the public, always sold on education in principle, be confident or satisfied with a troika management at odds within itself? For a decade or more, it has been told by one authority after another that deficiencies in educational programs and practices are imperiling the national safety and the attainment of national goals. There is a sensing of, if not familiarity with, the dictum of H. G. Wells that "human history is a race between education and catastrophe."

With this background, it doesn't suffice simply to say to the public— "give us the money and we will do our job." There is too much skepticism about the efficacy of current performance and about the capacity of the educators successfully to meet their confrontation with history. New programs by the educators and the approval of greatly increased funds by the public have to be developed simultaneously. But, what kind of programs? The greatest concern of the public about collective negotiations in education is not simply about whether teachers are entitled to "a better break" (having just read *Up the Down Staircase,* I believe they are), but whether the process will improve or decrease the chances of developing an educational program adapted to the needs of a changing world.

Various sectors of the "publics" have no hesitancy in letting school boards and school administrators know about their concerns. A recent report, made under the auspices of the Institute for Development of Educational Activities (financed by the Charles F. Kettering Foundation), concludes that the public is "far ahead of present-day educators" in a willingness to accept innovations in schools. In the public view, teaching machines and programmed textbooks should be used for "fact learning" and teachers should focus upon training students in how to think and to analyze situations. Technological change and increased productivity have become a part of today's life. The close relationship between extensive housing and welfare programs on the one hand and educational programs on the other is often better perceived by the public than by the educators. Indeed, the most burning current educational issue in many large urban areas concerns the extent to which the schools should now assist racial integration to further an equality of educational opportunities even at the risk of an impairment of total teaching effectiveness for the present. It might be added—even if that entails the loss of certain seniority rights of teachers to reject assignments at the so-called difficult schools. What constitutes the most urgent public interests can be highly controversial. It is often closely related to political factors. This is even the case as respects issues over more narrow interests, as when the citizens rally to fire the hapless coach whose team finished last in Little League Baseball or to protest about the corners designated for school bus stops.

The traditional organizational structure, i.e., the board-administrator-teacher relationship, has become increasingly ill-adapted to meet the public interests, diverse and conflicting, and the public has failed to respond to the simple argument that "nothing is wrong that more money won't cure."

The institution of collective negotiations is widely viewed as good for the teachers but as making the present educational service more costly to the public. Extensive changes in the relationships between school board, administration, and teachers is a concomitant, as well as changes in the relationship between these educational agencies and the public, but whether or not this improves the quality of education remains to be seen. After all, the primary function of any employee organization is to improve the well-being of its membership and to enhance their established rights. Nowadays this involves a minimization of the impact of change upon incumbents. Whether or not the effective performance of that useful—indeed necessary—function of employee organizations can be reconciled with the public demand for extensive improvements in the quality of education and in the productivity of educators is a momentous question. Even granting that satisfied teachers are an essential requirement for quality teaching, there are limitations to the proposition that what is good for the teachers is good for the students and, hence, for the public.

The diverse examples of the public interest in education noted at the outset of this paper have significant connotations for this present discussion. There are conflicts of interest between the public and the producers of goods and services in the public sector as well as the private sector. In our kind of a democratic society, the public interest is conserved by a latitude of consumer choice. This system is not without its costs. It can beget the production of bubble-gum and confetti in the private sector and the choice of snorkels in the public sector. But, by and large, freedom is worth far more than it costs.

The potency of the consumer power of choice has long been recognized, as well by employee organizations as by management representatives, in the private enterprise sectors. The extent to which consumers are voluntarily willing to buy a product and to pay a price under competitive conditions ultimately determines the job opportunities open to employees and the profits available to management. These are built-in restraints to serve the public interest. There is a somewhat different kind of competition between the agencies which provide essential governmental services. Each particular agency of government is convinced that priority should be given to its needs. Each agency typically seeks a relatively large share of the public funds, even at the cost of curtailment of other services. The public funds are limited despite a public acceptance of a higher tax rate than exists in most countries of the world. It is heady to contemplate what could be done with those taxes if their allocation for military activities could be significantly decreased.

Even so, I happen to hold the conviction that, in many states and cities (Pennsylvania and Philadelphia for example), the funds allocated for public education are woefully inadequate. I would even be willing to pay higher taxes for school purposes. My conviction, unfortunately, is not held by a sufficient number of fellow citizens who evidently assign priority to other needs, such as a new sports stadium, while being averse to further tax increases. My right and obligation is to work through the established democratic channels for a change in public sentiment. Union officials are pretty much in the same position when the membership demands a program that seems ill-advised to the leadership. They work within the framework of their democratic organization to change the sentiment.

In a democratic society, consumer choice as respects governmental services is ultimately exercised, not in the market place, but in the legislative authorization of laws to be passed, taxes to be levied, in budget expenditures to be made, and in loans to be floated. This is the final arbitrament of conflicts of public interests. The power of the consumer of government services is most clearly evident in those political jurisdictions where administrative budgets must be validated in town meetings. It is still very much present, though not so obvious, when the responsibility rests with legislative and executive officials who are usually quite desirous of being re-elected and fully aware that they might be dis-elected.

In short, the restraints of the market place and the restraints of the polling place are counted upon, in our kind of a society, to require the accommodation of particular interests to the interests and overall needs considered most imperative by the general public. It is in this competition between services that collective negotiations in the educational field, of necessity, must be developed in our kind of a political democracy. Lest you jump to the conclusion that I am naive about what goes on in the world, let me express an awareness of shortcomings in both restraints in making narrow and self-serving interests subordinate to the general welfare. However, the quest for government of, by and for the people cannot be abandoned without conceding defeat for the ideals which sustain us.

The ideas of the public and those of the school teachers are, more often than not, quite different about what constitutes equitable and viable terms of employment. School teachers have sometimes resorted to drastic means to get the public to change its collective mind. The teachers involved doubtless believed they were provoked beyond endurance. An example was the recent walkout of teachers in Louisville, Kentucky, when, for the fourth time in nine years, the voters rejected a school tax amendment which was necessary to provide salary increases. One could appraise this strike action, I suppose, a step for re-educating the public—as an example in adult education—or as the effective communication of a deep sense of grievance. The effectiveness of political democracy could be seriously impaired, however, if this kind of communication to the voters were generally followed by each group of public employees who believed that their wages were grossly inequitable. I am convinced that a far more effective system of communication to the public of its employees' needs can be devised and without risking an impairment of the processes of political democracy.

A possible approach was enunciated by a Commission on Collective Bargaining appointed by the New York City Board of Education in 1961. Following a short strike of New York school teachers, the Board of Education agreed to accept the "principle of collective bargaining." What did that mean? During Commission hearings, held to answer the question, representatives of more than ninety teacher organizations testified. The evidence was largely confined to the particular grievances and complaints of subgroups of teachers. The so-called unit of representation problem emerged as a formidable one. But, this is not the matter to which attention should now be directed. Invariably, each witness quizzically inquired: "Just how does this process called collective bargaining work in education? What is it?" In partial response, the Commission reported: "In respect of certain subjects,

the Board may make final decisions; as to others, particularly those calling
for the appropriation of public funds, its powers are limited since it can only
make recommendations of the total amount necessary for budgetary purposes. The Board and the employees' representatives can agree, nevertheless,
upon recommendations to the fund-providing agencies which both would be
obligated to support. There would thus be a combined judgment by those
directly responsible for the educational program of the funds needed for
them to discharge their responsibilities." If a combined judgment could
not be arrived at, the differences could be evaluated by one of those impartial boards to which resort is being increasingly provided, and its recommendations could be submitted to those who levy taxes and construct budgets.

I am sure in my own mind that the public would more likely be convinced of the need for greater budgetary allocations for educational programs by this kind of communication than by what is construed as coercion.

It seems obvious and elementary that the allocation of public funds for
education should be an integral part of the overall taxing and budgetary
decisions made by executive and legislative agencies. The complications of
not doing so seemed to me to be starkly apparent during the mediation sessions preceding consummation of the current two-year agreement between
the American Federation of Teachers and the New York City Board of
Education. These negotiations were carried out skillfully and with a keen
appreciation of rights and responsibilities on both sides of the table. The
terms of the agreement were, in my opinion, not only equitable to the school
teachers, but, in many ways, also improved the quality of the educational
process. There was, however, a lack of coordination with the budget-making
processes of the City. Negotiations for conditions of employment to be effective during the first year of the agreement were undertaken after the school
budget for that year had been approved. Allocations for various other necessary educational expenditures had already necessarily been made by the
Board. Only a residual share was left to provide for the teachers' needs. Collective negotiations cannot be carried out under such a limitation. Nor did
the residual share suffice to meet the minimum demands of the teachers'
organization. Additional funds had to be found somewhere or somehow and
their availability constituted a limitation on the negotiators. In marked contrast, the provision for teacher needs for the second year of the agreement
had to be specified without any assurance of what funds would subsequently
be made available by legislative agencies for the operation of the school
system as a whole. As one Board member expressed it: "We are mortgaging
our future." It could be argued that the Board had assumed a responsibility
for getting a bigger appropriation next year, but a failure to do so could
result in a contraction of services also essential to improved quality of
education.

A reconciliation between the needs of school teachers and other provisions for the improvement of the educational process as a whole is not possible if the amounts expendable in the school teachers' interests are computed either as a residual share after all other expenditures have been made or as a prior claim on a future unknown total budget. Avoidance of either situation, which can arise in negotiations with public employees generally, was an objective of recommendations made in the recently issued Report of the Governor's Commission on Public Employee Relations (New York). It was recommended that collective negotiations in governmental agencies be conducted prior to overall budgetary action by the legislative body. That body would then have before it a joint recommendation arrived at in collective negotiations or the recommendations of an impartial fact-finding board. The public interest will thereby be served by enabling the legislative body to carry out its governmental functions in an orderly manner.

This approach is predicated upon the assumption that just as collective bargaining in the private sector is subject to the restraints of the market place, so should collective negotiations in the governmental sector be developed under the restraints of political democracy and its governmental processes. The objective of collective negotiations is not to provide employees with the power "to write their own ticket" but to provide for their effective participation—and I emphasize effective—in the establishment of their terms and conditions of employment. Collective negotiations involve a concomitant obligation of employee organizations to accommodate the particular interests of their membership to the needs of society as a whole.

The adjustment to collective negotiations is a formidable undertaking for legislators, boards of education, school administrators, and teacher organizations. Together they have to invent the future. I am convinced that the task must be undertaken. Public interests have not been served by withholding from school teachers those employee rights of participation which have been accorded as a matter of law in the private sector. Inspired teaching and professional dedication is not compatible with government by mimeograph or with moonlighting as a way of life for teachers. The constructive contributions which teachers can make, on the basis of actual classroom experience, have not been adequately mobilized in the formulation of educational programs. There is a need for change in a system which, to a marked degree, measures teacher performances in terms of obedience, respect for authority, and adherence to bureaucratic rules and regulations as much as, or more than, in terms of intellectual achievement and a desire to experiment.

No longer should energies be dissipated in heated arguments about whether or not school teachers should be entitled to representatives of their own choosing. The dialogue on this point has been concluded. It should now progress to a consideration of these currently important questions: How can school teachers, as public employees, effectively participate in the establishment of their terms and conditions of employment so as to insure their equitable treatment? By what means can school teachers best contribute to improvement of the educational process? Some consideration has already been given to the first question. The second question also has perplexing aspects. It involves changes in the exercise of authority by the board and by school administrators and is complicated by the diversity of interests among the school teachers included within an "appropriate unit of representation."

In many states and cities, a considerable latitude is possessed by the board of education and administrative officers in allocating an approved school budget among a myriad of educational uses most of which require prompt and massive attention if public expectations are to be realized. The teacher organization is very much on the scene to protect the teacher interests and well-being. It will be aware of other pressing needs but the question of priorities in the allocation of limited funds can emerge as a conflict of major proportion. The low priority given to teachers' conditions when the allocation has been by unilateral decision of the administration is a major cause of teacher demand for collective negotiations. The high priority given to the improvement of the teachers' lot under collective negotiations can impede the provision for other needs.

The objective of collective negotiations is an agreement between representatives of employees and those charged with managerial responsibilities. It goes beyond giving teachers the mere opportunity to be heard or to be consulted. Collective negotiations limit the long-held latitude of school administrators to make unilateral decisions respecting the conditions under which school teachers carry out their vital functions. This prospect accounts for much of the resistance of school administrators to collective negotiations. The drive is for the making of administrative decisions within limits set by negotiated agreements. This means a drastic change in the way superintendents and principals have run things and this is what most employee organizations want. I once asked a teacher of long experience and outstanding reputation why she was such a staunch advocate of the teachers' union. Her reply was that during a strike of teachers, with arms waving, the school principal shouted accusingly at the pickets: "What are you doing to my school?" She added: "It isn't his school, you know."

From collective bargaining in the private sector, much can be learned about the importance of what is called the scope of bargaining, i.e., the necessary differentiation between those subjects which can and should be co-determined in negotiations and those subjects which should remain subject to unilateral determination by the management if it is to perform its essential functions. Some of the most critical labor-management conflicts have arisen over the making of this differentiation. Many of the conflicts were unnecessary. They were created by a managerial fear of any diminution at all in an all-inclusive managerial prerogative. The camels-nose-in-the-tent theory was espoused even when it became evident that outright authoritarianism caused such a loss of employee morale as to impair efficient performance. Even this seems preferable to some administrators to taking on an administrative partner, and not a silent one either but a striving one. Other avoidable crises in this area were created by drives of labor organizations for the right to participate in the making of decisions which, under existing circumstances, would greatly impair performance of the managerial function. These are classic examples of the dire consequences to all which have followed a taking over by the union of essential managerial functions. Collective negotiations are fashioned by the kind of restraint practiced by administrators and employee representatives in the exercise of their power in the joint relationship.

In this connection, the public either senses or is acutely aware of the fact that the primary function of an employee organization in collective negotiations is to enhance the status and well-being of its own membership. And, that membership can be extremely demanding in the performance expected of its representatives who, like legislators, can be dis-elected. The public, nevertheless, holds the view that an employee union should be operated in a democratic manner, i.e., it should be responsible to the membership. An agreement is not fully consummated until the employees themselves validate it.

The nature of the conflict of interests in this area is quite different in the public sector as compared with the private sector. In collective bargaining, company representatives are not under the constraints of securing specific approval of agreement terms from a higher authority. The agreement is directly between a politically oriented union (i.e., responsible directly to the membership) and company representatives with final authority. In the public sector, negotiations are between two political entities. Each party looks to a higher authority, the people represented, for a validation of its decisions by majority rule. Indeed, the governmental employing agency is bound to conform to such terms of employment as are mandated by the legislative bodies and may have to secure legislative approval for other terms to which it has agreed in collective negotiations. Negotiators for employee unions and employing agencies in the public service are thus subject to somewhat similar inhibitions. Legislative latitude can be delegated, in whole or in part, to a subordinate employing agency as in the case of the so-called authorities. Some school districts have been given independent taxing authority, although to a limited degree. Certain governmental agencies have been accorded the right to fix wages of skilled employees by use of the prevailing wage criterion. But, by and large, control of public employment lies with legislative bodies. It would be useful to study whether or not the present school relationship should be modified both as respects mandated items and the degree of latitude assigned to school boards by legislative bodies.

School boards and school administrators, then, are essentially held responsible by the public for expending funds made available to them for varied purposes—to build up run-down buildings, to create new physical facilities, to provide pre-kindergarten instruction and classes for those with exceptional ability, to help achieve equal educational opportunities irrespective of color. They have to save the dropouts and prepare an ever-growing number of students for college. Their problem is how to perform these functions demanded by the public while at the same time coming to terms with strong employee organizations committed essentially to the enhancement of teacher interests. The dilemma is sharp in the joint determination of conditions such as class size, contact hours with students, assignment to special classes and to difficult schools, unassigned hours and a host of other similar matters. A unilateral determination of these matters by the administration has not worked out but it does not follow that the well-being of the teachers should be the sole criterion for decision. Some of the most difficult problems of collective negotiations which affect the public interest in quality education are certain to be encountered in this area. In my opinion, the public interest requires the administrative agencies and employee organizations to be ready to utilize the services of outside fact-finding commissions to make recommendations when an impasse occurs between school agencies responsible for educational standards and teacher organizations responsible for enhancing the rights of the teachers. The public is entitled to an informed but outside judgment in such cases because this is public business. I would anticipate that the fact-finding board will be a far more common adjunct to collective negotiations in the public sector than it has been in collective bargaining in the private sector.

References have already been made to conflicts of interest in the legislative allocation of tax dollars to education and other essential governmental services as well as to the conflicts which arise in consequence of the differences in function of the managers of school systems and teachers' organizations. There is a third area of conflict of interests, i.e., within the ranks of the teachers themselves. The most obvious of these conflicts is in the role of teacher organization. On one hand is the thrust of the National Education Association to improve the state-mandated provisions of employment for the benefit of all school teachers in the state jurisdiction. On the other hand is the objective of the teachers' unions, which emphasizes the improvement of conditions for teachers under the jurisdiction of a particular school board. To be sure, the distinction is blurred more and more as teacher organization proceeds. The interests of the school teachers are related to both types of activities.

More fundamental conflicts of interest are related to the determination of school teacher status by reference to such criteria as length of service, college courses taken in education, and higher academic degrees acquired. Acceptable means have yet to be discovered for measuring differences in teacher performance or for taking "productivity factors" into account. Furthermore, identical terms of employment are usually specified for teachers whose preparation and abilities vary greatly—for example, to those who teach physics and to those who teach automobile driving. Perhaps these and related administrative practices have resulted from the long-established emphasis in teacher training in the colleges upon the methods of instruction rather than the mastery of subject matter. All of us are familiar with this conflict of views. A more immediate problem involving the public interest lies in the difficulty of securing a sufficient number of qualified teachers in emerging areas of great importance such as mathematics and physics. Should the entire salary level be increased to meet particular problems of recruitment? The established concepts of salary structure and administration obviously should be, at least, carefully examined to test their adequacy as a basis for improving the quality of education upon which improved educational results can be achieved. In doing so, there can be no failure to face the fact that many teachers have earned vested rights in a long-established system to which they have conformed. Would any change of the rules in the middle of the game be inequitable to them? They understandably expect their interests to be conserved in collective negotiations.

The point is that, in collective negotiations, the teachers' organization represents not only the common interests of all teachers but also a large number of particular interests, sometimes conflicting, among teachers. Intraunion mediation is a most exacting function of labor leaders in the private sector of the economy—both in resolving conflicts of interest within the membership and in gaining acceptance of priorities among common goals. All the demands of a membership can seldom if ever be fully satisfied. Exclusive representational rights have long been accorded to unions in the private sector as essential to the performance of these mediation functions.

There are, thus, many problems to be overcome in effectuating ways and means for providing participation rights to school teachers with due regard to the public interest. Assertion by school teachers of the right to strike, in my opinion, not only interferes with the fashioning of effective procedures but is viewed by the public as an infringement upon its fundamental interests. There is even a growing public intolerance of strikes in the private sector when the burden of stoppages is greater for third parties than it is for the participants. The public costs incident to a transit shut-down. are not dependent upon whether the system is publicly owned or privately owned. With growing intensity, there is a public demand for restrictions— beyond those specified in the Taft-Hartley Act—for limitations upon the generally accorded right to strike in the private sector. The question of strikes of public employees arises in an altogether different context—whether the right to strike should be extended to a management-employee relationship where it has always been withheld. In the United States the right of public employees to strike has never been authorized legislatively in any political jurisdiction. In many jurisdictions, including the federal government, the strike of public employees has been specifically declared to be illegal. Wherever strikes of public employees have occurred, they have been held by the courts to be enjoinable under the common law. There are some who question the desirability of these long-established policies. In our kind of a political democracy the way is open for people to seek a change in this present state of affairs through legislative enactment.

To be sure, this course of action is not a promising one for those who would have the strike approved as a part of collective negotiations. Yet, their protests have had far-reaching results. Belatedly the public has come to realize that a ban on strikes by public employees is not viable in the absence of alternate and effective procedures, other than the strike, to assure equitable treatment of employees. Regretfully, I conclude that this realization has come about mainly because of work stoppages and the threat of them. There is, moreover, unfortunate evidence that some governmental administrators tend, consciously or not, to rely upon the ban on strikes as a license for the arbitrary exercise of prerogatives and as immunity against their failures to negotiate in good faith with employees. The public onus for strikes in the governmental area should not always be limited to the employee organizations involved.

There are responsible union leaders who, fully cognizant of the differences between employee relations in the private and public sectors, nevertheless oppose an outright ban on strikes by public employees lest governmental administrators be in a position to deprive employees of their elementary participation rights. An outright ban on strikes, accompanied by penalties, would, they reason, interfere with the effective development of collective negotiations. They argue that the public interest in avoiding strikes by governmental employees will best be served by the creation of peaceful means for the settlement of differences but without a specific legislative ban on strikes. It is natural that they are not too concerned about the possibility of a wide swing of the balance of power in the opposite direction.

I suggest that a distinction should be drawn between work stoppages as an expression of civil protest against patently unfair treatment and their adoption as a regular way of life. The need for substitute means for settling differences has at long last been recognized. Their constructive development should, at least, be the next step for concentrated attention. Here is the necessary accompaniment of the no-strike policy which, for reasons expressed earlier, is needed to preserve the form of representative, democratic government upon which the basic liberties of all of us are dependent.

John Donne philosophized, many years ago, that "no man is an island." The idea can be extended in this century to the proposition that, in our closely inter-dependent society, no one special interest organization is an island or the center of a solar system. Ours is a meeting-of-minds society grounded upon the conviction that, after a negotiating confrontation, opposing interests can and will be accommodated by agreement. The future of our way of life largely is dependent, I believe, upon the institutional forms which are created to channel conflict, to make a confrontation of opposing interests possible, and to facilitate the reconciliation of those interests by agreement. In these terms, the current demand by public school teachers for more effective participation is in the established American tradition. There needs to be a better understanding all around about the many conflicts of interest, long existent but now sharply highlighted, which have to be channeled and reconciled in the operation of our school systems.

It has been my intention in this paper to phrase some of the questions involved and to suggest some of the criteria for possible use in dealing with them. If this paper is helpful in any way to persons who have the direct responsibility for achieving excellence in education, it will have served its purpose.

I-3

A FRAMEWORK FOR LOOKING AT
COLLECTIVE NEGOTIATIONS IN EDUCATION*

John H. Fischer

The problems that have beset public school systems in recent years are exceedingly complicated. They are neither attributable to a simple cause nor curable by a single solution. Yet the responses to all of the difficulties are inhibited and frustrated by a common condition that is widely recognized: The present forms of control and administration in public education are antiquated and obsolete. Within school systems new relationships have come about but the patterns by which they are maintained and managed are in need of careful study and, in many cases, fundamental change. The changes must be designed, however, neither to protect the status quo nor to advance partisan interests, but with the clear and unequivocal purpose of improving educational institutions and services.

To serve their purposes effectively, the relationships within and surrounding the educational establishment must be consistent with the special requirements that are imposed by the public interest, by the nature of the rights and duties of professionals, and by the particular character of the educational enterprise itself. Practices transferred from another field are likely to prove useful in schools and school systems about to the degree that the purposes and procedures of that field are similar to those of public education.

As a basis for my own approach to the problems of board-administrator-teacher relationships, I find it helpful to assert several basic premises. One is that the public school system, if it is not absolutely necessary to the achievement of universal education in our society, is by all odds the best mechanism we have yet conceived for the purpose. A second premise is that while in the operation of the schools the competence of professionals is essential, the control of policy must ultimately rest not in professional

* Summary of talk delivered on July 5, 1965 at the opening session of the National Institute on Collective Negotiations in Public Education cosponsored by Phi Delta Kappa and Rhode Island College, Providence, R.I. John H. Fischer is President, Teachers College, Columbia University.

hands but with the representatives of the public who are designated to act for the public. A third is that the professional who voluntarily serves in the schools accepts as a condition of his employment the obligation to help maintain and improve the institution in which he serves. A corresponding obligation to solicit, respect and use those contributions should likewise be honored by the employer.

In regard to all professional employees, three peculiar characteristics of a profession should be recognized by all concerned with the work of the school. One is that every practitioner is personally responsible for the quality of his own judgment and his performance as a professional and for the consequences of his own acts. The second is that no group can expect to enjoy the full status of a profession unless it is willing and able to establish and enforce standards of competence among its members. The third characteristic is the obligation of the profession, collectively and as individuals, to serve the public interest and promote the welfare of its clients.

Although the ultimate test of a school is the quality and effectiveness of the relationship between the individual teacher and the individual student, the right of teachers and other staff members to organize, to be respected in their organizations, to present their views, and to participate appropriately in the determination of policy must be recognized.

From these assumptions, views concerning the operation of employee organizations in education may be projected. If such a group is to share officially in influencing the work of the schools it should, as a condition of its participation, also share the responsibility for the quality of that work. This means deliberate effort in support of three basic tasks in which every good school is constantly involved: carrying to the highest possible level the development and learning of every student; strengthening in every feasible way the intellectual, social, and cultural well-being of the community as a whole; and equalizing educational opportunity and access to it.

Employee organizations do not carry these responsibilities alone. They must be accepted equally by those who act for the public in setting and administering policy. These groups must see that the coverage of the schools is inclusive, that their programs are relevant to the public interest and the requirements of the modern world, and that their procedures are effective in accomplishing their purposes.

The school board must see that staff selection is based on the capability of each person to perform his duties, to accept responsibility for performing them, and to share in the advancement of the institution and its program. They must see that each staff member is furnished with the physical facilities, the working conditions, and the assistants necessary to enable him to perform at his highest level. Working schedules should be set in realistic terms to permit staff members to perform at their best levels, and each person's compensation should reflect both his general professional status and the proficiency with which he performs his duties. Each staff member should have a voice in determining the conditions under which he works and should be given the safeguards necessary to protect his freedom and integrity as a professional worker.

Any system of relationships between boards, administrators, and staffs should be appraised in terms of criteria that reflect the nature of the educational enterprise itself as well as the proper concerns of the staff members. One possible group of such criteria might be set down as follows:
The pattern of relationships should

1. Advance the achievement of the purposes of public education.

2. Respect, as a matter of first priority, the interests of the pupils and the public.

3. Protect the freedom and respect the integrity of the individual staff member.

4. Provide systematically for the presentation of the judgment of teachers, individually and collectively, on matters of policy and practice, including questions of educational program as well as working conditions and compensation.

5. Provide for the systematic and equitable resolution of differences and the attainment of agreements.

6. Be based upon explicit understandings and agreements between the staff and the board as to their respective prerogatives and responsibilities.

I-4

COLLECTIVE NEGOTIATIONS AND PUBLIC POLICY, WITH SPECIAL REFERENCE TO PUBLIC EDUCATION*

Morton R. Godine

My credentials are somewhat tarnished since I wrote *The Labor Problem in the Public Service*. A teacher turned businessman and politician is hardly a description of an informed and objective participant who could be expected to contribute too much to this seminar. Perhaps I was invited to play a sort of reactionary relief role as a foil to your more progressive deliberations.

As a teacher I became interested in the public labor force—federal, state, local, white-collar, blue-collar, uniformed. It seemed paradoxical at that time—the late 1930's—that the New Deal which first brought an enlightened labor relations policy to the United States should have been so strangely myopic insofar as government workers were concerned. The new industrial democracy which transformed our private economy in so revolutionary a fashion found no parallel in the public bureaucracy. There were few voices in the liberal movement even aware of this paradox and none raised to remedy the manifest inequity. The government worker was forgotten and his interests were left to the ineffectual care of social clubs, or welfare groups, or to powerful lobbies seeking employee benefits through political pressures upon legislative bodies, but rarely if ever through collective negotiation. At the other end of the spectrum, or perhaps within the void always created in such situations, the irresponsible opportunists of the extreme left sought to exploit restive dissatisfaction from 1940 onward, albeit without too much success. Until recently there could be discerned only the glimmering of genuine efforts to achieve collective negotiations with public employers. The field accordingly seemed an inviting area to explore as a doctoral dissertation. One might even make a modest but real "contribution to knowledge," which is the formal if euphemistic designation of these

* A paper delivered on July 7, 1965 at the National Institute on Collective Negotiations in Public Education, cosponsored by Phi Delta Kappa and Rhode Island College, Providence, R.I. Morton R. Godine is Vice-President, Market Forge Company, Everett, Massachusetts.

lonely and arduous academic efforts. To my gratification the work was published and there were enough interested people to buy the first edition. There was not a second.

The role of the public administrator with respect to teachers parallels his responsibilities to all public employees. Government authorities throughout the United States have not yet accepted, as a matter of intellectual conviction or administrative desirability, the need for a vast extension of various forms of collective negotiations in the public work force. It is important to realize that participants in this impressive seminar do not reflect prevalent American thinking. The current attitude in the United States as regards associational effort of the public work force has hardly changed in the past generation. It is a rather democratically primitive viewpoint comparable to that of private employers prior to the passage of the first National Labor Relations Act. Moreover, these widely held beliefs are reinforced with several outmoded but still deeply felt convictions that the so-called sovereignty of public jurisdictions inherently precludes the possibility of effective negotiation with employees and by a traditional and uncritical acceptance of a widespread legislative pattern which rarely imposes an obligation upon officials to negotiate in good faith with employee representatives. Nor are administrators acting in less than good faith from a normal operational point of view when they invoke such legal obstacles. Municipal authorities are bound in most areas by laws which they do not make and which are not easily altered. It is neither the responsibility nor the practice of a municipality to alter laws unless its own interest is involved. In the normal course of municipal government the widest variety of questions arises, questions which are resolved in terms of the limits of its legal competence. Indeed, the principal function of the legal counsel of local governmental units is to define the scope of proper authority in terms of relevant statutes and regulations.

In the everyday course of municipal administration, an advisory opinion of legal counsel to the effect that a particular course of action is illegal or even of questionable legality is enough to conclude the issue insofar as action is concerned. Administration, public and private, inherently reflects a considerably lethargic attitude toward fundamental change in basic modes of conduct and procedure. Authorities will rarely make a real leap forward, especially in controversial areas that are not of direct concern or of readily discernible benefit to the jurisdiction. Such action as is forthcoming usually involves the distressingly slow legislative process with its attendant political compromises as well as the prior need for extensive educational efforts. Municipalities will not accordingly assume the initiative in furthering the techniques of collective negotiation. The present confused condition of the law and administrative procedures relating to employee organizations will only be amended, for better or worse, as a result of organized employee effort. It will not be sought by municipal authorities. They will remain quite content to leave things as they are. No union was ever called into being by the unilateral action of an employer unless it was a company union. The enactment of necessary legislation, permissive or mandatory, must be sought by public employees.

This area is of common interest to all public employees. Similar if not identical legislation would essentially cover the entire government work force, with the possible exception of police and firemen. It should be sought in concert with and not separately from the efforts of other employee groups, although such collaborative action does not preclude the separate organization of teacher and other employee groups. Public administrators may oppose such legislation as a political matter. It is doubtful if their opposition would reflect a major issue of principle. The substance of collective negotiation exists de facto in too many jurisdictions. The form is that which is most commonly lacking. Responsible organized employee activity should be able to gain such formal recognition if their programs are well-conceived and adequately presented for enactment or implementation.

The present status of collective bargaining in the public services is generally permissive. Employers may but are not obliged to negotiate or even discuss working conditions. Collective bargaining historically has never matured in an atmosphere of such permissiveness. In an unorganized work environment or in one of voluntary associational effort, the strong employer will prevail over the weaker individual or loosely organized employees. In aggressive and militant jurisdictions, the opposite may well occur and the work force could become the dominant group. In neither situation is there genuine collective bargaining in the bilateral sense but rather a resolution of power forces.

Municipalities desire to conduct their own affairs as free as possible from state direction and control. They will not voluntarily assume an obligation to engage in collective negotiations nor will they seek mandatory or permissive legislative sanction for such action. A frequent disposition of local officials is to welcome a lack of legal competence or to be reluctant to take advantage of any implied authority, that is, to act as would any employer who seeks to keep labor relations as easily and unilaterally manageable as possible. Hence state legislation making collective bargaining compulsory in local jurisdictions would serve conveniently to relieve public officials of the awkward predicament of voluntarily abrogating their managerial or allegedly sovereign authority.

The right to organize is a preliminary condition to employee participation in determining working conditions, but if the broader areas of recognition, arbitration, and agreement are left to local discretion, or in some cases specifically ruled illegal exercises of authority, the right becomes ineffective if not meaningless. New laws in Connecticut and elsewhere appear to provide the statutory framework for legitimate collective negotiation. A growing number of informal understandings or agreements of varying scope and authority have emerged in recent years to build a body of de facto experience of collective bargaining in the public service. Will they provide genuinely progressive arrangements from the point of view of the community's welfare as well as the teachers' interests, or will they comprise narrowly conceived and vocationally restrictive agreements indifferent to broad educational accomplishment? The accumulation of formal and informal, written and oral precedents is the basis of an ordered rational expertise to guide negotiation and agreement. The prevailing personnel pattern does not yet furnish a significant body of helpful experience in this field. An individual or ineffective group seeking redress in the simplest sense of the term may receive just treatment but in a completely unilateral fashion long discarded in private employment. This kind of relationship does not need formal administrative machinery; it necessarily presupposes its absence. Bilateral negotiation, however, requires for its proper functioning an explicit organizational structure. Effective representation of the teachers' interests and the community's needs cannot be developed without professional competence. Employee organizations have already acquired more than the rudiments of professional staffing on local, regional, and national levels of operation. School jurisdictions must develop comparable resources, although in small municipalities they often cannot afford full-time personnel staffs. In these instances, the pattern will be set by the larger urban and suburban jurisdictions and their agreements will prevail with necessary adjustments in the same manner as the unorganized segment of the private labor force follows the settlements reached by the dominant bargaining groups. The majority of school board members are amateur laymen and no match for professional labor negotiators. The public employer cannot leave the resolution of its employment conditions to part-time officials lacking professional skill and experience.

Professional personnel relations proceeding in good faith in this fashion are incompatible with a continuing resort to political pressure as a primary means to determine conditions of employment. Responsible government requires that public employees engage in collective negotiation and abide by its results or alternately proceed through current lobbying methods. They cannot employ both methods and bargain in good faith. A tentative agreement reached administratively which serves as a floor for subsequent political action designed to improve its terms is a denial of genuine collective negotiation. Public personnel authorities will quickly view bargaining under these circumstances at the administrative level as preliminary skirmishes to be resolved in the interplay of subsequent pressure-group activities. Responsibility for the substance of the public employment bargain will thus be transferred to political levels where it rests presently and the emergence of genuine collective negotiation will be forestalled.

Public employee associations in the federal government are eminently effective organizations which have engaged in extensive lobbying for many years. This is the conventional technique of the postal workers and of some white-collar employees who have developed influential and long-standing legislative contacts. It is doubtful if they would prefer to function in any other way, although there are precedents in the TVA, the Government Printing Office, and the entire blue-collar work force in the navy yards and army arsenals which provide extensive and illuminating evidence of vast areas of collective negotiation in federal service. The teaching profession or its organized segment appears to have demonstrated a firm preference for collective negotiation rather than political pressure wherever a real choice became available. It cannot legitimately pretend to vocational professionalism unless it views personnel administration from this viewpoint. The fact that teacher leadership seems oriented in this direction is one of the encouraging aspects of the emerging pattern of organized associational activity in this area of public service.

The school administrator as distinct from the public administrator occupies a special role in personnel management. A case study of recently evolved arrangements in the town of Brookline, Massachusetts, may provide an informative example of the search for progressive teacher-administrator relationships. The community is neither unique nor is it too typical. It does have its counterparts elsewhere in the country. A population of 55,000 is demonstrably committed to excellence in public education and is realistically aware that such standards demand substantial expenditures. The superintendent and staff are progressive in outlook. A consultation arrangement was recently established which falls considerably short of bilateral collective bargaining but embodies an even greater departure from the traditional pattern of personnel relations which had prevailed for decades. The specific distinctions are noteworthy.

First, the organization, inchoate as it may appear, is formally replacing sporadically held previous discussions. Secondly, continuing deliberation of issues has been instituted replacing last-minute discussions conducted in an atmosphere of crisis. Thirdly, the school authorities are represented by an assistant superintendent in charge of business and a director of personnel, as well as by the superintendent and representatives of the school committee. Teacher representatives are designated by the employee association. Until recently this was primarily a social group which presented what were essentially petitions to the superintendent or school committee, sometime prior to the Annual Town Meeting. Consultation was not established at prescribed intervals. Data presented for consideration customarily consisted of statistical tabulations designed to indicate that the salary scales lagged in certain respects behind those of comparable surrounding districts. Issues were not negotiated but were simply publicized with varying efforts to elicit popular support from the community at large as well as from the school committee. The procedure has been replaced by an established program of formal discussion well in advance of the final determination of employment conditions at the Annual Town Meeting.

An early and major accomplishment of this consultative arrangement was the establishment of a single salary schedule based upon objective qualifications rather than teaching assignment. The final arrangement was presented to the Town Meeting as a mutually agreed-upon settlement reflecting the full substance if not the form of collective bargaining in the conventional sense. A planned revision of teachers' salaries to keep them regionally competitive was the next basic objective which involved the administration and the teachers in a collaborative effort to prepare an index relationship of salaries covering all teaching classifications, from those with minimal to those with maximal educational and experience qualifications. The index permits a change in any base scale rate to modify the entire salary pattern equitably and rationally in a deliberate departure from usual across-the-board increases. Instead of flat increments in multiples of a stated number of dollars, salaries are adjusted by means of percentage revisions to an established comprehensive scale. The categories themselves, including the steps and levels of academic preparation, are always subject to individual or collective negotiation. The system is also designed to prevent too much of a closing of a rational differential between teachers' salaries and those of administrators, a frequent result of large flat increments.

This consultative pattern is an instructive example of creative personnel experimentation. It lies between full-fledged collective bargaining and employer domination of working conditions. Its strength is derived from its flexibility, which may well prove more acceptable in many jurisdictions than an unyielding insistence upon unqualified collective negotiation in the teaching profession. A militant intransigeance may close the door to fruitful experimentation and engender reactions which will deny to this segment of the public work force the promise and reality of industrial democracy.

The arrangements produce a considered sequence of proposals and counter-proposals. The opportunity is present for argument and the presentation and evaluation of supporting data on a continuing basis in a scheduled series of meetings. An atmosphere of genuine deliberation has replaced unilateral school board action or a political struggle. There is, however, no legal obligation to reach agreement. There are no procedures for arbitration. The school committee is still legally competent to make final official determination and recommendations to the appropriating authority. The key achievement is the creation of machinery manifestly susceptible of further modification and development in the direction of enhanced measures of collective negotiation.

Militancy as it affects relations between teachers and administrators is a recent phenomenon of growing and major significance. It has often emerged to challenge prevailing patterns of administrative behavior. Two attitudes have dominated official conduct in the past. The first and most common is one of benevolent paternalism which exhibits a sympathetic consideration of employee needs. Under such circumstances staff organizations are passive in outlook and action. Historically, their programs are generally social in orientation. Membership is optional and aggressiveness is considered unseemly. A less prevalent but still significant attitude among some administrators may properly be described as authoritarian. Teachers are discouraged if not prohibited from vocational self-expression, and by the standards of a free labor movement are in a condition of subservience. Neither of these positions is any longer a viable administrative posture. Democratic society demands effective vocational representation from which the public labor force cannot be justifiably excluded. Apart from this broader social imperative, the teaching profession is attracting a growing number of persons who will not be patronized by kindly "paternalism" nor intimidated by "authoritarian" domination.

These considerations acquire increasing relevance and urgency as a growing proportion of persons are engaged in service occupations as distinct from so-called "productive" employment. The teaching profession comprises a principal segment of the "service" sector of the working population. It is clearly becoming more articulate and its representatives may be expected to press their interests with increased vigor and militancy. Moreover, as conditions of employment improve and teachers acquire income commensurate with their professional status, more people will view teaching as an ultimate career rather than as a ladder to administrative advancement. They will not only be concerned with salaries and the perquisites of employment but with other questions such as their involvement in summer programs, in-service programs, opportunities for joint appointments with teaching colleges, classroom size, pupil discipline, academic freedom, and others of a vocational and professional nature extending throughout the educational field. All of these matters will increasingly appear legitimate areas of organized teacher interest. The fact that teaching is both a vocation and a profession provides the explanation and justification for teacher involvement in these areas. Commitments of this kind cannot be discharged without some kind of organized collective action which provides the only effective technique for the articulation and implementation of staff viewpoints and interests.

The multiplicity of school districts and the acknowledged unevenness in the American educational picture present major difficulties for teachers and administrators in the areas of potential collective action. In other countries, democratic as well as authoritarian, varying measures of centralized control are exercised over the general educational effort. Textbooks, curriculum, and conditions of employment are frequently standardized and uniform. In the United States the autonomy possessed by municipal jurisdictions has engendered a deeply cherished tradition of independence from external control. This unusual freedom has permitted much creative and fruitful experimentation in some areas, as well as a counterpart of inferior performance in others. The stultifying uniformity of a centrally directed bureaucracy has been avoided and the gains have probably outweighed the shortcomings. One of the latter, however, is the vast disparity among districts in achievement, resources, and outlook. The multiplicity of autonomous jurisdictions precludes the kind of comprehensive organizational effort which marked union activity in the private sector of the American economy. The provincial control of the educational establishment in Canada, for example, permits official relationship with teacher organizations on a province-wide basis. Such arrangements are practically inconceivable in the United States where legally constituted school boards require collective negotiation to proceed independently in each jurisdiction. From the teacher point of view, the obligation to negotiate separately with each jurisdiction is needlessly costly and time-consuming. Cooperative programs in the field of educational experimentation are difficult to develop and the very presence of independent authorities may act as a potential deterrent to broad acceptance of measures which would otherwise be deemed worthwhile. Regional efforts in curriculum development and educational television have already proven promising avenues of exploration and achievement. The precedents should be extended to other areas of educational administration. Neighboring and often similar communities should be able to negotiate at least basic conditions of employment in areas broader than local jurisdictions whose boundaries have only an historical and not a currently political or economic justification. The conglomeration of autonomous municipalities has burdened American local government with onerous economic and administrative anachronisms which have confounded efforts at a rational balance of program, income, and expenditure. State authority and the taxing power have been invoked as leverage to balance gross inequities, but the effort may be destined to failure if the relief is granted within an intrinsically and manifestly obsolete and irrational administrative milieu.

The role of the superintendent is frequently that of a communicator between the lay school boards and the teaching and administrative staffs. In matters, however, which concern a balance between the welfare and objectives of the teachers and the needs of the community, the superintendent's responsibilities appear to transcend those of a mediator seeking acceptable solutions. His is a primary loyalty and obligation which should not be compromised but rather explicitly formulated and understood. He represents the students in the interplay among the school committee, the public, and the teachers. The superintendent must be at liberty to support or oppose any side or combination of them if he feels that the quality of education and the welfare of the students are involved in the outcome of the consultative effort. If this position is valid, he should not belong to any effective bargaining unit which by definition is a power force directed toward the attainment of objectives which he must feel free to support or oppose as the occasion warrants.

The situation is more complicated at the level of educational middle management. Myron Lieberman is anxious to "zero-in" on the status of the middle administrator. Collective negotiation in the teaching profession has not yet emerged into a pattern clear or even coherent enough to provide guide points in this sensitive area. The National Education Association and the American Federation of Teachers reflect the radically divergent views on the issue. The trade union parallel generally espoused by the latter does not find a complete counterpart in the teaching field. Administrators at intermediate levels and the teaching staff share certain common interests but also have diverse and even conflicting ones. These require much more definition and evaluation than has been accomplished to date. Ultimately it should prove feasible to delineate the appropriate line of demarcation in terms of eligibility. It will probably extend beyond the teacher category to include numerous classifications but stop short, for example, of assistant superintendents in charge of personnel who obviously cannot bargain with themselves over terms of employment. Directors of guidance and other special service personnel are more readily eligible for membership in employee organizations, as are other segments of the administrative staff whose duties are predominantly educational in nature. This is perhaps the most relevant criterion. A persuasive case can be made for the inclusion of such personnel. They can make considerable contributions to responsible consultation. A rational and comprehensive determination of employment conditions may indeed be facilitated by their membership and impeded by their exclusion.

The school principal remains a key perplexing figure in this situation. His discretion and authority in hiring and firing would preclude him from union membership in private industry. If we define a principal, however, as an educator without teaching responsibilities, then he may reasonably be expected to support the instructional staff as its head teacher and stand with them in a representative capacity. This is perhaps an idealized view of a principal rather than the prevailing mode. In most instances, he remains an authoritarian figure in the midst of a passive but increasingly restive staff and to the extent that he is primarily a manager rather than an educator, the principal stands outside the proper scope of associational effort. As he assumes the role of a teacher without teaching responsibilities, his professional commitment would imply involvement and participation in the collective conduct of fellow teachers. The ultimate resolution of his status seems unclear at present and it is premature to seem to delineate his position in any categorical fashion.

Administrative participation in employee organization activity will depend largely on the extent to which organizational effort and programs are concerned with professional issues. The teacher organization which parallels in close fashion the union in private industry and whose perspective is confined to terms of employment matters is unlikely to attract middle management interest. This echelon will generally obtain wages and other employment conditions somewhat superior to the settlements reached for the teachers. Their "bread and butter" situation is determined increasingly by market considerations, and their services will be more highly evaluated as the improved quality of education in American life becomes a national objective of the highest priority. Their turnover is less than that of rank and file teachers and their professional status is more secure. The quality of education within their jurisdiction is their primary vocational concern, for it is by this standard that their careers are judged and advanced. They may accordingly be expected to support associational activities that are genuinely directed toward the improvement of educational standards and achievement. The aspirations of the middle echelons of the educational structure envisage a professional career status for its members. These objectives demand collective effort to obtain income and other working conditions commensurate with the value of their vocational contribution. With the exception of the principal, the majority of the personnel, which comprises increasingly specialized occupations of a professional nature, is neither destined nor inclined by training and temperament to assume top administrative posts. Their professional and job concerns coincide largely with those of the rank and file instructional staff. To the extent that employee organizations create programs and pursue courses of action calculated to enhance the quality of educational accomplishment, they will not only summon the support of teachers and various levels of the administrative staff but respond in a positive and constructive fashion to some of the critical challenges confronting the educational profession.

I-5

POWER AND POLICY IN EDUCATION*

Myron Lieberman

My concern in this article is power and policy in education. I use the term "power" to mean capacity to influence the behavior of others. Such capacity varies from person to person, from group to group, and from situation to situation. My generalizations on the subject do not assume mathematical precision. They are statements of general tendency, frequently subject to more exceptions and qualifications than I shall provide here.

As I use the word, "power" denotes a relationship between people. We can, of course, refer to a person's power over his physical environment, and this is a perfectly legitimate use of the term. We also agree that power over the physical environment is often an important basis for power over people. For example, the power to change the course of rivers or to pollute the atmosphere with radioactivity is an indirect but immense source of power over people. However, power over the physical environment is not the kind that concerns me here, however important it may be in other contexts and for other purposes.

It often happens in education and elsewhere that A and B have some power over each other. For example, a superintendent may have the power to fire, hire, transfer, and promote teachers. The teachers, once hired at least, may eventually have some power over the actions of the superintendent. For instance, even though the superintendent may have the power to fire teachers, the latter may be able to rattle enough skeletons in the educational closet to exact an extremely high price for any such exercise of administrative power—in some cases, a price so high it is not paid.

Power has many sources—legal authority, technical or administrative skill, attractive personality, good looks, money, and so on. All the usual

* Paper delivered in the Frontiers of Educational Thought Series sponsored by the School of Education, Indiana University, and published in September, 1964, under the title, *Power and Professionalism in Teaching,* Vol. 40, No. 5, Bulletin of the School of Education, Indiana University. It is used here by permission. Myron Lieberman is Director of Educational Research and Development, Rhode Island College.

sources of power are present in education. However, any source of power may be limited in a given situation. Money may have no influence upon the person who chooses a life of poverty. Not everyone can be moved by tears, by sex, by law, or even by the threat to life and limb. Persons who can be influenced on some occasions by any or all of these things may not be subject to their influence—or be subject to the same degree—on other occasions.

A common fallacy is to identify power with the abuses of it, and to assume that power is used only for selfish ends. Thus, many persons think of teacher power solely in terms of its impact on teacher welfare. More power for teachers means more money for them; less power, means less money for them. There is some truth in this view, but it is a dangerously short-sighted one. A group which is too weak to protect its immediate welfare interests will usually be too weak to protect the public interest as well. Teachers need power to protect academic freedom, to eradicate racial segregation in education, to secure more and better instructional materials, and to do many other things that have little or no relationship to teacher welfare. If teachers are weak, they cannot protect the public interest in education. This is why the weakness of teachers as an organized group is one of the most important problems in American education today.

Some people regard teachers as a powerful group. A wide variety of evidence has led me to an opposite conclusion. Admittedly, some of this evidence is rather subjective. For example, I have never met an influential political leader who regarded teachers' organizations as a particularly important or influential lobby. Consider for a moment the 1962 election in California for the office of State Superintendent of Public Instruction. In this election, a former school superintendent, Max Rafferty, was elected State Superintendent of Public Instruction in California against the opposition of every important teachers' organization in California, including the California Teachers Association, the largest and most powerful state association of teachers in the country. Although powerful, the association was not powerful enough politically to prevent the election of a person regarded by the CTA itself as opposed to many of its basic policies. Mr. Rafferty's election over the opposition of teachers' organizations can hardly be regarded as unique; it is doubtful whether a single important politician in the United States owes his position to the National Education Association or the American Federation of Teachers (the two national teachers' organizations) or depends upon them as a major source of support.

The internal evidence about the National Education Association and the American Federation of Teachers (and their state and local affiliates) also seems to me to be quite inconsistent with the view that these are strong organizations. In 1959, the NEA, then with over 667,000 members, conducted a study of its affiliated local associations. The study showed that about 80 per cent of the associations sent two or fewer communications to their school authorities during the entire year, and that about 90 per cent received two or fewer communications during this period from their school authorities. Seventy-five per cent of the associations did, however, participate in social activities during the year—more than in any other kind of activity.[1]

In this connection, we must include the American Association of University Professors on the list of "paper tigers." In fact, an important cause of weak teachers' organizations is that the teachers have such a poor model in the American Association of University Professors. For the most part, the professors have trained the public school teachers in organizational impotence and naiveté. Teachers must look elsewhere for their examples and their inspiration if they are to achieve and exercise the power appropriate to their tasks in society.[2]

We should also realize that the leaders of teachers' organizations may have a vested interest in avoiding widespread acceptance of the view that teachers' organizations are weak. After all, the paid staffs of teachers' organizations want their dues-paying members to believe they are getting something for their money. For this reason, they tend to use organizational journals and conventions to persuade teachers that their organizations are effective. The contrary point of view has relatively little opportunity to present its case to the rank and file.

Instead of arguing about whether or not teachers' organizations are powerful, suppose we phrase the issue this way: Regardless of whether we characterize these organizations as weak or strong, what are the reasons they are not more powerful than they are? Agreed, there are several explanations as to why they are not, but what are the most important reasons and what should be done about them?

At any level, the weakness of teachers' organizations in a specific case might be due to inadequate leadership, lack of members or money, inadequate program, or any of the reasons underlying organizational weakness generally. What we are looking for are the most basic causes, those that go farthest in explaining teacher weakness in the widest variety of situations and over the broadest geographical area.

One such cause is the public attitude that strong teachers' organizations would, *ipso facto*, be harmful to the public interest. Teachers' organizations are viewed solely as a means of raising the level of teacher welfare. A higher

[1] Research Division, National Education Association, *Local Education Associations at Work,* The Association, Washington, D.C., 1960.
[2] Lieberman, Myron, *The Future of Public Education,* University of Chicago Press, Chicago, 1960, Ch. 10.

level of teacher welfare would presumably require higher taxes. Therefore, the way to prevent higher taxes is to prevent the rise of strong teacher organizations.

Another important factor is that many private employers compete with the government for personnel. Naturally, these employers do not want the conditions of competition to favor public rather than private enterprise. Thus, in addition to the higher taxes that would result from higher levels of support for government personnel, these employers have an additional incentive to prevent the rise of public employee organizations strong enough to raise substantially the level of compensation in public employment. It is a myth that government is a model employer; if anything, the conditions of government employment lag behind those in private employment.

Because the strength of teachers' organizations is viewed largely in terms of their impact upon taxes, there are widespread, if inarticulate, objections to encouraging, or even permitting, the growth of strong teachers' organizations. The unfortunate but predictable consequence is that conditions of private employment tend to be superior to those of public employment. Obviously, if organizations of public employees are restricted in ways that do not apply to organizations of persons in private enterprise, it is only a matter of time before the greater freedom and strength of the latter result in superior conditions of employment in the private sector.

It is possible to analyze this situation from several standpoints. We could, for example, question the simplistic notion that the public does not pay for higher levels of compensation in the private sector of the economy. Realistically, it appears that the public pays for these as much as it does for higher levels of compensation in public education or the postal service. We could also question whether it is in the public interest to have conditions of employment in the private sector superior to those in public employment. It is difficult to visualize how the public gains from a situation in which conditions of employment in such vital areas as education and public health are inferior to those in advertising, liquor, and cosmetics industries. The public certainly should have the right to decide this issue, but it is doubtful whether it is currently being resolved on the basis of adequate data or full insight into the long-range ramifications of the issue.

The most fundamental objection to weak organizations of public employees is that such organizations are conducive to a totalitarian society. Put positively, strong organizations of public employees are essential to a democratic society. Only the narrowness of popular thinking on the subject prevents wider understanding of this crucial point.

In the normal course of events, public employees are likely to be among the first to recognize incompetence or corruption among the public administrators. The public employees are likely to have many constructive suggestions for improving the quality and efficiency of public services. Nevertheless, it is only to be expected that some of their exposures of managerial inefficiency or corruption, or their constructive suggestions generally, will be greeted with managerial hostility or indifference.

The crucial point is that, if the organizations of public employees are dominated by the public administrators, the organizations will be unable to protect the public interest. The public employee who has no job protection and no organization strong enough to protect him from administrative reprisal is unlikely to challenge administrative inefficiency or corruption or make valid suggestions which run contrary to administrative thought. If the organizations of public employees are weak, they are unable to mobilize public opinion to effectuate needed reforms and legislation.

This is especially true of education, where teachers' organizations reveal a striking inability to mobilize public support for adequate books and supplies, academic freedom, educational research, and a host of other things that would be clearly in the public interest. This is why, in the long run, the weakness of teachers' organizations is more important than the state of public opinion. The latter could be modified by an effective teachers' organization.

The attitudes of the public, important as they are, in specific situations are not the crucial cause of teacher weakness. Public attitudes themselves have causes. The actions and policies of teachers' organizations are one of the most important, if not the most important, of these causes. Therefore, while public opinion may be an insuperable barrier to the achievement of teacher power at any given time, we cannot regard public opinion as the last word on the subject. The crux of the problem is not with the public but with the organizational naiveté of teachers, their bumbling and fumbling organizations, and their appalling leadership. Progress must start here, not with the public.

As I previously pointed out, the weakness of teachers' organizations reflects an irrational but widespread public fear of strong organizations of public employees. Another cause, however, is the notion, cultivated by our "experts" in school administration, that education should be "nonpartisan." Their argument is that "education is a unique function of government. It should not be subject to political wars, such as revolve about highways, liquor control, civil rights, housing, and so on. Education must be insulated from politics."

Now, if "keeping the schools out of politics" means that school systems should not be used to provide jobs for various political machines, I agree. If it also means that the day-to-day administration of the schools (the choice of textbooks, the selection of teachers, and similar matters requiring specialized knowledge) should be left to full-time educators, this too is sound. But to many educators, "keeping the schools out of politics" means keeping even matters of basic educational policy out of politics. Politics, in this view, are unclean, and schools should be protected from their corrupting influence. This, in my judgment, is impossible and undesirable. What is spent for education is as legitimate a matter for political debate and decision as is what is spent for public health, urban renewal, or national defense. Indeed, all of these items compete with one another in some measure, and if the proponents of greater educational expenditures do not exert themselves politically, the schools will not get enough.

We may put it this way. Some issues are both educational and political, just as some issues (e.g., medicare) are both medical and political. The nonpartisan approach to school board elections and/or appointments has tended to blur the distinction between educational issues such as the selection of instructional materials, which should be solved within the professional community, and such political issues as the level of public support for education, which should be resolved by the electorate.

A recent study revealed that in 42 states all or some members of local school boards are elected by popular vote. In 35 of these states, all the elections were on a nonpartisan ballot; in four others, some school boards are elected on a partisan and some on a nonpartisan ballot. The "nonpartisan" nature of school board elections usually carries over into the timing of such elections. Seventeen states hold school board elections separately from any other elections. Six states hold school board elections concurrently with other nonpartisan elections, and four hold them concurrently with partisan elections but on a separate ballot. Many others have some type of legislation governing school board elections to ensure that education does not get entangled with "partisan politics."

This pattern of separating education from politics has the approval of most professors of school administration, who believe that state-wide educational policies should be formulated by a state board of education elected at large on a nonpartisan ballot. They also think these nonpartisan boards should appoint the chief state school officer, and this is what more and more states are doing. Political scientists, on the other hand, generally favor having the governor appoint the chief state school officer. They argue that gubernatorial appointment increases the chance that educational needs will get a hearing at the highest levels of state government, and that, if the state commissioner or superintendent is insulated from politics, he will be less likely to generate sufficient support for his program in the legislature. It is their contention, and I agree with it, that state educational executives are in politics whether they like it or not, and that the problem is to make them effective, not to bind their hands with the wrappings of "nonpartisanship."

After all, what is a "nonpartisan" election? In practice, it is one in which the candidates do not use the labels "Democrat" and "Republican."

The theory seems to be that a school board election, whether state or local, should merely choose the "best man" and rely on their "nonpartisan" judgment about how the schools should be run.

My conviction is that the nonpartisan approach to school board elections weakens teachers' organizations. As long as they remain nonpartisan, teachers can only sermonize about the values of academic freedom instead of retiring politicians who support censorship of textbooks. A few showcase examples of power at the polls would do more for academic freedom than all the pompous pronouncements ever issued by teachers' organizations. A politically-conscious teachers' organization would provide funds, literature, and workers for candidates who shared its point of view. The endless number of state and national teachers' conventions now devoted to assorted drivel could be infused with political spirit and training.

When educators talk about keeping the schools out of politics, they really mean that in an ideal community the public would agree with the educators about how the schools should be run. But in the real world no such agreement can be counted on, as Mr. Rafferty's election in California illustrates. It is unrealistic for educators to preach that education is and ought to be a nonpartisan activity on 364 days out of the year, and then expect to be effective at the polls on election day, the most crucial of the 365 during the year. We desperately need to end this schizophrenia, and I believe it should be ended by clear recognition that some educational issues are necessarily political and will not be resolved the way teachers want them resolved unless the teachers as a group become politically effective.

When educators describe education as a nonpartisan activity of government, they reveal more than their own political naiveté and incompetence. Teachers who do not understand the dynamics of American politics cannot teach it to others. As a friend of mine put it, citizenship education starts with the Constitution, ends with the ballot box, and leaves out everything in between. Thus the most disturbing thing about the fallacy of nonpartisanship in education is not teacher failure to generate adequate financial support for education, important as this is. It is that we have no reason to expect a group as politically naive as teachers to provide students with real insight into the dynamics of American politics. As for the professors, it may be noted that Mr. Eisenhower did not seem to suffer greatly from the fact that his opponent was widely regarded as the choice of the eggheads. Personally, I have never confused the class of professors with the class of intellectuals, but it seems to me that the support for Mr. Stevenson from both these groups was the subject of derision and ridicule in other circles.

Because teachers fail to recognize the political dimensions of their problems, they tend to be ineffective even on those occasions when they do participate as a group in the political arena. Let me illustrate by comparing the legislative strategies used in education with those used in other fields.

Today, the federal government pays 90 per cent of the costs of the interstate highways being constructed all over the country. The expenditures under this program run into the billions. When this legislation was before Congress, the business interests that stood to gain directly from it were extremely active. Automobile manufacturers, oil companies, and construction companies supported the highway program, which went through Congress like the proverbial juggernaut.

Some educational legislation which would be good for the country would also provide greater profits for certain businesses. For example, there is a pressing need for more instructional materials per pupil—more textbooks, more films, more laboratory equipment, and the like. Many communities are confronted by a severe shortage of classrooms. How do teacher organizations try to generate support for these things? By appealing to PTA's to write letters to their congressmen. This is all right as far as it goes—but it has not, does not, and will not go far enough.

What should teachers do? They should go, for example, to the textbook publishers with a message like this: "Last year your firm got two per cent of the textbook market and made five hundred thousand dollars. Here is a bill which would provide twice as much money for textbooks as was spent last year. If this bill passes, and you retain your present share of the market, you will sell twice as many books and make over a million dollars. Therefore, we are asking you to get behind this bill in every way you can. As a starter, we are asking you—and all other textbook publishers—to contribute an amount equal to one half of one per cent of your textbook profits to help get this bill passed. In addition to your financial contribution, we are asking you to get in touch with legislators A, B, and C in your state, and explain to them the importance of this bill to the economic health of your firm and your employees."

The same sort of approach should be used with all firms which benefit directly from educational legislation. Instead of relying upon humanitarian appeals, the teachers should find out who would make money from educational legislation and get their active support for it. Obviously, some organization has to coordinate and direct overall strategy in these situations. Teachers' organizations should be playing this leadership role, but the NEA and the AFT are too moribund to proceed this way. NEA leadership seems to regard recognition of the important role of self-interest in political and educational matters as un-American, cynical, or evidence of lack of ideals. Many commerical firms doing business with the schools would probably be reluctant to accept AFT leadership on legislative matters, but there is little danger that they will be tested on this score. The AFT has such a doctrinaire attitude toward businessmen in education that it may take decades for the

Federation to identify and use those elements of the business community—and they are substantial—who would support higher taxes for education. The unpleasant prospect is that teachers will continue to rely primarily upon ineffective appeals to PTA's "for the sake of the children" and ignore appeals to businessmen for the sake of the dollar. And they will continue to get nowhere, as they have in the past.

Many people agree that teachers should have more power, but they show an appalling naiveté about how teachers are to get it. A major fallacy here is the notion that teachers must wait until they are accorded more respect by the public, or until they are more deserving of power. Then, it is thought, legislators and school boards and administrators will give it to them, in the form of control over entry, a greater measure of academic freedom, and the like.

This is what I call the "oven theory of power." It posits a public which is like a housewife taking a roast out of the oven to see if it is ready. Unlike roasts, however, the teachers are never ready and they are invariably put back in their oven to mature a little more. "You are not ready for greater power"—this is the epitaph on innumerable requests by teachers for more power over professional matters.

The approach is very similar to the situation concerning civil rights. How often, for example, have legislators asked whether Negroes were "ready" to vote, to go to school with white students, to drink from the same fountains, and to use the same washroom facilities? Almost invariably, those who regard "readiness" as a relevant concept seem to find the Negroes are not ready, just as those who raise this issue in education almost always come to the conclusion that teachers are not ready.

Giving power to those not ready for it is likely to result in irresponsible uses of power. Thus the idea that it is important to see whether teachers are ready for power is readily understandable. Nevertheless, I am convinced that this line of thinking is fallacious, at least in the context of our educational situation.

In the first place, power is not usually *given* to a group. It is *taken* by it. More precisely, the public does not actively give power to a group; rather, it acquiesces to a taking of power by the group. The difference is not semantic hairsplitting. It lies at the very roots of teacher weakness.

If we look at individuals and groups who have achieved positions of power, we find that their acquisition of power was the result of an active drive to get it. Senator Kennedy did not wait until the people thought he was "ready" to be President. He actively sought the presidency. To whatever extent his readiness for power was an issue in the minds of some, he directed an extremely effective campaign to resolve it in his favor. The American Medical Association did not wait until the public thought doctors were ready to control entry to medicine and medical education. Instead, in the early 1900's, it embarked upon a vigorous drive to strengthen the Association's control over medical licensure and education, to mention just two areas in which it currently exercises a controlling voice. The unions did not wait until they were deemed ready for collective bargaining and greater power. They acquired these things by an active campaign. By the same token, the teachers will not have power thrust upon them nor will they achieve it by becoming "more deserving." Occupational groups do not become less deserving of power because they actively seek it; indeed I would be prepared to argue that groups which do not contend for power are, on the whole, no more likely to use it effectively in the public interest than groups who actively seek power. This does not mean that every group which contends for it should have it or will use it for the common good, but only that we must eliminate the attitude that the use of power is something too nasty to contemplate in a good society.

Let me review briefly the major points I have tried to make. First, I have tried to provide a feasible definition of power and to explain the educational significance of this concept. I have suggested that teachers do not have a great deal of power and have identified some of the reasons for this conclusion. These reasons include public opposition to strong organizations of public employees, the notion that education is and ought to be a nonpartisan activity of government, teacher failure to capitalize on the self-interest of other groups, the misguided notions of professionalism which prevail among teachers, and fallacies in the strategy and tactics employed by teachers to achieve their objectives. Other important reasons, such as unrestricted administrator membership in teachers' organizations, have not been discussed because they have received more attention elsewhere. My concluding thought is that the task of increasing the power of teachers as an organized group, and of simultaneously ensuring that their power is exercised in the public interest, is one of our most crucial educational problems and deserves the most careful consideration by everyone concerned about the future of American education.

I-6

PROFESSIONAL PERSONS IN PUBLIC ORGANIZATIONS*

Ronald G. Corwin

Advances toward a better comprehension of man's role in society await the discovery of fruitful questions to ask. The development of sound methods and validated knowledge, for which there is much demand currently, hinges directly on this more fundamental problem.

CONCEPTUALIZING ORGANIZATIONAL CONFLICT

The Individual Versus the Organization

A perennial question which philosophers and social scientists alike have asked in one way or another concerns the individual's conflict with society. Hobbes stated the question bluntly in terms of individuals versus other individuals: "How is society possible in a state of war of all against all?" Since such frightful issues were first raised, social scientists have become sophisticated enough to realize that man is basically a group-centered creature and hardly in a constant state of warfare with his fellows. On the contrary, critics complain of the opposite, an "organization man" with little independent will of his own.[1] With this prospect of conformity in view, contemporary scholars have posed the issue in a slightly different form —the individual versus the organization.

Contemporary literary and social critics have been aware of the apparent problems that organizations have posed for individuals. The influence

* Revision of a paper written for a conference on "Developments in Professional Staff Relationship: Research and Practices," sponsored by the U.S. Office of Education, Washington, D.C., May 27-28, 1964. The author acknowledges with thanks the thoughtful comments of Russell Dynes, Willard Lane, and Robert Howsam. The article is reprinted by permission from the *Educational Administration Quarterly,* Vol. I, No. 3 (Autumn, 1965), pp. 1-22. (Footnotes have been renumbered.) Ronald G. Corwin is Assistant Professor in the Department of Sociology and Anthropology, The Ohio State University.
[1] William H. Whyte, *The Organization Man* (New York: Simon and Schuster, 1956).

of this issue is quite apparent in American literature. Plots of many current novels analyzed by Friedsam center around the fact the hero is a bureaucrat.[2] The dilemma posed in such novels as Wouk's *The Caine Mutiny* is that, while the employee ought to be able to afford the luxury of his own integrity, bureaucracy increasingly erodes his intellectual responsibility and compromises his moral integrity. Social scientists also have formulated the issue in a similar way. Argyris' work, for example, is based on a presumed conflict between the needs of "mature" individuals for independence, variety, and challenge and the demands of organizations for dependent and submissive employees.[3]

Toward An Organizational Conception of Organizational Problems

Such statements of the problem pit *the* individual against *the* organization. There are, however, serious disadvantages in this way of formulating the problem. One disadvantage stems from the component of "the individual" in the equation; it prompts analysts to explain what are essentially *organizational* problems in individualistic terms. This approach deflects the focus of attention from the central problem of organization to philosophical speculation on the nature of individuals, which is a residual problem from the standpoint of organization theory. Given this formulation, the person in trouble is defined either as a hero or a maladjusted personality, depending on one's point of view. But personality seems to be significant precisely *because* a given way of organizing is taken for granted; if a specific organization is assumed to be legitimate, then noncomformity will, by definition, appear as a personal "maladjustment."

Still other problems are associated with conceptions of organization that seem implicit in this way of formulating the issue (individual versus organization). The organization is portrayed as an overbearing entity, a unified set of values and goals which are in opposition to personal values and needs. This unitary conception of organization is fostered by two common implicit preconceptions of organization held by those who study organizations: (1) institutional favoritism and (2) organizational bias.[4] Institutional favoritism refers to the exaggerated attention that customarily is given to legitimate institutional ideals embodied in an organization. For example, theorists tend to focus almost exclusively on educational values in schools, religious values in churches, or efficiency in

---

[2] Hiram J. Friedsam, "Bureaucrats as Heroes," *Social Forces,* XXXII (March, 1954), 269-74.

[3] Chris Argyris, *Personality and Organization* (New York: Harper and Brothers, 1957), 50-51.

[4] Cf., Willard Lane and Ronald G. Corwin, *Foundations of Educational Administration: The School as a Complex Organization* (New York: The Macmillan Company, 1967).

businesses. Correspondingly, with a few exceptions, value conflicts within each of these settings have been neglected.[5]

This institutional perspective tends to emphasize the static image implicit in the very concept of organization. Not only does the study of structure tend to be preferred over process, but structure itself is conceived statically; earlier formulations of structure as a set of "positions" (of teachers, administrators, etc.) obscured the role conflicts or tensions built into each position. Subsequent developments in role theory have helped to correct the impression that structure is necessarily consistent, but the almost exclusive attention to the normative quality implicit in the concept of role (or expectations) has continued to distract attention from the perplexing discrepancies that exist between role conceptions and actual behavior. Finally, little attention has been given to longitudinal studies of the outcomes of role conflicts; consequently little is yet known about the forces within organizational structure itself that produce systematic changes in roles.

The term organizational bias refers to the related prominence given to a presumed set of overriding organizational goals. If it is assumed that it is "normal" for all personnel to work toward a set of organizational goals, then conformity to a rational decision-making model is also "normal"; and, conversely, nonrational behavior can only be attributed to "abnormal" sources. Hence, given these assumptions, any behavior which does not conform to the organizational logic—i.e., the logical means for fulfilling the organization's official objectives—is difficult to explain except in terms of "problems" and personal deviations. Consequently, all forms of behavior which do not "fit" the assumed logical structure are usually grouped into a *residual* category—that is, a category consisting of elements which have little in common except the fact that they don't correspond to the logic. Whenever behavior cannot be explained in organizational terms, it is explained in such residual categories as accident, circumstance, personality, or that amorphous creature bred for the purpose, "informal organization."

To summarize, when the logic of organization is taken for granted, behavior unsuitable to the organization in question tends to be explained in individualistic rather than organizational terms. The problem is that organizational tension, despite its prevalence, cannot be incorporated into existing models of organization in other than a residual way.[6]

---

[5] Callahan's study, which analyzes the effects of business principles on education, is a notable exception. See Raymond E. Callahan, *Education and the Cult of Efficiency* (Chicago: University of Chicago Press, 1962).

[6] For criticisms of social scientists' neglect of conflict models, see: Ralf Dahrendorf, "Out of Utopia: Toward a Reorientation of Sociological Analysis," *American Journal of Sociology*, LXIV (September, 1958), 115-27; Jessie Barnard, "Where Is the Modern Sociology of Conflict?," *American Journal of Sociology*, LVI (July, 1950), 11-16; also, Dennis H. Wrong, "The Oversocialized Conception of Man," *American Sociological Review*, XXVI (April, 1961), 183-93.

Professional Versus Employee Principles of Organization

There is another alternative. Using a different line of reasoning, behavior that is deviant in one form of organization may be seen as conformity in another. It is well known, of course, that the bureaucratization of American society is one of the fundamental developments of this century and that bureaucracy presently represents a dominant form of organization. Drucker, in fact, has termed this an "employee" society; that is, one in which the rights and obligations between employers and employees (i.e. those who work for another for wages) determine the character of the society.[7] As individual employers have disappeared, these relationships increasingly have been defined by impersonal administrative principles.

However, it is equally true that the social forces which have produced this bureaucratic society have also created alternative forms of organization. Professional principles constitute a prominent but competing way of organizing an employee society.[8] In a professional-employee society, the fundamental tension is not between the individual and the system, but between parts of the system—between the professional and the bureaucratic principles of organization.[9]

Dual professional and bureaucratic principles have been evolving in teaching for some time. The employee status of teachers has been reinforced, first by a strong tradition of local, lay control over educators, and then by the subsequent growth of complex school systems, which have required more administrative control to maintain coordination.

At the same time, the growth of systematic knowledge in teaching and a firm sense of responsibility for students' welfare supports teachers' claims to an exclusive monopoly over certain aspects of teaching, which is the basis of a *professional image* that points teaching in quite another direction. Behind professionalization is a "drive for status," or the efforts of members of a vocation to gain more control over their work—not only more responsibility, but more authority.[10] For decades teachers have subscribed to the

[7] Peter F. Drucker, "The Employee Society," *American Journal of Sociology*, LVIII (January, 1952), 352-63.

[8] Cf., Ronald G. Corwin, "The Professional Employee: A Study of Conflict of Nursing Roles," *American Journal of Sociology*, LXVI (May, 1961), 604-15.

[9] Parsons has warned of the dangers in analyzing occupational behavior on the basis of individual motives. See Talcott Parsons, "The Professions and the Social Structure," *Social Forces*, XVII (May, 1939), 457-67.

[10] The term profession is conventionally applied to a set of structural characteristics (i.e., an organized occupational group with a legal monopoly over recruitment and knowledge); but most of what might be called professional behavior is in fact the striving of a group to achieve the right to claim the title of a profession. In other words, to study professions is to study process. See also Howard S. Becker, "The Nature of a Profession," *Education for the Professions*, Sixty-first Yearbook of the National Society for the Study of Education, Part II (Chicago: University of Chicago Press, 1962).

idea that they have professional obligations (such as staying late to work with students) ; now they are demanding professional rights as well (such as the right to select their own teaching materials and methods).

Professional associations were, of course, originally formed in order to free vocations from lay control; and the efforts of teachers to professionalize are no exception. The process of professionalizing publicly supported vocations, then, is likely to be militant. It represents a challenge to the traditional ideologies of control by laymen and their administrative representatives. The professionalization of any vocation (including school administration) will involve boundary disputes among laymen, the professionals, and public administrators. These boundary disputes, it should be noted, also infect the vocation itself, breaking it into segments or coalitions which compete among themselves: one, a small but active militant leadership group, spearheads the movement, while other coalitions constitute small groups of supporters and the opposition. Each segment then attempts to control the conditions of work in terms of its own definitions.

In teaching, the immediate issues concern the amount of autonomy which teachers should have over the selection of textbooks, over methods, and over curriculum development. But the underlying issues are not peculiar to teaching. One issue concerns the appropriate role of professional-employees in complex organizations. A second involves the place of experts in a democracy. In a sense, this conflict between expertise and democratic principles has already been waged by administrators of public organizations. In these struggles, on the one hand, the growth of knowledge has almost forced laymen to forego their right to make many technical decisions; but on the other hand, many people feel that ultimately only public control will safeguard public interests. Militant professionalism, then, is intended to compromise both the control that administrators have gained over public education and the control traditionally exercised by the lay public.

Despite the efforts of many occupations to professionalize, the characteristics of complex organizations do not uniformly support professional behavior. In fact, there is evidence from a variety of settings that inconsistencies between professional and employee principles are responsible for tensions. As one example, the professional roles of physicians in the military have been found incompatible with the bureaucracy in which they operate.[11] The professional person's self-conception as an individual capable of critical ability with capacity for original thought could be only superficially followed in the structure of the military organization, according to McEwan, who believes that the bureaucratic principles on which the military is organized— such as standardization of positions and superordination-subordination by

[11] William J. McEwan, "Position Conflict and Professional Orientation in a Research Organization," *Administrative Science Quarterly,* I (September, 1956), 208-24.

rank—are, in practice, incongruent with the need for creative thinking and peer relations that prevail among professionals.[12] The principal of delegating authority seems inconsistent especially with the idea that professional authority is independent of the sanctions applied by a particular organization.[13]

Professional-Employee Role Conflicts

Bureaucratic principles can serve as a point of departure for conceptualizing organizational role conflicts.[14] These principles include: (1) specialization of jobs, (2) standardization of work, and (3) centralization of authority. Each may be visualized as a separate continuum, ranging from more to less bureaucratic (see Table 1). The configuration of these variables influences the opportunity that members of an organization have to act professionally in their relations with clients, colleagues, the administration, and the public, and the amount of pressure that is exerted on them to behave as bureaucratic employees in these relationships.[15] For example, group practice of medicine is characterized by a highly specialized but uncentralized form of bureaucracy. On the other hand, school systems probably do not differ from factories in degree of centralization, or even of standardization, but they differ fundamentally in level of specialization of their personnel. Therefore, because of these different configurations of bureaucratic principles, different types of tensions would be expected in schools, medical centers, and factories.

As professionals, teachers are expected to defend the welfare of students, even against *organizational* practices that are likely to be detrimental; so professional teachers will be disposed toward supporting school consolidation and toward defending the right of students to read significant American authors such as Steinbeck or Faulkner, and they will adjust their teaching to the unique capacities of their students. As bureaucratic employees, however, they will be expected to subscribe to the expectations of the administration and the community. Hence, it is possible for a teacher to be successful as an employee while failing to fulfill professional obligations, or vice versa.

Some of the tensions arising from these bureaucratic principles are

[12] There is also a hierarchy among professionals, but it has a different basis of authority; and communications between ranks of professionals are more nearly reciprocal.

[13] Walter I. Wordwell, "Social Integration, Bureaucratization and Professions," *Social Forces*, XXXIII (May, 1955), 356-59.

[14] Of course, there are many similarities between professional and bureaucratic expectations, but the differences will be the focus of this discussion.

[15] For an empirical study showing low inter-correlation among these variables, see Richard H. Hall, "The Concept of Bureaucracy: An Empirical Assessment," *American Journal of Sociology*, LXIX (July, 1963), 32-40.

TABLE 1

Contrasts in the Bureaucratic- and Professional-Employee Principles of Organization

Organizational Characteristics	Bureaucratic-Employee Expectations	Professional-Employee Expectations
Standardization		
Routine of Work	Stress on uniformity of clients' problems	Stress on uniqueness of clients' problems
Continuity of Procedure	Stress on records and files	Stress on research and change
Specificity of Rules	Rules stated as universals; and specific	Rules stated as alternatives; and diffuse
Specialization		
Basis of Division of Labor	Stress on efficiency of techniques; task orientation	Stress on achievement of goals; client orientation
Basis of Skill	Skill based primarily on practice	Skill based primarily on monopoly of knowledge
Authority		
Responsibility for Decision-Making	Decisions concerning application of rules to routine problems	Decisions concerning policy in professional matters and unique problems
Basis of Authority	Rules sanctioned by the public	Rules sanctioned by legally sanctioned professions
	Loyalty to the organization and to superiors	Loyalty to professional associations and clients
	Authority from office (position)	Authority from personal competence

illustrated in the case of *specialization*. As Gouldner observes, much orga-nizational tension can be attributed to the fact that administrators frequently supervise and evaluate professional subordinates who are more compe-tent in their work than they.[16] This situation, in turn, raises such questions as whether the criteria for promotion should be seniority and loyalty to the organization or professional skill and competence, which is difficult for non-specialized administrators to evaluate. The problem of evaluation is com-pounded by the fact that the reputations of professionals are based on the opinions of their colleagues outside the organization. Blau and Scott report that of the social welfare workers they studied, those who were most closely oriented to their profession were also less attached to the welfare agency, more critical of its operation, and less confined by its administrative pro-cedures.[17] On the one hand, the expert is expected to be loyal to the orga-nization, and on the other hand, his primary identification often is with groups on the outside. (However, there also exist locally oriented profes-sionals who are primarily concerned with the opinions of their peers in the organization.)

Similar tension exists between the professional and his client, for while professionals are obliged to serve the best interests of their clients and to provide them with needed services regardless of other considerations, they are not obliged to accept their advice; professionals develop ways of rationalizing their clients' evaluations of them. This indifference to clients' opinions poses a problem in public organizations like public schools where neither the professional nor the client has much choice in entering the relationship.[18]

Second, *standardization* presents another problem, not because it is in-compatible with individualism, but because it probably discourages creative and original thought, which is so necessary if organizations are to adapt to changing environments. Watson concludes, for example, that team work is a substitute for creativity, and is responsible for much mediocrity in academic institutions.[19] From the short-run perspective in which adminis-

[16] Alvin W. Gouldner, "Organizational Tensions," *Sociology Today,* ed. Robert Merton *et al.* (New York: Basic Books, 1959), 400-28.

[17] Peter Blau and W. Richard Scott, *Formal Organization* (San Francisco: Chandler Publishing Company, 1962), 244.

[18] The factor of choice is an important control mechanism for both clients (who can boycott professionals from whom they receive little benefit) and for professionals (who can do a more effective job with clients who have faith in them). Private prac-tice, however, overcompensates for the first problem, because of the professional's dependence on private fees; and bureaucratic employment accentuates the second problem. The fact that teachers are arbitrarily assigned students who are compelled to accept the service is a serious strain on the teacher-student relationship.

[19] Goodwin Watson, "The Problem of Bureaucracy, a Summary," *Journal of Social Issues* (December, 1945), 69-72.

trators and workers see their daily problems, predictability and consistency often appear more convenient than change and the risk of applying new ideas. (It is interesting, for example, that usually it is not sufficient to demonstrate that a proposed change will be no *worse* than the existing situation; change is avoided when possible.)

However, despite the complaints of professionals, standardized procedures do have advantages for them. From his examination of school systems of varying degrees of bureaucratization, Moeller concludes that, contrary to his expectations, standardized systems can provide teachers with a sense of power that does not exist in systems where there is a lack of policy; for policy reduces particularism and increases predictability. Hence teachers demand rules, especially in dealing with other groups such as students.[20] What the professional employee resists is the imposition by outsiders of rules which do not support him; even then, rules are preferred to their absence unless the group has such power that it can maintain its interests without them. The major difference between professional- and bureaucratic-employees in this respect is the established ideology which grants professionals the right to make the rules, and which sanctions the diffuseness of the rules that are made.

In considering the procedures by which rules are established, the third bureaucratic dimension, *centralized authority,* has been introduced. The problems of centralized authority, however, are more extensive than the mere question of the organizational level at which rules are made. For the very basis of authority in complex organizations is involved: bureaucratic and professional principles provide different ways of legitimating authority.[21] In bureaucratic organization, one derives his authority primarily from the position that he holds. He may be competent in the profession, but the amount of deference that is due him is based directly on his rank rather than on, or at least in addition to, his personal or technical competence. In bureaucracies, a superior has the right to the last word because he *is* the superior.

The notion of hierarchical authority, on the other hand, is not central to professional organizations; the last word presumably goes to the person with greater knowledge or the more convincing logic. In other words, the professional employee, in comparison with the bureaucratic employee, distinguishes between his obligations to accomplish his work and his obligations to obey; the bureaucratic employee is hired to "do what he is

[20] Gerald H. Moeller, "Relationship Between Bureaucracy in School Systems and Teachers' Sense of Power" (Unpublished Ph.D. dissertation, Washington University, 1962). Centralized authority systems support professional autonomy by resisting outsiders (as when principals defend teachers against interfering parents) and by refusing the use of essential facilities to competing groups.

[21] Gouldner, *op. cit.*

told," while the professional already knows what he is to do and how to do it. Thus, the professional's loyalties are split between the organization and the profession according to these competing bases of authority.

In this connection, when Peabody compared school employees, police officers, and welfare workers on the degree to which each group stressed each basis of authority, he found that the most striking contrast among the three groups was in the relative importance that the elementary school teachers attached to the professional basis of their authority.[22] Yet, their typical reaction to conflict was acquiescence to the authority of position, particularly among the less experienced members of the sample.

However, this presumed tension between professional and bureaucratic principles of organization will vary systematically with different types of organizations. Two variables are especially important: the *complexity* of the organization, and the degree of *technical* specialization that employees have achieved. Specialization gives employees power; the more specialized they are, the less competent are administrators and laymen to supervise and evaluate them. On the other hand, the more complex the organization, the greater the need for internal coordination, which enhances the power of administrators whose primary internal function is coordination. Lay control is challenged simultaneously by the development of both conditions; and at the same time the concurrent development of specialization and complexity has fertilized the soil for conflict between administrators and professional employees.

The implication is that if a particular organization is structured around several, often divergent but legitimate principles, then the personnel in it can legitimately disagree on the appropriateness of each principle.

SOME PRELIMINARY RESEARCH FINDINGS

In view of some of these considerations, a research project was outlined to explore some of the implications of possible tensions among professional-employees in the public schools.[23] The general working hypothesis was that professionalization in bureaucratic organizations is a militant process.

[22] Robert L. Peabody, "Perceptions of Organizational Authority," *Administrative Science Quarterly,* VI (March, 1962), 463-82.
[23] Ronald G. Corwin, *The Development of an Instrument for Examining Staff Conflicts in The Public Schools,* U. S. Office of Education Cooperative Research Project No. 1934, Department of Sociology and Anthropology, The Ohio State University, 1964. The research reported here was supported through the Cooperative Research Program of the Office of Education, U. S. Department of Health, Education, and Welfare in cooperation with The Ohio State University.

Methodology

In the conceptual model, the teaching position was visualized as a product of the teacher's role expectations concerning students, the public, administrators, and colleagues. Professional and bureaucratic (or employee) role conception scales containing items pertaining to each of these role expectations were constructed and administered to 284 teachers who represented seven secondary schools of varying sizes (from 9 to 120 teachers) located in Ohio and Michigan. Each scale consisted of Likert-type pretested items derived from the focal concepts: centralization, standardization, and specialization. The professional orientation scale contained sixteen items and the employee orientation scale consisted of twenty-nine items, selected from among those judged by a panel of sociologists to be relevant to the several dimensions of each concept. These dimensions were referred to as "subscales."[24] Possible responses weighted on a five-point scale ranged from "strongly agree" to "strongly disagree." Using critical ratio tests and scale value difference ratios, the final set of items proved to be internally consistent, in the sense that they discriminated between groups of respondents whose total scale scores were in the extreme quartiles.[25]

Each major scale also discriminated between respondents who exemplified logical extremes (high versus low) of professional and of employee conduct. Criteria found to be associated with the extreme professional groups included a combination of levels of education, time devoted to reading journals and number of journals subscribed to, number of articles published, and professional activities; extremes of the employee groups were identified from a combination of loyalty to the administration as rated by principals, expression of agreement and disagreement with criticisms toward the organization and administration, and absenteeism. Also, a group of university high school teachers, who technically are members of the university faculty, and whose professional orientation is reputedly high, scored at the expected extremes of each scale. The employee scale differentiated among the means of the set of seven schools in the sample, and the professional scale differentiated between the means of the two extreme schools.

Total professional scale scores of the sample were not significantly correlated with total employee scale scores, which bears out the conceptual

[24] *Employee Orientation "Subscales"*: Administrative orientation, loyalty to the organization, competence based on experience, interchangeability of personnel and standardization of work, stress on rules and procedures, and public orientation. *Professional Orientation "Subscales"*: Client orientation, orientation to the profession and professional colleagues, competence based on monopoly of knowledge, decision-making authority, and control over work.

[25] The corrected split-half reliability of the employee and professional scales is .85 and .70, respectively.

model hypothesizing professional and employee expectations as part of independent systems. The absence of correlation between the two major scales suggests that analysis of the way respondents organize their professional and employee conceptions is of promising importance for studying role conflicts. A significant difference was found in the proportion of the faculties at each school who were simultaneously highly committed to both conceptions, simultaneously low on both, or simultaneously high on one and low on the other.

In addition to the scale analysis, 143 teachers were randomly selected for open-ended interviews and were asked to describe friction incidents involving themselves or other staff members. Respondents identified 326 separate incidents, which were then classified by methods of content analysis as to the openness of the conflicts, the type of issue, and the parties involved.[26]

There was general consensus within schools on the frequency with which different types of problems have created incidents, although not all incidents described were specifically corroborated by a second respondent. Many of the incidents which were not directly corroborated were mentioned by "reliable" respondents, i.e., those who did report at least one corroborated incident; nearly half of the incidents are either corroborated or reported by reliable respondents. The frequency with which corroborated, reliable, and non-corroborated types of incidents were mentioned is not significantly different, as tested by chi square.

It was found that the number of conflicts reported in a school increased directly with the number of the staff interviewed, but this was not related to either the size of the school staff or to the proportion of the staff interviewed. Therefore, in order to avoid a measure of conflict rates which is a simple function of the number of interviews, the number of incidents reported per interview is the index of organization conflict rates that was used.

This method of computing the rate of conflict was compared to a "global tension" measure in the questionnaire which asked "how much tension" exists between each of thirteen types of role partners in each school (e.g., teacher-administrative role, teacher-teacher role, etc.). The alternatives ranged from severe to none. There was a direct Spearman rank order correlation of .82 between the total number of incidents reported per interview and this global measure of tension. The rank order correlation between this global measure and the rate of "open or heated discussions or major incidents" reported per interview was even higher: .93. Also re-

---

[26] An "incident" is defined as a description of a discrete episode in which a verbal complaint or attack was made against a person or group. A single episode was considered to be one incident regardless of the number of teachers involved or the number of times it was reported.

spondents were asked to indicate "how much tension exists" between them and each other member of the faculty. When schools were ranked only on the basis of the proportion of faculty mentioning "severe" tension, the rank order correlation with the number of "open or heated discussions or major incidents" per interview was .86, and with rate of "open or heated discussions or major incidents per interview" that specifically involved teachers and administrators it was .89.

The rates of conflict computed from interviews also correlated with other independent measures of conflict, such as the frequency with which respondents reported that their contacts with the principal have involved disputes, the proportion of teachers checking at least one negative statement about their principal, and the proportion of teachers who mentioned that compliance impresses their principal.

Types of Conflict

Approximately forty-five per cent of all the incidents involved teachers in opposition to members of the administration; about one-fifth of these disputes were "open" discussions involving direct confrontations of parties in an argument or "heated" discussions (as judged by content analysis), or "major incidents" including a third party in addition to those teachers and administrators initially involved; this is a larger number of open conflicts than reported among teachers themselves. About one-half of all incidents involved *groups* of teachers (teachers' organizations in seven per cent of the cases).

Twenty-four per cent of all conflict incidents fell in the categories of classroom control, curriculum management, and authority in the school; these incidents embraced such issues as the use of proper teaching techniques and procedures, changing the curriculum and selection of textbooks. About half of these involved administrators (Table 2). Of the 159 incidents that were in the open, about one-fourth were with the administration over these issues of authority.

Professional Militancy

There was a significant rank order correlation ($r_s = .91$) between the mean professional orientation of the seven schools and their rates of conflict per interview. The seven schools also were grouped into three categories on the basis of their rank on mean professional orientation (2-high, 3-middle, and 2-low schools) (Table 3). The two high-ranked schools (combined) reported a rate of open or heated discussions or major incidents per interview several times as great as that of the low-ranked schools (.4 compared to 1.9 interview). There was a parallel ranking of such incidents that specifically involved the administration. The reverse also

TABLE 2

Frequency of Occurrence of Incidents Involving
Authority, the Distribution of Scarce Rewards,
and Values, by Level of Intensity

Type of Issue Involved	Number of Open or Heated Discussions or Major Incidents	Proportion of All Incidents*
I. Authority, Total	81	**48.7**
A. Over the classroom		
1. with respect to superiors (curriculum management and authority over classroom)	35	17.4
2. with respect to subordinates (student discipline and problems)	23	15.6
B. Within the school		
1. with respect to superiors (authority over school)	7	6.8
2. with respect to public (school-community relations)	2	1.8
3. with respect to peers (disputes among teachers' organizations)	14	7.1
II. Distribution of Scarce Rewards, Total	48	**25.2**
A. Teachers' economic and job status (salary problems, distribution of physical facilities and job status)	23	13.1
B. Scheduling problems	21	10.4
C. Economic status of the educational program (school finances)	4	1.5
III. Value Conflicts, Total	26	**22.1**
A. Moral, ideological and interpersonal issues	9	8.6
B. Educational philosophy	3	4.9
C. School policy	14	8.6
VI. Unclassifiable (Insufficient Information)	4	**3.9**
Total Number	159	—

* Based on total number of incidents of all types, including complaints and impersonal competion. N = 326.

TABLE 3

Rates of Conflict in Schools Whose Faculty Have
High, Middle and Low Professional Orientations

Level of Professional Orientation	Rate of Incidents Per Interview			Rate of Open, Heated Discussions or Major Incidents Per Interview			Rate of Open, Heated Discussions or Major Incidents Per Interview Involving Teachers and Administrators		
	Number		Rate	Number		Rate	Number		Rate
	Conflicts	Interviewed		Conflicts	Interviewed		Conflicts	Interviewed	
High Schools 3 and 7 $\overline{X} = 58.69$	93	27	3.44	50	27	1.85	24	27	0.88
Middle Schools 1, 5, and 6 $\overline{X} = 57.17$	131	83	1.58	94	83	1.13	38	83	0.46
Low Schools 2 and 4 $\overline{X} = 56.76$	102	36	2.83	15	36	0.42	4	36	0.11
Total	326	146	2.23	159	146	1.08	66	146	0.45

tended to be true; schools with higher rates of conflict had higher mean professional scores than schools with lower professional orientations.

Finally, persons who held simultaneously high-professional and low-employee orientations had higher rates of conflict than persons who held low-professional and high-employee orientations, or any of the other possible role combinations (Table 4). Nearly half of the group with combined high-

TABLE 4
Organization of Status Conceptions and Rates of Conflict

Status Organization	N	No. of Conflicts Per Person	Per Cent Involved	
			1 or More	2 or More
High Professional—High Employee	67	0.61	.34	.16
High Professional—Low Employee	60	1.27	.47	.28
Low Professional—High Employee	59	0.56	.29	.14
Low Professional—Low Employee	71	0.89	.31	.17

professional and low-employee orientations were involved in one or more incidents, and about one-fourth of them were involved in two or more incidents. This finding illustrates that it is as important to ascertain what a group is *against* (low-employee orientation) as to determine what it is *for* (high-professional orientation).

The weight of evidence from this very limited sample suggests that there is a consistent pattern of conflict between teachers and administrators over the control of work, and that professionalization is a militant process. In future phases of the study, larger samples will be collected. Also, more intensive analysis of concomitant variations between professionalism and organizational variables eventually will help to assess the relative significance of each type of variable in relation to conflict.

IMPLICATIONS

Complex Authority Systems

It seems likely that if the sources of organizational tension are structural, then potential solutions to organizational problems also will be found at that level. Hence, use by administrators of more benevolent methods in working with teachers will not necessarily solve the problems unless these administrative practices are supplemented with structural changes. Many school boards and administrators today are talking about "allowing" teachers to participate more in the decision process. However, teachers appear to want the authority to make certain types of decisions, not merely the opportunity to become involved with some stages of decision-making at the discretion of the administration. The problem with so-called "democratic" administration is that the participation of subordinates usually continues to be at the discretion of the administration. As an uncertain privilege, the opportunity to participate may be withdrawn or withheld in practice. Lefton, Dinitz, and their associates, for example, found that when wards in a hospital were operated according to so-called "democratic" principles of administration, the actual result was far from democratic;[27] moreover, professionals working in this situation, where only an illusion of democracy was perpetuated, were more frustrated and negative than those working in wards that were admittedly less democratic. Hence, those who regard the problem simply as one of creating "good administration," ignore the very condition that professionalization is designed to remedy—that, under benevolent authoritarian administration, the status of the teachers' authority still depends on the discretion of the administration.

When the problem is viewed as one of organization, it becomes apparent that the teachers' professional authority will be in jeopardy until it is supported by the structure of the organization itself. For example, in one study dual lines of authority which developed between physicians and administrators in a hospital helped to minimize professional-employee conflicts.[28] On the one hand, the hospital administration maintained the right to make certain administrative decisions, such as scheduling and chart review, and the right to give advice. However, physicians reserved the right to accept or reject administrative suggestions about patient care. It was up to the physician actually attending the patient to make the final decision. Physicians interpreted the official right of the administrator to supervise as the right to "advise" rather than to make the decisions. This consulting relationship was even more acceptable because respected physicians held the administrative positions. Whether or not physicians accepted advice with which they disagreed depended on whether they considered the sphere of authority in question to be administrative or professional in nature. Although following administrative regulations was not very important to physicians when these regulations conflicted with their professional tasks of taking care of patients, they did otherwise comply with them; for, by complying in strictly adminis-

[27] Mark Lefton, Simon Dinitz, and Benjamin Pasamonick, "Decision-Making in a Mental Hospital: Real, Perceived, and Ideal," *American Sociological Review*, XXIV (December, 1959), 822-29.
[28] Mary E. W. Goss, "Influence and Authority Among Physicians," *American Sociological Review*, XXVI (February, 1961), 39-50.

trative spheres, physicians gained freedom from administrative responsibility, which they considered to be onerous.

Goss, the author of the study, concludes that although the hierarchical organization of the hospital in which professionals work might appear to conflict with the essence of professional autonomy, in fact the hospital avoided this conflict by using this kind of separation of spheres of authority.

In thinking of organizations, administrators often seem to have had in mind a stereotype implicitly based on the military bureaucracy, which they have attempted to apply wholesale to virtually every type of organization, under the myth that a central office must have authority over every decision throughout the organization. This myth can bridle professionals, who have firsthand acquaintance of their clients' problems and who have specialized *training* for dealing with them, but who have insufficient *authority* over the way clients are treated. Conversely, those who are most removed from the operating level are put in the impossible position of being held *responsible* for the decisions that must be made there. Moreover, these discrepancies among authority, competence, and responsibility have more significance for professional-employee organizations than, for example, for factories or prisons.

Perhaps more than any other factor, the myth that a central office must stand responsible for every decision throughout an organization is now deterring administrators from considering alternative designs by which organizations could be adapted to accommodate the fact of professionalization.

Administrative Training Programs and Conflict

The prospect of growing conflict among professionals within school systems also is likely to transform traditional leadership functions of the school administrator. Increasingly, his functions will involve mediation between groups; his job will be less that of "directing" the organization, as legal theory stipulates, and more one of just holding it together sufficiently to enable the professionals to improve their own effectiveness. His influence will be felt, but less directly than formerly, by the support that he gives to, or withholds from, the innovations that his subordinates suggest.

If conflict is a routine and normal occurrence within the administrative process, then administrative training programs should address themselves systematically to the proper role of conflict—its positive as well as its negative functions. Yet, to the extent that conflict has been fully recognized, it probably has not been considered with the intent of redefining administrative roles in terms of these conflict functions. Training programs seem to have focused on ways of limiting and managing conflict by screening people on the basis of their backgrounds or personality tests or teaching-group dynamics in hope of establishing cooperative and harmonious relationships among people on the job. However, in the first place, the disadvantages of such harmony have not been thoroughly explored; nor have the boundaries within which conflict can fruitfully occur been established. And secondly, it is possible that even the most peaceable, reticent person will become militant when he is operating under certain pressures. Perhaps it is these pressures that school administrators, especially, need to understand.

Evaluating Professional Employees

Finally, many administrators lack a coherent philosophy for evaluating their professional employees and for guiding their own conduct with respect to professional employee conflicts. The principal fact is that the teachers who are the most loyal employees, and the ones who make the administrator's job easier, are not always the most professional teachers. Conversely, those professionally oriented teachers who also want to be good employees are likely to receive little recognition, but endure much blame, for the moral responsibility that they do demonstrate when they are forced by an administrative regulation or by public fiat to compromise one set of principles in the interests of their school's or their students' welfare. What is to be the fate of a teacher who is guilty of "insubordination" while attempting to protect his students from a textbook or a curriculum guide which he believes would be ineffective, or detrimental, to students? How will an otherwise competent teacher who leaves the building early be treated? The same issues, of course, apply to administrators. Will a superintendent who has been requested by a school board to violate a professional ethic (e.g., fire a competent teacher for prejudicial reasons) dare to be insubordinate?

The answers to these questions depend upon the relative merits of professional and employee norms. The question of merit is in part a value judgment, but it is also partly an empirical question. Are professionally oriented teachers more effective? The answer, of course, depends on the criteria used to assess effectiveness. Are professionally oriented teachers better liked by students and parents? Do they have a better grasp of subject matter, and do they communicate more effectively? Perhaps professionally oriented teachers are not superior in all these respects. But, one hypothesis does merit further consideration. That is, professionally oriented teachers, in comparison with less professional ones, can be expected to protect the interests of clients against both bureaucratization and the special interests of laymen. For example, because classroom teachers interact daily with slum-school children, they are probably under greater direct pressures than the central city administration to adapt the organization to the problems of this unique clientele and environment; increased professional autonomy for these teachers might tend to alleviate those discriminatory practices otherwise fostered by standardization.

Professional norms also can counteract community pressures to maintain an outmoded curriculum or to censor the literary works of major American authors. More generally, because many professionals have less reason than administrators to be committed to a particular form of institutional structure, with the support of a strong organization they would be in a more opportune position than the administration to exercise leadership in changing the structure. Also in this regard, if more autonomy were granted to professionals (especially the younger ones trained recently), who may be partially insulated by the administration and their own professional organizations from outside pressures, the diffusion of those educational innovations most in harmony with professional values might be accelerated; and, conversely, teachers would be in a better position than administrators to resist adverse outside pressures.[29] If so, then the preference of administrators for loyal, compliant employees may be in conflict with their responsibilities as professional educators.

CONCLUSIONS

In conclusion, while individual personalities do become involved in conflicts, the individual-versus-the-organization hypothesis has obscured some potential contributions that studies of conflict can make to organization theory. A more fruitful approach to the problem focuses on the contrasting organizational principles which individuals uphold. From this perspective, one function of conflict is to defend conflicting but valued principles and to effect creative compromises between them. Group conflicts, in other words, function as "checks and balances."

Yet, although traditional theory has been concerned with divisions of labor, and more recently some attention has been given to distinctions between formal and informal organization, the conflicts among other largely ignored structural divisions, such as professional and employee modes of organization, have been relatively neglected. Moreover, to the extent that organizational structure has been recognized as a potential source of conflict, it often has been with the intent of showing only that the known principles of organization have not been applied, as in the case where illogical work flows have been discovered.

[29] At the same time, of course, while professional autonomy can protect clients, professions in a status struggle also can jeopardize the interests of clients because of their own self-interests, special viewpoints, and status hierarchies. For example, most professions seem to give preferential treatment to clients with more power. Similarly, in our study of conflicts between teachers, reported above, it was clear that teachers were competing with each other for students for their extracurricular activities in order to enhance their own positions, and apparently at the expense of the students' welfare in some cases.

Behind the current interest in professional-employee organization is the idea of process, the simultaneous professionalization and bureaucratization of American society. It is not possible to consider the problem of organization without considering the possibilities and probabilities of organizational change. In considering potential reorganization of large-scale systems, administrators will have to take into account one of the most powerful phenomena of our times—the professional organization of employees.

II

THE LEGAL AND POLITICAL FRAMEWORK FOR COLLECTIVE NEGOTIATIONS

This section includes articles which analyze the legal and political background of collective negotiations in public education.

Most private employees in the United States have been guaranteed by law the right to form organizations and to bargain collectively with their employers since the National Labor Relations Act (Wagner Act) of 1935. The National Labor Relations Board (NLRB), a federal agency, was established by the Wagner Act to administer the federal statutes relating to collective bargaining in private employment. One of the most important functions of the NLRB is to investigate claims that employers or employee organizations, or their representatives, are not obeying the law.

As public employees, teachers are excluded from federal legislation regulating private employment. The extent, if any, to which school boards are required to negotiate with teacher organizations is a matter for state rather than federal legislation. Unless teachers are satisfied to accord each local school board the right to refuse to negotiate with the duly chosen representatives of the teachers, the latter must seek state legislation which would require boards of education to negotiate with teacher organizations. In several states, such legislation has been enacted, although it does not always conform to the wishes of all the teacher organizations affected by the legislation.

The article "State Politics and the Public Schools" is from a book of the same title by Nicholas A. Masters, Robert H. Salisbury, and Thomas H. Eliot. The authors examine various pressures exerted by educational lobbies, especially state teacher organizations, on state legislatures. Although the article does not deal with collective negotiations statutes directly, it illustrates the legislative milieu in which such statutes must be considered. The article also includes valuable insights on the effectiveness of state teacher organizations, especially in the area of teacher welfare. The book from which the article is taken is a pioneering study of the dynamics of state educational legislation and should be read in its entirety by persons interested in this subject.

Since legislation on collective negotiations for teachers is still rather limited, judicial decisions and attorney general rulings in this field are particularly important. Wesley A. Wildman's article examines the legal status of collective negotiations in states where no laws are applicable. He also gives some background of the development of collective bargaining in private employment. As an attorney and director of "The Study of Collective Action by Teachers" at the University of Chicago, Wildman is well qualified to discuss the legal aspects of collective negotiations by teachers.

Regardless of the common law in this field, school boards have been generally unwilling to negotiate with teacher organizations. For this reason and others, teacher organizations have lobbied strongly for state legislation which would require school boards to negotiate with duly chosen teacher organizations. Donald H. Wollett, a lawyer who has served as co-chairman of the Committee on Law of Public Employee Relations of the American Bar Association and has taught at several universities, discusses the importance of state legislation regulating collective negotiations in public education. Wollett has also served as an attorney and consultant to the Urban Project of the NEA.

In 1965, six states (California, Connecticut, Massachusetts, Michigan, Oregon, and Washington) passed laws requiring school boards to negotiate with teacher groups. Rhode Island enacted such a law in May, 1966, and Wisconsin was the only state that had such a statute prior to 1965. All eight statutes vary widely in scope and enforcement provisions. Arvid Anderson analyzes the Wisconsin statute and develops criteria for future legislation in his article entitled "State Regulation of Employment Relations in Education." As one of the three commissioners of the Wisconsin Employment Relations Board (WERB), Anderson has been deeply involved in state regulation of teacher collective negotiations for several years.*

Inasmuch as statutes providing for collective negotiations are relatively new in public education, it is important to study their effects to date. Two articles have been included for this purpose. In one, Robbins Barstow, a staff member of the Connecticut Education Association, analyzes the Connecticut negotiations statute; in the other, Hyman Parker, chairman of the Michigan Labor Mediation Board, examines the Michigan statute. The last article in this section provides an overview of collective negotiations in Canadian education by Tom Parker, the executive secretary of the Nova Scotia Teachers Union.

---

* The complete text and an analysis of the other statutes (except for Rhode Island) may be found in *Collective Negotiations for Teachers: An Approach to School Administration* (Chicago, Ill.: Rand McNally, 1966), pp. 47-54, 447-65. See also "Recent Legislation Affecting Collective Negotiations for Teachers," by Michael H. Moskow, *Phi Delta Kappan,* XLVII (November, 1965), pp. 136-41.

II-1

EXCERPTS FROM STATE POLITICS AND THE PUBLIC SCHOOLS*

Nicholas A. Masters, Robert H. Salisbury, and Thomas H. Eliot

The purpose of this study has been to determine how and by whom power is exercised when decisions are made concerning public schools at the state level in three midwestern states, without implying that they are typical or atypical. The book deals directly with only certain aspects in the political process where education and politics meet. We excluded decision-making concerning higher education entirely because, in that policy area, different groups initiate demands which are handled in substantially different ways. A large part of the politics that inevitably surrounds state administrative decisions, particularly in the areas of teacher certification, school accreditation, textbook selection, vocational education, and the administration of federally supported programs, was left virtually untouched and remains virgin territory for future inquiries. The influence patterns that emerge in negotiations between the city school systems of St. Louis, Kansas City, Chicago, and Detroit, and state officials, were only tangentially discussed. We designed this project assuming that each state should be examined as a separate entity before we could make any meaningful generalizations or comparisons.

Of necessity, we restricted the project to selected aspects of state politics, mainly those decisions that must ultimately be approved in the legislative arena. Attention was focused on the 1961 sessions in the three states. The dramatic contrasts among the states we studied illustrate the importance of discussing the politics of education with a clear understanding of the variations in policy processes that occur from state to state. Our efforts reveal that there are almost as many variations as there are uniformities.

In view of the massive effort that is made today to provide educational opportunities, the obviously increasing role which the states play, and the

* Nicholas A. Masters, Robert H. Salisbury, and Thomas H. Eliot, *State Politics and the Public Schools* (New York, N.Y.: Alfred A. Knopf, 1964), pp. 261-80. Nicholas A. Masters is Professor of Political Science at Pennsylvania State University; Robert H. Salisbury is Professor of Political Science at Washington University; and Thomas H. Eliot is Chancellor, Washington University.

demands for uniform standards and equality of educational opportunity, we need to know who is doing what, how. It is more evident now than ever before that educators must face political realities, as well as problems concerning the improvement of educational instruction. For they, too, as this study has attempted to show, *must compete for scarce resources.* However, this book is not designed as a guide for political action or as a source for answers to political complexities. Our study has been exploratory and our conclusions are explanatory rather than prescriptive.

SOME HYPOTHESES

At this point we should like to set forth certain *a posteriori* hypotheses with the understanding that new data must be collected to test them. In this chapter, we have focused on generalized statements in order that our findings may have wider applicability. The points we wish to emphasize are not mutually exclusive, so some repetition is necessary.

The Power Structure

Public school decisions are made within a clearly identifiable power structure in which the influence relationships are clearly established, or in a political arena where power is fragmented, resulting in a high degree of uncertainty for the particular interests which are making claims.

The routine way in which most state public school decisions are made and the regularity with which certain procedures are followed in Illinois and Missouri clearly indicate the existence of a power structure in each of these states. The existence of such structures is one thing, what makes them "work" is another matter. Our data suggest that the key to understanding the Illinois and Missouri patterns, although they take different forms, lies in an appraisal of how these structures fit into each state's political system. Although it is true that the School Problems Commission (SPC) in Illinois and the Missouri State Teachers Association (MSTA) in Missouri are the focal points of power, their power is exercised within the bounds imposed by their respective state's political system. In essence, these two agencies have become such integral parts of the systems in which they operate that the personal judgment of their leaders or members, as the case may be, frequently become the policies.

In Michigan, we found only the remnants of power structure in public school matters, although attempts were being made to forge a new one. The strains and stresses within this state's political system, coupled with the emergence of *strong independent* groups directly concerned with the public school policy (the two phenomena are not unrelated), have destroyed any sem-

blance of continuity and predictability in Michigan as to final policy outcomes, especially in the area of finance.

Given these influence arrangements, then, what additional characteristics of the process may be cited to explain the nature of public school decision-making? The following general statements are designed to highlight
these characteristics.

The Role of Responsible Leadership in the Power Structures

*Those who seek to influence public school policy work within a frame-
work or "an area of permissible negotiation" established or set by the "responsible leaders"—a leadership that includes both legislators and the
governor.* In Illinois and Missouri the responsible leaders, those with the
power to say "You can go this far and no farther," work together and enjoy
highly developed and long-established interrelationships, although they may
occasionally disagree. The responsible leaders include in both states the governor and "key" members of the legislature. In both Illinois and Missouri,
the education interests are, for all practical purposes, a "part" of this leadership, having sufficient influence and resources to help design and shape the
total political climate in which final decisions are reached or the proposals
for change are judged and acted upon. In both states, the claims of the
majority of education interests are given a high degree of legitimacy, but it
is a legitimacy that is constantly in jeopardy.

In Michigan, as we have seen, the "responsible leadership" itself is fragmented, with the governor and legislative leaders frequently being at odds.
In the period we observed, the public school interests, divided among themselves, remained apart from the responsible leadership, almost as if they had
to be deliberately excluded. Moreover, one segment of this leadership, the
Republican leaders of the Senate, had sufficient influence to set boundaries
on expenditures that left no room for negotiation. In brief, then, what we
are saying is that public school interests encounter the "responsible" leadership which lays out the playing field and sets the rules of the game of competing for scarce resources; in order to be effective, school interests must
persuade or become part of this leadership. To be sure, this is a nebulous
concept, but it is designed to characterize nebulous situations.

Organized Use of Unorganized Opinion

*Relatively few public school policy proposals entertained in the legislative
halls of the three states studied result from general public pressures or from
wave-like "public" protests.* We observed none and no one suggested that any
issues have ever come up this way. Normally, general concern or expression
of opinion that is presumed to emanate from the public is significant only

when the organized interests themselves *use it or are able to use it* as a key element in making their claims upon governmental agencies. Whenever MSTA tries to secure some major innovation, such as the adoption of a foundation program, it carefully cultivates and in fact creates committees composed of prominent Missourians from all walks of life to help build support. Such effort is largely behind the scenes. Similarly, in Illinois the Illinois Education Association (IEA), with the assistance of various other interests, circulates petitions among the public for presentation to the governor or legislative bodies. It also arranges conferences composed of prominent Illinoisians to advocate solutions to school problems.

The situation in Michigan is slightly different, in that in view of the conflicts, generating public support or widespread interest has often appeared as the only alternative to deadlock. The passage of the continuing appropriations act in 1959 resulted from the education interests' successful efforts to mobilize widespread citizen support, an effort that was given considerable stimulus by the first Soviet Sputnik. Precisely what constitutes widespread support or what legislators interpret as public pressure not only varies with the individual legislators but rests to a large extent on how each sees the political world in which he must live. This latter point is, of course, true in all three states.

Controversy

Issues concerning public schools can and do become highly controversial, despite the fact that there are no organized anti-school groups.[1] Conflicts occur over how much additional money the states can afford to spend on schools, how reorganization of school districts will affect particular locales, the extent of state as compared with local responsibility for financial matters, racial integration, state responsibility for teacher welfare, transportation of parochial students, etc. The nature and extent of the conflicts will, of course, vary with the issues.

The very fact that education issues involve conflict, potential or real, is clearly illustrated by the pattern of decision-making and non-decision-making in each of the states studied. In Missouri, many potential conflicts are contained within a private group, the MSTA, but they are not allowed to escape into the legislative process. The SPC in Illinois was created largely as a result of chaos and continuous controversy over policy alternatives, and it too has found ways to contain conflicts or minimize their disruptive effects. In Michigan, the efforts have been made to create an analogous mechanism

---

[1] Among professional educators in Michigan, the Friends of the Michigan Schools is often referred to as the public schools' number one enemy. But this group, as its title suggests, does not regard itself in this light and counts among its allies many professional educators from the state's small rural school districts.

primarily through an Educational Council, but the major issues in that state are too broad in scope and affect too many decision-makers to be contained. In short, in Michigan, when the governor disagrees with the state legislature —or some effective veto element within it—the state has no machinery and no group has the resources (or the ability to use them effectively) to act as an intermediary to "ready" decisions for final approval by the powers that be. Approval may still be forthcoming, but it seems mainly to be a hit or miss proposition.

The Red Flag of Finance

Issues that involve basic changes in the revenue structure or involve substantially increased expenditures for education purposes can activate groups that are capable of exerting strong counter pressures and manipulating strong consensus-building symbols in opposition to the proposed changes or increases in expenditure levels. Characteristically, such groups do not oppose the schools *per se*. On the contrary, they will frequently acknowledge that schools need additional funds, although such admissions do not necessarily temper the tone of the opposition. These groups, in the main, base their attack on political themes such as fiscal responsibility, balanced budgets, and that "taxes are already too high."

The politics of public schools in Michigan provides the most dramatic support for this generalization. In that state, for example, school proposals encountered stiff resistance from groups and individuals that were not opposed to the schools but which were opposed, frequently vehemently opposed, to *any* increased expenditures. In 1961 lobbyists representing General Motors, Ford, and Chrysler managements and conservative-oriented senators and representatives responding to their own personal ideologies, as well as to outside pressures, expended considerable time and effort to keep taxes down and expenditures at as nearly present levels as possible when the school groups, as well as others, were asking for additional funds.

The unity and effectiveness of the SPC in Illinois were almost destroyed by an attempt of some of the commission's members to increase substantially the expenditures under the state's foundation programs. The normal practice in Illinois has been to ask for only moderate increases, determining *in advance* how much opposition there might be.

Moreover, in a sense, the MSTA in Missouri operates tactically in the same manner as does the SPC. Representatives of that organization try to avoid proposals that might activate this type of opposition, and if they seek substantial changes, they start an elaborate process to obtain consensus before conflict arises. But despite its predominant position, the MSTA has not always been successful in containing the opposition. The initial effort to secure increases in state aid in 1959 through an increase in the sales tax earmarked for schools is a case in point. In that instance, opposition came from two normally conflicting sources—the state Chamber of Commerce which was opposed to any increase in taxes or expenditures and the state AFL-CIO, which was opposed to an increase in the sales tax.

Proposing the Programs

The groups and individuals who articulate the policy proposals, the innovators so to speak, are those who have a direct or tangible stake in the outcome of the decisions.

In the three states we surveyed, however, no one single pattern emerged in this regard. In Missouri, policy proposals emanated primarily from a single interest group, the MSTA. In Illinois, the professionals shared the policy articulation process with SPC legislators and gubernatorial appointees who had achieved the status of experts in their own right. In Michigan, policy proposals emanated from various organized interests which often found agreement among themselves impossible.

Despite these important variations, in each of the states we surveyed the major group was the state affiliate of the National Education Association; namely, the MSTA in Missouri, the IEA in Illinois, and the Michigan Education Association (MEA) in Michigan. These groups have a relatively high degree of organization, a principal spokesman, a wealth of information about school needs, and generally favorable access to at least some points in the *formal* decision-making structure.

Education association representatives in each state assiduously try to prevent their organizations from being labeled political action groups. All regard the systematic presentation of information about school needs as the most useful manner in which to approach political officials. Professional expertise and "objectivity" are regarded as the most important resources of influence of each group. Each group expends a vast amount of effort to influence policy and calls upon some extremely able people to support its views. Each group would prefer not to activate its members or to pressure a legislator in any overt way. Whenever possible, all avoid identifying and allying with other groups that are not directly concerned with education and which compete in the legislative arena. Obviously, as we have attempted to demonstrate, each of these three principal interests has had to accommodate its policies and strategies to fit its own state's political system and thus in a sense, too, each group is similar.

The tactic of using information, of presenting the facts of their case in the best possible light, is based, in the main, on the assumption that groups that claim to be above politics, that claim to be neutral and objective and that as a matter of course refuse to take sides when other interests are battling, cannot go much further than this without taking the risk of being labeled political. Anything beyond persuasion is a strategy reserved for "desperate" or "critical" situations. By labeling these situations "desperate" or "critical" they indicate their desire that additional efforts not be regarded as merely politically inspired.

With the exception of the teachers union, other education interests—the School Board Association, School Superintendents Association, the PTA, etc.—rely more heavily on other means to secure legislative objectives. But for the most part they leave it to the NEA-affiliated groups to determine and articulate the demands. Michigan is the exception. Explaining Michigan's more pronounced fragmentation presents a problem. The answer seems to be that each group in Michigan perceives itself as having a greater stake in the outcome than do the comparable groups in the other two states. But this may beg the question, "Why is each specific group more independent?" On the surface at least it appears that the state's greater role in financing public schools allows for a more comfortable independence and opens the way to each group to pursue its own special interest, which may be incompatible with other interests. Also the unambiguous refusals by the state legislature seem to create uncertainty as to where new efforts should be directed. In brief, failure to achieve results has its divisive effects. Of equal significance is the MEA's sensitivity to competition from the Michigan Federation of Teachers (MFT). To meet the competition, MEA places greater emphasis on its teacher welfare proposals, which in turn alienates the school board and superintendents' organizations.

Even though the extent of fragmentation of interests varied in each state, with Michigan clearly on one end of the continuum, Missouri on the other, and Illinois somewhere in between but closer to Missouri, there is in each state a subtle pyramiding of power *in terms of who articulates the demands.* This power lies predominantly in the hands of the official spokesmen for the organized interests, the professionals, who are limited only by what the political system will allow or (just as importantly) by what they think it will allow. Exclusively lay interests have little to say about what is needed, although they may have a great deal to say about what is finally gotten. The Farm Bureaus of Illinois and Michigan are active and concerned, but their concern lies in the area of school district reorganization and has diminished as reorganization has been accomplished. These groups repeatedly said it was "up to them to decide what was needed," and by "them" they meant the professional associations or groups. This may be distressing news for those who believe education should be the chief bulwark against concentrated power and may raise some knotty questions for those who believe that democracy requires a wider diffusion of responsibilities. But the grooves of influence are deep and have been carefully channelled out. The interests are like a closed club, displaying a pattern of influence that constantly repeats itself. Yet, although the professionals pull the strings, they must pull people instead of puppets.

The Rule of Favorable Access

The extensive commitment of virtually all groups within society to the maintenance of a system of public education facilitates access of the public school lobby to decision-makers. In each state surveyed, legislators frequently singled out the education interests as the most powerful in the state. This image seems to rest largely on the single fact that education groups have a considerable symbolic advantage that virtually insures access. That is, the sentimental appeals used by education groups—"doing something for the children," "young people are the future of America," etc.—even if sparingly used, are most difficult for politicians to resist or counter, if indeed there is a desire to do so. It would be difficult to suggest that education is not operating in the public interest, even though some legislators may privately hold this view. Moreover, the presence of professional educators in every local community, coupled with the fact that many local superintendents and educators are prominent in their communities and are backed by fairly active and prestigious groups such as the local PTA, League of Women Voters, etc., insures the education groups to which they belong virtually guaranteed access to elected officials who represent these areas in the state legislature. *However, the lack of political sophistication, failure to recognize the realities of politics, or just plain inertia on the part of its members frequently prevents an organization from utilizing its maximum resources.*

Teachers' unions, which enjoy relatively limited access on the state level, access usually confined to urban Democratic legislators, are a general exception to the favorable access rule. The developmental pattern of teachers unions indicates that they are primarily big city organizations with few locals in the less urbanized areas of the state. At least this was the pattern we observed in Illinois and Michigan and, in an embryonic way, in Missouri. State legislators bring out the point that because teachers' unions are affiliated with other segments of organized labor, they enjoy less social prestige among their colleagues, particularly among Republicans and rural or outstate Democrats, than do the other education groups. The generally unfavorable position among the school interests of the Illinois and Michigan Federations of Labor, and their limited relationships with the state legislatures, exemplify the widespread resistance to unionism of white collar and professional workers.

Minimizing Conflicts and Reducing Goals

Based largely on the mythology that education and politics should be kept apart, a major goal of education interests is to have governmental decisions affecting public schools made in a routine manner; that is, they desire a process in which all decisions are highly predictable as to their outcome, even if this means the sacrifice of certain policy alternatives or acceptance of less desirable results. Efforts of the major education interests concerned with finance and reorganization are clearly in this direction. The high level of confidence the interests in Illinois have in the SPC, the efforts to form an effective Educational Council in Michigan, the dominance of MSTA in Missouri despite its clear policy of incremental gains and restricted demands, all suggest a desire not to engage in a process that would require competition with other groups each year in the legislature. Continuous competition and agitation for legislative action would make it appear that professional educators, including the representatives of organized interests concerned with legislation, have abandoned the high ground of professional neutrality. In short, the less direct and open involvement in *political* decision-making the better. This may seem to involve ordinary political bargaining, but it is more than this. It is a desire for *safety* that permeates the thinking.

In Missouri, for example, the predominant group, the Missouri State Teachers Association, *avoids* raising certain questions, particularly in the area of teacher welfare, in order to minimize conflict within its organization between teachers and administrators, and, by refraining from raising issues that rival legislators would oppose, to maximize its chances for gaining other objectives. The SPC in Illinois deliberately sets aside those questions that it regards as explosive and concentrates on areas where immediate results can be reasonably assured. With the possible exception of the Illinois Federation of Teachers, Illinois education interests have not only willingly and enthusiastically supported this approach, but are indeed an integral and official part of the machinery.

In Michigan, on the other hand, where the goals of education interests are similar, the results are not the same. A neat, clear separation of education from conflict is the ultimate aim of groups such as the Michigan Education Association, but several factors present in Michigan and not present to the same extent in either Illinois or Missouri, have thwarted this objective. First, all attempts at unity in Michigan have failed. Second, Michigan differs, and not insignificantly, because the state government has been more generous in the past in its support of public education in general and the public schools in particular than either Illinois or Missouri—or for that matter most other states. Affluence seems to have made education interests disagree about how hard to push for further improvements. It has also allowed legislators to refer constantly to "Michigan's favorable position among the states," whenever faced with new demands for greater appropriations. This factor was clearly evident in 1961, when several groups were advocating different proposals as the absolute minimum necessary for a sound public school system.

Third, in Michigan the education interests feed their demands into a political system rife with conflict, much of it partisan in nature. In Missouri, there is a relative absence of deep divisive forces, particularly those of party. In Illinois, the SPC is engineered in such a way as to weed out or reconcile the divisive forces in that state before there are any eruptions, particularly those of party or those that emanate from the historic Chicago-downstate division. In short, the pattern of decision-making involving most major state education decisions in Illinois and Missouri is set and locked. But in the Michigan political system, differences run deep over fiscal matters and consequently touch all policy areas. Thus, conflicts over education can hardly be avoided. It should be pointed out, however, that if the conflict in Michigan is an extreme case because the state's total activities are the subject of controversy, it is only the extreme of a conflict that may exist in any state political system.

Group Leadership

Direct participation in the decision-making process by the representatives of organized education interests frequently forces them to tailor or alter their programs in order to produce consensus or sufficient support for their adoption; or it may serve as means for such representatives to take positions that might otherwise be impossible because of internal dissension. In short, knowledge of the political process enhances the control a representative of a group has over the aims, direction, and priorities of the group itself. It would be a mistake in this study not to single out certain key individuals who are constantly adjusting group demands to fit their assessment of the realities of politics. In the states we surveyed it was Everett Keith (MSTA's executive director), Lester Grimm (IEA research director, emeritus, and SPC member), Dick Adams (MEA lobbyist) and Max Cochran (legislative representative of the Michigan state superintendent) who acted both as brokers and innovators, attempting to transfer organization ideals into reality. This does not suggest that these and other officials of organized interests operate as free agents, yet their knowledge of organizational views and membership desires, combined with their working relationships on a day to day basis with political officials, serve as a dual shield, allowing their independent judgment in effect to become the policy and strategy of their respective groups. We can reasonably suggest that certain discrete or personality variables play a crucial role in each state.

Little Political Currency

With few exceptions political officials feel that efforts in behalf of education offer few of the traditional prizes; therefore they avoid direct involvement. The only exceptions to this rule are those legislators who achieve the status of experts in this policy area and who count education interests among their principal bases of support. Although in this study we did not quantitatively measure legislators' attitudes on this subject, our fragmentary evidence strongly suggests that the overwhelming majority find advocacy of public school causes not particularly advantageous, or to use their own jargon, not to contain much political currency (voter appeal, patronage).

With even less evidence, we can suggest some reasons for this. First, education is itself a highly specialized area and most legislators feel that to deal with it substantively requires some background in and familiarity with an education enterprise itself. Few legislators have this type of experience. Second, legislators must be reelected. In the states we covered, where racial and religious issues do not intervene to any disruptive extent, everyone is generally in favor of schools or is pro-school in attitude. Thus, a legislative candidate who is for better schools is not unique. Rather, he is expected to be so disposed. Third, education is a policy area that offers few payoffs. Education interests do not endorse candidates or contribute money, and they generally refuse to get entangled in any campaigns unless they are trying to defeat a perceived foe. Other groups engaged in the policy process are not so inhibited or restrictive in their activities and may and do offer private inducements to secure support. And lastly, patronage is largely unavailable to legislators whether they champion school causes or not. This is of special significance in Illinois, where most downstate legislators of both parties view the patronage at their disposal as a necessary ingredient for a successful political career.

All this means that public school policy questions are handled in a different way from other policy areas. Legislative decision-makers who are experts on education are open to persuasion; they *do* pay attention *even though* there are few other inducements. The other legislators, recognizing that education must be financed and improved, will usually go along, *providing* the tensions among education interests themselves and within the larger political context are not so great as to make support inconsistent with their own and their constitutents' views, as was the case in Michigan during 1961.

Role Specialization

Because of the limited political opportunities education seems to offer to ambitious politicians, role specialization within the legislative branch has become a vital aspect of state politics as it relates to the public schools. In each state, several legislators, usually one from each party in each house and several more, have become the recognized experts and the ones upon whom education interests rely most heavily to carry their proposals through. Insofar as we have studied it here, the extent of role specialization varies. It was much more pronounced in the Illinois legislature than in the Missouri legislature, largely because ten Illinois legislators were also members of the SPC.

Missouri and Michigan relied on fewer legislators, but in Michigan the absence of an expert or a legislator committed to representing school needs in the state senate greatly hampered all attempts to influence that body. "We didn't have anybody to carry the ball," was the way one group official put it.

Ineffective State Superintendents

The politically-elected state superintendent departs too widely from the norm of professional neutrality to be an effective, independent force, except perhaps in a state such as Florida, where the elected superintendent is a member of the state cabinet system and has political bargaining powers far beyond those of his counterparts in Illinois or Michigan. The elected superintendents in Illinois and Michigan serve interests that are committed to "professionalism." Thus, whatever firepower they may have stemming from their political contacts is effectively muzzled. This was true in both Illinois and Michigan, where the state superintendent either was influential through SPC or attempted to be influential through an Educational Council established through his office. The situation in Michigan contrasts with Illinois, however. In Michigan, the elected superintendent, being a Democrat, has been closely aligned with the teachers union movement, which obviously strains his relations with the MEA. Nevertheless, this has not erupted openly because the entire staff of the department, with one exception, is on permanent civil service tenure and enjoys close ties with the MEA regardless of who fills the top position. His elected status as a Democrat has also severely curtailed or limited his influence with Republican leaders who have controlled both houses of the state legislature. In Illinois, SPC membership has allowed the superintendent to exercise influence that otherwise would have been impossible. But whatever influence he does exercise is of little consequence to him politically; that is, a state superintendent cannot build a political record on SPC accomplishments. Yet in both states the aim is to make the state education department or office appear to be professional and nonpartisan.

The political role of the appointive head in Missouri contrasts markedly with the roles performed by the elected superintendents. Hubert Wheeler, the incumbent since the office was created in 1945, does not attempt to influence either the legislature or the governor directly. He has no program to present to the legislature nor proposals to make to the public. The present incumbent conceives his role as that of a professional educator concerned exclusively with administrative duties. He contends that any attempt to participate openly would meet with strong disapproval, not only from the education interests he serves, but from the state board to which he is directly responsible. Instead he relies on his close connections with the MSTA as the way in which he can influence policy matters. The extent to which he exploits these ties rests upon certain discrete variables, primarily the incumbent's assessment of a situation and the reception he receives from the personalities who govern the MSTA.

The conclusions of this study are tentative. The study has attempted to demonstrate that there is no great distance between professional educators and politicians, and that political activity of education interests will probably increase as the need for resources increases. If the professional educators' article of faith that politics and education should be kept apart is ever taken literally, then professional educators will be totally unprepared for what awaits them. But this is not to argue that attempts to divorce school questions from politics are unrealistic. Quite to the contrary. It has been just such attempts that have led to the type of policies and decision-making structures that have been adopted. True, as long as public schools remain *public* schools, they cannot escape political decision-making. However, the *very desire* to place public school questions above any conflict is itself an integral part of the process of decision-making.

Our experience with three midwestern states reveals that the political issues which questions of public school policy generate become entangled in varying degrees with the many processes and patterns of conflict and resolution in the total state political system. When such studies as this are made in other states, we anticipate that certain dimensions of conflict not found in our states will affect education policy. A cursory examination of other states suggests several salient areas of investigation:

First, political scientists might investigate the degree and nature of conflict between teachers' unions on the one hand and state and national NEA groups on the other. Involved here are the public school teachers' self-perceptions as professionals and their attendant modes of behavior. Who is to represent the teachers? Are classroom teachers to be lumped, for purposes of vocational identification, with school administrators? Or must the classroom teachers, on the basis of shared attitudes and common occupational objectives, organize apart from the administrators, who do not share the same attitudes and objectives as their staffs? If the latter, do classroom teachers lose their status as professionals? Or do they make their profession more cohesive and homogeneous? In either case, what is the effect on their political influence?

Teachers' unions are not yet a significant factor in two states we studied; Michigan is the exception. However, conflict between the unions and the NEA affiliates might be more pronounced in states such as New York, Pennsylvania, or California. In cases where such conflict is highly developed, we would expect a greater emphasis on teacher welfare on the part of both groups in an effort to attract and retain membership. Such a situation would weaken or strain the alliance between the state NEA affiliate and the state school boards association, as is the case in Michigan and possibly New York and Pennsylvania.

Second, political scientists might investigate the entire web of conflict patterns in other substantive policy areas in terms of their effect on educational policy and the way they render futile educators' efforts to keep politics and education separate. The controversial question of the separation of church and state still remains an unresolved issue in public school policy information.

Third, political scientists might study the racial problem as a possible cause of further conflict situations for the NEA as it competes with teachers' unions for the loyalties of American teachers. As long as NEA support depends on affiliates which are segregated—as in Florida, Texas, Georgia, North Carolina—this may give the teachers' union movement greater currency in the North and Midwest. And, of course, de facto and de jure segregation in our public schools is a burning political issue.

Finally, political scientists might study the potential conflict—if indeed it is just potential—between higher education and the public schools in their competition for scarce resources. For example, are we to accept without scholarly investigation the explanation that NEA's last-minute, well-mobilized opposition to a college aid bill in the Eighty-seventh Congress was predicated on the fear that the bill would "establish a precedent for Federal aid to private elementary and secondary schools"? Or again, what is the nature of the political tension between community (as opposed to state-supported) junior colleges and state-supported institutions of higher education that maintain far-reaching extension programs?

This book has dealt with the question of the relationship of politics to education—a basic issue that affects all Americans. The problem has been most succinctly stated in these words of J. K. Galbraith:

> Education, no less than national defense or foreign assistance, is in the public domain. It is subject to the impediments to resource allocation between private and public use. So, once again, our hope for survival, security, and contentment returns us to the problem of guiding resources to the most urgent ends.[2]

---

[2] *The Affluent Society* (Boston: Houghton Mifflin, 1958), p. 355.

II-2

LEGAL ASPECTS
OF TEACHER COLLECTIVE ACTION*

Wesley A. Wildman

Local collective activity among public school teachers is clearly increasing. The policy-making school boards and the policy-executing administrators view such activity by teacher organizations as a means to assume greater power over policy formulation and decision-making areas traditionally considered the unilateral responsibilities of boards and administrators.

As the drive for formal collective negotiation relationships gains impetus across the country, administrators, boards, and teachers will become more concerned with what the law says in a particular jurisdiction—what can or must they do in regard to the key aspects of a formal collective employee-employer relationship? Anyone concerned with public education in the United States must understand the implications for education that are inherent in the attempts currently being made to provide organization and bargaining rights for teachers similar to those enjoyed by employees in private enterprise. Many state legislatures are under increasing pressure to pass legislation to provide and implement these rights. Educators will be called upon to make knowledgeable judgments and decisions regarding the differences in policy betwen the NEA and the AFT on the question of the applicability to education of traditional private sector labor relations procedures and concepts.

So far educators have shown little awareness of the possible ultimate significance for the schools if the key elements of private sector collective bargaining are extended to the relationships among teachers, administrators, and school boards within a school system. They have yet to engage in meaningful dialogue about this issue. Those concerned with the teaching and practice of administration are playing only a negligible role in the important events that are shaping the future of teacher-board-administrator relationships in the United States.

* This article appeared originally in the April, 1955 issue of *Theory into Practice*. It is reprinted here by permission. Wesley A. Wildman is Director of "The Study of Collective Action by Teachers" at the Industrial Relations Center, University of Chicago.

Because of space limitations, I shall deal only briefly and in an elementary fashion with what may be, to the uninitiated, a complex and bewildering problem, marked by strange terminology and concepts, whose application to education is not always clear. I shall first examine the assumptions underlying collective relationships in our private economy and the key aspects of policy and practice supporting and implementing these relationships. This will provide a basis for comparison that will help us understand where the law now stands in regard to teacher bargaining across the country, and where current proposals might take us if they are widely adopted.

Collective bargaining in industry is essentially a power relationship and a process of power accommodation. The avowed theoretical purpose and practical effect of bargaining in industry in this country has been to grant employee organizations an increased measure of control over the decision-making processes of management. The essence of bargaining is compromise and concession-making on matters where there is a conflict between the parties in the relationship. The bargaining relationship is a bona fide one if each party retains the right and ability to inflict loss on the other in the event of failure to reach an agreement as to how they shall live together for a specified period. While much problem-solving may take place in negotiations—particularly at the beginning of a bargaining relationship in public employment—true, mature collective bargaining in either industry or school systems is much more than an elaborate structure of communications or a new type of formal procedure designed to resolve problems to the mutual satisfaction of the parties concerned.

The theory and practice of collective bargaining are based on two assumptions: that there is a significant and continuing conflict between the managers and the managed in any enterprise, and that there will be a strong identifiable community of interest and consensus within the employee group in regard to items and areas of judgment over which there will be conflict with the managing authority. The establishment of a formal collective employee-employer relationship often sets in motion certain processes that tend to change these underlying assumptions into self-confirming hypotheses.

Providing an employee organization with a significant number of the key elements of collective bargaining supports and encourages the bargaining relationship, grants the organization power that it can wield in the collective relationship, and results in the institutionalization of the conflict that is presumed to exist. These key elements of private sector bargaining —some provided by law and others evolved through practice—are as follows:

1. The right to organize. Employees are permitted to organize without influence or coercion from either management or labor. Machinery is provided in our federal legislation and in some of our state labor relations statutes for impartial adjudication of charges that the employees' right to organize is being interfered with either by management or by a labor union.

2. *Designation of a majority representative.* Under federal law, the National Labor Relations Board has the authority to determine what classes and groups of employees shall be included in a given bargaining unit. An election is then held to determine the majority representative within the unit. The proper composition of a bargaining unit may present many problems in industry, but almost invariably all levels of supervision are excluded from the rank and file unit. *Exclusive representation,* which is granted to the majority representative, allows the majority representative organization to represent *all* employees in the bargaining unit—regardless of whether they voted for the union or whether they join the union. The alternative to exclusive representation is an impracticable arrangement, with management having to face many organizations, all of which have different requests and demands for small groups of the total number of employees. Yet the total group of employees must be governed by a uniform set of rules and policies relating to wages, hours, and other conditions of employment.

3. *Union-shop or "union-security" provision.* This provision in a collective contract between the union and the employer states that all employees must join the union within thirty days after being hired or lose their jobs. Federal laws permit such a requirement, although the states have the option to adopt "right-to-work" laws, which forbid such an agreement between an employer and a union. At present, nineteen states have "right-to-work" laws, which make most "union-security" provisions illegal.

4. *Dues checkoff.* This provision allows union dues to be deducted from employees' paychecks and sent directly to the union. The union-shop and the checkoff clauses are important to the union, since they can determine whether or not the organization will have a sufficient membership and financial base to operate adequately.

5. *Bargaining and signing an enforceable agreement.* The duly authorized union has the right to insist that the employer meet and bargain concerning wages, hours, and other conditions of employment; the union also has the right to insist that any agreement reached must be incorporated into a written, legally binding document. Under federal law, management and the union are required to negotiate "in good faith," but they are not required to reach an agreement. If agreement is reached, however, either party may insist that it be put in writing. The requirements of "good faith" bargaining have become very complex; moreover, the concept of "wages, hours, and other terms and conditions of employment" has been expanded constantly, by the NLRB and the courts since passage of the Wagner Act, to make an even greater number of items subject to "good faith" bargaining.

6. *Grievance processing, terminating in binding arbitration.* This is the

crucial procedure that constitutes the heart of a majority of labor agreements in industry. It provides for the peaceful settlement of disputes that arise over the application or interpretation of the contract during its term. When a dispute cannot be settled by the parties themselves through the grievance procedure, it may be submitted, under an arbitration clause, to a neutral third party for final determination. Binding arbitration may also be used to determine some or all of the terms and conditions of a collective contract itself, if the parties have reached an impasse in negotiations; but this practice is relatively rare in the United States.

When there is an agreement to submit all unresolved disputes to binding arbitration during the life of the contract, there is often a clause that denies the union the right to strike while the contract is in force.

7. *The strike.* This is the union's ultimate power prerogative, which it may exercise in an attempt to force agreement in the event of a bargaining impasse with the employer; the employer, of course, has the right to refuse to employ labor on the terms and conditions demanded by the union.

Any or most of these seven elements of bargaining may be extended to teachers (or other public employees) by state legislation, municipal ordinance, or voluntary adoption—depending on the local legal picture—by a board of education or other public employing agency. It should be noted, however, that it was not until the Wagner Act that management and labor in large sectors of our economy came to face each other across the bargaining table as two opposed collectivities in a relationship marked by a rough "equality of bargaining power" between the parties. If experience in the private sector of our economy is any guide, it may be that formal, mature collective bargaining relationships will not become dominant in public education in the United States unless the procedures and concepts supporting meaningful collective employee-employer relationships are made available to teachers, probably by state legislation.

No judgment is being made here as to whether collective bargaining or professional negotiations are inevitable or desirable on a widespread basis in American education. In my opinion, we do not yet know the extent to which the assumptions concerning employee-employer conflict in industry are applicable to or true for the public education system. We do not yet have sufficient analyses of specific collective negotiation relationships between boards and teacher groups that weigh both the utilities and disutilities inherent in every such relationship. Such analyses would help guide us in making judgments about the impact of collective bargaining on the school system, conceived as an institution of client-centered professionals offering their services to the public. Research is not yet available to show whether the type and degree of conflict found in school systems needs or deserves institutionalization through establishment of a formal collective employee-employer relationship.

To return to our survey, where do public employees—including teachers —and public employers stand in regard to the salient characteristics of industry's collective bargaining? The trend in many states is to make an increasing number of key elements available to public employees through court decisions and laws, or at least to sanction many of the procedures and practices of bargaining, if a public agency sees fit to embrace them voluntarily.

In a few states, the public employees' *right to organize* is prohibited by law. During the past few decades, however, opposition has decreased, and fifteen states now recognize the right either in their laws or constitutions. Court decisions and executive orders indicate that in the majority of the states public employees have the right to join organizations of their own choosing. Although a state may limit or circumscribe the right of organization for certain purposes, it is widely assumed that blanket prohibition against public employee organizations would create grave constitutional difficulties; the trend is clearly in the other direction.

Wisconsin is the only state at present that grants public employees the right by statute to designate a *majority representative* and the right to have exclusive representation status.[1] Some authorities believe that without laws to authorize exclusive representation it would be illegal to grant such status to an employee organization, since it would interfere with the employee-citizen's constitutional right to petition his government. Attempts have been made to avoid this objection in public employment labor agreements by reserving the right for the individual employee to present his grievance and to insist on meeting individually with his employer if he wishes to make his concerns known.

Although these two crucial features of a bargaining relationship are not widely available to public employees *as a matter of right,* the concepts of majority representation and exclusive representation have been extended in practice to public employee organizations on a voluntary basis by the many public employing agencies, including school boards, across the country. In many jurisdictions where public policy seems to encourage some form of bargaining, the laws and courts are silent on the questions of majority representation and exclusive recognition; in many of these jurisdictions it would seem to be implied, however, that public employing agencies that wish to adopt such election and recognition procedures are free to do so. For exam-

---

[1] For a discussion of the legal aspects in Wisconsin, *see* "Collective Bargaining with Teachers under Wisconsin Law," [by H. W. Story in *Theory into Practice,* IV (April, 1965), pp. 61-65.]

ple, in March 1964, the Attorney General of Michigan was asked for an opinion on the following question:

> Does the Board of Education of the school district of the City of Detroit have the authority in its discretion to recognize as exclusive negotiating representative for the purpose of carrying out the procedures outlined by the Board that association of teachers which receives a majority of the teachers' vote at a representation election?

The Attorney General replied:

> The Board of Education of a school district may, in its discretion, recognize for the purpose of resolving differences concerning salaries, status, teaching conditions, personal welfare or other related problems, as the exclusive representative that association of teachers which receives a majority of the teachers' votes at a representative election.

This opinion may well foreshadow a trend.

Numerous governmental entities have refused—through laws and court decisions—to sanction the *union shop* in public employment on the ground that requiring union membership as a condition of employment is irrelevant to or inconsistent with the concept of merit. Court cases in several states indicate that it is illegal for a board of education in those jurisdictions to sign a rigorous union security agreement. A number of states that recognize the right of public employees to join labor organizations also provide for the right *not* to join in the same law. In at least ten states, the use of union-shop provisions in public employment agreements has been declared illegal by law, court decisions, or attorney generals' opinions. In some states, "right-to-work" laws, which neither include nor exclude public employees, may be interpreted as denying union-shop provisions in public employment.

Voluntary *dues checkoff,* authorized by individual employees, is fairly common in public employment. Dues for all types of employee organizations are deducted from paychecks in many states and local communities. Numerous state and local governments have legally authorized payroll deductions for public employees.

As for the *right to bargain,* defined as the right merely to meet and talk with the public employer, nearly a third of our states now provide by statute that municipal employers may or must meet with employee representatives and allow for the presentation of employee proposals or grievances. A few states prohibit "negotiation" between public employees and employers. In most of the states, however, there are no applicable statutes and employers are probably free to undertake consultation or bargaining-type activities with their employees, if they wish.

Laws or court decisions in seven states provide the public employer with the right to enter into contracts with the organization representing his employees, if he wishes to do so. However, at least twelve states have laws, court decisions, or attorney generals' opinions declaring that public agencies cannot sign collective agreements with the employees, and that to do so, in the absence of statutory authorization, constitutes an illegal delegation of authority. This is still the majority view.

Even where bargaining or signing collective agreements is not illegal per se, the question remains as to whether such a signed agreement has any legal force or effect. In most states, it would appear that if a school board, for instance, signs a collective agreement with an organization of teachers, the board retains the right to nullify unilaterally the agreement or any part of it, and that, in such event, the teachers would find it difficult or impossible to gain relief in the court. In some cases, the ultimate power of the board to ignore the contract, if it sees fit, is specifically provided for by a clause in the contract in an attempt to avoid attack on the entire negotiating procedure in which the board has engaged.

The doctrine of illegal delegation of authority—which has been so potent in forestalling collective bargaining between public employers and employees—is under attack in both theory and practice. The doctrine has been gradually relaxed, as discretion has been granted increasingly to administrative officials throughout government in recent years, and it appears that the doctrine's demise as an effective block to negotiating activities in public employment is reasonably certain. It has been pointed out that the act of bargaining per se does not seem to constitute any delegation of authority by the public employer agency engaged in the bargaining. The requirement to bargain, even under federal labor laws applicable to private industry, does *not* carry a corollary requirement to abdicate responsibility, to capitulate on any given demand, or even to reach an agreement. It should be noted, though, that while concessions and compromises are not demanded by the legal concept of "good faith" bargaining, it is a practical fact that, in the context of the power relationship that marks true collective bargaining, matters discussed for the purpose of mutual decision-making are often compromised if they become subjects of dispute between the parties.

Boards and administrators who are about to begin negotiations with teacher organizations are often concerned about what they can, should, or must bargain about. The essentially political nature of the legislative determination and control of salaries and other conditions of employment for public employees makes the problem acute in most jurisdictions. In some teacher negotiating situations, the administration, if not the teacher organization, seems confident that headway has been made in defining those areas that will remain "managerial prerogatives," not subject to bargaining, and those matters that are "fair game" for the bargaining table. However, consideration of the following does not make one confident that hard and fast rules on what is or is not negotiable are likely to be forthcoming quickly on the teacher bargaining scene: The dynamics of any union-management relationship demand an ever increasing scope for union action and concern; under the laws applicable to private industry, the concept of "bargainable subject matter" has constantly expanded; and teachers, because of their professional relationship with the school system, are concerned with and knowledgeable about a vast range of the school's problems and activities.

There has been a trend in the last decade to provide some at least rudimentary *grievance procedures* to handle individual employee complaints in public employment. A public employee's right to present a grievance is protected by law in six states, and specific grievance machinery has been established by statute, executive order, or municipal ordinance in at least ten other areas. In most cases, the final step in the grievance procedure consists of nonbinding (advisory) arbitration, mediation, conciliation, or fact-finding. Grievance procedures have also been adopted voluntarily by numerous governmental employing agencies, including many school systems. Often these procedures have been adopted in the absence of any relationship with a collective employee organization.

Agreements in public employment to submit disputes to *binding* arbitration often meet the same objection—illegal delegation of authority—as does the signing of a collective contract. However, a number of recent court cases indicates a progressive relaxation of the prohibition against binding arbitration in governmental operations. Public agencies may soon have the recognized right to agree to submit to arbitration questions of liability under an existing agreement—e.g., grievances over the interpretation or application of the collective agreement. It is not likely, however, that they will be permitted to submit questions of policy to binding arbitration—e.g., basic terms and conditions of a collective agreement—in the foreseeable future.

The legislative and judicial positions on the question of *strikes* by public employees are quite clear. Both the federal government and the states, through laws and virtually unanimous court decisions, prohibit strikes by public employees. This is likely to remain the situation, despite the belief of some public employee unions that public employees in noncritical service areas should be allowed the right to strike. The problem of what to do in the event of a bargaining impasse when strikes are illegal is the single, most important issue relating to the extension of collective bargaining to public employees. Various forms of fact-finding and binding and nonbinding arbitration have been proposed, and experimentation in the states is sure to follow. Even though a teacher organization may not have the strike weapon in case of an impasse, it is far from powerless. It is free to operate in the glare of publicity and the expectations of the community. As negotiating procedures become established in local school systems, it seems probable that teacher organizations will find power alternatives to the withdrawal of services.

Although state laws, court decisions, and local ordinances provide the legal framework for teacher bargaining activities, mention should be made of President Kennedy's well-known Executive Order No. 10988 (January 1962). This Order provided for the recognition of, and collective bargaining by, organizations of federal employees. The Department of Labor is given the right to determine majority representatives, exclusive recognition is provided, written agreements may be signed, arbitration is advisory only, and the union shop and the strike are forbidden. The Order is being implemented in many departments of the federal government, and it may serve as a legislative pattern for the states.

Teacher groups, administrators, and boards of education are making pragmatic, flexible adjustments to particular circumstances in many communities—despite the chaotic, nonuniform state of the law applicable to teacher bargaining, the ambivalent attitude of school administrators toward collective action by teachers, and the opposition to formal shared control by the National School Boards Association. The relationships and procedures used to communicate and accommodate conflict are as diverse as the various autonomously administered school systems in which they have developed. A great variety of procedures and structural relationships, effecting more or less formal interaction, consultation, and negotiation, are being used by boards, administrators, and teacher groups. Many different subjects and problems are being discussed, bargained, and resolved, and in many cases the agreements are put in writing. These varied developments in numerous school systems and their impact on the educational process will deserve detailed analysis in the coming years.

Forces are at work, both within and outside education, that have the potential of providing greater impetus and opportunity to public employees —including teachers—to establish formal collective relationships with their employers. As a result, there may be a widespread extension of bargaining in education. All who are concerned with public education must give increasing attention to this phenomenon, its dynamics, its language and concepts, and its probable consequences.

II-3

THE IMPORTANCE OF STATE LEGISLATION*

Donald H. Wollett

The subject of this paper is the role of state legislation in professional negotiation. In analyzing this topic, it is important to understand the essential objectives of state legislation pertaining to professional negotiation. Such objectives are set forth in the NEA publication entitled *Guidelines for Professional Negotiation.*[1] According to the *Guidelines,* there are six essential things that need to be established as basic elements in a professional negotiation program.

First, there is recognition of the professional organization, the local, as the representative of the teachers. Second, there is the establishment of the proposition that these representatives of the teachers will meet with the board or its representatives and exchange views, that each will listen to the views of the other and negotiate in an effort to reach a mutually satisfactory understanding or agreement. Third, that the subject matter of those negotiations will reach beyond such welfare matters as salaries and will embrace all matters of mutual concern. Fourth, that if there is an impasse in these negotiations, there will be some procedure set up to deal with that situation. Fifth, that the procedures for settling an impasse will be professional and not labor-oriented. Sixth, that there will be special rules and regulations tailored to fit the profession of education. For example, that negotiating or bargaining units will not be fragmented into high school teachers, junior high school teachers, elementary school teachers, or subject-matter teachers, etc.; that unit determinations will take into account the fundamental proposition that the profession is unified around the certificate to teach.

These are, I take it, the main objectives, and the question is how to accomplish them. Significant accomplishments toward these six main objec-

---

* Adapted from a paper delivered at the NEA Conference on Professional Negotiation in Chicago, September 10, 1964. Donald H. Wollett is a partner in the New York law firm of Kaye, Scholer, Fierman, Hays, and Handler.
[1] Office of Professional Development and Welfare, *Guidelines for Professional Negotiation* (Washington, D.C.: National Education Association, 1965).

tives have been described in this conference, accomplishments through the process of agreement, that is, voluntarily, on a school-district-by-school-district basis. Something in the neighborhood of 120 written professional negotiation agreements are on file with NEA. Many more are in existence, but that many are on file with NEA. Each of these agreements does not contain all of these six essentials, but all contain some, so there has been significant progress on a voluntary basis. While the number of agreements is not as great as we would like, that does not minimize this accomplishment. This is hard work, and those who have accomplished these voluntary arrangements are certainly entitled to the gratitude of all of us.

There is another kind of voluntary action which has been used in Connecticut and perhaps in other states. I am familiar only with Connecticut where, working with the State Board of Education and other components of the educational complex, our association obtained the State Board's approval of a document called "Working Relations Between Boards of Education and Teacher Organizations." This is not a binding kind of thing and has no compulsory force on local school boards, but it has persuasive effect in establishing uniform criteria for school boards that wish to accept them. Perhaps most important of all, to the extent that these procedures are adopted they establish an educational custom and usage. I emphasize that because this can be very important when the day comes—as a matter of fact, it's here now—when more and more litigation and judicial decisions come down. Educational practice, as actually established, should play a great role in the disposition of legal questions. This is another form of voluntarism, but at the state level, rather than at the district level.

The only other way to attain our objectives that occurs to me is the involuntary method where professional negotiation is established, not by voluntary agreement, but by legislative mandate. We do not have any such legislation at the moment, as far as I know. We do not have any state laws which deal with professional negotiation as such.

THE CASE FOR LEGISLATION

What is the case for legislation as a method for accomplishing our objectives? Or, to put it negatively, why should we not stick with the voluntary methods that have been tried with success? I think there are several reasons that make the case for seeking state legislation. First, state legislation will *accelerate* the process of establishing professional negotiation, substituting for voluntarism the mandate of law. It will no longer be a matter of choice, it will be a matter of compliance. Let me say in that connection that I was interested to note that the resolution of the NEA Department of Classroom Teachers in Seattle was very much like the resolution passed by the NEA

Representative Assembly, except that it said the right of professional negotiation should be mandated by law.

Second, and I think this is the principal argument for legislation, let
us analyze the difficulties of accomplishing our objectives voluntarily.

As I see it, when we talk about professional negotiation we are talking
about two things fundamentally. We envision what one might call a countervailing force of organized teachers which asserts professional pressures equal
to lay pressures generated by other groups in the community; by this process,
the organized profession becomes a full partner with the board of education
in forming and shaping local school policy. The second thing I see is that
professional negotiation is a vehicle whereby teachers acquire greater on-the-
job dignity and independence in performing their functions as the heart of
the public school enterprise; for example, an effort by teachers through this
process to escape from the performance of demeaning and degrading chores
in the cafeteria, or to end "snoopervisory" practices which are outmoded
even in assembly-line industry.

RESISTANCE TO VOLUNTARY ACCEPTANCE

I have mentioned these fundamentals because I think that here lie the
seeds of much of the resistance, much of the problem, in terms of gaining
voluntary acceptance of the professional negotiation procedure. Some school
boards welcome such a procedure, as many already have, and doubtless many
more will; but others, and I suspect most others, will resist it for a good many
years. It seems to me that the reasons for this are rather clear. In the first
place, the process in varying degrees, depending on whether it is a Level I,
II, or III Agreement, poses a threat to local autonomy and lay control, or at
least it is so regarded. Whether in fact it is such a great threat may be
argued in a given case, but is likely to be looked at as involving in some
sense, at least, a usurpation of the school board's authority. School boards
(and superintendents, to the extent that they are delegates of board authority) are jealous of their sovereignty.

Second, professional negotiation procedures threaten notions of ortho-
dox line and staff management where authority must always coincide with
responsibility.

Next—and this reason hadn't occurred to me until I was made ac-
quainted with it by people from Connecticut—the process may turn out to
be too effective. Here is the illustration: In Meriden, Connecticut, an election
was held early last school year which our local affiliate won rather handily.
It entered into professional negotiation with the Meriden school board,
and through this process finally accomplished the largest salary increase in
the history of the Meriden district, ranging from $300 to $700. These in-

creases necessitated a special tax; and the board had some second thoughts about this after the negotiations were consummated and decided that it was too effective, so they de-certified the professional association. Voluntarism is not going to work where school boards have this mentality. Professional negotiation has to be established by law.

There is another source of resistance worth mentioning. We run into it often, particularly in the large urban communities where trade unions are strong. School boards and superintendents may be fearful of the professional negotiation process because it involves recognition of the professional association, usually to the exclusion of the AFT; and they are fearful that this will alienate the AFL-CIO structure in the community and make it more difficult to get favorable voter action on bond referenda and tax levies. I think this is one of the reasons for the stalemate situations we now find in such cities as Seattle and Los Angeles. How does one go about overcoming this resistance? It seems to me that if you want to overcome it in the reasonably near future, the answer has to be state legislation. You can continue to try to accomplish your objectives by voluntary agreements, but it's a hard road and I'm afraid a long one.

One other thing I want to say on this point. I suspect that some superintendents, perhaps many superintendents, would welcome a professional negotiation agreement but are unable to sell the idea to their school boards. Or perhaps they don't even want to take it to school boards for fear the school boards will say, "Look, the teachers teach. You run them. That's what you are hired to do and let's not have any of this nonsense." Or it may be that the school boards are fearful that the people in the community to whom they are accountable might say, "What is this nonsense? You were elected to the school board to run the school system. Now you are turning it over to the teachers." I mention this because if legislation were enacted, superintendents and school boards who are of a receptive mind but are unable to move into this kind of arrangement for the reasons I have indicated would do so. They would have to do so, and they would be completely off the hook as far as accountability to their constituency is concerned. An appropriate analogy is to civil rights legislation, where an executive officer—a mayor or a governor —may be unable to follow his own conscience in these matters if he wants to survive politically. But once there is a law, he is off the hook.

DANGERS OF NON-LEGISLATION

There are dangers in not having legislation. Now we in the NEA—and this is clear in our objectives—want among other things to be free of labor law precedent. We want to be free of labor law concepts which fragment bargaining units. Most of you are familiar with the Richfield case, which arose under the labor laws in Minnesota and involved exactly that issue. In that case we had a happy result. But there is a danger here. Concepts of what is an appropriate bargaining unit—drawn from the national Labor Relations Act, or from the state Labor Relations Act, or from rules and regulations of a state mediation board—will be applied to the field of education. The result may be to divide education into separate units for secondary teachers, elementary teachers, English teachers, shop teachers, and so on.

Another reason why we are concerned about the exclusion of labor law precedent from this area is that we object to the automatic exclusion of administrators, not only from the bargaining unit, so they are disenfranchised, but also because they may be excluded from all boards and committees and positions of influence in state and local associations. That issue was litigated in Wisconsin a year ago. It had a happy result for us also, at least so far as administrative membership is concerned. But the problem is not settled by one decision.

Moreover, we want educational channels to resolve impasses and to settle grievances. We don't want a labor arbitrator, although he may be a splendid adjudicator in a discharge case between the automobile workers and a truck manufacturer. We don't want him, despite his expertise in labor relations, to determine class size, for example. This is something he is not likely to know anything about. Nor do we want a state mediation board, no matter how highly qualified the members of it may be. We don't want them deciding, for example, where a salary dispute between a school board and a teacher association has come to them, whether the increase is to be across the board, on the basis of an index, or on some other basis. We regard these matters as educational problems to be solved by people whose competence lies in that field. This is another reason for wanting educational channels rather than labor channels.

In the absence of legislation, which is the current situation, what kind of precedents today are in fact being built? Let's take a look at the record and see what's happening around the United States in terms of the shape and direction of the law, in the absence of legislation of the kind we would want. The only statutory law that is being applied is in Wisconsin. Where did the law come from? It came from labor sources, UAW and others. These are very powerful forces in Wisconsin. It's a labor statute; it's labor in origin; it's labor in orientation; and, in the main, it's labor in administration. This is not a criticism of the members of the Wisconsin Employment Relations Board. It is just a statement of fact; that is their expertise, that's their experience, and, under the statute, that's their job. You can't criticize them for doing their job. But those are the precedents that are being built.

The vacuum is being filled with many, many decisions out of Wisconsin involving duty to bargain, involving bargaining units, involving whether supervisors can vote, involving whether administrators may belong to state associations, and whether or not you can send your literature to superintendents and let them distribute membership cards or let them distribute them through the schools. All of these things are being decided today at an ever-increasing rate. You can see the possible implications in other states. As problems come up, people in other states—and the courts—look to see what's happening in Wisconsin where the only experimentation is occurring. Judges, like most of us, take some comfort in seeing what the other guy is up to, especially if they can say, "Well, he has had more experience with this than I've had." That's the kind of law that is being developed in the absence of any education legislation dealing with this matter.

And what kinds of customs and usage are being developed, aside from law, in terms of local school board determinations? In the absence of law, determinations as to what kind of procedures will be followed are being made by local school boards, whose members are not knowledgeable in this field. They are usually under severe political pressure. They do the best they can. They reach for whatever they can and put together something which they think makes some sense. This is the kind of pattern and usage that is developing. The criteria for unit determination—that is, voter eligibility—have varied widely, depending apparently upon political rather than policy considerations. This has raised, I may say, some rather serious suspicions of gerrymandering. In Detroit teaching supervisors were excluded; a department head who teaches many hours a week couldn't vote. This was a more rigorous rule than was applied by the Wisconsin Employment Relations Board in Milwaukee. That cost us a lot of votes in Detroit, not enough to make the difference in the election result, but a significant number. In Yonkers, administrators were arbitrarily excluded from participation in the election, without any hearing, without any opportunity to present the evidence, without any opportunity to argue our case. This cost us enough votes to keep us from winning in Yonkers.

Let me give you a second example. There has not been uniform recognition of the right of organizations to full freedom in selecting the persons to sit at the bargaining table, after the election, or after the establishment of the negotiation procedure. I mentioned Detroit. In Detroit negotiators representing the teachers have to be employees of the system or on leave. Outsiders are excluded. That knocked out the executive secretary of the Detroit Education Association. He had never worked in the Detroit system. One school board, Yonkers, in setting up the rules for the election campaign even attempted to exclude everyone except the Yonkers teachers from participating in the campaign, from saying anything. We got the superintendent (this was his idea) to change this ruling, but it took some doing.

Here is another example: Determinations concerning the running and managing of elections have sometimes been hit-or-miss. It is very important to maintain the integrity of the secrecy of the ballot, to prevent coercive pressures around the polling places, to have the polling places open in locations and at times where and when people can easily vote, so you get a good turnout. The policies actually adopted constitute a crazy-quilt pattern. In some instances the school board has run the election itself. That was the case in Cleveland. There was a little hanky-panky there, we think. Again, not enough to make a difference, but disturbing. In other places inexperienced persons have been delegated by school boards to run and manage elections. In Yonkers and in New Rochelle, it was the League of Women Voters. They did a good job, but they don't know anything about running elections. They are fine ladies and conscientious—sincere and honest—but this is not their cup of tea.

Policies or procedures have often been established unilaterally by school boards. They don't listen to what we have to say. They don't listen to what the other side has to say. They don't call in educational experts and ask them what they have to say. They go ahead on their own without anything that could be identified as a fair hearing, or even the semblance of a fair hearing, and that's what happened in Cleveland. The school board reversed a year-long policy of opposition to any kind of effective teacher representation, without notice to anybody except the union encamped behind the door; scheduled an election in seven days; and did not make a definite ruling even on voter eligibility, or prescribe any election rules, until four days before the polls actually opened. Now, what kind of a process is that, to decide a matter as serious as the determination of a negotiating agent?

The elections themselves have been conducted under a widely diversified set of rules. Some school boards have said the winner has to poll a majority of those voting. This is the usual rule. New Rochelle is an example. Others have said that a plurality of votes is enough. This was the rule in Cleveland. Some have insisted upon a two-thirds majority. East Hartford, Connecticut, is an example. One school board (Yonkers) required a majority of all those eligible to vote.

The significance in practical terms of being recognized as the bargaining representative has varied widely. One board—this is Cleveland again—denied that the election winner would have any negotiating rights, so what the election established in Cleveland I haven't the slightest idea. Why they had that election except to help the union have a propaganda victory, I don't know. Other boards have indicated their willingness to bargain but have attempted to restrict the subject matter to wages and other welfare matters. Again, Yonkers is an example; they don't want us to talk about anything else, just money, just fringe benefits—an utter negation of the professional aspects of our program.

These are the kinds of customs and usage that are developing in the United States in the absence of law, and I find it very disturbing. I can't make any sense out of what is developing. It doesn't fit any coherent pattern; it has no rational basis; but this is what is happening and what I am afraid is going to continue to happen until some legislative guidelines are set down.

Another situation concerns me. This is where, as in Cleveland, there is a strong, competitive union local. We are at a disadvantage in Cleveland, where the union is putting pressure on the board to get one set of procedures and we are putting pressure on the board for another set. There are no applicable laws in the state. The board has a free hand to do what it wants to. And in a Cleveland-type situation where the AFL-CIO is strong they are able to mobilize more pressure on the board than we are. The power structure in the community, the opinion-makers that you might suppose would come to our side and help, remain dishearteningly neutral. But the trade unions don't suffer from this ambivalence; they know that the AFT is their outfit and they are with it, as they were in Cleveland. My point is that where the battle is a competitive thing and the union is in the picture, to let the battle be confined to the local community is a mistake. Particularly is this a mistake in a highly unionized city, where the central labor council is strong, not only in terms of economic muscle but in terms of political influence. By permitting the conflict to be confined that way, rather than broadening it to the state arena where in almost every instance we are strong and the state federation of teachers is weak, we cripple ourselves. One of the ways to shift this kind of thing, in terms of rules and regulations and precedents and so on, from the local level, where it is subject to the vagaries and diversities of local determination, into the state arena where we are strong, is to enact legislation that will introduce some uniformity and good sense and achieve our objectives.

Now a final reason. The American Federation of Teachers has already introduced considerable legislation, and is going to introduce more. I have in my hand the report to the Industrial Union Department, AFL-CIO, by its president, Walter P. Reuther; and he says, among other things: "Teacher organizing progress has already proved that this area must be further enlarged. In this connection, efforts must be directed toward winning legislation permitting collective bargaining. With such legislation, a growth potential will be virtually unlimited."

Mr. Reuther is bold, imaginative, and frank. He has said legislation will be introduced. This is not an idle promise. It will be done, at least in those states where the unions think they have a chance of getting successful action. If this is true, and it is, our adversaries are going to introduce their kind of legislation which, I take it, will be like the Colorado bill, or the Wisconsin statute. What should we do?

Rather than for us to be on the defensive trying to stop the enactment of that kind of legislation, is it not better to beat them to the punch and introduce the kind of affirmative legislation we want? Is that not better legislative strategy and does it not present a better image to our teachers, so that they know what we are for, not merely what we are against?

If we are really for professional negotiation, we have to fight for legislation that will make it a meaningful reality to 1,500,000 teachers—sooner, not later. If I read the signs correctly, the teachers in this country are demanding action, not talk; positivism, not negativism. We have a superior product, and we must market it, not by sneering at collective bargaining for teachers, but by demonstrating superiority with superior performance. That means that we must have legislation—now.

II-4

STATE REGULATION OF
EMPLOYMENT RELATIONS IN EDUCATION*

Arvid Anderson

Justice Holmes in one of his memorable dissents stressed the wisdom of allow-ing states to make "social experiments that an important part of the commu-nity desires, in the insulated chambers afforded by the several states."[1]

Currently, at least nine states, California, Connecticut, Massachusetts, Michigan, Minnesota, Oregon, Rhode Island, Washington, and Wisconsin, are engaged in various social experiments as to whether the principles and practices of collective bargaining can be transferred from the private to the public sector. Five of these states, Connecticut, Massachusetts, Michigan, Rhode Island and Wisconsin, have adopted laws to be administered by state labor relations agencies for their municipal employes. However, the states of Connecticut and Rhode Island, as well as California, Oregon and Washing-ton, have adopted separate statutes regulating teacher-school board relations.

The variations in these statutes and in their administrative machinery will serve as laboratories and guides to the rest of the nation for the estab-lishment of orderly procedures for the resolution of school board-teacher disputes. The statutes are based on the premise that employment terms in the public service, including wages, hours and conditions of employment, are essentially political decisions, hence a system of collective bargaining based upon informed persuasion rather than on economic weapons will be per-suasive upon the body politic and upon the employe organizations to resolve impasses.

Most of these labor relations statutes protect the right to organize and the right of employes to be represented in collective bargaining by repre-sentatives of their own choosing; provide for the determination of questions of representation; establish the duty to bargain; establish certain unfair labor

---

* Adapted from an address by Commissioner Arvid Anderson, Wisconsin Em-ployment Relations Board, at the National Institute on Collective Negotiations in Public Education cosponsored by Phi Delta Kappa and the University of Pennsyl-vania, Philadelphia, Pennsylvania, June 23, 1966.
[1] *Truax vs. Corrigan*, 257 U.S. 312, 1921.

practices for municipal employers and municipal labor organizations; and, in the event of impasses, make available mediation services and provide for fact-finding with public recommendations which are non-binding, as an alternative to the right to strike. The fundamental question to be answered by these legislative experiments is whether the principles and practices of collective bargaining which have been developed and protected by law in private employment can be transferred in whole or in part to public employment, while at the same time prohibiting the right to strike. Our five-year experience in administering the Wisconsin statute indicates that the tentative answer is yes, but the experiment is still in progress. Some authorities believe that the development of collective bargaining is unlikely without the strike weapon. Perhaps they are right, but our experience in Wisconsin suggests that collective bargaining can work even though strikes are prohibited. We have had five strikes by public employes in the past 4½ years, some more serious than others. Other strikes have been threatened. I do not suggest that Wisconsin law has abolished strikes but so far it has avoided serious prolonged strikes in public employment. Whether this record will continue remains to be seen.

A declaration of rights for municipal employes was passed in 1959, and in 1962 the Wisconsin Legislature enacted a comprehensive labor relations statute for all municipal employes. In May, 1966, the Wisconsin Legislature passed a comprehensive bargaining bill for state employes. This bill will be effective as of January 1, 1967. The prospective law allows collective bargaining by public employes on all matters except wages and other matters specifically governed by civil service.

The 1962 statute requires the Wisconsin Employment Relations Board (WERB) to administer the state labor relations code for state and local public employes. Up to June, 1966, the WERB received 478 cases involving municipal employes. Of this number 46 cases involved teachers. During the four-year period following enactment of the statute, the board conducted 30 representation elections among teachers. Locals of the Wisconsin Education Association were certified as the majority representative in 18 cases; locals of the Wisconsin Federation of Teachers were certified in 10. In two instances, no representative was chosen. In addition to the formal certification issued by the WERB, the Wisconsin Education Association claims that its locals have been formally recognized by boards of education in approximately 100 school districts. The Wisconsin Federation of Teachers also claims that its local affiliates have achieved recognition in a number of districts.

Other activities of the WERB include seven prohibited practice cases, one of which was pending in June, 1966. The board has been involved in seven mediation cases, including four cases in which formal recommendations of a fact-finder have been issued involving teachers. Mediation was effective in five cases, including four which went to fact-finding. The findings of the fact-finder were not accepted in toto, but served as the basis for settlement. Overall, of some 102 fact-finding petitions filed from 1962 to 1966, only 30 fact-finding reports were actually issued. The vast majority of cases were settled before the fact-finders made their recommendations by collective bargaining by the parties, by mediation, and/or by informal investigation by the board. In the course of determining whether a dispute warrants the appointment of a fact-finder, the WERB assigns a staff member to conduct an informal investigation or a formal hearing. In a substantial number of cases WERB representatives have been successful in resolving the dispute during the course of such informal investigation.

Many questions need to be resolved under the Wisconsin statutes. Some will require judicial interpretation or legislative changes. For example, the majority of the WERB (a three-member board) has held that the obligation to bargain is voluntary on the part of the municipal employer and thus not subject to an unfair labor practice charge, but that a refusal to bargain in good faith is a dispute subject to fact-finding with recommendations.[2] I dissented from that decision and also from a holding that a school board could grant a check-off to a minority employe organization as well as to the certified exclusive bargaining representative. It is my view that a dues check-off can only be executed with the exclusive majority representative.[3] These cases are now on appeal.

In my view, there are three basic areas of employer-employe disputes. One is recognition. In private employment, representation elections resolve the question of whether or not a labor organization does in fact represent a majority of the non-supervisory employes in a particular bargaining unit. This procedure, with some modification, has been adopted in public employment. The second major area of labor disputes involves grievances arising during the term of a collective agreement. In private employment, such grievances are resolved by final and binding grievance arbitration in approximately 95 per cent of collective bargaining agreements. There has been a very slow acceptance of grievance arbitration in the public service, but provisions for such arbitration are now being included in an increasing number of public labor agreements.

The third major area of dispute in public employment involves the terms of a new labor agreement. In private-sector collective bargaining, mediation and the strike are the means by which impasses over contract terms are resolved. In the public sector, it is hoped that such impasses can be resolved without resort to strikes by the use of advisory arbitration, fact-finding with recommendations, mediation, or, in some instances, compulsory

[2] *City of New Berlin,* Decision No. 7293, 3/24/66.
[3] *Milwaukee Board of School Directors,* Declaratory Ruling, Decision No. 6833-A, 3/24/66.

arbitration. In any case, recognition, grievances over working conditions, and impasses over new agreements are areas of dispute in school board-teacher relationships, as well as in private employment.

As previously pointed out, some states have already, and affirmatively, answered the primary question of whether collective bargaining for public employes shall be protected. These states have concluded that there is a need for orderly procedures to resolve employer-employe disputes in public employment. This does not mean that states which have not enacted legislation in this area have no problems over teacher-school board relations—they just do not have orderly procedures for dealing with them.

The second question is what legislation and what administrative machinery will facilitate collective bargaining in public employment. I define collective bargaining as the mutual obligation of employer and employe representatives to negotiate in good faith at reasonable times about their wages, hours, and working conditions. Specifically, I describe the collective bargaining table as being supported by four legs; the first is wages and all other economic benefits; the second is seniority; the third is grievance arbitration; and the fourth is union security.

Thus far, I have repeatedly used the term "collective bargaining" rather than the term "professional negotiation." This is not because I prefer one term over the other, but merely as a background for what I am about to say. Based upon my experience in Wisconsin, including experience at the negotiating table with representatives of organizations affiliated with the National Education Association and representatives of locals affiliated with the American Federation of Teachers, I am unable to find any substantive difference between collective bargaining and professional negotiation with respect to the four items which I have mentioned. There are differences in semantics, in tactics, and in methods which would cause teachers and school administrators to prefer one organization over the other, but I have failed to observe a substantive difference with respect to the four major objectives which both organizations pursue at the negotiating table. For example, some negotiators prefer the term "salary" rather than "wages"; the term "length of service" or "tenure" rather than "seniority"; the term "complaint procedure" rather than "grievance procedure"; the term "organization security" rather than "union shop." Basically, both the NEA and AFT are talking about the same conditions of employment, regardless of whether they "negotiate" or "bargain." I also have difficulty finding substantive differences between "withholding of service," "organization-declared professional study days," "strike," and "sanctions."

My only one real quarrel with the term "profession" as applied to teaching is that teachers are not paid as professionals. According to the statistics in Wisconsin, which are not greatly different from those prevailing elsewhere in the nation, the average earnings for teachers are just about equal to the average annual earnings for industrial workers in the state, slightly above $6100 per year. This is far below the average earnings for the skilled workers who build schools; it is approximately half the earnings of over-the-road truck drivers. Teachers' earnings, of course, do not compare with such professional employes as engineers, doctors, or lawyers.

A *Wall Street Journal* article about a year ago described teachers as the "Under-achievers in the collective bargaining process, who were rapidly moving to the head of the class." I would agree that they are under-achievers, but I disagree that they are rapidly moving to the head of the class. I am pleased to acknowledge, however, that teachers have found out that there is a course offered in the subject.

A source of concern to school administrators and state agencies regulating collective bargaining in public education is that NEA and AFT locals, as representatives of professionals, want to negotiate on matters not within the traditional scope of collective bargaining. The NEA asserts a right to negotiate over "all matters which affect the quality of the education program," and the AFT asserts a right to negotiate on "anything that affects the working life of the teacher." Such concepts clearly affect educational policy and are much broader than salaries, hours, and terms of employment. That these objectives are broad is understandable because most teachers, as professionals, are dedicated persons interested in the education of the whole child, rather than being interested in their occupation merely as a means of livelihood. However, the objectives of their professional organizations will affect the scope of negotiations.

One of the major arguments advanced for separate negotiations legislation governing school board-teacher relationships is that the problems of education are unique. This uniqueness is illustrated by the existence of school boards which, in many instances, have separate budget and taxing powers. On the other hand, the threat of strikes is not unique to teachers and is hardly justification in itself for establishing special procedures for dealing with teacher-school board relationships. Work stoppages by non-teaching personnel, such as custodial employes or school lunchroom employes or playground custodians, may also interfere with school operations. Furthermore, a strike by teachers hardly poses any greater threat to public health or safety or to the public interest than a strike of policemen, firemen, nurses, hospital attendants, or public utility employes. I make no argument that such groups of public employes should have the protected right to strike. The point is, however, that those who advocate special procedures for resolving teacher-school board disputes have the obligation not only to show the unique qualities of their particular occupation, but also that the establishment of such special procedures will help to meet all employer-employe relationships in their field, rather than just a portion of them.

It is also argued that relationships between teachers and administrators

are unique and require that supervisors not be excluded from teacher bargaining units, as would be expected under labor relations statutes. Experience
in Connecticut and a few other states which permit supervisory inclusion
in bargaining units will provide a better basis for deciding whether there is
a basic conflict of interests between supervisory participation in employe
organizations and the responsibility of the supervisor to carry out school
board policy.

In a recent paper, Wesley Wildman commented that teacher organizations which desire to change the pattern of lay control of education in this
country and which want to diminish the power of administrators will seek
to absorb the administrative hierarchy into the teacher group.[4] Wildman
also commented that some school board associations confronted with collective bargaining would prefer to have it modeled on the traditional pattern
with their policy-implementing administrative staff left wholly intact and
out of the rank-and-file organization. Wildman concludes that all-inclusive
bargaining units may pose a threat to the traditional role of school boards.
Wisconsin experience to date would confirm this belief.

In a significant unfair labor practice case, the WERB determined that
a school board committed an unfair labor practice when it refused to renew the teaching contract of the chairman of the local teacher welfare
committee on the ground that the teacher was too active and too vigorous
in pursuing the teachers' demands.[5] In this case, the school board acted
upon the recommendation of the superintendent of schools, who in turn
acted upon the recommendations of supervisors who had been influenced
by the superintendent. The discharged teacher even wanted to negotiate
directly with the school board rather than allow the superintendent to
conduct the negotiations for teachers. The complaint protesting the discharge
of the teacher was filed by 24 fellow teachers against the superintendent,
the principals, and the school board. The decision of the WERB ordering
the reinstatement of the teacher was reversed by the State Circuit Court
on the ground that the school laws of Wisconsin give school boards, rather
than our labor relations statute, the primary authority in the determination
of school employment policies.[6] This is a legal question which has to be
resolved by the Wisconsin Supreme Court, where the case is now on appeal.
In addition thereto, the Circuit Court concluded that if the school board

---

[4] "Representing the Teachers' Interests," Wesley A. Wildman, Director, Labor-
Management Projects, Industrial Relations Center, University of Chicago, delivered
at the Industrial Relations Research Association Annual Spring Meeting, May 7,
1966.
[5] *Muskego-Norway Consolidated Schools Joint School District No. 9, et al.,*
Decision No. 7247, 8/19/65.
[6] *Muskego-Norway Consolidated Schools Joint School District No. 9, et al.* v.
Wisconsin Employment Relations Board, Waukesha County Circuit Court, 3/1/66.

had a valid ground for refusing to renew the contract of the teacher, such ground would override any findings that the school board violated the Wisconsin employment relations statute in refusing to renew the teacher's contract because he was active on behalf of his fellow teachers in collective negotiations.

In the same proceeding, the WERB found that the school board, through the superintendent as its agent, violated the employment relations statute by threatening a teacher with loss of pay if the teacher failed to attend the convention of the state education association. The board concluded that such threat violated the rights of the teachers to refrain from organizational activity if they so desire.

Potential conflicts between supervisors and teachers can be presented in another way. Suppose a teacher who wishes to protest the denial of his request for transfer to a different school wants the teachers' association to represent him in protesting that denial. Suppose further that his principal is the president or a key officer of the local teachers' organization. With whom should the teacher file his grievance? There is no easy answer to this question. It is often suggested that in such instances of potential conflict, the supervisor is an important officer in a local teachers' organization, it is unlikely that his fellow teachers and supervisors, who also may be officers and members, will overrule him.

Admittedly, there is a considerable community of interest in salary schedules between supervisors and teachers, but even here there are some conflicts. Naturally, supervisors and principals want to establish salary schedules strong enough to recruit and retain qualified teachers. This reflects credit upon them and upon the school system. On the other hand, when there is not enough money to go around, which is normal, conflicts inevitably develop between the superintendent and the principals and the teachers whom they supervise. Should the money available be spent at the hiring level to recruit new teachers? Should it be spent at more experienced levels to retain qualified teachers and thus reward experience and advanced degrees? Should the money be spent at supervisory levels?

Possibly the resolution of conflict growing out of supervisory membership in employe organizations lies in permitting organizations of supervisors to use the employment relations statute and in forbidding the affiliation of such supervisory organizations with any organizations which also enroll employes whom they supervise. Regardless, anyone who thinks problems of supervisory employes are unique to education has not studied the problem in police, fire, nurses', and engineers' organizations or any other employe associations at the local, state, or federal level.

Previously, reference was made to differences between the negotiating objectives of teachers' organizations and the objectives of other public employe organizations. These differences have led to conflicts over the scope of bargaining. The professional employes have traditionally been consulted by the school administration on the curriculum and teaching materials to be used in the school system, but such consultation does not necessarily require negotiation or an agreement. Similarly, matters of class size affect not only working conditions but also educational policy. The WERB is now confronted by the question as to whether the school calendar is a negotiable subject. An unlimited right to transfer, based on seniority and assuming no questions of qualifications are involved, would permit teachers to transfer from less desirable teaching assignments in so-called difficult schools or in racially segregated schools, or from other older neighborhoods, thus weakening some of the schools which are most in need of experienced teachers. To what extent should supervisors make teacher assignments which override the individual teacher's right to exercise his preference? All of these matters affect the quality of the educational program as well as the individual rights of teachers. Whether the administration of teacher employment is entrusted to a labor relations agency or to an education agency will not make these decisions any easier, but it may mean educators will better understand the problems in some instances.

In preparing this paper, I asked representatives of school boards, teachers' organizations, and school administrators to give their views on whether or not administration of the Wisconsin statute conferring negotiating rights upon public school teachers should have been entrusted to an educational agency. Out of ten responses from individuals who were most candid in their answers, I found none who were convinced that the assignment of the labor relations function over education to a state labor relations agency had been a mistake. This is not an argument that the job could not have been done by an education agency, but it is significant that the executive secretary of the Wisconsin Education Association, an organization which had initially favored assigning such responsibilities to an education agency, now opposes such a change. All of the respondents emphasized the problems of understanding the educational system, but they felt that such understanding was secondary to an acceptance of orderly procedures for resolving employer-employe disputes in education. Some of the respondents stressed that the qualifications of the personnel administering the statute were far more important than the administrative machinery established to carry out the objectives of the statute. Some respondents suggested that the practice of using advisory committees composed of representatives of educational agencies had been a constructive step to understanding the problems of education.

From 1962 to 1966, members of the WERB have appeared at numerous school board conventions, conferences with school board administrators, conventions of the Wisconsin Education Association and of the Wisconsin

Federation of Teachers, and at institutes sponsored at the University of Wisconsin. The WERB staff has held hundreds of conferences and interviews with different school groups and individuals, explaining the objectives and purposes of the Wisconsin employment relations statute. The job of education has been a two-way street, and the WERB has learned a great deal about educational administration in the process. The effective administration of any labor relations statute and availability of competent mediation services at the state and federal levels have required experienced labor relations experts to learn a great deal about the field in which they are expected to assist.

Perhaps the biggest advantage of assigning the responsibilities for administration of an employment relations statute covering all state and local public employes to a single state agency is that single-industry agencies created to assist employers and employes in solving their day-to-day problems can become assimilated into the industry or dominated by it. As a result, these latter agencies are not in a position to exercise independent judgment. This has been the major criticism of the administration of the Railway Labor Act. In its early days, the Railway Labor Board made great contributions to railroad labor peace, but it has not been an effective instrument for resolving major conflicts between railroads and railroad employes in recent years. State legislatures should also take a look at the national labor policy in the Landrum-Griffith Act. This act contains special amendments to govern the construction and garment industries, makes special provisions for watchmen or guards, and recognizes the right of professional employes to have separate bargaining units.

Any employment relations statute in the public sector will have to take account of the division of powers in government and the impact of such division on the authority and scope of negotiations. The separation of the legislative and executive functions with respect to the decision-making power over employment conditions makes it difficult for government to furnish an effective negotiating team with the capacity to say "yes" or "no" at the negotiating table. Unless such a bargaining team is established with authority to effectively recommend action to the school board or other final legislative body, the bargaining process will break down. Budget deadlines and civil service or special statutes for teachers also affect the negotiating process, but this is also true for other public employes.

The course of collective negotiations for public employees is a political judgment for each state to make. On the basis of Wisconsin experience, I suggest that legislators considering negotiations statutes, whether for teachers only or for all public employes, should specifically provide for:

1. The right to organize.
2. The right to exclusive representation by the majority representative.
3. A clear designation of the role of the supervisor.

4. The duty of the public employer to recognize the majority representative.

5. The right of the public employe organization to negotiate collectively.

6. The duty to negotiate in good faith by both the public employer and the public employe organization.

7. Machinery for the enforcement of employment contracts.

8. A system of grievance arbitration to determine disputes arising during the term of the employment agreement.

9. Mediation services to resolve impasses.

10. Fact-finding with recommendations or advisory arbitration to resolve impasses as an alternative to the right to strike.

11. Prohibition of strikes but discretionary authority to take remedial action in case strikes do occur.

If public employment relations statutes contain the basic framework outlined above, and if they are administered by persons who believe that public employes have a right to organize and to negotiate, then the statute will have a good chance of working no matter which agency is assigned the responsibility for administration. Needless to say, the administrators must also believe that the balancing of employer-employe relationships will not only improve the economic status of the employes, but also improve the quality of our education system.

It is essential that advocacy of collective negotiations for public employes not be misunderstood to mean the transfer of unilateral determination of the conditions of employment from the public employer to the public employe organizations. What I am advocating is that a balancing of public employer-employe relationships by negotiation is in the public interest. If this can be achieved, and it has been achieved in the private sector, then our political democracy can be strengthened by the improvement in the salaries, hours, and conditions of employment in the public sector.

Negotiations are not a panacea for all of the shortcomings in education. Rather, they are an instrument which can be used by school administrators and teacher organizations for improving the quality of education and the quality of our society. Collective negotiations in education can make a contribution to fulfilling the promise of the twentieth century to become the century of the educated man. Those who share these convictions should join in the social experiments now abounding throughout the country and make whatever contribution they can to improve our educational system. The next decade should tell us whether these social experiments are one of the answers to improving the quality of education. I think the answer is going to be yes, and I hope educators everywhere will want to play a part in the experiment.

II-5

CONNECTICUT'S TEACHER NEGOTIATION LAW:
AN EARLY ANALYSIS*

Robbins Barstow

Public Act No. 298 of the 1965 Connecticut legislature established a new era in teacher-board relationships in this state. For the first time it entitled teachers in every one of Connecticut's 177 towns and school districts to negotiate with their employing board of education, *not by sufferance but by right*.

On June 18, 1965, Governor John Dempsey signed into law "An Act Concerning the Right of Teachers' Representatives to Negotiate with Boards of Education." Six months later, local teachers organizations in more than sixty towns embracing well over 50 per cent of the state's 30,000 teachers had already gained formal recognition under the law as exclusive negotiating representatives. By the end of June, 1966, over 90 per cent of the teachers in the state were operating under the statute's provisions. In all but two cities, the democratically chosen negotiating organization was a local education association affiliated with the Connecticut Education Association and the National Education Association.

One year is too short a time for a full assessment of the effect of a new statute. Nevertheless, the first twelve months under Connecticut's teacher negotiation law have revealed significant trends which offer the basis for an early analysis.

As of June 30, 1966, a total of twenty-five teacher representation referenda had been conducted under the Connecticut statute. In addition, exclusive recognition had been established in other towns by a "designation agreement" signed by the local school board on petition of a majority of the certificated professional employees.

By the end of the 1965-66 school year more than twenty overall group contracts regarding salaries and other conditions of employment had been

* Adapted for inclusion in this volume from an article published in *Phi Delta Kappan,* March, 1966. Robbins Barstow is Director of Professional Development, Connecticut Education Association.

negotiated and signed by local teacher organizations and boards of education. (Before the law only four such contracts had been in existence in Connecticut, all secured by CEA-NEA-affiliated local associations.) The first comprehensive agreement to be executed under the statute was signed on January 17, 1966, by the New Haven Teachers League (CEA-NEA) and the New Haven Board.

ELECTION RESULTS

Local education associations affiliated with or supported by the CEA and NEA won twenty-three of the twenty-five referenda conducted during 1965-66. In the first election held under the law, on September 8, 1965, the Hartford Federation of Teachers (AFL-CIO), gained exclusive negotiating rights in Hartford by a slim plurality vote over the Hartford Education Association. In the last election of the first year, on June 1, 1966, the New Britain Federation of Teachers defeated the New Britain Education Association. In between these two referenda, local education associations were victorious in twenty-three straight elections.

CEA-NEA associations were chosen as exclusive representatives in such cities as Bridgeport, Bristol, East Hartford, Manchester, Meriden, Stamford, Stratford, and Waterbury. All but two of the school districts where elections were held had more than 100 teachers, and most had staffs of between 400 and 1,400.

One of the most hotly contested elections, however, taking place on December 2 in the small town of Chaplin, involved a total of only 11 teachers. The final vote of 6 for the Chaplin Teachers Association (unaffiliated), 4 for the Chaplin Federation of Teachers, AFL-CIO, and 1 for neither, attests to the seriousness of the issue in this community. In fact, both state organizations poured staff, money and materials into the fray in efforts to swing the vote one way or the other. One local teachers' meeting was actually attended by three outside federation representatives and two CEA staff members!

How do the election results in Connecticut under Public Act 298 compare with the results of previous elections held in the two years preceding the statute's enactment? CEA-NEA affiliates won all eight of the pre-statute referenda in Connecticut; but in towns where AFT locals were listed on the ballots both times, the votes in the second contests gave the associations greater margins of victory than in the first elections. Association partisans interpret these results as evidence of teacher satisfaction with association representation and as a trend away from the AFT in Connecticut towns where CEA-NEA affiliates have won exclusive representation rights by the election route.

LEGISLATIVE BACKGROUND

Connecticut's "Right to Negotiate" law was originally sponsored and introduced by the CEA, which secured the passage of a breakthrough professional negotiation bill by the House early in May. The state federation of teachers and the AFL-CIO sought at first to block its passage in the Senate by the substitution of a collective bargaining bill for teachers under labor auspices. The statute finally enacted was hammered out in the heat of controversy and involved substantial amendments to the original bill. On every basic point of difference, however, between CEA-advocated "professional negotiation" provisions and federation-advocated "collective bargaining" provisions, the CEA position prevailed.

Because of the political pressures under which the final version was produced, the draftsmanship of Connecticut's teacher negotiation law is less than perfect. Some of its language is ambiguous and inconsistent, and litigation may well be required to clarify certain provisions. Nevertheless, despite imprecisions in wording, the Connecticut statute does embody a pattern of basic principles which distinguishes it at various points from teacher negotiation legislation enacted through 1965 in other states. The enumeration of these principles, together with an analysis of certain key ones, may offer a basis for further consideration in relation to the possible enactment of similar legislation elsewhere.

SIXTEEN PRINCIPLES

Significant principles embodied in the Connecticut teacher negotiation law are:

(1) It applies exclusively to teachers and boards of education, and does not lump them in with other public employees.

(2) It operates within the framework of the state department of education, and not the state department of labor.

(3) It covers all certificated professional employees of local boards of education below the rank of superintendent, and does not include the superintendent or non-certificated employees.

(4) It provides for employee representation through organizations, not through staff committees.

(5) It provides for exclusive representation by one organization on majority decision, and not proportionate representation.

(6) It allows exclusive recognition by majority designation where no competing organization files in opposition, and does not require an election in every school district.

(7)   Where two organizations seek exclusive recognition, it provides for majority choice by secret ballot election, not by membership count.

(8)   It provides for elections to be conducted by an agreed upon "impartial person or agency," not by the local board of education.

(9)   It provides for unit self-determination, and neither requires all negotiating units to include administrators nor requires all to exclude them.

(10)   It requires boards of education to *negotiate* with the selected teacher representatives, not merely to meet and confer. (It avoids, however, any use of or reference to the term "collective bargaining.")

(11)   It requires boards of education to negotiate with any representatives the teachers designate, not merely with local employees.

(12)   It provides for negotiations concerning "salaries and all other conditions of employment," and does not limit negotiation solely to economic policies.

(13)   It requires the "execution of a written contract incorporating any agreement reached if requested by either party," and does not leave negotiated matters to unilateral board adoption.

(14)   It specifically prohibits use of the strike weapon by teachers to effect a salary settlement, but it sets no statutory penalties.

(15)   It provides for mediation of disagreements or impasses by the state commissioner of education, not by the state labor mediation board or by a general public employee relations board.

(16)   It provides further recourse if mediation by the education commissioner fails, and establishes procedures for the appointment of a three-member advisory board of arbitrators for fact-finding and non-binding recommendations to both parties to secure a final settlement.

Five of the foregoing principles are elaborated upon here.

Separation from Other Public Employees

The first principle was regarded by the CEA as of paramount importance in Connecticut. The 1965 Connecticut legislature enacted another public employee landmark bill in addition to the teacher negotiation law. Public Act No. 159, the "Municipal Employees Relations Act," applies to all municipal employees "except . . . certified teachers," and extends to them a modified form of collective bargaining under the jurisdiction of the state labor department.

The CEA had exerted determined efforts over a period of many years to assure that teachers would not be lumped in with other public employees and that legislation affecting teacher-board of education relationships would be separate legislation, designed exclusively to serve educational needs and interests. The strongest kind of united-front insistence by state educational groups on this issue finally culminated in the twofold legislative breakthrough in Connecticut in 1965—one act for all municipal employees except teachers, and an entirely separate act governing teachers and boards of education alone.

Education Rather Than Labor Framework

The CEA took a similar position in relation to principles number two and fifteen outlined above. It was felt to be of crucial importance that teacher negotiation legislation provide for problems to be resolved and procedures developed through an agency specifically and exclusively established to deal with educational matters. The question of whether teachers and school boards should operate within the framework of the state department of education or under the state department of labor was a key controversy between the CEA and CFT forces in the 1965 legislature. The principle prevailed in Connecticut that professional school employment relations should be regulated by the state education agency.

As an outcome of the passage of the Connecticut teacher negotiation law, it was announced in November, 1965, that approval had been secured by the Connecticut State Department of Education for a federal grant of some $33,000 under Title V (Strengthening State Departments of Education) of Public Law 89-10 to be used for "Consultative and Regulatory Services in Teacher Board of Education Negotiations and Mediation." The Connecticut State Board of Education planned to employ at least two new full-time educational consultants specifically for the purpose of helping to implement Public Act No. 298 under educational auspices.

Education Commissioner Mediation

By the end of the 1965-66 school year a total of sixteen teacher-school board impasses had been submitted to the commissioner of education for mediation under the Connecticut act. Of these, eleven had been successfully resolved through the commissioner's mediation, one had been settled through subsequent referral to a three-member board of arbitrators, and four remained pending.

The first major dispute had occurred in the town of Stratford, where the Stratford Education Association had been elected on September 22, 1965, as the exclusive representative for all five hundred professional staff members. After two months of meetings in the face of an early budget deadline, and with full support from the CEA and NEA, the SEA formally submitted to the state commissioner of education the persistent disagreement over pay scales which had developed. The SEA charged the Stratford school board with lack of good faith in salary negotiations.

The issue was culminated in two lengthy mediation sessions in early January in the Hartford offices of the education commissioner. At these sessions, the Stratford teacher and board representatives finally reached agreement on a salary settlement which was subsequently approved by the staff as a whole and the full board of education. Schedule increases agreed to for 1966-67 ranged from a $500 jump in the bachelor's minimum to a raise of $950 in the maximum teacher's salary, and included similar gains for administrative personnel.

Local negotiations immediately resumed on a host of other items which had been submitted to the board by the SEA. On February 15 a comprehensive agreement was signed covering all professional employees of the Stratford board below the rank of superintendent. It incorporated the mediated salary settlement and twenty-five other articles including a detailed grievance procedure providing for binding arbitration in the final step.

Impartial Election Agency

Principle number seven enunciated above calls for the determination of majority choice by a secret ballot election where two organizations seek exclusive recognition in any one school district. The Connecticut statute sets certain basic election ground rules, and it specifically provides, as noted in principle number eight, that any teacher referendum called for under the act shall be conducted by a mutually agreed upon "impartial person or agency."

During the first year under the Connecticut law, the American Arbitration Association (AAA) was accepted by both NEA and AFT locals, as well as local boards of education, to conduct election contests. Out of the twenty-five elections held under P. A. 298 during the school year 1965-66, a total of eighteen were conducted by the AAA. In the eighteen AAA-conducted elections, rules and procedures for voting were determined for each separate town at one or more joint meetings of representatives of the school board and the competing organizations, presided over by an AAA staff representative. No two sets of rules were identical, but a general pattern evolved for the conduct of these elections. This pattern was specifically adapted to the circumstances, requirements, and concerns of teachers and their organizations.

The fact that each election was conducted by an agreed-upon, outside, impartial agency, with rules jointly determined, precluded any objection or challenge to the legitimacy of the vote. Such criticism had been voiced in previous Connecticut referenda held before the law was enacted. The use of the AAA in all contested major elections under the act made it possible to take advantage of developing educational precedent and served to increase confidence in the procedures for all concerned.

Types of Representation Units

Perhaps the most unique and significant element of Connecticut's teacher negotiation law is its procedure for unit determinations. The resolution of the problem of unit of representation embodied in Public Act No. 298 is that of *local self-determination within categorically defined limits.* The statute neither requires the inclusion of administrative personnel in every negotiation unit nor requires their exclusion from every unit. It leaves the decision to those involved in each school district.

Three types of representation units, *and only three,* are provided for under P. A. 298:

(1)   a unit comprised of the entire group of all certificated professional employees of the local board below the rank of superintendent;

(2)   a unit comprised solely of all certificated professional personnel employed and engaged in positions requiring only a teaching or special services (guidance counselor, etc.,) certificate; and

(3)   a unit comprised solely of all certificated professional personnel, below the rank of superintendent, employed and engaged in positions requiring an administration or supervisory certificate.

Thus the teachers and administrators in every Connecticut school district now have the option of either going it together or each group going it alone in negotiating with their school board. Moreover, the statute is so constructed that a majority of either group can veto any joint approach. Only if *both* a majority of the teachers and special services personnel *and* a majority of the administrative and supervisory personnel petition and/or vote for a single, all-inclusive negotiating unit can such a unit be established. If either a majority of teachers or a majority of administrators call for a separate negotiating unit, such a separate unit must be set up, and the other group has no alternative but to constitute a separate unit itself if it wishes to negotiate under the law. All arrangements are subject, however, to annual revision and change.

BI-UNIT ELECTIONS

The machinery devised to implement this unit self-determination provision of the Connecticut law in competing organization towns involves the holding of what is referred to as a *bi-unit* election. A bi-unit election is one in which teachers and administrators take part in a simultaneous election, but each group uses separate ballots in a separate voting place to select a negotiating representative. The same organization or different organizations may be selected to represent each group.

Under the Connecticut statute an election must be held in any school district (but not more than once a year) if a petition is filed with the state commissioner of education by twenty per cent or more of the employees either in the entire group of certificated personnel or in either of the two separate categories. In every instance where petitions for both entire-group and separate-unit elections have been filed in the same town, bi-unit elections have been mutually agreed to. The AAA has prepared separate ballots for teaching and administrative personnel, with the stipulation that: "In the event the results of the election by both separate units shall result in the election of the same representative organization, such organization shall be declared and certified as the exclusive representative for the entire group, comprising both units, of the certificated professional employees of the board of education."

Most CEA-NEA local associations have been committed to the concept of a single all-inclusive negotiating unit, partly on the premise that the larger the unit the greater the power at the bargaining table. They have also taken the position, however, that an all-inclusive unit can function effectively only if it can demonstrate without doubt that it commands the support of a majority both of classroom teachers and of administrative personnel. Therefore, the bi-unit election procedure has been supported in order to secure a separate, secret ballot poll of each of the two basic groups which make up the all-inclusive association's membership and which would have to back up its negotiations. In almost all such elections during the first year, the choices on the ballots have been, for the teachers: the association, the federation, or neither; and for administrators: the association or "no organization."

BOTH ALL-INCLUSIVE AND SEPARATE UNITS

Of the twenty-five teacher representation referenda held in Connecticut during the first year under Public Act No. 298, eleven were bi-unit elections. In all of these eleven, a majority of both teachers and administrators voted for the education association, and the unit of representation thus became a single, all-inclusive one. In six other Connecticut towns, elections were held on an entire group basis without separation or contest, so the result was one negotiating unit for all personnel below superintendent in these districts also.

On the other hand, in four Connecticut communities, including both Hartford and Chaplin, teachers petitioned for a separate election for teaching and special services personnel only, and no elections were held for administrative and supervisory personnel. In four other towns the teaching personnel and the administrative personnel each petitioned separately for separate elections. The result in these districts was the certification of different organizations to represent the two categories of employees.

Thus the outcome of the first twenty-five representation referenda held in Connecticut under P. A. 298 was seventeen towns having all certificated personnel below the superintendent represented in one all-inclusive negotiating unit, and eight towns having teachers represented in a separate negotiating unit not including administrative and supervisory personnel. A similar division took place among the towns where employees secured exclusive recognition by designation petition in the absence of any competing organization. Under the majority of such designation agreements, the negotiating unit recognized was an all-inclusive one embracing the entire group of certificated professional employees below the superintendent. There were a limited number of towns, however, where classroom teachers and special services personnel petitioned for and were granted designation in a separate unit excluding administrators.

CONNECTICUT A TESTING LABORATORY

It is apparent, therefore, that two types of negotiating experience will be gained simultaneously under the Connecticut law. Because of this, Connecticut during the latter half of the 1960's will in a real sense be a proving ground and testing laboratory for two contrasting theories regarding collective negotiations in education. One theory is that teachers and administrators have such conflicting interests that they cannot negotiate satisfactorily together with the same employer. The other theory is that teachers and administrators have common interests to such a degree that they can negotiate most effectively on a joint basis as part of a single unified group.

Connecticut's Public Act No. 298 could scarcely have been designed more appropriately to test these two theories against each other. The statute is so constructed as practically to compel the certificated professional employees of every board of education in the state to come directly to grips with this central issue and to make a decision one way or the other. If they wish to negotiate under the law, they must do so either in an all-inclusive unit or in two separate units, one comprised of teachers and the other of administrators. No half-way measure or other division is allowed.

Already a wide variety of internal organizational machinery has been developed to handle negotiation problems and procedures, particularly in local associations representing all-inclusive units. A basic ground rule in most such cases has been that the majority of the association's negotiating team should be classroom teachers but the team should include at least one administrative representative. Undoubtedly, no single pattern or structure will be universally adopted, and different situations will be found to yield best results through different means.

Nevertheless, when five or ten years have gone by in Connecticut under P. A. 298, if either the all-inclusive type or the separate type of negotiating unit proves through experience to be significantly more effective and comes to prevail in the great preponderance of Connecticut school systems, then that type of unit may be judged to be the one which, as a general rule, may best serve the teaching profession in the United States.

ALL-INCLUSIVE CONTRACT IN NEW HAVEN

It is interesting to note that the first comprehensive group contract to be negotiated in Connecticut under Public Act No. 298 was executed, not by a teacher-only unit such as that in Hartford, but by the all-inclusive unit in the city of New Haven. In an early bi-unit election, 79 per cent of the teachers voting and 76 per cent of the administrators voting, on separate ballots, had selected the New Haven Teachers League to represent all of the 1,075 professional staff members in the city in negotiations with the New Haven Board of Education.

The League negotiating team, which included administrative staff representation, commenced formal negotiations with the New Haven Board in late September. With extensive CEA staff and NEA legal counsel assistance, the teachers' efforts extended over a four-month period and culminated on the evening of January 17, 1966, in the signing of a binding, 48-page document by the official representatives of the League and the Board. Previously on the same day, both groups in separate meetings had officially ratified the proposed contract as developed through the negotiation process and recommended for ratification by all members of the League negotiating team and the Board president.

The group agreement thus executed between the parties extends over a three-year period and covers all professional personnel except the superintendent of schools. The contract contains a total of twenty-five separate articles, plus appendices listing salary schedules for all teachers and for all principals and other administrative-supervisory staff members. It provides for an average salary increase per teacher of more than $1500 over the three-year period. It includes extensive new fringe benefits applying to all professional personnel, and a detailed grievance procedure terminating in *final and binding arbitration*. Other employment terms spelled out in the agreement deal with such items as severance pay, personal leave, sabbatical leave, duty-free lunch periods, transfers, assignments, promotions, class size, teacher load, faculty meetings, textbook selection, preparation periods, teacher aides, clerical assistance, teacher specialists, and dues deductions.

The pattern established by this initial, all-inclusive New Haven agreement, and by the similar Stratford contract executed one month later, has already set significant precedents. Such agreements are clear evidence of the positive results for education and the profession which may be expected from the new era in teacher-board of education relationships launched by Connecticut's 1965 teacher negotiation law.

II-6

THE NEW MICHIGAN LABOR RELATIONS LAW AND PUBLIC SCHOOL TEACHERS*

Hyman Parker

On July 23, 1965, Governor George Romney signed into law Act 379 of the Michigan Public Acts of 1965, which constituted a basic revision of the Michigan Public Employment Relations Act. At the time the bill was signed, Governor Romney issued the following statement:

> The bill is the most basic revision of the act since its adoption in 1947. The major provisions of the bill give public employees, primarily at the local level, the rights of organization and of collective bargaining.
>
> It also eliminates automatic penalties for striking employees but permits public employees to discipline striking employees, to the extent of discharge, with the employees having the right of appeal to circuit court.
>
> I have given this bill the most careful consideration of any of the hundreds of bills adopted at this sitting of the Michigan Legislature.
>
> It is apparent that public employees in our state and throughout the nation are demanding and deserve a greater voice in their own working conditions than we have historically given them.
>
> The procedures called for in this revision of the Hutchinson Act will give them this greater voice, while at the same time leaving the ultimate determination in labor relations matters with public employers.
>
> These procedures importantly retain the prohibition against strikes by public employees, a prohibition which I wholeheartedly support in the interest of retaining always and without interruption the service to which the public is entitled.

The Act applies to all public employees, including persons "in the public school service." For the first time, the law declares it lawful for public employees to organize in labor organizations and to bargain collectively with public employers through representatives of their own free choice. Duly designated representatives of the employees in the appropriate unit

* Written especially for inclusion in this volume. Hyman Parker is Chief Mediation Officer, Michigan Labor Mediation Board.

are held to be the exclusive representatives of all public employees for the purposes of collective bargaining.

The Act establishes an election procedure patterned in many respects after the National Labor Relations Act. Public employees or organizations acting in their behalf may secure representation elections by filing petitions with the Michigan Labor Mediation Board. In addition, a public employer may file a representation petition for election where one or more individuals or labor organizations claim to be recognized as the bargaining representatives.

The Act also provides for decertification elections in which a group of employees assert that the labor organization which has been certified or recognized is no longer their representative.

The Labor Mediation Board encourages the parties to enter into agreements for consent representation elections, in which case, the parties must agree upon the appropriate bargaining unit and other matters. In the event a consent election cannot be obtained, a formal hearing is scheduled and the Board will issue an appropriate order determining the contested issues, including the designation of the appropriate bargaining unit.

The Act prohibits the conducting of an election within twelve months following a previous valid election. Run-off elections may be conducted in cases involving more than two choices, where none of the choices on the ballot received a majority vote. Such elections will be conducted between the two choices receiving the two largest number of votes. In addition a so-called re-run election may be ordered by the Board where conduct improperly affected a prior election. The Act also provides that a collective bargaining agreement will bar an election unless it is for a period of longer than three years.

If the employees' organization wins the election, the public employer is required to bargain collectively with the representatives so designated. Refusal to bargain collectively in good faith constitutes an unfair labor practice which can be remedied by the Board by the issuance of "Cease and Desist Orders" after a formal hearing.

The new Act, also for the first time, establishes so-called unfair labor practices which are designed to protect employees in their right to self-organization. The Act declares it unlawful for a public employer:

a)   To interfere with, restrain, or coerce employees in the exercise of their rights of self-organization.

b)   To create, initiate, dominate or interfere with the formation of a labor organization.

c)   To discriminate in regard to hire, terms or other conditions of employment for the purpose of encouraging or discouraging membership in a local organization.

d)   To discriminate against a public employee because he has given testimony or instituted proceedings under the Act.

e)   To refuse to bargain collectively.

Enforcement of violations of the Act is secured by filing "Charges" with the Labor Mediation Board which usually results in a formal hearing before the Board or a Trial Examiner. The Board, if it finds that the charges are supported by the record, will issue Cease and Desist Orders. Such Orders may be enforced in the courts or may be appealed by any of the interested parties.

The Act continues the prohibition against the right to strike by public employees. However, the previous harsh penalties of automatic discharge have been modified in order to permit the public employer either to re- move or otherwise discipline a striking employee. A disciplined or discharged employee may secure review of the employer's decision through the courts.

The amended Act continues to authorize the Labor Mediation Board to intervene and mediate grievances. The request for mediation may be initiated by the collective bargaining representative or the public employer. Where an appropriate request is filed, the Board will assign a staff mediator to assist the parties in arriving at a mutually agreeable settlement of the issues.

In addition, the amendments leave untouched the fact-finding pro- cedure for public employees. Such procedure is invoked where mediation has failed to resolve the matters in disagreement. The law authorizes the Board or its agents to conduct Fact-Finding Hearings and to issue non- binding Findings of Fact and Recommendations which may be publicized.

The limited experience of the Labor Mediation Board has demonstrated the effectiveness of the new Act in terms of representation elections. Peti- tions have been filed by affiliates of the Michigan Federation of Teachers and the Michigan Education Association. Frequently, both organizations will appear on the ballot and the results of the election will determine the bargaining representative.

It is still too early to evaluate conclusively the effect of the new Act in terms of public school teachers. However, the legislation does afford a method for reconciling the competition among teacher organizations for sole collective bargaining rights.

(The following paragraphs were added in August, 1966, to take into account the Michigan experience during 1965-66 under the Michigan Pub- lic Employment Relations Act.)

On July 23, 1966, the Michigan Public Employment Relations Act was one year old. One observer characterized 1966 as "The Teachers' Revolution," and "The year the teachers went to war for higher wages, better working conditions and a voice in educational policy." Although the dust of the battle has not yet settled, the one-year period has established a number of trends.

Despite the fact that strikes are prohibited under the act, nine school districts in Michigan were struck during the year for a period of one to nine days. The strikes were settled after school boards either filed a suit for injunction and/or invoked mediation.

Of approximately five hundred school districts in Michigan, a majority has either granted voluntary recognition to a teacher organization or has had a representation election supervised by the Michigan Board. Collective bargaining between teacher organizations and school boards has resulted in substantial increases in teachers' salaries and improvements in non-economic matters. Indications are that future negotiations may center on such non-economic items as curriculum development, class size, and transfer policies.

During 1965-66, collective bargaining was impeded by several factors. The most important were lack of experience on both sides, reluctance on the part of school boards to yield traditional management rights, the demand by teacher associations to correct all inequities by means of the first contract, and the financial inability of school districts to meet collective bargaining demands. The latter factor may necessitate an attempt to secure new sources of revenue by school districts.

In Michigan, property owners have been reluctant to vote additional millage. Naturally, this has created deadlocks in collective bargaining. There is a movement for "fiscal reform" in school finance. Such reform is designed to emphasize another form of taxation, such as a state income tax, instead of the property tax as a major source of school revenues.

During 1965-66, the Michigan Labor Mediation Board was actively engaged in intensive night and day mediation conferences between teacher organizations and school boards. The Board's efforts at mediation were usually successful, but some school districts may experience work stoppages during 1966-67.

During its first year of operations the Public Employment Relations Act appears to have taken three courses. The first involves sole collective bargaining rights under the act. Although teacher organizations historically have engaged in discussions and conferences with school administrators, such informal arrangements have been converted to legal collective bargaining relationships. This was accomplished either through voluntary recognition of a teacher organization by a school board or through the filing of petitions for election with the Michigan Labor Mediation Board. Subsequent elections resulted in board certification of a teacher organization as the sole collective bargaining agent of the teachers in a particular school system. In either case, there has resulted a mandatory duty to bargain in good faith. This new concept has required a reorientation in the attitudes of both school boards and teacher organizations.

A number of unfair labor practice charges have been filed by teacher organizations against school boards. The charges often allege refusal to bargain in good faith and interference with the formation and administration of teacher organizations. Most of these unfair labor practice cases have been settled either through hearing and board orders or by withdrawal where settlements have occurred as the result of collective bargaining and mediation.

The third development is in the process of collective bargaining and, where necessary, mediation and fact-finding. The negotiation of a first agreement in public as well as private employment has always been difficult, to say the least. Teacher organizations have attempted to secure not only salary adjustments, but also improvements relating to non-economic items. As previously mentioned, lack of experience and immaturity in the collective bargaining process have complicated negotiations. Nevertheless, it is anticipated that the parties will eventually learn to live with one another in a collective bargaining relationship so that the problems of accommodation may be minimized.

II-7

COLLECTIVE NEGOTIATIONS IN CANADIAN EDUCATION*

Tom Parker

My purpose in this paper is to provide an overview of collective negotiations in Canadian education. In doing so, I hope to clarify in some measure an area of relationships that, in my opinion, is of paramount importance to the future of the educational systems in both the United States and Canada.

In Canada we are opposed to the master-servant approach in board-teacher relationships. We believe in collective bargaining for teachers. We believe teachers should have a voice not only in determining their conditions of employment but also in defining educational goals and shaping educational policy. This requires recognition by both provincial (state) and municipal levels of government. To achieve this recognition we have succeeded, over a period of three decades of struggle, in developing all-inclusive province-wide teacher organizations embracing classroom teachers and principals alike. Before discussing collective negotiations in detail, it will be profitable to dwell briefly on the development of our teacher organizations and the political structure of the country in which they operate.

STRUCTURE OF GOVERNMENT

The government of Canada has a federal structure embracing ten provinces. Its powers and responsibilities are distributed between the federal government on the one hand and the provinces on the other hand.

Under the terms of the British North America Act of 1867, which established Canada as a Dominion, each province has been given the exclusive right to make laws in relation to education. In turn, all of the ten provinces except Newfoundland have delegated much of this responsibility for education to municipal units of government. While the costs of education are shared by the province with municipal authorities in varying pro-

* A paper delivered at the National Institute on Collective Negotiations in Public Education cosponsored by Phi Delta Kappa and Rhode Island College, July 7, 1965, Providence, R.I. Tom Parker is Executive Secretary, Nova Scotia Teachers Union.

portions depending on the grant structure in each province, the responsibility for education, including the engaging, dismissing, and terminating of the contracts of teachers, has been turned over to the individual local boards. This applies in all provinces except Newfoundland, where the teachers are engaged and paid by the province.

As might be expected, the ten provinces vary widely in population, size, and wealth. This has resulted in inequitable educational loads as between one province and another. A similar imbalance exists within each province between one municipality and another because of limiting local tax sources. This is an important factor in explaining the wide range in salaries paid to teachers from province to province and from municipality to municipality. Federal support for public education is limited to the field of vocational education, in which substantial grants are available for both capital and operating costs.

TABLE I
Province of Canada
(1961 Census)

Province	Area	Population (in thousands)	Seats in Legislative Assembly
British Columbia	366,255	1629	52
Alberta	255,285	1332	63
Saskatchewan	251,700	925	55
Manitoba	246,512	922	57
Ontario	412,582	6236	108
Quebec	594,860	5259	95
New Brunswick	27,985	598	52
Nova Scotia	21,068	737	43
Prince Edward Island	2,184	105	30
Newfoundland	156,185	455	42

TEACHER ORGANIZATIONS

Before the First World War teachers in most parts of Canada had some form of teachers' organization, either provincial or local in character. They were, however, largely ineffectual and frequently dominated by provincial inspectors or superintendents.

Following the War and during the depression years, in the economic struggle to survive, teachers quickly became more aggressive and better organized. In this struggle for economic survival and professional recognition the province of Saskatchewan achieved a very significant breakthrough in 1935 when it persuaded its government to pass legislation providing statutory or compulsory membership. A year earlier the Saskatchewan teachers had approached their government and had been told that if they could increase their voluntary membership from 45 per cent to 70 per cent they would get their professional act. During the ensuing year they raised their membership to 71 per cent with 91 per cent declaring themselves in favor of the proposed legislation. A year later Alberta also obtained statutory membership. As early, then, as 1936 there were two provinces in Canada where membership in the teachers' organization was a condition of employment. With a 100 per cent membership and a relatively substantial and stable income, there was a terrific potential for power and influence.

This development in Saskatchewan and Alberta created great interest in all the other provinces where the pros and cons of statutory membership were given full debate. It was, however, not until six years later that any other province was able to get a similar membership setup. In 1942 both Manitoba and New Brunswick obtained statutory membership, followed in 1944 by Ontario. The remaining provinces obtained their legislation later in the 40's, with the exception of Nova Scotia, which did not get full automatic membership until 1953. Table II shows this development, together with the kind of membership obtained.

TABLE II
Membership: Provincial Teacher Organizations

Province	Year Implemented	Compulsory[1]	Automatic with Write-out[2]	No. of Members (1964–65)
British Columbia	1947	x		14,961
Alberta	1936	x		15,300
Saskatchewan	1935	x		10,137
Manitoba	1942		x	8,650
Ontario	1944	x		61,941
Quebec (PAPT)	1945		x	6,035
(PACT)				2,100
New Brunswick	1942	x		6,049
Nova Scotia	1953		x	7,100
P. E. I.	1945		x	1,150
Newfoundland	1951		x	5,168

[1] Compulsory—all belong.
[2] Automatic with write-out—all belong except those who write out within a given time.

In summarizing, then,

1. Each province in Canada has only one teachers' organization (Quebec is an exception).

2. All qualified teachers are required to belong (except in five provinces where, if they do not wish to be a member, they must write out within a given time).

3. In each province the provincial government recognizes only one voice for teachers. Quebec is an exception where, up to the present, there have been two Commissions. The Protestant Commission recognizes the Provincial Association of Protestant Teachers. The English Catholic teachers are represented by the Provincial Association of Catholic Teachers, and the French Catholic by the *Corporation Instituteurs et Institutrices Catholiques*.

4. Each provincial organization is relieved of the task of soliciting membership each year and can devote its time and energy to more important tasks.

5. Each provincial organization has a steady working budget, the amount depending, of course, on the fees set. Fees in most provinces are deducted at source.

COLLECTIVE NEGOTIATIONS IN CANADA—GENERAL

Six of the ten provinces in Canada have statutory provision for collective bargaining. These provinces are British Columbia, Alberta, Saskatchewan, Manitoba, Quebec, and my own province, Nova Scotia.

Three of these provinces—British Columbia, Manitoba, and Quebec—have provision for arbitration proceedings and compulsory awards in the terminal stages. In the other three provinces the findings of a conciliation board or commission are not binding on either party.

Five of the provinces—British Columbia, Alberta, Quebec, Manitoba, and my own province, Nova Scotia—provide for a conciliation or mediation officer who may be used during the negotiation procedures.

Only one province, Alberta, gives formal recognition to the right to strike. Saskatchewan reserves the right to strike if the findings of the conciliation board are rejected. Manitoba legislation prohibits teachers from striking. In Quebec, a 1965 amendment to the Labor Code now gives teachers the right to strike. I have not seen this latest piece of legislation but I understand it includes a 60-day "cooling-off" period which restricts the effectiveness of the strike as a weapon.

Nova Scotia uses coincidental resignation in place of the strike when it is necessary to take further action following a board's rejection of conciliation findings.

Recognition of local bargaining units is specifically included or implied in the collective bargaining legislation of British Columbia, Alberta, Saskatchewan, Manitoba, Quebec, and Nova Scotia. In three of the four remaining provinces—Ontario, New Brunswick, and Prince Edward Island—

while not provided for by statute, there is in actual practice recognition of bargaining units. Local bargaining does not take place in Newfoundland, where a provincial salary scale is in effect.

This general information is summarized in Table III below.

TABLE III
Legislation Re Collective Bargaining of Teachers in Canada

Province	Legislation for Collective Bargaining	Arbitration Binding Awards	Conciliation Not Binding	Act
British Columbia	x	x		Public Schools Act.
Alberta	x		x	Alberta Labour Act.
Saskatchewan	x		x	Teachers' Salary Negotiation Act.
Manitoba	x	x		Public Schools Act.
Ontario				
Quebec	x	x		Labour Code.
New Brunswick				
Nova Scotia	x		x	Nova Scotia Teachers Union Act.
P. E. I.				
Newfoundland				

COLLECTIVE NEGOTIATIONS IN CANADA— PROVINCE BY PROVINCE

So far I have attempted to give you a general picture of negotiations across Canada. Most of you will want to know in greater detail the situation which exists in those provinces which have succeeded in obtaining statutory provision for collective bargaining. For this purpose I intend to use a summary prepared in 1964 by the Research Division of the Canadian Teachers' Federation, with which all ten provincial organizations are affiliated.

Summary of Negotiation Machinery as Outlined in the Legislative Acts of Six Provinces

1. British Columbia. Where no agreement exists respecting teachers' salaries, the local school board fixes the schedules applicable to all classes of teachers in that district. If negotiations are requested for schedules to go into effect the following calendar year, they take place between the board and the teachers between September 20 and October 31. On or before September 20, either party may initiate negotiations by submitting a notice to the other requesting a change in the existing agreement.

If negotiations are begun at this time, but no agreement is reached by October 31, the matter is put into the hands of a conciliator chosen by mutual agreement. If the parties cannot agree, then the Minister may appoint a conciliator. An agreement reached through the conciliator by November 14 is accepted by the school board and considered binding for the following year.

If no agreement is reached, the dispute is referred to a Salary Arbitration Board composed of:

a) one member appointed by the school board;

b) one member appointed by the teachers;

c) a chairman selected by the two arbitrators already appointed or, where the arbitrators cannot agree upon a chairman, by a judge of the Supreme Court of British Columbia.

If one party fails to appoint an arbitrator by November 25, a judge of the County Court appoints one for that party.

Arbitration proceedings must be concluded before December 31. The decision of the Arbitration Board is final and is binding on the school board. The resolutions go into effect the following day, January 1, for the whole calendar year.

This same method of conciliation and arbitration can be employed in the case of several school boards and the teachers in their districts. The decision of the Arbitration Board is binding for all who originally entered into negotiations.

2. *Alberta.*   Under the Alberta Labor Act, the Alberta Teachers' Association is the bargaining agent for all Alberta teachers. A collective agreement between the teachers and the board in any bargaining unit is legal and binding only after it has been signed on behalf of the ATA. In most cases, the teachers of a bargaining unit negotiate with their board and effect a settlement at the local level in a lawful, but not in the strictest sense legal, manner. If deadlock occurs, the ATA appoints a representative of the bargaining agent who meets with the board in further attempts to reach settlement.

If negotiations break down at the bargaining agent level, either party can request the services of a conciliation commissioner, an employee of the Board of Industrial Relations, who attempts to effect a settlement between the parties. If he is not successful, a conciliation board is usually appointed. This consists of a representative of the teachers, a representative of the board, and a mutually acceptable chairman. If the award of the conciliation board is rejected by the teachers or the board, a strike vote may be taken. If it carries and a strike takes place, it will be legal under the Alberta Labor Act.

3. Saskatchewan.   In Saskatchewan, the committee selected by a group of teachers to bargain collectively for salaries must be certified by the Saskatchewan Teachers' Federation. A certificate to this effect must be sent to the appropriate school board not later than November 1. The negotiating committee may include one member who is not part of the bargaining unit.

Application to negotiate by either the teachers' negotiating committee or the school board must be made between November 1 and January 15 of any academic year. Either party must honor an application to negotiate within thirty days of receipt. Any agreement reached during subsequent negotiations is applicable for the following school year and continues in effect until revised under the terms of the Teachers' Salary Negotiation Act. In the event of a breakdown in negotiations, either party or both may apply to the Minister of Education for a Board of Conciliation consisting of three persons:

a) one member appointed by the teachers;

b) one member appointed by the school board;

c) a chairman selected by the other two members.

Unless both sides accept the conciliation award, the decision of the Board of Conciliation is not binding and the right to strike is reserved in the event of its rejection by the teachers.

4. Manitoba.   The Province of Manitoba has established a Collective Agreement Board, whose authority it is to supervise the operations of all negotiations concerning teachers' salaries. It is composed of:

a) a chairman, the Deputy Minister of Education;

b) one member representing the Manitoba School Trustees' Association;

c) one member representing the Urban School Trustees' Association of Manitoba;

d) two members representing the Manitoba Teachers' Society.

The term of office for each member is three years, with the proviso that no more than two members change each year.

The bargaining agent for the teachers in a school district is the local. A local may consist of "any group of the members" of the Manitoba Teachers' Society (MTS). It may consist of the teachers in one school district only, or it may consist of teachers of as many as twenty or thirty school districts. The local must have a school district listed in its constitution before it can require the school district to meet it to negotiate an agreement covering the teachers in the district.

The teachers' business agent is the general secretary of the Manitoba Teachers' Society. His duty is to do the "paper work" required by the local, and to offer advice and assistance if requested. He cannot initiate any action on his own authority. He must have a request from the local in the form of a resolution from a meeting of the local.

In order to be qualified as the bargaining agent, a local must submit to the Procedure for Certification. The local must supply the following to the Collective Agreement Board:

   a) the charter and the constitution of the local which lists the schools in the local;

   b) evidence that the majority of the teachers at the local meeting wish the general secretary of MTS to become the business agent;

   c) evidence that the majority of teachers in each district wish the local to become certified for their district.

This is done on forms specified by the Collective Agreement Board. Thus, it is possible for a local to become the certified bargaining agent for nine school districts out of ten, but not for the tenth, because a majority of teachers in the tenth district do not wish the local to become certified to bargain for them. When a local has been certified for bargaining, the school board must deal exclusively with a committee of the local on all matters concerning the agreement. No individual teacher may bargain for himself. A local's certificate may be revoked by the Collective Agreement Board if, in the opinion of the Board, the local no longer represents the majority of teachers in the district for which it was certified.

If there is a collective agreement in force, the local gives written notice to the school board between one and three months before the agreement expires. This letter should contain a statement of the amendments proposed by the local, and should initiate the negotiations meeting.

In the event of a breakdown, either side may apply to the Minister of Education for the services of a conciliation officer, who shall hold as many meetings with both parties as are necessary until they are brought to agreement, or until he thinks none is possible. He then closes his case and either party makes a request to the Minister of Education for a Board of Arbitration.

A Board of Arbitration consists of three members appointed by the Minister:

   a) one outside member is nominated by the local society;

   b) one is nominated by the Trustees;

   c) the members nominate a chairman from a panel previously selected jointly by the Manitoba Teachers' Society and the Trustees' Associations.

The Board of Arbitration has the power to make a decision which is final and binding on both parties, i.e., on the board and on all teachers in the school district. It can summon witnesses and require them to give evidence under oath. It can demand the production of documents and any other evidence it wishes.

5. *Quebec.* In the province of Quebec, up until this year disputes between school corporations and their employees were heard and ruled on by councils of arbitration composed of three members. The school corporation and the employees, or the association authorized to represent them, each recommended a member to the Minister of Education, who subsequently appointed them to the council for a maximum period of two years. The third member, who represented the public and acted as president of the Council, was appointed by the Lieutenant-Governor. All decisions of the councils of arbitration were binding on both parties and could not be revised by the courts.

You will note that I have said "up until this year." A new Labor Code, implemented in December, 1964, and Bill 15, passed by the 1965 Legislature but not yet printed by the Queen's Printer, give teachers the right to strike and school boards the right to lock out. However, these rights are so limited by such restrictions as boards of inquiry, court injunctions, time limits, etc., that these rights are really of little practical value. Moreover, so I am told by Patrick McKeefrey, secretary of the PACT, in the final stage the dispute has to be referred to a Board of Arbitration with compulsory awards, as before.

6. *Nova Scotia.* Negotiations between a local of the Nova Scotia Teachers Union and the school board begin when either party writes a letter to the other requesting that negotiations be entered into. If the board refuses to meet with the teachers, the teachers may request that the Minister of Education appoint a mediator. This may be done. Should no settlement be reached through these negotiations the teachers can ask for a conciliation commission, which must be appointed.

Each side appoints one member. The two members then choose a third, or, in the case of disagreement, the third is appointed by a judge of the County. For the purpose of conducting an inquiry, a conciliation commission has all the powers of a commissioner appointed under the Public Inquiries Act. Within one month, the commission, unless both parties agree otherwise, must submit a report of its findings and recommendations to the Minister, the union and the school board. Each side is free to accept or reject the findings of the conciliation commission.

Summary of Practice in Four Provinces Where Salary
Negotiations Are Not Governed by Provincial Statutes

1. *Ontario.* In Ontario, there are no provisions for negotiation of teachers' salaries contained in the provincial legislation. Traditionally, how-

ever, local teachers' groups bargain collectively in all but the smallest boards. There seems to be a gentleman's agreement between teachers' organizations and boards that strikes will not take place. However, when negotiations break down, other techniques are occasionally used by the teachers to bring about a satisfactory settlement. These include use of the grey list or pink list; on which all teachers are advised of the breakdown in negotiations and informed that their organization does not approve of their signing contracts with the board or boards involved. In addition, limited use has been made of mass resignations as a means of effecting a settlement.

2. New Brunswick.   No negotiation procedure is spelled out in provincial legislation. However, teachers in large boards customarily bargain collectively for salaries. If negotiations fail, the New Brunswick Teachers' Association will, upon request, negotiate on behalf of the local group. There is no provision for conciliation.

3. Prince Edward Island.   No provision is made for collective bargaining under provincial statute in P.E.I. However, teachers in the two largest centers, Charlottetown and Summerside, do bargain collectively for salaries.

4. Newfoundland.   Since Newfoundland has a provincial salary scale, local collective bargaining does not take place.

RELATED QUESTIONS

Up to this point in my paper I have confined myself very largely to a description of the conditions existing in Canada with respect to collective negotiations by Canadian teachers. I am sure my audience has a number of questions and perhaps it would be appropriate to anticipate and attempt to answer a few of them. It should be kept in mind that while my answers are personal, they are nevertheless based on my knowledge and experience of conditions across Canada.

Union or a Profession?

What are our teacher organizations in Canada? While this question is sometimes posed by our members, it is more frequently asked by school boards and the public generally. Actually it is an academic question. We are professional in the sense that we are concerned with teacher education, standards of admission, and quality of service, and yet we do not hesitate to acknowledge and use techniques which have been developed and perfected by organized labor. Does it matter what people call us?

Are Teachers in Canada Affiliated with Organized Labor?

At the present time no teachers' organization in Canada is affiliated with labor. For a period of years, beginning in 1943, the B. C. Teachers' Federation was affiliated with the Trades and Labor Congress of Canada, but in 1956 it broke this affiliation. Its reasons were primarily economic. It was believed that the considerable sum spent in affiliation fees could be spent more effectively by the federation directly and that there was little direct benefit from continued affiliation. In the 1940's both Ontario and Nova Scotia seriously considered affiliation. The latter province actually went so far as to hold two province-wide referenda within a period of three years, one against and the second one for, by a small margin in both instances. The executive at that time wisely chose not to act on the results of the vote. Teachers in Canada are not against organized labor but they believe that their objectives can only be obtained through their own efforts and that there will be less public confusion if they make these efforts independently except for the support of fellow teachers in their neighboring provinces and across Canada.

What About Sanctions?

Teachers cannot bargain from a position of weakness. Effective negotiations are possible only when both parties recognize the strength of the other. School boards have authority to terminate the employment of teachers. In turn teachers must have a balancing power. In Canada we employ the technique of strike in some provinces and mass resignation in others. Armed with such a weapon, teachers can sit down at the bargaining table and know that their presentations will be considered and not ignored. On the other hand, the use of such a weapon does not take the place of negotiations. On the contrary, it must be used rarely and only with sound judgment.

What Does the Public Think About Teacher Strikes?

The answer to this question varies from province to province. In my own province of Nova Scotia we had two wildcat strikes which our provincial body chose to support in spite of opposition from sections of our membership. The press at that time as well as large sections of the public attacked the teachers for unethical action, breach of contract, etc. Largely as a result of this opposition to strike expressed by the press, the public, and sections of our own membership, we have since adopted and use the technique of mass or coincidental resignation. But probably it is not fair to assess the public attitude towards strike in a province where the technique is not used by teachers. Let us take Alberta instead, where, you will recall, it is legal for teachers to strike.

In April, 1964, the government of Alberta appointed a special committee "for the purpose of reviewing procedures for collective bargaining between trustees and teachers with a view to recommending such procedures and legislative enactments as it may conclude are necessary and desirable in the public interest."

The committee had thirteen public sittings and received submissions from teachers, trustees, and labor unions, as well as individuals. Whether or not teachers should be allowed to strike was discussed in almost every submission. In its report to the legislature made early this year, the committee, having assessed the feelings of the public and parties involved, listed as its number one recommendation "that the government enact no legislation which would deny the teachers the right to strike." This recommendation and the fact that the government of Alberta, during the sitting of its 1965 legislature, made no changes in the existing statutory provisions for collective bargaining between boards and teachers would seem to indicate that the public in general accepts the premise that teachers should have the same right to withhold their services as does any other employee group in our society.

Another indication of attitude towards teacher strikes is reflected in changes in the Quebec Labor Code implemented in September, 1964, which include provision for teacher strikes and school board lockouts. (Before a strike the code requires a 60-day "cooling-off" period.)

What Do We Mean by Coincidental Resignation?

In each province in Canada there is a set date (in some provinces two dates) during the year when the teacher or board gives notice of termination of service to become effective at the end of the school year. For example, in Nova Scotia the date of notice of termination of individual contract is March 31, with the actual termination becoming effective on July 31.

Coincidental or mass resignation occurs when all or a majority of teachers employed by a board individually submit their resignations because of dissatisfaction with conditions of employment or with the results of negotiations. Before such action approval is first obtained from the provincial body. Following such action, every member is notified by mail and may be reminded by daily notices in the press that unsatisfactory working conditions prevail in the particular area. The result of such an action is that the school board is unable to recruit a staff for the opening of school at the opening of the next school term. In the majority of cases a settlement is reached before the opening of the next school term. Where a settlement is not reached, the school or schools remain closed. In this sense coincidental resignation is really a delayed strike.

The technique of coincidental resignation is not as "clean" as that of the strike, and, since several of those who resign will not return to the school system because they have accepted positions with other boards without waiting for the termination of the dispute, it generally has a temporary adverse effect and sometimes a very serious effect on the operation of the particular school system for the next two or three years. On the other hand, despite these drawbacks, the use of coincidental resignation by teachers is accepted by the public, press, etc., in many parts of Canada which have a very strong reaction against the idea of teacher strikes.

What About the Incidence of Strikes and Coincidental Resignations?

Neither technique is used often and the work stoppage resulting from their use is negligible. In Alberta between 1942 and 1963 there were seven strikes totalling 82 school days lost. In one instance no school days were lost, so the 82 is actually limited to six jurisdictions. For these jurisdictions the percentage loss works out to 0.3 of one per cent, and if the whole province is considered, the percentage of school days lost works out approximately to 0.012 of one per cent. I do not have comparative figures for coincidental resignation, but they would be no greater since most of these disputes are resolved before the opening of the next school term.

What Do Teachers in Canada Think About Compulsory Awards?

I would have to admit that our thinking on compulsory awards is varied. In those provinces where compulsory awards do not apply to teachers, the reaction of those regularly involved in negotiations is generally against the compulsory awards restriction.

In British Columbia, Manitoba, and Quebec, where the statutes provide for compulsory awards, the attitude towards this provision is mixed. While some say it has been good for the teachers, others maintain that it jeopardizes "bargaining in good faith," since there is a tendency for one or both parties to go through the motions of collective bargaining, counting on the board of arbitration to resolve their problem at the appropriate time. J. A. Sprague of the British Columbia Teachers' Federation sums it up in these words:

> Too frequently under British Columbia conditions, the negotiation pattern is one of an obstinate group of teachers facing an obdurate school board, drifting through the mere passage of time into a hastily arranged hearing before a hurried and harried arbitration board which makes a poor best of a bad job under impossible conditions. Such a procedure cannot solve the real problem; at best it postpones for a year the search for a solution.

Are Local Negotiators Given Any Special Training or Help?

Yes, this is done in a variety of ways. First of all, most provinces have one or more persons on their staff who have been especially trained in economics, which is another word we use for salary negotiations. Mr. Fergusson, the economic member of our NSTU staff, has spent four sessions at the ATA (Alberta) Economic Seminar. Another person on our staff has been there three times.

These persons in turn are expected to transmit their knowledge and skill to local negotiators and are continuously available to locals at every stage of negotiations.

In several provinces the effectiveness of the staff's service in the collective bargaining is increased and extended by the use of a corps of economic consultants who have been carefully selected from various parts of the province. They have been selected for their past work in local negotiations. They are given special training, and are used as liaison men and to assist in local negotiations when requested.

The preparation each year of an economic handbook for negotiators and regularly distributed economic bulletins and newsletters also help to give local negotiators the know-how as well as knowledge of up-to-date developments and negotiations across one's own province and in other provinces, too.

CONCLUSION

In presenting this outline of collective negotiations in Canada, I have overlooked many details because I wanted to give you the picture as a whole. I have also ignored the many problems we face in Canada in this area of collective bargaining.

I appreciate that your political, social, and educational situation is much more complex in the United States than is ours in Canada, and I know that the techniques developed in one country, province, or state cannot be used by another without substantial modification. I have, therefore, no advice to give or words of wisdom to drop.

In summing up, I might say that if we have had reasonable success in our efforts in collective bargaining it has been because of some or all of the following factors:

1. Through our statutory membership we have achieved a status which closely parallels that obtained by organized labor when it has achieved what it calls a "closed shop."

2. Our membership embraces in one organization all (or practically all) teachers and principals employed by the school boards.

3. Most of our provincial organizations have fee deductions at source.

4. A majority of the provinces have collective bargaining machinery established by law and accepted by school boards.

5. Several of the provinces have developed effective techniques for the application of sanctions where necessary.

6. All recognize the necessity of continuous effort in this area of

collective negotiations. The memberships are constantly reminded that an agreement reached is not the end in itself. After an agreement has been signed it still has to be made to work. At the same time, preparations must be started at once for the next sessions at the bargaining table. Collective bargaining is a perpetual process.

ORGANIZATIONAL APPROACHES TO COLLECTIVE NEGOTIATIONS

The collective negotiations movement in public education has its origins and chief sources of power in the dynamics of teacher organizations. The rivalry between the American Federation of Teachers and the National Education Association is an important part of these organizational dynamics. Beginning in the early 1960's, these two organizations rapidly developed both the theory and practice of collective negotiations in public education. The different traditions and allegiances characteristic of the two organizations have given them different outlooks and somewhat different goals. There are factors, however, which force both organizations to adopt similar objectives and tactics as they become more deeply involved in collective negotiations. This fact can be observed not only in Section III but in the section on strategy and tactics and in the section on issues and problems.

No better spokesmen for the positions of the NEA and AFT could be found than Allan M. West and Charles Cogen, respectively. West was brought to the NEA in 1962 after proving his ability as a leader and demonstrating his understanding of the potential of group action while executive secretary of the Utah Education Association. He headed the new NEA Urban Project, a coordinating agency designed to deal with the complex educational problems stemming largely from the fast pace of urban growth in America. The Urban Project was frankly designed, among other things, to help local associations develop collective agreements favorable to teachers and to win representation elections vis-a-vis the AFT. West was elevated to assistant executive secretary of the NEA for field operations and urban services in 1964, a position he still holds.

Charles Cogen led the United Federation of Teachers, the New York City local of the AFT, when it forced the New York City Board of Education to conduct a representation election and then went on to win the election itself. He was president of the UFT when it achieved its trail-breaking first written agreement with the New York City board in 1963. The UFT rapidly became the leading local teacher union in the United States, and Cogen rode to the presidency of the AFT in 1964 on the crest of the UFT's prestige and success.

The article by George Strauss provides some interesting observations on the effectiveness of the American Association of University Professors. Interested readers might find it profitable to contrast Strauss's article with Chapter X of Myron Lieberman's The Future of Public Education, *which is also devoted to the AAUP.*

In response to the increasing use of collective negotiations in public education, other educational organizations have also taken positions on the issues involved. These positions have sometimes been adopted reluctantly and belatedly and with an inadequate understanding of the collective negotiations movement. One important exception to this generalization is the 1965 policy statement of the National Association of Secondary-School Principals. Benjamin Epstein, principal of Weequahic High School in New Jersey, is the author of the NASSP statement. His article in this section summarizes the NASSP position and his reactions to the role of the principal in collective negotiations.*

Although collective negotiations are inherently a result of teacher initiative, the school boards' response to it is of the utmost importance. As executive director of the National School Boards Association, Harold Webb has been in an excellent position to assess school board reactions to the collective negotiations movement. Although the position outlined in his article clearly is no longer applicable in many states, it does reflect the prevailing view of many school boards.

The collective negotiations movement has placed new pressures on school superintendents. For several years they have struggled individually and collectively to formulate policies in this area. The next selection, taken from a 1966 policy statement of the American Association of School Administrators, deals primarily with the policy problems of negotiations as they impinge upon school administrators. Although inadequate time has elapsed to assess the impact of the AASA statement, it will probably influence many school administrators to accept some form of collective negotiations in public education.

Finally, because Canadian teacher organizations have had longer experience with collective negotiations and have developed strategies and techniques still unfamiliar to U.S. teachers, we have included an article describing the role of Canadian teacher organizations in collective negotiations. Arthur Kratzmann writes from his point of view as executive director of the Alberta School Trustees' Association, an organization of Canadian school

---

* The official statement of the NASSP is set forth in Benjamin Epstein, *The Principal's Role in Collective Negotiations* (Washington, D.C.: National Association of Secondary-School Principals, 1965).

boards which one might expect to oppose effective group action by teachers. Interestingly enough, Kratzmann admires the Alberta Teachers' Association for its ability to take militant action for teachers and for education. His article includes some interesting observations on how teacher organizations in the United States might increase their effectiveness as organizations of professional employees.

III–1

THE NEA AND COLLECTIVE NEGOTIATIONS*

Allan M. West

A planning committee recently discussed at considerable length whether to make the title of an assigned conference speech "The Teacher Rebellion" or "Why Are Teachers Raising Hell?"

I find there is a good deal of misunderstanding about the answer to this question. Some would dismiss the current ferment among teachers as a jurisdictional fight between two organizations. Others have said that it is being caused by a group of young radicals trying to wrest control of the schools from the elected authorities. Both of these views are superficial and false.

The current unrest among teachers is a natural response to a combination of a number of social forces in our society. And since the public school is society in miniature, these forces are having some profound effects upon schools and those of us who work in them.

If we are going to deal with these forces successfully, we must take a hard look at our present practices and be prepared to make some changes in our thinking and in the way that we work with each other. Let me identify briefly a few of the developments which illustrate why collective action in public education is a timely topic, and why we must change some of our old concepts and methods.

In the first place, our public school enrollments are growing rapidly. Between 1930 and 1964 our pupil population increased from 26 million to 42 million. But this is only part of the picture. While our elementary population was increasing from 22 to 27 million, our high school population increased from 4 to 15 million, and it costs more—about one and one-half times more —to educate a high school pupil than an elementary pupil.

Increased enrollments have caused a corresponding increase in the size of our teaching staff, and most of these new teachers are recent college graduates coming in at the bottom of the salary scale. This means that the av-

* Paper presented on April 2, 1965 at the Midwest Administration Center, University of Chicago, Chicago, Illinois. Allan M. West is Assistant Executive Secretary for Field Operations and Urban Services, National Education Association, Washington, D. C.

erage age of our teaching staff is being reduced. In the five years between 1956 and 1961, the average age of our teaching staff was reduced by two years. Moreover, during this same five-year period the proportion of men teachers has increased from 27.5 per cent to 31.3 per cent of the total teaching staff. In 1956, 53 per cent of the men teachers were under thirty-five. In 1961, 62 per cent were under thirty-five.

Today's teachers have more college training and fewer hold substandard credentials. The proportion of our teaching staff holding bachelor's degrees or better has increased from 60 per cent in 1947-48 to 90 per cent in 1963. The proportion holding master's degrees or higher in that same period has increased from 15 per cent to 25 per cent.

So our younger teaching staff is also better trained and more masculine. Today's teachers have a new spirit which is demanding a voice in determining what goes on in the classroom. They want to be full-fledged members of the school team. They want to be treated as responsible professionals. They want to be consulted about problems which affect them. They are saying: If we can be trusted to teach the boys and girls of the community, we should be trusted to help make the policies which determine the quality of education which they receive.

This need for recognition, this desire to play a more responsible role in school policy making, is at the bottom of many of the eruptions that have taken place in the past few months. This new breed of teacher is impatient. He does not want to wait for the benefits which he honestly thinks he deserves. He is not aware of the battles that have been fought and won in the past. He wants benefits now. He is more concerned with what an organization can do for him in the next six months than he is in what it has done for him in the past century.

School systems are also changing. Thirty years ago we had about 130,000 school systems in the United States. Today there are only about 25,000. Illinois offers a dramatic example of the changes taking place in our school systems. Since 1940 the number of school districts in Illinois has been reduced from 12,000 to 1,390.

Today's school is larger and more impersonal. The social distance between the classroom teacher and the administrator is greater. In larger school systems we tend to have less confidence in each other. We do not know each other well. We communicate in writing where formerly a teacher and an administrator could iron out problems with a personal conference. As systems become larger we become inhibited by rules. The superintendent ceases to be an individual; he is a name on the bottom of a memorandum. Bigness, depersonalizing of the school system, and bureaucracy have given greater significance to the local unit. More teachers feel powerless as individuals to change conditions. Formal grievance procedures are needed to correct gripes that at one time could be settled informally.

There are also important changes taking place in the culture of our local communities. In rural areas with the mechanization of the farms young people have left to seek their fortunes in the cities and suburban areas.

In the growing urban and suburban areas problems are more complex. Large urban communities are more bureaucratic, less responsive to the needs of the citizens, and a new culture and a different scale of values is developing.

There are fewer white Anglo-Saxon Protestants, and more Jews, Negroes and Catholics with different social philosophies. There are greater demands for services because of growth, and there are greater frustrations due to inability of the community to respond to the needs of the citizens. The changing population is bringing with it needs for more water systems, rapid transit lines, welfare services, police, fire and health protection. All of these demands bring with them greater competition for the tax dollar, and in many communities frustration is a way of life for all who seek to meet new conditions with outmoded governmental machinery.

There was a time when most problems which teachers faced could be solved by the state associations through legislative action. Minimum salary laws were enacted requiring the local board of education to meet certain minimum requirements by statute. Mandatory minimum increments were added.

Tenure laws and retirement laws were passed by the legislature at the initiative of state education associations. This left little in the salary area for the local associations to do in areas when districts were small. But as districts have become larger, teachers are finding a need for a more vigorous and articulate voice in the local community to deal with the more impersonal board of education and administration, and to persuade the local community to recognize and meet school and teacher needs.

Current social changes also reveal some weaknesses in our past legislative approaches. Traditionally we have made allocations in terms of so many dollars per child, or classroom units. We now see that some children require more dollars than others. The question, therefore, is not simply one of equalizing educational opportunities through the distribution of a certain uniform number of dollars per child. It is also a matter of measuring differences in needs among children to be served by the public schools, and providing the dollars necessary to compensate for past failures of the home, church and community, if we are to meet the individual needs of pupils.

These are just a few of the forces which in combination account for the emergence of proposals to formalize procedures and tap the resources of our teaching staff. These are the forces which cause teachers to insist upon their recognition as full-fledged members of the school team with some assurance that their voice can be heard where policy decisions are made. These are some of the forces which have moved them to insist that they be considered in policy making as a *right,* rather than as a favor bestowed upon them by a benevolent administration or board of education. It is a matter of self-respect.

In the past few months we have seen explosions in big cities, suburban, and even rural areas. In my opinion these explosions have taken place as a result of one or a combination of the following factors: accumulated frustrations of teachers because of their inability to meet their own standards in the classroom, a desire for a stronger voice in policy making, a protest against the impersonality of bigness and bureaucracy, a protest against arbitrary administration, or a protest against community inaction in the face of mounting school needs.

TRADITIONAL APPROACHES

Both professional organizations and teachers' unions exist to bring about changes. Obviously the methods used by each group will be different, since the philosophies which motivate the two groups are different.

Traditionally the union has devoted its efforts almost exclusively to the local school system. On the other hand, the professional organizations have emphasized action on *all three levels*—LOCAL, STATE and NATIONAL.

State associations exist in every state. Each has a paid staff, and in most states the "teachers' lobby" is numbered among the most effective lobbies on Capitol Hill.

The nature of the school enterprise is such that more than two dollars out of every three available to the schools for operation and maintenance go into the salary budget. It is just that kind of an operation. Therefore, if the legislatures can be persuaded to appropriate more dollars to schools, a good share of them will go into the salary budget. A school is a service enterprise in which professionally trained people provide services to children. It is, therefore, appropriate that the salary category should account for most of the operating budget. There is little flexibility in the typical school budget. Maintenance of buildings can be postponed. But it is a small part of the total budget and a short-sighted way to "save" money. It has been the policy of professional organizations to work aggressively with state legislatures and the federal Congress to put more dollars in the hands of local boards of education. Local units then have had the task of seeing that teachers' salaries receive a fair share of the revenue.

Therefore, by joining with other organizations interested in the schools including the administration and local school board, the chief task of the state association has been to promote legislation which would improve the financing of the schools, protect the tenure of teachers, provide adequately for their retirement, protect against legislation which will cripple the schools, and promote that which will improve the quality of the school program. These services of the state associations have been backed up by the Research Division of the National Education Association and the work of a host of state and national committees and commissions which provide specialized information and a forum for sharing successful experiences and developing uniform legislative goals. Local associations have been involved in the legislative effort by taking part actively in the election of legislators, persuading them after election to support good school measures, and making certain that teachers share equitably in the fruits of the legislation.

These state legislative programs must continue and remain strong. The constitutions of the several states place the primary responsibility for schools upon the state legislature. Teachers must continue to have an articulate voice in its deliberations. They must also be active in the political arena to elect legislators who will support good school legislation. In recent years the importance of strong leadership at the national level to secure good school legislation from the federal Congress has become dramatically clear and increasingly important. While federal funds still comprise a small share of total school revenues, the percentage of federal funds has increased significantly.

The growing size, complexity and impersonality of local school systems have added a new and important dimension to that traditionally performed by the local unit. It is clear that professional associations must devote more effort to strengthening local associations and improving community relationships. This has been recognized and a great deal of effort is now being made by professional associations to strengthen them. Local units must engage in a growing variety of activities required to give a voice to teachers in the local community above and beyond that required to support state and national programs.

The unions have approached the problem differently. They have borrowed procedures from industry through which to apply pressure on the local board of education. The theory is that if sufficient pressure is applied locally, and, if the local board of education cannot grant the relief requested, it will be sufficiently uncomfortable to seek relief from the higher levels of government.

Unions are not equipped to work on all three levels. They do not have either the organization or the strength. They have no state organizations in most states, and none which are comparable in strength to the state education associations. If the president of the American Federation of Teachers accurately defines the policy of the AFT, there appears to be little distinction between the procedures which it considers to be appropriate for industry and those which are appropriate for teaching in the public service. Charles Cogen, in an interview with Peter A. Janssen of *The Philadelphia Inquirer,* following his election in 1964, said that he hopes ". . . to use all of the devices available to trade unions because after all we are a trade union. These include strikes if necessary, picketing and rallies."

Because of the great differences in the purposes, resources, philosophies and structures of the two organizations, it is not surprising that they should adopt different methods of operation. The union relies chiefly on force applied at the local level. The professional association relies chiefly on persuasion at all three levels—local, state and national.

It is only natural that the associations see strength in the cooperative approach to the solution to school problems. It is based on the belief that teachers, school boards and school administrators have differences, but they also have many common and overriding mutual interests. It is, therefore, possible to agree to disagree on some things, and to agree to cooperate on others.

The professional organization believes that it can serve teachers best by remaining independent of organic connections and resulting loyalties to non-educational organizations. Such ties inhibit its policies and prevent it from putting the interests of teachers and education *first* in its considerations. Affiliations with labor organizations also carry with them obligations which are frequently in conflict with the first-priority goals of teachers. It is also our belief that by remaining independent of other groups the professional organization will have the freedom to work for school and teacher advancement with any and all interested groups, including organized labor. Such independence makes it possible for the professional organizations to focus upon and give top priority to matters of education, and education alone. It also relieves the professional organization of any obligation to support non-education programs and to respect picket lines on questions which are external to the schools, and that might alienate groups which otherwise might be persuaded to support school measures.

An example is the recent action by the American Federation of Teachers to have removed from the schools textbooks and encyclopedia sets produced by the Kingsport Press of Kingsport, Tennessee. Included in the AFT's blacklist of 170 titles are such well-known and reputable publishers of textbooks as: Grossett and Dunlap; Harper and Row; Holt, Rinehart and Winston; Alfred A. Knopf; J. B. Lippincott; McGraw Hill; Charles E. Merrill; Random House; Charles Scribner and Sons; Field Enterprises Educational Corporation; and Grolier, Inc.

The reason given by AFT to ban these books from schools was their disagreement with the labor policy of the Kingsport Press. This action by the 49th convention of AFT was obviously taken to pay the debt incurred by the teachers' union for the acceptance of financial and other help from the other AFL-CIO unions. This obligation which unionized teachers assume is too high a price to pay. And it is not necessary. Independent teacher groups the nation over are negotiating better contracts without sacrificing their professional integrity.

Albert Shanker, president of the United Federation of Teachers, in response to a letter published in the *New York World-Telegram and Sun* of April 8, 1965 stated that unionized teachers must help other unions achieve their objectives so that they can get the support which teachers need when they are in trouble. Charles Cogen, president of AFT, stated this policy in his address to the 49th convention in August, 1965 in these words:

> Every AFT member knows the practical need for making sure that our brothers and sisters in other unions are "there" when we need them. They will be ready to help us if we are "there" when they need *our* support. Such solidarity is imperative, even though we know that the labor movement, including ourselves, has some shortcomings.

I believe in trade unions. I believe in collective bargaining. But I believe that trade unions are wrong for teachers because the cost of labor support can be the loss of the teachers' professional integrity and freedom to teach. This is illustrated by the Kingsport Press incident.

SOME INDICATIONS FOR THE FUTURE

In the past two years approximately 400 formal agreements have been negotiated, establishing a procedure for employer-employee relationships in school systems throughout the country. A greater proportion of those recently negotiated are Level Three agreements. By this I mean agreements which contain a complete procedure involving (1) a recognition of the association as the spokesman for all teachers; (2) a definition of the procedures under which negotiation with the board of education and administration shall take place; and (3) a provision for resolving an impasse if it should develop. It is no secret that considerable resistance has come from school boards based chiefly on the claim that give-and-take negotiation and advisory appeals procedures encroach upon the legal prerogatives of the board.

Recently Commissioner Arvid Anderson of the Wisconsin Employment Relations Board said:

> . . . examples are evident that governmental units at all levels, both with and without express legislative sanction, have been engaged in the

practice of collective bargaining in the manner described for a long time. The best example is the fact that [President Kennedy] issued Executive Order 10988 . . .[1]

Acceleration of the adoption of formalized procedures by boards of education can be expected. I also see a lessening of resistance to procedures for the resolving of an impasse as an encroachment upon the legal authority of the board of education. Boards of education have the legal responsibility for the adoption of school policy, but boards of education can arrive at that policy in any way they choose. In the days ahead I see an acceptance of the idea of give-and-take discussions for negotiations by boards of education recognizing that teachers have a right to participate in a responsible way in the formulation of school policy. I think our experience to date shows that the powers of boards of education are broad enough to permit them to involve teachers in the decision-making process if they want to do it. The legal argument is usually an expression of the reluctance of the board to give up the practice of unilateral decision making.

Legislation for Professional Negotiation

Some form of professional negotiation legislation was proposed in at least 14 states in 1965. New laws were passed by legislatures in eight states. Let me suggest five reasons why I think that more and more states will turn to the legislative route.

1. State legislation will increase the number of agreements much more rapidly than is possible under the voluntary approach. With legislation, school board acceptance of professional negotiation will be a matter of compliance rather than a matter of choice. Legislation will also permit separate treatment for school personnel rather than blanketing them into laws which do not recognize the special character of the school. An important example is the law passed by the 1965 Washington State Legislature. This law provides for (1) the inclusion of all certificated personnel in the negotiating unit; (2) a broad definition of the subject matter of the negotiation which goes beyond the limits of the narrow definition of the labor law; and (3) a procedure for resolving an impasse which is separate and apart from the channels provided by the state labor law.

2. The voluntary approach has more appeal for those districts with the most enlightened personnel policies. Therefore those systems which need professional negotiation most are likely to be the last to adopt it voluntarily.

3. State laws assure teachers of their *right* to take an active part in the

---

[1] Arvid Anderson, "The Developing State of Collective Bargaining for Public Employees." Address to Conference on Public Employment and Collective Bargaining, University of Chicago, February 5, 1965.

process of school policy making. They recognize that teachers have a legitimate role to play in the formulation of the policies which affect them. They give teachers greater on-the-job dignity, security, and independence in performing their functions at the heart of the public education process.

4. Legislation can establish a uniform set of rules for the procedure of give-and-take negotiations to operate, which will apply in all school systems in the state. A uniform set of conditions will stimulate the perfection of the process by permitting sharing of experiences among the different school systems.

5. The establishment of legal authority for the meaningful participation of teachers in policy making removes the legal, or sovereignty, argument which has been a major obstacle to securing voluntary acceptance of professional negotiation.

Unit Definition

A question which has arisen in the past, and will likely arise in the future, concerns the appropriate definition of the negotiating unit. Ideally all members of the professional staff have an identity of interest centering on (1) the skills and training which are common to all; (2) the professional commitment to a high-quality school program; (3) the agreed-upon standards of professional practice; and (4) salary and fringe benefits which apply to all professional personnel such as retirement, insurance, and sick leave (all of which override partisan interest generated by their positions in the school hierarchy).

To the extent that this identity of interest prevails, the conclusions seem inescapable: all persons holding professional certificates or permits issued by the state agency, with a possible exception of the superintendent, should be members of the unit, even though they may perform supervisory or administrative functions. This principle was followed in all referendums held in Connecticut, and is practiced by the teachers in Canada.

However, in many school districts, particularly large ones, realities may not conform to the ideal. Classroom teachers may desire representation independent of administrators. The determining factor in any school system should be the desires of the professional personnel concerned. Custom, established practice and membership patterns usually provide the evidence of the desires of the membership.

Some will argue that an all-inclusive unit is inappropriate. And in some instances it is. However, this decision should follow the desires of the local members. Great strength can be given to an organization if an all-inclusive unit can be formed with complete freedom for teachers to participate in discussions without inhibitions. Some will argue that a classroom-teacher-only unit will be more militant.

In the last year one of the most militant demonstrations of determination on the part of educators to improve their conditions was the effort made by the Utah Education Association. It would be difficult to find a person more militant than the president of that association. He was a high school principal. Yet the policy-making apparatus of that association is in the firm control of classroom teachers. The inclusion of administrators in its membership and in active participation has given strength to the organization. At the height of the activity, boards of education, not classroom teachers, attempted to force administrators out of the association. Some boards of education tried to insist that administrators give their complete loyalty to them and withdraw from the association. But the administrators held their ground and remained in the association. The association enrolls better than 90 per cent of all certified personnel in the state. This solidarity gave great strength to the organization in the legislative and political activities which led to the substantial improvement of the school program and paved the way for the removal of national sanctions on March 15, 1965.

Some unions have had similar experience with all-inclusive units—notably the Typographical Workers and the Building Trades. Efforts have been made by management to force the separation of supervisory employees, but without success. Forcing a uniform standard upon all local units *could be* playing management's game rather than serving the best interests of the employees.

The National Union of Teachers in Great Britain is an independent professional organization enrolling over 242,000 school personnel. It has a long record of militant action to improve the status of teachers and promote popular education. Reference is made to the source of NUT's militance in an article in the *Monthly Labor Review* for September, 1964, as follows:

> . . . Two-thirds of all NUT members are women teachers, but it is the head teachers of both primary and secondary schools who, though numerically a much smaller group, dominate the national executive of the Union and also play a leading part in local association politics. The drive towards "trade union" tactics, and towards militancy, comes mainly (though not exclusively) from assistant masters who comprise an important section of the Union, while this insistence on "professionalism" and respectability stems largely, though by no means entirely, from those enjoying the highest status in the profession—the headmasters and headmistresses. This is as far as broad generalization can go. . .[2]

Separate units for classroom teachers and administrators is justified if teachers feel that their active participation in organization affairs is being

[2] Walter Roy, "Reaction of Organized Teachers to Crisis," *Monthly Labor Review,* September, 1964, p. 1022.

restricted in the all-inclusive unit. Separation can also be justified if adminis-trators attempt to use their administrative authority to influence association policy. But the mere inclusion of administrative personnel in the unit does not prevent it from being militant in the pursuit of its goals. Moreover, those who argue against the inclusion of administrators fail to recognize that when employees become more highly skilled or professionally trained, they tend to identify more closely with the purposes of an enterprise, and differences be-come less marked as skills and training increase.

Exclusive Representation

The organization which has the support of the majority of the profes-sional staff should be their exclusive representative. The professional nego-tiation process seeks agreement on policy matters. Since there can be only one policy, there should be only one teacher representative. I suggest that we will see wide acceptance of this principle as more and more teacher organizations press for formalized procedures.

The chief strength of the concept of exclusive representation is that it encourages responsible behavior. Experiences of the past three years with joint committees or a multiplicity of organizations speaking only for their members argue for the selection of an exclusive representative. Joint com-mittees are torn with organizational rivalries. They frequently provide a forum for minority groups to make unreasonable demands in an effort to attract membership from the uncommitted.

The designation of an exclusive representative to represent all teachers of a school system does not prevent the minority organization from pressing its views with the superintendent and board of education.

Experience indicates that the minority organization does not dissolve when a majority organization is awarded exclusive representation rights. For example, in Detroit where the professional association lost an election last year it has increased its membership and it is a stronger organization now than it was before the election.

Scope of the Negotiations

If we are to attract the kind of imaginative, creative and resourceful teacher we would like for our schools, we must create the conditions which will attract this kind of individual. The truly professional teacher wants freedom to exercise independent judgment as a professional. Teachers as other persons will generally react in terms of the way in which they are treated.

Dr. Francis S. Chase, in a study of over 200 school systems in 43 states, sought to determine what administrative polices and prac-tices tend to increase the satisfactions which teachers experience in their work. From replies from 1784 teachers he generalized that:

One of the most important contributors to the satisfaction which teachers take in their work and the enthusiasm which they feel for the system in which they are working is a sense of professional status, responsibility, and freedom. Freedom to plan one's own work was rated as the most important potential source of satisfaction by all groups of respondents. It was given the highest possible rating for satisfaction by 77 per cent of teachers in elementary schools, 75 per cent of those in secondary schools, 69 per cent of the men teachers, 78 per cent of the women teachers, over 80 per cent of the superior teachers, and nearly 69 per cent of the below-average teachers.

The interviews supplied further evidence of the importance of this factor. Again and again teachers who were enthusiastic about the system in which they were working praised their freedom to experiment, to adapt programs to the needs of their pupils; or cited as important to satisfaction the fact that they were regarded as competent to make their own decisions and to work out their own procedures.

. . . Freedom to plan one's own work is given the highest possible rating by more than three-fourths of all respondents, and achieves a considerably higher average rating than any other factor.[3]

While I think most teachers desire to participate in the establishment of salary schedules, class size and other conditions of work, they also want a voice in other aspects of the program which influence the quality of education.

Precedents, traditions and habits have grown up in industry concerning the subject matter of negotiations. Certain subjects have been labeled management prerogatives. Others have been designated areas in which workers have a legitimate interest. Generally speaking, employees in industry have the legal right to negotiate only on those subjects which come under the general heading of wages, hours and working conditions.

When it comes to education, these precedents, traditions and habits are irrelevant. One of the earmarks of a professional group is the recognition of its responsibilities beyond the limits of self-interest. This includes the responsibility to the general welfare of the school system. A professional group should be permitted to negotiate with the board of education on matters which affect the quality of education other than those covered by the narrow definitions in labor law. This philosophy is based on the belief that the case for improved teacher welfare rests on the necessity for improving the quality of public education generally. Teachers have an interest in the conditions which attract and retain a better teaching force. They are concerned with

[3] Francis S. Chase, "Factors for Satisfaction in Teaching," *Phi Delta Kappan,* November, 1951, p. 130.

in-service training programs, class size, selection of textbooks, the kinds of programs available for emotionally disturbed, physically handicapped children, and other matters which go beyond the limited industrial definition. In a recent survey in one big-city school system it was found that the one problem which was of greatest concern to teachers was the lack of adequate provision for emotionally disturbed children. Professional associations are uniquely equipped and backed by resources to bring to bear on negotiations the expert services necessary to make good decisions. The specialized services of the many departments, special projects, and research departments of the state and national associations enable the association to make contributions in many areas having a bearing on the quality of education which are not available to any other organization.

Sanctions

Sanctions have proved to be effective. We have recently had four dramatic examples of the success of sanctions in winning results for teachers without violating professional responsibilities. In Utah; Waterbury, Connecticut; Little Lake, California; and Oklahoma, sanctions focused public attention on conditions in the schools which needed correction. This ability to capture public attention and define school problems in concert with effective public relations programs and political action made it possible for the people of Little Lake, California, to turn out of office a majority of the school board, secure the resignation of the superintendent, and remove the conditions for which the sanction was applied. In Waterbury the sanction defined the issues which made it possible for the people of Waterbury to elect a new mayor and secure through political action the remedies needed to correct the situation which called for the sanction.

In Utah the sanction was a means of dramatizing the problem and appealing to the pride of the people to take corrective action. They responded by electing a new governor and a majority of the legislature in a campaign which emphasized education. The legislation is estimated to provide a $450 increase for teachers this year, $250 more next year, and it will add other benefits which will affect the quality of education. This is in addition to the more than $600 received last year.

Speaking to a statewide meeting of Utah teachers on March 19, 1965, Governor Calvin Rampton acknowledged that sanctions had brought about an awareness of the needs of education and the kinds of problems to be faced.

In Oklahoma sanctions provided the stimulation whereby both legislative action and a successful referendum made it possible to correct the conditions which caused their imposition.

At the beginning of the 1965 legislative session the Governor of Oklahoma offered the Oklahoma Education Association an increase of $50 per teacher. Instead of this token $50 raise, every teacher in Oklahoma will get a minimum salary increase of $350 and many of those in large school systems will receive $800-$1,000 and more.

Sanctions do not violate the provisions of teaching contracts. They are completely under the control of the teaching profession. They can be escalated in stages. Safeguards are built into the sanctions to provide that they be applied only after an investigation or field study has been made by a competent national agency. They are applied only as a last resort and after opportunity has been provided for corrective action.

As we work with sanctions I expect that we will learn a great deal through experience. It is, therefore, important that we proceed with a pragmatic view toward them. However, on the basis of experience to date, they show great promise as a means of securing public attention for school problems and providing a motivating force to bring about corrective action.

The effectivenes of sanctions emphasizes the need for responsibility in their use. The association does not assume this responsibility lightly.

Grievance Procedures

There is a need, especially in our larger school systems, for improved and more effective formal grievance procedures. I am convinced that some of the explosions that are occurring in education are a result of the accumulated frustrations of teachers. Many of these frustrations could be relieved if teachers had easy access to machinery for resolving problems which result from differences in the interpretation or administration of school policies. Little problems become big problems if they go unresolved.

School systems without satisfactory provisions for handling grievances run the risk of having dissatisfaction become acute and explode into a major incident. Moreover, the lack of grievance procedures can outweigh and cause teachers to forget about many favorable conditions. Often school administrators are unaware of the needs for grievance procedures. When one becomes an administrator, he no longer participates in the boiler-room sessions where grievances are aired.

A grievance procedure should have six general characteristics:

1. The term "grievance" should be clearly defined so that a teacher may have fair notice of when the procedure can be invoked.

2. The procedure should be easily accessible to any person who thinks he has a grievance, and its use should be encouraged by the administration.

3. The procedure should have prescribed time limits within which the grievance must be processed at each stage.

4. The procedure should guarantee the grievant independent representation at all stages.

5. The procedure should guarantee the grievant protection from administrative coercion, interference, restraint, discrimination or reprisal by reason of having filed and processed his grievance.

6. The procedure should terminate in a full and fair review, where the grievant so desires, by an agency which is in no way beholden to or prejudiced against any party in interest.

The needs for formalized employer-employee relationships *are coming*. They are coming because they are necessary to personalize and make more effective employer-employee relationships in education. The task of teachers, administrators and school boards alike is to devote our best thinking to the task of developing procedures which will recognize the unique nature of schools, and best represent sound public policy. None of us has yet had enough experience to be confident that we have *all* the answers. But pioneering can be an exciting adventure.

III-2

THE AMERICAN FEDERATION OF TEACHERS AND COLLECTIVE NEGOTIATIONS*

Charles Cogen

In April, 1965, as president of the American Federation of Teachers, I addressed a telegram to the president of the Department of Classroom Teachers of the National Education Association. I proposed that the DCT and the AFT engage in a dialogue for the purpose of establishing a nationwide "Code of Observance" for the conduct of teacher representation elections. What we in the AFT were seeking was a united front of teachers in establishing uniform rules for choosing local exclusive negotiating representative organizations, regardless of whether the organization chosen by the teachers was an AFT local or an association affiliated with NEA or its state branches.

Increasingly, educational commentators have proposed that the AFT and the NEA merge into one organization. We would not rule out such a possibility. The AFT favors "teacher unity"—but there are fundamental points at issue between the two organizations, and many of these revolve around the question of the proper relationship between teachers and their employing boards of education. We reasoned that if teacher unity in an organizational sense is not possible, at least we ought to be able to agree on the rights which teachers have, and we should stand united in our insistence that these rights be recognized by boards of education. Within this framework the two organizations could then compete for teacher support.

Our efforts to establish a common framework of teachers' rights as employees were rebuffed by the Department of Classroom Teachers. Instead, the DCT supports legislation defining the negotiating relationship on a state-by-state basis. We consider this action irresponsible and harmful to teachers. It seems motivated more by the desire of the associations to maintain the organizational status quo than by any consideration for improving

---

* An address by Charles Cogen, President of the American Federation of Teachers, on July 8, 1965, to the National Institute on Collective Negotiations in Public Education cosponsored by Phi Delta Kappa and Rhode Island College, Providence, R.I.

the status of teaching as a profession. At best the state-by-state approach can only result in a patchwork of unsatisfactory compromises, achieved after decades of effort, and it is likely to lead to a prolonged guerilla war in which teachers become embroiled in unproductive attacks against each other while the great issues confronting the schools are neglected.

If there were to be a nationwide negotiating code, what would it look like?

WHAT A NATIONAL CODE FOR TEACHER NEGOTIATIONS WOULD INCLUDE

In general, the AFT favors the same sort of relationship between teachers and their boards of education as that which has been established for employees in the private sector through the National Labor and Management Relations Act.

We favor the principle of exclusive recognition of a single bargaining agent. We are opposed to "members only" bargaining, in which two or more organizations have separate but equal rights to negotiate with the board. We are opposed to "joint committees," whether they are chosen on an organization basis or by direct election of individual committee members.

We favor recognition of the organization which achieves a majority of those voting in a secret ballot election, where there are two or more organizations vying for such recognition. We are opposed to recognition on the basis of membership lists, except where only one organization is seeking exclusive recognition. Even here, due notice should be given so that any other organization could force an election upon making a sufficient showing of interest.

We favor "continuing recognition" until such time as a significant proportion of the members of the negotiating unit petition for a new election. We are opposed to required annual or biennial elections of negotiating agents.

We favor negotiating units composed of non-supervisory educational employees only. We are opposed to units composed of "all certificated employees," including principals and other administrators and supervisors.

We would place no limit on the scope of negotiations, the items which are subject to the bargaining process. Anything on which the two parties can agree should become a part of the agreement; anything on which they cannot agree will, of course, not appear.

We favor written agreements between boards of education and negotiating agents. These agreements should should be legally binding.

We favor development of a code of unfair labor practices and definitions of what constitutes good faith negotiations.

We favor according teachers the right to strike; we are opposed to anti-strike laws, and we are opposed to the use of injunctions in teacher-board disputes.

We favor the use of skilled mediators to resolve impasses. We are opposed to compulsory arbitration of negotiable items.

We favor individual grievance procedures, with outside arbitration as the final step. We oppose grievance procedures which place the board or the superintendent in the position of final arbiter.

Any nationwide teacher-board relations code would include the items I have noted. Many variations in detail are possible and these we are perfectly willing to discuss and even compromise on, but it is obvious that even the compromises least advantageous to teachers and most favorable to those who are in the management end of the school enterprise would constitute a tremendous advance in teachers' rights. Neither the AFT nor the DCT-NEA could bind its local units to any such code, of course, nor would agreement between the two teacher organizations mean that all boards of education would accept the code. Most local teacher organizations, however, want guidance, and many boards of education are willing to help establish some order in what is now a chaotic situation. At the very least we have an obligation to set standards of right and wrong in this field.

APPROPRIATENESS OF LABOR-MANAGEMENT CONCEPTS TO EDUCATION

Some educational commentators decry the trend toward collective negotiations on grounds that bargaining between teachers and their employer is not appropriate to education. Teaching, they say, is a profession, and education is not a business. Now, some might deny that teaching is, at present, a profession, and everyone can agree that education is not a business in the usual sense, but semantic arguments of this sort advance us very little.

Teachers certainly are *employees* of the board of education, regardless of their professional status or the lack of it, and if one were to place a schematic drawing of the staff structure of a typical private business corporation of comparable size, the little boxes and circles would be about the same for each. The same stresses, strains, and conflicts which exist in such structures in private enterprise are also to be found in enterprises owned by the public, whether they be school systems, fire departments, or bus lines.

The "non-profit" argument, too, is fallacious. Schools are just as much in the marketplace for their share of consumer dollars as any manufacturer of automobiles or safety pins. People pay taxes because they want schools, just as they put up $3,000 for a new automobile or 10¢ for a packet of pins because they want these things. Boards of education and superintendents are elected and employed to produce education, and their obligation is even set forth by law. Their success, like that of private managers, is measured by an equation in which public approval is balanced against costs.

Many superintendents, principals, and other supervisors and administrators resent efforts to classify them as "management," as though there were something disgraceful about the term, and most of the opposition to applying established labor-management concepts to education comes from this quarter. Their attitude is reflected by the non-union associations, and a large "literature" of circumlocutions, rationalizations, and anti-labor propaganda has emerged from the effort to avoid labor-management terms and concepts. Yet, ironically, one of the most widely read educational magazines among administrators and school board members is *School Management*.

SUPERVISORS AND ADMINISTRATORS SHOULD NOT BE IN TEACHERS' UNITS

A basic labor relations tenet is that management employees should not be in the same bargaining units as non-supervisory employees. There can be no question about the predominantly managerial status of a school superintendent. Even legislation sponsored by the various non-union state associations excludes superintendents from the bargaining—or negotiating—unit. As to principals and others in middle management, the determining questions are "how much discretionary power?" and "with whom does he identify?" Two categories are debatable. Teaching department heads, for instance, who have little discretionary power and who in the main are treated as teachers, probably should be included in the bargaining unit. Assistant principals, who usually exercise the authority of the principal, and who are usually paid or given other benefits based upon those given principals, probably should be excluded.

Only in a few of our largest cities is there anything approaching a civil service merit system for the selection of administrative personnel, and even where such a system operates the superintendent retains a great amount of power in determining who gets promoted. The standard practice in private enterprise of allowing the chief executive a free hand in the selection of his subordinates has been applied to the educational enterprise. The increasing tendency to require specialized certificates changes the status and power factors very little. Getting a certificate is a matter of getting the credits. In some cases, acting appointments are made and then confirmed after the person chosen has acquired his certificate.

Basing the salaries of administrative personnel on percentages of the teacher salary, or "indices," does not materially change the concept we have been discussing. True, under an index, every time the teachers get a raise the administrators get one too, which ought to produce friendly feelings toward teacher salary campaigns. But when hard negotiations begin, or a strike occurs, and the order comes down from the superintendent to tighten the rules or cross the picket line, it is a rare administrator who will uphold the teachers' cause.

The supervisors' salary index idea is bitterly resented by many teachers because the very people who try to curb teacher action end up by benefiting the most from teacher success. Also, the index freezes a status relationship which many teachers do not acknowledge.

The relationship existing now between supervisory personnel and teachers is superordinate-subordinate, not primarily collegial.

In normal employee-employer relations, those who have authority to hire and fire, settle grievances, or make specific job assignments are excluded from the employee bargaining unit. Placing these positions firmly on the management side acts to check possible abuses of power, and allows non-supervisory employees to make group decisions without being subjected to undue influence and undemocratic pressures from supervisors. We would see no objection to middle management administrators and supervisors forming bargaining units of their own, but these should be separate from those for non-supervisory personnel.

We in the AFT think it unwise—even downright silly—to ignore the experience which has been amassed in labor-management relations over the years. The principles and concepts which have evolved apply to industries of widest possible diversity, and there is no reason to segregate educational employees and attempt to establish a new body of rules for them. In fact, teachers can only lose from such a development.

ORGANIZATION, NEGOTIATION, AND PROFESSIONALISM

Effective organization, negotiating rights, and greater professionalism are all parts of the same problem with which teachers are now confronted. It is worse than useless to have the *right* to negotiate where teachers have no *power* to negotiate, and the development of rights and power by teachers must be accompanied by a much higher degree of involvement in matters of professional concern.

Most administrators would agree with this last statement, at least in principle; where they would disagree is on the question of priority. The administrators would say, as some Southern governors say about civil rights: "They aren't ready for it. First they have to show that they know how to handle these rights and privileges."

Many of us in the AFT might, in turn, agree that teachers must be much more willing to accept responsibility for matters which they all too often abjure, but progress in this direction will come as a concomitant to the increased power and rights of teachers rather than as a prerequisite. As teachers achieve improved status, more able and aggressive individuals will be attracted to enter—and remain in—the profession. As teachers become more "professional," they will achieve greater power and more rights. I do not want to add to the torrent of definitions of professionalism which has spewed forth from lecturers, panelists, writers, and after-dinner speakers over the decades. When I use the term I am referring to our commitment as teachers to accept responsibility, to welcome innovation, and to be firm in our insistence on proper standards so that the quality and quantity of education is constantly improved and enlarged.

This sort of professionalism can develop only in a society of equals, in which all have an equal responsibility in the common enterprise.

Collective negotiation is the logical, practical, and meaningful way to develop greater professionalism among teachers. In the past, when teachers depended primarily upon public relations, research, lobbying, and paternalism, their progress toward professionalism was tortuously slow. As they assume the new rights and responsibilities which go with collective bargaining —or collective negotiation—their progress is speeded up.

Those who seek to place limits on the scope of teacher bargaining are basically anti-professional. A professional insists on professional standards— conditions of work which permit him to use his professional skills to the greatest advantage. In New York City, the Board of Education representatives take the position that the proper size of a class is not a proper subject for negotiations, while the union asserts the right of its members to exercise their collective professional judgment on this question. Would a doctor allow a hospital superintendent to determine the time he can spend with each patient, or the number of patients on whom he must operate in an hour?

What should be the "professional" role of the superintendent of schools in the negotiating process? The NEA, in its rapidly expanding literature on "professional negotiation," talks of the "dual role" of the superintendent. The superintendent does have a "dual role"—but the duality is not quite the kind meant by the NEA. Rather than one role as advisor of the board and another as advisor of the teachers, the two roles of the superintendent are both management in function. On the one hand he is an administrator, responsible for the efficient operation of the educational enterprise. On the other he is an educational leader, responsible for making policy recommendations to the board of education. The superintendent has as great an obligation to negotiate on professional matters as on business affairs.

In a clothing factory, the workers negotiate about wages, fringe benefits, and conditions of work, but garment workers are not expected to set clothing styles. Teachers, however, as professionals, have an obligation to exercise their professional judgment—to share the educational policy-making function.

I look for a great expansion in the effective scope of negotiations between teachers and school management. Obviously class size, number of classes taught, curriculum, hiring standards, textbooks and supplies, extracurricular activities—in fact, anything having to do with the operation of the school—is a matter for professional concern and should thus be subject to collective bargaining. The fact that these items also involve budgetary arrangements is an added reason for including them in the scope of bargaining.

Teachers can, through local and eventually state-wide and possibly national negotiation, even use their collective power to control standards of entry into the profession.

SOME LEGAL PROBLEMS

In many states during the past few years we have run into legal obstacles to establishing the right of teachers to negotiate. Sometimes these obstacles have been created by boards of education and sometimes they have been created by the non-union associations.

In Taylor Township, Michigan, a teacher, using the same law firm retained by the Michigan Education Association, obtained a restraining order prohibiting recognition of any exclusive bargaining representative which might be chosen as a result of a forthcoming election. The election was held, after a two-month delay, but on an advisory basis only. The Board of Education has thus far refused to enter into an agreement with the Taylor Federation of Teachers, which received a majority of the votes.

In Detroit, legal obstacles to exclusive recognition delayed a representation election in 1964 and nearly precipitated a strike. The election was held, and the union won, but one of the stipulations under which the election was authorized by the Detroit Board of Education was that a new election would be held in a year. On the eve of the second election, the Detroit Education Association sought a court order to grant administrative and supervisory personnel the right to vote in the election. When the judge refused to rule immediately, the DEA withdrew from the ballot, and a committee representing the union was then recognized as the exclusive bargaining agent for the teachers. The legality of any agreement in Michigan is still in doubt. Yet peculiarly enough, in April, 1965, in Hamtramck, Michigan, the board ratified a written agreement reached between its negotiating committee and that of the union.

In New York, the status of the exclusive recognition of the United Federation of Teachers has been upheld by the State Commissioner of Education, but the contract between the board and the union has not yet been tested in court. This is probably due to the fact that the contract contains a compulsory arbitration feature on grievances, as a final step, which tends to make it self-enforcing, and also to the no-strike clause, which is the union's *quid pro quo* in making the contract. If the board breached the contract, the union could consider itself free of its agreement not to strike during the duration of the contract.

Many boards of education fall back on the doctrine of "sovereignty" to deny teachers bargaining rights. They say that signing a contract would restrict their freedom to act during the duration of the contract. Not infrequently, as in St. Louis, Missouri, associations have reinforced the board's view that exclusive recognition is illegal.

There are really very few recent court decisions as to the legality of exclusive recognition. Unfortunately, state attorneys general tend to repeat court doctrine and opinions of their predecessors in office which were handed down prior to the growth of unionism among government employees during the past decade.

The fact remains that in spite of adverse legal opinions, the number of written and unwritten collective bargaining agreements based on exclusive recognition is increasing at a very rapid rate. We in the AFT are inclined to proceed on the assumption that boards of education can enter into exclusive bargaining agreements if they want to, and that in most states attempts to obtain statutory sanction for such arrangements are apt to raise more problems than they solve.

THE IMPASSE PROBLEM

I wish to conclude my remarks by stating our view toward the problem of resolution of impasses in negotiations. We believe that work stoppages by teachers should be a last resort in attempting to resolve such impasses. Every possible effort to reach an agreement should be made before a work stoppage occurs. However, we also believe, as does the NEA, as evidenced by its sanctions policy, that work stoppages by teachers are morally justifiable under certain circumstances.

AFT locals are urged to follow the normal procedure of collective bargaining. When an impasse occurs, they usually resort to some sort of public appeal—a public demonstration; informational picketing; leaflets; newspaper, radio, and television advertisements; and marshaling of support from the labor movement and parent and civic organizations. If these efforts fail to move the board from its position, the members often set a strike date.

We strongly advocate the use of skilled mediators in attempting to resolve negotiating impasses. In addition to his experience and skill, the impartiality of the mediator must be above question. We do not think that most state superintendents of public instruction qualify for the mediation role on either count. Few have had mediation training or experience, and even the "fairest" state superintendent is apt to have a pro-management bias. Perhaps standing educational mediation panels could be approved by state teacher organizations and the state school boards association. Mediators for any particular situation could then be chosen from this panel.

In most cases when a strike date is set, a settlement is reached before the deadline. However, there are occasional impasses which are settled only after the walkout occurs. Few of these work stoppages have lasted more than a day or so. Teachers have shown great reluctance to use the strike to resolve an impasse, and one reason for this hesitancy is that in most states a strike by public employees is enjoinable, either under a specific anti-strike statute or under common law. The lurking fear of court action, added to the distaste of many teachers for such drastic action, has limited the willingness of teachers to strike. Teachers' strikes tend to be more in the nature of demonstrations to call public attention to the points at issue.

Legally, no one can be forced to work. A group of public employees who are determined enough can withstand court fines and jailings of their leaders and threatened loss of vested rights, just as the social workers in the New York City Welfare Department did in January of 1965, and when they do, they usually win. However, teacher groups are only now approaching such solidarity. In the meantime, methods of avoiding the legal entanglements of anti-strike laws and injunctions should be explored.

The most desirable step toward giving teachers bargaining power in negotiations would be to outlaw the use of the injunction in teacher-board disputes, just as the Norris-La Guardia Act outlaws injunctions in labor disputes in the private sector. The Michigan Board of Education recently declared in favor of granting teachers the right to strike, but widespread acceptance of the right to strike is not an immediate likelihood.

Perhaps the best avenue to explore is the "no contract, no work" concept.

When teachers understand that they are to work only under the terms and conditions of a collective bargaining contract—or professional negotiation agreement, if you prefer—no formal action would be required to set a deadline for a work stoppage. Lack of contract or the acceptance of a contract is a self-evident fact, and teachers would simply act accordingly. Certain types of picketing, advertising, and communications are usually subject to court restraint, but no court can force a union to sign an agreement. So long as teachers remain true to the no-contract-no-work principle, a legally permissible work stoppage can be carried on.

In some respects the no-contract-no-work policy is similar to the code of ethics approach of Myron Lieberman and others, and it also bears strong resemblance to the sanctions approach of the NEA, at least as projected in the Utah and Oklahoma situations.

If teachers have a code of ethics involving standards of salaries, class sizes, teaching program loads, and other vital matters, and agree that they will teach only under these ethical conditions, a work stoppage is implicit when conditions fail to meet these standards. The difficulty with this approach lies in its rigidity. There is such a variation in the ability of local school districts to provide adequate professional conditions that either exceptions would have to be made or the code itself would be so substandard as to be meaningless in many situations. The code of ethics could have meaning if considered in conjunction with local collective negotiations and the no-contract-no-work principle, however.

The sanctions approach of the NEA has possibilities for development into an effective professional weapon, but in its present formulation it has many pitfalls and drawbacks. The basic idea underlying sanctions—that teachers should not work in districts which do not maintain adequate professional standards—is sound. It is the same principle underlying the no-contract-no-work idea. However, if a district is not a fit place in which to teach, all teachers—those presently employed as well as applicants for teaching positions—should refuse to teach there. We see no moral or logical defense for condoning teaching by those who are already there while new applicants are urged to go elsewhere.

Furthermore, this strangulation approach is unduly attenuated and a great deal of harm can be done to the children and to public education in general while the process runs its course.

Another problem with the sanctions idea is that of "who invokes and who revokes." An impasse occurs in local negotiations, or in a state educational program. The local or state association declares in favor of sanctions. Then an investigating team comes in, ostensibly to make an evaluation of he professional conditions which prevail. In actuality the "evaluation" is a sort of under-the-table negotiation in which local teachers as a collective force are removed from the process. Let us presume, however, that following the evaluation sanctions are applied in their most extreme form and teachers are encouraged to pick up their goods and chattels and teach elsewhere (a vengeance harder on the avenger than the avengee). Who decides the point at which conditions have become acceptable? And then does everybody move back into town?

Compared with a strike or a no-contract-no-work policy as a way of resolving an impasse, sanctions are slow, uncertain, potentially harmful to children and the schools, difficult to enforce, a hindrance to teacher involvement in the problems which concern them, and lacking in democratic controls. If sanctions procedures could be modified to correct these defects, what would emerge would be essentially, a no-contract-no-work policy.

In all the foregoing I have avoided mention of arbitration as a method of settling negotiating impasses. While we favor arbitration to enforce an agreement once it is negotiated, as a final step of a grievance procedure, we are opposed to its use in negotiations for a variety of reasons which are too lengthy to go into here, and which I have outlined in a brief policy paper available from our office.

CONCLUSION

I now come back to my original thesis: The principles involved in establishing collective negotiation are too important to be settled on the basis of organizational advantage. Rather, the two organizations ought to make every effort to agree on these principles and mutually uphold them. We must never lose sight of the fact that it is the *teachers* whom we represent and serve. Any temporary organizational advantage which might seem possible by pursuing some expediential course which is contrary to sound principles of teacher-board relationships will be swept aside as teachers march toward their goal of greater dignity and professional status.

III-3

THE AAUP AS A PROFESSIONAL OCCUPATIONAL ASSOCIATION*

George Strauss

The purpose of this article is to examine the American Association of University Professors as an occupational association or quasi-union. Two recent issues of the *AAUP Bulletin* make such an analysis easier by setting out the organization's past, present, and future problems. One issue includes an article by Walter P. Metzger on the "Origins of the Association," which has just passed its fiftieth birthday.[1] The other is largely devoted to a Self Survey Committee report which deals with recent trends and makes recommendations.[2]

My thesis here is that the AAUP, like many other occupational associations, suffers from a mixture of objectives and a tension between economic goals and those which are more purely professional, even altruistic, in nature.[3] In recent years its efforts have been directed toward the dual objective of defending academic freedom and raising academic salaries. At the moment, when conditions in both areas seem to have improved, it faces the dilemma of deciding whether to be primarily "a professional association whose members are dedicated above all to the advancement of higher education ... and ... who conceive that their personal interests ... are ... to be furthered only as subservient to this larger aim,"[4] or an "action group dedicated without apology to serving the interest of our members exclusively."[5] This difference as to objectives leads to disputes over composition and con-

* Reprinted from *Industrial Relations*, Vol. V, No. 1, (October, 1965), pp. 125-40. George Strauss is Professor of Business Administration and Research Economist, Institute of Industrial Relations, University of California, Berkeley.

[1] Walter P. Metzger, "Origins of the Association," *AAUP Bulletin,* LI (June, 1965), pp. 229-37.

[2] "Report of the Self-Survey Committee of the AAUP," *AAUP Bulletin,* LI (May, 1965), pp. 99-209.

[3] The two articles and this reveiw deal with AAUP at the national level, although much of the association's most effective work is done by local chapters. Many of the national problems discussed here occur locally as well.

[4] "Report of the Self-Survey Committee of the AAUP," p. 191.

[5] *Ibid.,* p. 197.

trol of the organization and over the means by which its ends shall be achieved. The professional stance seems most appropriate for professors in prestigious (usually private) institutions, while the interest group stance is more in accord with the needs and interests of those in the less well-known institutions engaged in mass education.

AAUP UNTIL 1956

As Metzger's article explains, higher education seethed with ferment during the late nineteenth century and early 1900's. The number of colleges, universities, and students grew at unprecedented rates. The graduate school system was established, universities were largely secularized, and professors ceased to think of themselves as a branch of the ministry and began to look for an identity of their own.

The AAUP grew out of this ferment. Significantly, it was founded by the leading practitioners of the profession, not by administrators or under-privileged professors at the bottom of the status ladder. The founders' purpose was to protect the academic freedom of individuals against unjust discharge, but they were also interested in developing the occupation of professor into a profession closely modeled on that of the "true professions," medicine and law (and, in so doing return to the position which professors held in the medieval university).

The objectives of the AAUP founders have a very familiar ring for students of occupational associations. Fearing "the debasement of the currency of the Ph.D. by uncontrolled and ceaseless issue," they proposed that the AAUP "take hold of professional education ... standardize graduate requirements ... and even accredit—and discredit—the graduate schools in line with the therapeutic precedent which had recently been set by the AMA." Indeed, "some would have had the association reduce the irrationality of the market by setting up an employment agency," i.e., a hiring hall.[6]

The AAUP founders, like professionals generally, yearned for a greater degree of self-government. There was some suggestion that university faculties should help select their boards of directors, and there was considerable feeling that faculty should be consulted in all matters of educational policy. In addition, there was "broad agreement that the association should promulgate and enforce a code of professional ethics."[7] This code would not only

---

[6] Metzger, op. cit., pp. 232-33.

[7] To John Dewey, "the primary concern of the new organization would be the development of professional standards. ... 'I am confident,' he said, 'that academic freedom cannot be more than an incident of the activities of the association in developing standards. ... The existence of publicly recognized and enforced standards would tend almost automatically to protect the freedom of the individual and to secure institutions against its abuse." "Report of the Self-Survey Committee of the AAUP," p. 160.

deal with the employee-employer relationship but also would be concerned with the "relationship between professor and student, between scholar and the world at large, and between scholar and scholar." For example, "the medical code opposed the patenting of medical discoveries; the academic code might take a stand against the patenting of scientific discoveries."

The structure of the new association reflected its founder's interests. Besides Committee A (Academic Freedom and Tenure), there were committees established on appointment and promotion, recruitment to the profession, classification of universities, and ethics. In 1916, Committee T on self-government was established. This committee issued a statement calling for direct communications between faculty and trustees, joint selection of the university president, and faculty participation in all budgetary decisions which might bear on teaching.

Of the various committees, only Committee A flourished. The AAUP's other functions atrophied. A placement bureau was established and then abandoned. Committee T died. The code of ethics was never written. By 1956, "an objective observer would say that the AAUP was Committee A."[8] It is clear that in seeking to be a full-bodied professional association the AAUP had bitten off more than it could chew and had therefore concentrated its efforts on the area which had greatest membership support, the defense of academic freedom.

The AAUP achieved notable victories on the academic freedom front over the years, but by 1948—as Communist witch hunts started across the nation—its influence had started to decline, and by 1955 its strength was at a nadir. This was due in part to the failing health of the general secretary who had served for 20 years. More important, "for several years, the association had suspended public activity in the area which from its very beginning had been the center of its activity, viz., the clarification and defense of academic freedom." In the opinion of many members it failed to stand up against McCarthyism and to take sufficiently firm positions on the critical academic freedom issues of the moment: the loyalty oaths and the discharges arising from legislative investigations of suspected Communists.[9]

THE NEW MILITANCY

The years 1955-56 saw the association's fortunes revive. The 1955 annual meeting went into near rebellion. A new general secretary was elected, and a generally new administration began to take vigorous action. A firm position was taken to the effect that discharge should be based primarily on

[8] Metzger, *op. cit.,* p. 236.
[9] "Report of the Self-Survey Committee of the AAUP," p. 103. AAUP investigating teams did continue their activities and their interest contributed, to some extent, to the protection of academic freedom during this difficult period.

specific proof of unfitness for academic responsibilities and that "unfitness cannot be inferred by association." Committee A entered into a flurry of activity. An all-time peak was reached in the number of published investigations and institutions censured for violations of academic freedom. Among the administrations censured during this period were those of the University of California, Ohio State, Rutgers, Temple, and Fisk. Aided in large part by changes in public opinion as the anti-Communist hysteria of the early Fifties subsided, the association was able to point to notable improvements in academic freedom by the early Sixties.

The AAUP's new look also extended to activities which were primarily economic, of the kind traditionally performed by trade unions, such as improving salaries and strengthening job security. There was, as well, some new interest in the professional functions envisioned by the founders.

Economic.   By 1959, the association was able to devote some of its attention to the economic sphere. Relative to national per capita income, the salary of full professors had dropped 47 per cent since 1939.[10] Hewing to their concept of the association's role as being primairly professional, only a small number of the association's founders wanted it to deal with the salary issue, possibly because of "fear of the trade union label, plus certain lingering inhibitions inherited from a cleric past."[11] Although Committee Z on Economic Conditions was established during the post-World War I inflation, this fact-finding body had "merely proved through anonymous statistics that professors were being repeatedly immiserated by further inflations and a great depression."[12] In 1959, under the leadership of Fritz Machlup, the committee instituted an ingenious Self-Grading Survey. Colleges and universities are asked to report various salary information, including minimum and average earnings for each rank of professor.[13] On the basis of these data, each institution is graded from AA to F in terms of previously announced standards. These standards are raised each year with the expectation that salaries will double over a 10-year period.

The survey has been outstandingly successful. The number of institutions making reports tripled over a 5-year period, and today almost every institution of note permits publication of salary data once generally considered confidential. Success of a more tangible sort is shown by reported salary increases which average in the neighborhood of 6 per cent a year. The committee's effort undoubtedly helped raise salaries in some institutions, but the

[10] "Table 3. Academic Salaries Compared with U.S. Per Capita Income," in "The Economic Status of the Academic Profession: Taking Stock," *AAUP Bulletin,* LI (June, 1965), p. 250.

[11] Metzger, *op. cit.,* p. 233.

[12] *Ibid.,* p. 236.

[13] Where institutions refused to cooperate, the local AAUP chapter was encouraged to collect this information from individual faculty members.

primary reason for rapidly increasing faculty salaries has been the burgeon-ing demand for manpower and its relatively restricted supply.[14]

Committee A has ventured increasingly beyond academic freedom to tenure (or job security). More explicit "Standards for Notice of Reappoint-ment" have been promulgated, and it has frequently intervened in cases of late notice of dismissal given to nontenured professors.

Professional.   A professional code of ethics has at last been drafted. A revived Committee T on faculty participation in university government has proposed a statement of principles which it hopes to issue in conjunction with the American Council on Education. Meanwhile, the committee has investigated institutions whose self-government is deficient and has published reports singling out two such institutions for criticism. AAUP spearheaded the successful attempts to win repeal of the disclaimer affidavits required of students under the National Defense Education Act, and Committee S on Faculty Requirements for the Academic Freedom of Students has proposed standards of student freedom considerably more liberal than exist on many campuses. The Committee on University Teaching and Research has investi-gated educational TV.

ALTERNATIVE OBJECTIVES

Where does the AAUP go from here? Informal reports and the litera-ture suggest that there is debate between a group which thinks of the AAUP as primarily a professional organization and a group which wishes it to be a militant interest or pressure organization working in large part for economic objectives.

The professional view.   This view holds that having had considerable success on the economic and academic freedom fronts, the AAUP should now give greater emphasis to professionally oriented objectives, such as in-creased faculty self-government and the development of standards of ethical conduct. They deplore the use of "untraditional academic pressures . . . [and] tactics and pressures alien to the contemplative mind . . . in this era of the ultimatum."[15] The temptation to act "merely as an agency for the pro-tection of group interests . . . must be sternly resisted if the association is to

[14] The AAUP still felt a need to rationalize economic self-interest in professional terms. As an association president put it: "We are a professional organization and intend to remain such, with our foremost aim the general improvement of standards and the maintenance of freedom and research. The economic improvement of the profession is a means to that end." Bentley Glass, "An Invitation to Membership: The Half of One Per Cent Club," *AAUP Bulletin,* XLIV (Winter, 1958), p. 714.
[15] Address by William P. Fiedler, general secretary, in *AAUP Bulletin,* LI (June, 1965), pp. 313-14.

discharge its function as custodian of the interests of higher education and research."[16]

On the whole, this group comes from the older, better established institutions. Members of their chapters are generally well off. Demand for faculty exceeds supply in many fields. Salaries have been increasing rapidly. Research funds are plentiful. Dissatified professors find it easy to switch jobs. Academic freedom and faculty self-government are accepted. The main problems are rapid growth, impersonal university administration, and the need to protect high professional standards from dilution.

The Self-Survey Committee's report is generally consistent with this view. It suggests that salary goals should be based on "sensible grounds" and that the "association cannot defensibly" seek salary hikes without also working closely with university administrations to raise money. "The collective bargaining concept as adopted from the industrial and commercial world," it warns, is too "limited and rigid," and runs the "real danger of separating the community artificially and unnecessarily into 'bargaining' components."[17]

Perhaps symptomatic of the committee's approach are its strong recommendations that a committee be established "to hear and judge complaints of unprofessional conduct against [association] members" from which "one could expect a common law governing academic responsibility to arise and obtain acceptance." The Self-Survey Committee argues:[18]

> Whereas the association has long practiced, and in a sense perfected, a technique for bringing offending institutions into account, it has no parallel procedure directed against its members who are guilty of violations of good academic practice . . . . If the professors . . . really constitute a profession worthy of the name, it would seem incumbent upon the association, as an organ of the profession, to police its members, as do the legal and medical professions, visiting reprimands upon those found to have acted improperly, and in extreme cases expelling them from the association. . . . The AAUP . . . is false to its avowed purpose if it relinquishes the claim to be the most competent of all authorities to set standards of conduct and to play a major role in the enforcement of them.

The militant view.   Supporters of this view tend to come from newer institutions of less renown. Many are just emerging from the status of teachers' colleges or from the control of state or local agencies mainly concerned with primary and secondary schools. Faculties in these schools aspire to the status and privileges enjoyed at longer established institutions. For them the battles for academic freedom and economic security are still to be won. (In

[16] "Report of the Self-Survey Committee of the AAUP," p. 191.
[17] *Ibid.*, pp. 176-77.
[18] *Ibid.*, pp. 101-102.

California, for example, there is a struggle at the state college level for faculty self-government and at the junior college level for tenure.) Some of the militants come from chapters subject to sharp competition from other associations and unions.

Supporters of the militant view (whether from newly established institutions or not) generally view the AAUP as too slow to act. "National AAUP has projected an image of itself as a genteel, impeccably objective, rather remote, and essentially reflective as opposed to an executive (active) body," two Kent State professors charge. Instead, it should change itself to an action group, frankly devoted to self-interest.[19]

ORGANIZATIONAL COMPOSITION AND CONTROL

These differences in objective are naturally reflected in struggles for control. Three recent issues are indicative of the conflict.

Election procedure. At present, members of the AAUP Council are elected by the membership as a whole, although provision is made for equitable recognition of all geographical regions. As a consequence, argue the militants, council members are elected on the basis of reputation in their disciplines (rather than association service) or even reputation of the colleges from which they come; were elections held on a regional basis, presumably the men who work at the precinct level would have a greater chance of winning. But supporters of the status quo argue that change would promote weaker responsibility to the profession as a whole.

State and regional conferences. During the Twenties, the association developed a plan to create nine regional conferences which were to act as intermediate bodies between headquarters and the local chapters. Since an increasingly important function of the intermediate bodies is to deal with problems affecting public institutions at the state level, the regional conference is giving way to the state conference. Some conflict arises here, too. Those who think of the association as primarily an interest pressure group would like to expand the conferences' scope and financing. Those who see the association as chiefly self-regulating see little function for the conferences.

Membership standards. If AAUP is to be a professional organization along the lines of the American Medical Association, then it should restrict membership to those who meet rigid standards. If it seeks to be an economic

[19] V. Edwin Bixenstine and James Karge Olsen, "Must AAUP Change Its Image? An Open Letter to the Ad Hoc Self-Survey Committee," *AAUP Bulletin*, L (September, 1965), pp. 285-88.

pressure group, it should recruit as widely as possible. Prior to 1919, the AAUP required 10 years of academic employment for admission, plus nomination by three members and approval by two-thirds of the council. Over the years, these entrance requirements have been progressively liberalized. The issue at the moment concerns junior college faculty. Fearing that some junior college faculty lack "professional consciousness," a minority report of the Self-Survey Committee recommends that applicants from junior colleges should meet special standards not required of those from four-year colleges. Naturally, the opposing argument is that this is hardly the means to strengthen the association at the junior college level.

The two sides differ, too, over the role of AAUP members who become administrators. Seen from the militant viewpoint, there may be conflict of interest if administrators are permitted to be active in association affairs. The opposing view objects to a "psychological differentiation between 'us' and 'them' which is unhealthy for a community of scholars."[20]

TRADITIONAL WEAPONS

The AAUP's traditional weapons have been persuasion, negotiation, and, where these fail, unfavorable publicity. The militants believe that the present approach is cumbersome and ineffective. Their opponents argue that great caution is required if AAUP's findings are to receive credence within the profession—and that present procedures are generally adequate. Let us look at these traditional means and then examine the conditions under which they are effective.

Particularly in the area of academic freedom, the association prefers to negotiate general principles with other associations and to win acceptance through consensus. The guiding "Statement of Principles on Academic Freedom and Tenure" was developed in 1940 jointly with the American Association of Colleges (in a sense, an employers' association). Over the years the statement has been endorsed by more than a score of learned societies. By now, procedures consistent with it have been incorporated into the rules of most major universities. In general, the AAUP has been reluctant to adopt such statements unilaterally. Thus, it has withheld endorsement of a proposed statement on faculty participation in university self-government in the hope that it could be issued jointly with the American Council on Education.

If these joint statements can be considered as contracts reached through bargaining, then the AAUP also has a grievance (professional term: investigative) procedure. This procedure is set in motion by a complaint which goes through a number of stages—informal investigation, formal investigation by a special committee, publication of a report, and if all else fails, formal cen-

---

[20] "Report of the Self-Survey Committee of the AAUP," p. 116.

sure of the administration concerned.[21] Throughout the procedure, every effort is made to negotiate a satisfactory settlement of the complaint. The vast majority of complaints are so settled and the association serves fairly effectively as a policeman of academic freedom.[22]

Committee T, on faculty self-government, has copied Committee A's techniques. Committee T investigates institutions alleged to have abridged faculty rights and uses the threat of a published unfavorable report as a cudgel to win concessions from administrations with which it deals.

In the salary area it was not possible to arrive at generally accepted standards which would cover all cases. As a consequence, Committee Z could not emulate Committee A directly, by specifically censuring institutions whose salaries are substandard. Both committees, however, make use of the same ultimate weapon, unfavorable publicity. As Metzger puts it, "Committee Z now exposes through self-inquiry and capitalizes on the power of invidiousness by naming and rating institutions."

How effective is unfavorable publicity? Judged by the reported efforts of some censured administrations to be restored to AAUP's good graces, censure must carry a considerable sting in many cases, particularly when the demand for good professors exceeds the supply. And yet, as the militant emphasize, reliance on this single weapon weakens the organization's overall power.[23]

The militants also argue that the censure procedure is much too slow. At least three years normally elapse between the initial complaint and the final vote of censure. Furthermore, to preserve its impact, the ultimate sanction must be used sparingly. If too many institutions are censured, the shame of being singled out for reproach is lessened. As the AAUP enlarges and tightens the standards which it seeks to enforce, the number of instances in which institutions fall afoul of these standards tends to increase. Consequently, the Self-Survey Committee recommends that the association institute graded degrees of "reproach," with censure reserved for the most serious cases.

[21] For a careful and critical analysis of this procedure, see "Report of the Self-Survey Committee of the AAUP," pp. 145-60, and "Report by the Special Committee on Procedures and Disposition of Complaints Under the Principles of Academic Freedom and Tenure," *AAUP Bulletin,* LI (May, 1965), pp. 210-21.

[22] A recent article describes the association's procedures as that of a "mediation agency." James Allan Belasco, "The American Association of University Professors: A Private Dispute Settlement Agency," *Industrial and Labor Relations Review,* XVIII (July, 1965), pp. 535-53. Metzger's characterization of the association as "the avenger of academic crimes" (*op. cit.,* p. 237) is strong, but more to the point. The association conceives of its function as upholding the law, not just being an intermediary.

[23] From time to time various suggestions have been made to make the censure sanction more effective. Presumably a censured institution will have greater difficulty in recruiting new faculty. The preamble to the list of censured institutions suggests, but does not require, that members not accept appointments to such institutions. Recently some members of the more militant wing have suggested that "tenure insurance" (a form of strike benefit) be established. In effect, this would encourage professors to resign from censured institutions by reimbursing them for lost pay and other expenses while they look for a new job.

The real problem here is that the association's choice of weapons rests on the assumption that there is a professional community which includes both administrators and rank-and-file professors and that members of this community are concerned with maintaining their good reputation within it. If this is so, a formal vote of censure or exposure of unprofessional practices should mobilize sufficient adverse opinion within the profession to force the erring member to mend his ways.[24] This assumption is most realistic in institutions where academic values are well-established. However, the association has been relatively weak in areas marginal to the profession, such as technical, theological, and Negro schools, and in the South. (Perhaps the administrations of "aspirant" institutions, such as junior colleges, may in fact be more influenced by AAUP's opinion than are the administrations of schools whose reputations are already secure. However, there is little evidence to support this view.)

As the percentage of educational costs borne by the taxpayer continues to grow, the key educational decision-makers, particularly in the salary area, may increasingly be politicians and budget bureau technicians. These people may well be the "significant other" to whom association appeals in the future must be addressed. One wonders to what extent legislators, for example, will be willing to accept the legitimacy of the values (such as academic freedom) which the AAUP takes for granted—or to what extent they will be influenced by the scholarly dignity of current AAUP reports.

If the analysis above is accurate, then the differences as to means are not matters of philosophy alone, but reflect differences in objective conditions between elite and mass educational institutions.

WHAT ROLE FOR THE AAUP?

The AAUP's founders hoped it would grow to be an all-embracing professional society which would perform the full range of functions performed by such "pure" societies as the American Medical Association. The AAUP has not fulfilled such a function. In the first place, it has not gained universal support. Only about 30 per cent of those eligible have joined, and membership is extremely low in many prestige schools. At Harvard, Yale, and Cornell, for example, the membership rate is below 15 per cent.

The mere fact that professors are employees, not self-employed, makes it harder for AAUP to legitimize the claim for self-regulation. Furthermore,

[24] The Self-Survey Committee recommends that each chapter establish a Professional Standards Committee to judge unprofessional conduct, but it does not discuss what is to happen once the committee finds a member guilty. Does this make the condemned man an outlaw whom the university administration may discharge without further ado? Or will the committee's curse be so awesome that the erring member will repent on the spot? Or what? I have known professors so cussed that they might court censure just to prove their independence.

many professors feel first loyalty to their discipline[25] and their discipline's scholarly society—a society which may typically include nonacademicians. Indeed, one may argue that professors do not constitute a profession. Although doctors, lawyers, and school teachers specialize, each profession has its own common body of knowledge and practice in which every specialist is presumably skilled. No such interchangeability exists among professors. A Ph.D. in biology or chemistry, moreover, fits into a wide variety of employment. No special further training or entrance examination is required to become a professor. Although all physicians are M.D.'s, and all lawyers must pass the bar exam, a very significant number of professors are not Ph.D.'s.

The Self-Survey Committee described the AAUP as "a professional association, whose members are dedicated above all else to the advancement of higher education."[26] Although many professors have a teaching orientation, the leaders of the profession are more likely to be devoted to the advancement of knowledge, not higher education as such—just as lawyers may be devoted to the law, not to courts. It is fair to say that the typical professor thinks of the AAUP not as his professional society, but as an interest group primarily concerned with his employment relationship. The AAUP's leaders may talk about professional advancement as the association's proper goal, but in practice, as discussion at the AAUP annual meetings indicates, they find subjects such as salary ranges and academic freedom somewhat more meaty fare than improving standards of teaching. (More recently, to be sure, there has been concern with a nonemployment issue, student political rights.)

The Bar Association and the AMA have won for themselves the right to regulate their professions as a whole. Despite the Self-Survey's recommendations, few AAUP members look upon AAUP itself as an instrument of self-government. Instead, they think of AAUP as a means by which they can get self-government at each individual campus—for example, through establishing and strengthening faculty senates. At schools such as Harvard, Yale, and Cornell, self-government is well-established and the AAUP atrophies, no longer being needed as a channel of expression.

AAUP to date is primarily an interest group. Yet, it is not a purely economic interest group. It can be argued that in the AAUP context academic freedom has boiled down largely to job security for tenured faculty and lengthy termination notice for those without tenure. Yet this is far from fair. Throughout AAUP's history its greatest concern has been to protect professors who have expressed unpopular opinions or engaged in unpopular acts. Its primary function has been to protect the nonconformist. It has not been strenuously involved in cases which center over differences as to a man's competence or over technical failure to follow due process.

[25] See Alvin Gouldner, "Cosmopolitan and Locals: Toward an Analysis of Social Role," *Administrative Science Quarterly*, IV (December, 1957), pp. 281-306.
[26] "Report of the Self-Survey Committee of the AAUP," p. 191.

What of the future? My guess is that as the center of power in American higher education shifts from the elite private institutions to the integrated state systems of mass education, the AAUP will increasingly be involved on the economic front and that its tactics increasingly will be those of lobbying. On some issues the more militant view won the majority support of the 1965 annual meeting, although the council and the standing committees generally seem to be more professionally oriented.

An ever-increasing proportion of the academic profession is working for publicly financed universities, and higher education is taking up an increasing proportion of our state budgets. Salaries have been going up at a rapid rate, but it is questionable whether this rate of increase will continue, particularly in public universities. Taxpayers and legislators may show increasing resistance as the salaries of top-ranking professors begin to approximate the highest paid by the state. In many states questions are being raised about teaching loads and outside income. Academic "workloads," not easily measured, are widely misunderstood by state legislators. To some extent, salary increases are tied to those of janitors and prison guards. To be sure, professors may continue to get higher increases than other groups, but in doing so they will compete against other claimants who feel that they have a case at least as good as the professors. Political muscle pays off on the legislative front, not merit alone or tight scholarly logic.

If this argument is correct, professors will learn, as have other civil servants, that they need an interest group to represent them. Some argue that eventually professors will turn to the American Federation of Teachers. I do not think this likely unless the AAUP fails.[27] Not only does the AFT call itself a union, but even worse, it represents school teachers; professors will resist identification with either. Thus, the trend will be, as in Germany, to make the AAUP more like a civil service association—though with a strong emphasis on academic freedom. Where other governmental employees engage in collective bargaining, AAUP chapters will probably engage in bargaining, too.[28]

[27] There is always the possibility that two occupational associations will arise, one representing the occupation generally, the other the majority employed in public institutions.

[28] The Self-Survey (p. 177) recognizes that "There may ... be situations and circumstances where, because of legal or administrative patterns or demands of the immediate environment, organizations or representatives of the faculty are officially designated as collective bargaining units. Where this is the case a chapter or conference of the association might be so designated in preference to some less representative or desirable agency. ... [But it] should oppose the designation of any group short of the faculty as a whole, in its corporate capacity, as an *exclusive* bargaining agent. ... [And bargaining should be] confined to the few matters that can most nearly be handled through such direct negotiations ... and pursued without pressing any threat of ultimate sanctions.

III-4

THE NASSP AND COLLECTIVE NEGOTIATIONS*

Benjamin Epstein

In analyzing the impact of collective negotiation on principals, there are several broad areas to be considered. First, I want to present some general thoughts about the impact of collective negotiation on teacher relationships with administrators, especially principals. Second, I would like to outline briefly the official position taken this year on the subject by the NASSP and published in the form of a short pamphlet. Third, using some current agreements, I would like to illustrate briefly the worries of principals with, and objections to, certain phases of current trends in negotiations, and also some caveats that need to be raised concerning these trends. Finally, I would like to explain why the process of collective negotiation can be approved and supported by principals, especially if some of their reservations can be overcome.

At the present time, public education in the United States is moving through massive mutations. The effects of the civil rights movement, television, the war against poverty, the population explosion, the external critics of schools of all shades of opinion, the impact of national curriculum designers (such as the PSSC, SMSG, BSCS, CBA, and CSG), Operation Head Start, the organizational rivalry between the AFT and the NEA, the urban-suburban dichotomy, Title I of the Elementary and Secondary Education Act of 1965, and many, many other mutagenic influences have created a period of difficulty and uncertainty, and have led to massive innovation in American education within less than a decade. Educational innovations in the structure of schools, their instructional content, and often even their physical appearance are beginning to make schools both unrecognizable and incomprehensible to those who were knowledgeable about education only a very few years ago. Overhead projectors, language laboratories, data processing, phonetic alphabets, structural linguistics, ungraded schools, higher horizon programs, public pre-kindergarten classes, programmed instruction,

* Revision of paper delivered on June 22, 1966, at the National Institute on Collective Negotiations in Public Education cosponsored by Phi Delta Kappa and the University of Pennsylvania, Philadelphia. Benjamin Epstein is Principal, Weequahic High School, in Newark, New Jersey.

are but a handful of the items that cause the observer to wonder about what has happened almost overnight.

Among these widespread changes, there is also widespread evidence of immature, awkward, but rapidly emergent new patterns of relationships between teachers, administrators, supervisors, and school boards. These new patterns are partly an outgrowth of the general restiveness in the world and in our nation today. In addition, they are reactions to a long period of practical neglect of schools, at a moment in history when exaggerated lip-service is being paid on all sides to the fundamental need for quality education as the underlying basis of the good future for our society, in terms of its ability to promote cultural, moral, material, intellectual, and aesthetic well-being.

The emerging patterns are also signs of a new breed of educational practitioners, who are determined to be professionals rather than merely wage-earning craftsmen. These patterns are evidenced by increased boldness and militancy on the part of teachers in asserting themselves, and especially in demanding that they be an essential part of educational policy- and decision-making on the basis of recognized right rather than as a result of occasional invitation. Finally, these patterns are marked by acts which demonstrate that the collective strength of teachers can paralyze the operation of schools if teacher demands for recognition and status continue to be ignored.

As a result, we have begun to see the increasing use of strikes, boycotts, sanctions, refusal to perform extra-curricular services, picket lines and mass demonstrations in school districts all over the nation. Because the problems of large urban centers are more pressing and difficult, and because the size of the teaching staff creates greater collective strength and more impersonal relations between teachers and school administrators in large districts, this new militancy of teachers has appeared more often in a big-city environment. It has, however, also been evident in such less urbanized regions as Utah, Oklahoma, and suburban New Jersey and Michigan.

This surge of teacher self-assertion is patterned very closely after the model of American trade unionism. This is true regardless of whether the surge is led by teachers affiliated with the labor movement through the AFT or by those who claim an austere professional independence by way of the NEA and its state and local affiliates. The movement calls for exclusive recognition of the organized group in the majority as the spokesman of teachers. It insists on the right to negotiate "in good faith." It seeks to incorporate jointly agreed upon conclusions into written agreements. It endeavors to play as significant a role as it can, not only in advancing the welfare of teachers but also in setting up policies which affect other aspects of education. It demands elaborate machinery for redress of grievances and for guaranteeing the precise execution of teacher agreements with teacher employers, the school boards.

The upsurge of teacher militancy is raising questions about many traditional hierarchical practices in public education. At the same time, it is forcing a redefinition of the powers, the authority, and the range of discretion of school boards, of the central school administration which operates through the office of the superintendent and his staff, and of the immediate administrator-supervisor, the school principal (plus his staff of department heads, vice-principals, and administrative assistants, where such exist).

Increasingly, and very often with a paradoxical and nostalgic apologia to their dedication to "the united profession," the teachers have come to regard the superintendent and the principal either as adversaries or impediments in their struggle for bargaining power. Sometimes with—but more often without any—rancor, teachers are coming to look upon the superintendent, the principal, and the remainder of the administrative-supervisory staff less as colleagues, less as their educational leaders, less as patriarchal and venerable figures from whom to seek guidance and help, but more as managerial representatives of the employer who are barriers to the free exercise of the teachers' collective professional will.

This new set of teacher attitudes is reflected in demands for increased rights and privileges, as well as for the establishment of new limits on traditional board and administrative discretionary control and authority over teachers. These demands plus the new relationships they produce become formalized sooner or later and are being put into writing as agreements, contracts, or joint teacher-board memoranda of policy.

In practice, such determinations of new policy and procedure are typically made as an outcome of direct, face-to-face negotiations between the spokesmen of teachers and the school boards per se rather than with any intermediaries. While the superintendent may be designated as the board's negotiator so that he plays an essential part in the process, it is also possible and has happened that he sits out the negotiations on the sidelines, acting as an expert consultant rather than as a proposer or determiner of policy.

In May of 1966, Aaron Cohodes, Editor of *Nation's Schools,* published an open letter in that journal to Dr. Harold Spears, Superintendent of Schools in San Francisco and President of the AASA. In it, Cohodes argued that superintendents must recognize the reality of teacher attitudes towards them. He said:

NEA is as militant and strike-happy and sanction-oriented as are the teacher unions. Like teacher unions, NEA does not want administrators among its members. Unlike teacher unions, NEA is stuck with them. But not for long. Each year, NEA grows ominously close to tossing them out. It has no choice. Supervisors, especially superintendents, not only represent management, they are management. To expect AASA and NEA to function sensibly as one organization under one roof is like expecting the

National Association of Manufacturers to sign up as a division of AFL CIO. We should live so long.

The role of the principal in the pioneer phases of teacher-board negotiations and joint policy-making has as yet not become clearly defined or established. There are some who would argue that principals should have no role at all. In some localities, the principal has been included as part of the general teachers' organization and joins in the negotiations as part of the teachers' negotiating team. There is, however, a contradiction inherent in such an arrangement. It is inevitable that in seeking to expand their own role in the decision-making process, teachers will and must try to diminish any influence which restricts that role; thus there exists a dilemma for any principal or principals' group that wants to be an integral part of a teachers' negotiating unit. In so acting, the principal is, whether he is willing to admit it or not, put into the position of assisting in the narrowing and lessening of his own authority and power to carry out the educational and administrative functions for which he is always held responsible, not only by law but also by the school board and the community—functions which increase constantly and need greater executive control.

In other localities, superintendents and school boards have invited principals and other administrators to serve either as consultants to or participants on the administrative team that is part of the negotiations. Such inclusion has resulted from foresight or unhappy experience. Clearly, when principals are excluded, the decisions which emerge may gratify certain teachers and relieve school boards of threats of drastic teacher actions, but may also be unmanageable, impractical, or actually harmful in the day-to-day operations of a school.

In many localities, there has been no involvement of principals in the decisive phases of agreement-writing. The teacher organizations do not want principals to be a part of the negotiations while the school board and superintendent find it expedient to yield to keep principals away from the bargaining table. Under these circumstances, principals and other administrators have begun to feel themselves in the middle of a squeeze play in which their responsibilities and duties are increasing while their power and authority are slowly or rapidly chopped away by the agreements and policies that result from board-teacher negotiations. It is not difficult to understand, therefore, that principals, especially those who are in larger school systems, have begun to discuss and to request negotiating privileges for themselves and, in some cases, written agreements to protect their own status.

It is increasingly apparent that not only the curriculum, the physical structure, the organization, and the procedures of our schools are in a period of intense flux, so are all staff relationships, including the prerogatives, the stratifications, and the hierarchies of administrative authority. We should, therefore, consider what changes have already occurred as an outgrowth of teacher-board agreements. Because such agreements are still a new phenomenon, they can at best only presage a trend. That trend will probably reflect full pendulum swings in one direction and then swings in the other, until some new golden mean (which Webster's dictionary defines as "the way of wisdom and safety between extremes") is attained. We are still only at the beginning of the swing in which teachers seek to release themselves from traditional board-administrator authority. Such authority —whether democratically or autocratically administered—is regarded as a roadblock to be removed by teacher bargaining power. Thus, teachers seek the feeling of having achieved power themselves rather than feel they have been given privileges by others.

It is too soon to predict what new equilibria will emerge. We do not know how relationships between teachers and principals will ultimately develop within our schools. It is, however, strongly probable that such relationships, even in the most cordial circumstances, will be more circumscribed and more formalized within a framework of rules spelling out many phases of school life in greater detail. Trends suggest that, while tightly defined and negotiated limits governing teacher conditions of employment will protect teachers from capricious, arbitrary, and autocratic treatment, nevertheless the flexibility, the creativity, the artistry, and even the individuality of the teacher within the teaching situation and that of the administrator to give unfettered leadership will be reduced considerably. Trends also suggest the possibility that the desire of teachers (and administrators even more so, believe me!) to rid themselves of the effects of bureaucracy and its miles of red tape may result in even greater rigidity and obeisance to new legalisms and formalisms. The constraints of the written agreements may come to replace those of the board rules, superintendent's directives, and principal's bulletins—only more so!

With this general description of the milieu in which a new approach to staff relationships is being molded, let us examine the position of a strong national organization of administrators, the NASSP, on the problem.

The NASSP declared that:

1. The schools belong to the people, not to the educators. The people, through their voting power, their legislatures, and their school boards have and should continue to retain final control over their schools and to oversee the education of their children. They have the right to expect that those whom they employ to provide that education are capable, well-trained, and perform their functions effectively.

2. Those employed by school boards, in turn, have rights to good compensation at appropriate levels of training and responsibility. They

have rights to proper conditions of work, reasonable hours and work loads, and dignity of personal treatment.

3.   School board employees should no longer be forced to seek rights as humble petitioners before a sovereign agency which, like the king, can do no wrong. Instead, they must have the same rights as employees in private enterprise to negotiate with their employers in good faith, to seek mutual solutions or compromises, and to have their conclusions incorporated in a contract or agreement which is accorded faithful adherence.

4.   Laws, where needed—and they are needed in most states—to permit collective negotiations are desirable and welcome. (I personally would go further than NASSP and say that such laws are necessary and should be enacted as mandates to school boards by state legislatures to negotiate in good faith.)

5.   Teachers have a right, as do private employees, to organize and be exclusively represented by organizations which, in free elections, establish that they speak for the majority of employees for whom they negotiate.

6.   Teachers must be free in their choice as to whether they will join or not join any particular organization. They should have this right of free choice with no duress or pressure, actual or implied, of any kind placed upon them either by school boards or their administrative and supervisory superiors, no matter how altruistically motivated.

7.   In all negotiations, the chief administrative officer of a school system, and the school board's chief educational advisor, the superintendent, must be an integral part, serving as an expert consultant, as a guardian of the interests of the children in the schools, as a wise mediator, and as an active initiator of recommendations.

8.   It is increasingly apparent that both AFT and NEA affiliates at the local level do not want to include principals as part of their negotiating unit (e.g., New York, Newark, New Rochelle, Philadelphia). Principals are beginning to realize that, while they have a great many common interests with teachers, teacher pressure at the local level inevitably seeks to curtail their prerogatives and limit their authority while it constantly increases the principals' work load and responsibility. Principals are, therefore, questioning their own membership in local teacher organizations.

Last month, after lengthy debate, the Public School Principals Association of Newark adopted the following resolution without dissent. "It is the policy of the Public School Principals Association of Newark, New Jersey, that its members do not belong to *Local Teachers' Organizations.* Furthermore, the Public School Principals Association is the only official spokesman for the principals of Newark." Though I am its president, I was not the one who proposed this statement of policy. It was the experience of all of us, in a period which included two representation elections, two strikes, and one written contract that led to this new attitude.

Principals are beginning to seek a clearly defined role at the bargaining table. Since so very much of all negotiations between teachers and school boards in one way or another impinges upon the principals' functions and status, principals are pressing for participation in the negotiations—less and less as part of a general professional unit and more and more as an independent unit at the negotiating table or as part of the administrative team involved in negotiations—the latter more usual in small communities, the former in larger school systems.

9. NASSP deplores the widespread absence of mediative and arbitrative machinery. Such absence often leads to strikes, boycotts, sanctions, and other end-of-the-rope measures used by teachers with growing frequency to deal with impasse situations. NASSP strongly advocates enactment of legislation to provide for mediation and fact-finding. It has taken no position as to whether such machinery should be in the hands of state labor mediation agencies or state departments of education.

Most NASSP members would, I believe, prefer that the negotiations statutes be administered by educational agencies. Personally, I do not consider this as significant a problem as it has been made to seem in some quarters. Such statutes could be effective in either a "labor" or an "educational" agency. Much of their administration could successfully be undertaken by an outside agency such as the American Arbitration Association. The mechanism is needed more than arguments as to who operates the mechanism.

10. As employees, teachers and administrators, together or separately, have every right to negotiate for their welfare needs and should be able to do so as much as any group of private employees. In addition, as professionals, they should be helping create the policies and practices in their area of expertise. But these policies cannot emerge from negotiations—they must come from research, training, and experience. It is one thing to negotiate a teacher's daily work load; it is another thing to equate this work load, necessarily and always, with the concept of class size. The latter should be determined by standards other than a negotiated compromise based upon some arbitrary number such as 30 or 15 or 25. Some classes of 18 pupils may demand far harder teacher labor than others with 75 pupils.

The NASSP strongly supports the inclusion of teachers as well as administrators in a partnership with school boards to develop educational policy. It would certainly accept the concept that teacher and administrator organizations negotiate with school boards on the ways of creating and structuring that apparatus within a school system for guaranteeing—by right rather than invitation—the inclusion of representatives of these groups in such policy development. On the other hand, it cannot accept the concept that the policies themselves always be the outcome of negotiation. The NASSP agrees, for example, that teachers be guaranteed an important part in the selection of textbooks and other materials of instruction, but it does not agree, for example, that a local NEA or AFT affiliate should use bargaining power to force the inclusion of a list of approved texts as part of a negotiated written agreement, or to demand that a particular projective test should be given by the school psychiatrist.

These, then, are the main items of NASSP policy salted with some of my own views. Why do principals want to become involved in the negotiations and the agreement-writing? To put it simply—they are very much involved in the decisions which are made and want to speak for themselves when they are so involved. But putting it simply isn't enough.

In the first place, principals are worried about the fact that in many agreements they receive inequity of treatment. Let me cite as an example the grievance procedures set up in the first Newark agreement between the Board of Education and the Newark Teachers Association. As of the time of preparation of this paper, no successor agreement had been negotiated. There are four steps in the grievance procedures. At Level I, the teacher and principal only are involved. If the teacher is dissatisfied, he asks the Association to proceed on his behalf to Level II, which is the Superintendent plus one Board member. If the teacher is still dissatisfied, the grievance goes to Level III, the full school board. If he disagrees with this decision, he appeals to Level IV, an outside arbitrator named from a panel of arbitrators, who then renders an advisory decision. But, interestingly enough, if the principal is dissatisfied with the decisions at Level II or III, no provision of any kind is made for permitting him to appeal. He has lesser rights than the teacher. Incidentally, in the writing of this grievance procedure, as in the whole agreement, the NTA's negotiator was an attorney made available to the local association by the NEA. The outcome stands in contrast with the UFT agreement in New York City, wherein the principal is permitted to appear at all appellate hearings and present his own views. The grievance procedures in the first Newark agreement have not only changed the status of the principals, but they have gone further and removed from him the same rights to due process which they have given others. It is easy to see why principals are opposed to such processes.

Second, principals find certain items being written into agreements to be unmanageable and impractical. As an example, consider the New Rochelle agreement dated November 24, 1964. NEA took such pride in this agreement that it published and distributed the agreement widely. It is even included in full in a book by three staff members of the NEA.* Article

---

* T. M. Stinnett, Jack Kleinmann, and Martha Ware, *Professional Negotiation in Public Education* (New York: The Macmillan Company, 1966).

II, Section 2f, says: "Participation in extra-curricular activities for which no additional compensation is paid shall be voluntary. At the same time, the teachers recognize that their responsibility to their students and their profession requires the performance of duties that involve the expenditure of time beyond that of the normal school day." How does one enforce the clause concerning teacher responsibility if and when they refuse to volunteer? Think about getting faculty members out to PTA meetings or evening dances, or school plays. If a teacher does not "volunteer" for such after-school activities, may the principal submit a grievance to the effect that the teacher has been remiss in recognizing his responsibility? And if the principal can initiate a grievance, what can the association do about it? Or can the principal rate the teacher as uncooperative when it is clear that the word "voluntary" also means the right not to volunteer. The answers to these questions do not seem very clear.

Consider another clause from the first Newark agreement: "Teacher assignments shall be made without regard to race, creed, color, religion, nationality, sex, or marital status." In general, this is a noble and desirable provision. But if a principal had been there while it was being written, he might have pointed out that sex can't be disregarded in the assignment of physical education teachers. Maybe the teachers don't know it, but there could be considerable trouble if a male teacher entered a girls' gymnasium locker room to break up some minor squabble between two girls. So I and every other Newark principal deliberately violate this part of the agreement. As yet, no grievance has been presented on this score. Of course, the clause wasn't meant to force principals to ignore sex in teacher assignments wherein the sex of the teacher is a legitimate factor to be considered. The clause was designed to prevent discriminatory practices. But that is not the way the agreement reads, at least to me.

Another point is that some items included in certain agreements are, in my opinion, educationally harmful and professionally unjustifiable. These items may eliminate certain gripes of teachers, but one is not sure that the gripes were justified in the first instance. To illustrate, there is one section in the Newark agreement that reads, "Building faculty meetings after the teachers' working day shall not normally be longer than 45 minutes from the start of the meeting and shall not be scheduled more often than once a month except in emergencies." By the way, the term "emergency" is not defined. Secondary principals might think about this provision while in the midst of preparing for an evaluation by a regional accrediting association. Needless to add, "emergency" evaluation by a regional accrediting association can be subject to conflicting interpretations.

In the UFT agreement in New York City, there is a very detailed description of a policy known as "rotation." One item in that policy provides that on each elementary grade level, classes should be divided into two categories, "difficult" and "less difficult" in terms of reading achievement. (I'd say it would have been even better bargaining to classify them as "difficult" and "more difficult.") If a teacher had one of the two last year, this year she gets the other kind. The reason given for this practice, and I quote, is "In order to make certain that teachers are not frozen into positions which are relatively easy or difficult." Why does the UFT object to a teacher having it "relatively easy?" But where do the pupils come in? Most principals would be chiefly concerned with the problem as to which teacher can do the most for a particular group of children. In the hands of the right teacher, the more difficult group may be far less of a problem, and yet that same teacher might be less effective in a faster moving class. But if a principal dares place a teacher where his knowledge, observations, and experience indicate the teacher will do the best job, the principal may have a grievance on his hands. It really doesn't make good educational sense to put a school system and its supervisors into a straitjacket merely because over the years some teachers have thought that the grass is greener in their neighbor's class.

Many similar examples could be cited, but the point is probably clear by now. Every example cited is the product of justifiable complaints of teachers. These complaints grew out of conditions that needed correction. But the corrections should provide solutions and not create new problems.

As principals, we are far less concerned with retaining some illusory sense of majesty and power status than we are in seeing to it that the authority which we must have in order to provide maximum service to students is not reduced to the point of ineffectiveness. While such an outcome might be a pleasant retaliation for the unnecessary and petty bossism of an occasional misguided administrator, the diminution of necessary administrative control and authority is bound to hurt the best interests of teachers themselves.

Principals see no ominous threat to themselves in collective negotiations. They do, however, strongly assert that their own absence from such negotiations is indefensible. Their presence would produce more workable and more satisfactory agreements. Principals might even ask for some items for teachers that the teachers themselves would be apt to overlook.

Principals welcome the concept of formal across-the-table negotiations between teachers vis-a-vis their employers, the school boards plus their administrative and supervisory staffs of superintendents and principals. We believe that such negotiations will bring greater dignity to the teaching profession as well as greater respect for teachers by others and by teachers for themselves.

Principals know that teachers have a great deal to contribute collectively in creating policies for improving education and should have the right to help fashion those policies. Principals feel that as teachers become decision-makers, they will grow in responsibility; they will even have to reach the point where they, rather than colleges or state certification boards, will determine the qualifications and professional behaviors required if those who wish to enter remain in the profession. We have already seen that negotiations in many areas have brought about better salaries and improved working conditions for teachers—and have brought them about faster than the previous procedures.

Many teacher organizations have not merely been interested in self-serving demands but have also sought to make the total school system better able to serve the needs of youngsters.

Principals deplore the fact that, at this early stage of its development, the process of collective negotiation has too often been accompanied by misunderstandings and suspicions between teachers and their administrators. Of course, this is a sign of the infancy of the collective negotiation movement. We have faith that it will mature rapidly. While that's happening, we don't want to get stuck by the diaper pins.

III-5

THE NATIONAL SCHOOL BOARDS ASSOCIATION AND COLLECTIVE NEGOTIATIONS*

Harold Webb

Charles Keller said the only way to study an organization is to see how it got that way.

Perhaps, as a starting point, it would be wise for me to review briefly the developments which have led to the present era of board-superintendent-staff relationships, and follow with a detailed analysis, review, and clarification of National School Boards Association policy relating to collective negotiations.

The growing militancy of teachers is perhaps not so much an indication of basic conflict with school boards as it is the result of a significant change in the spirit of the nation's teachers in the last decade.

John Hopkins, in a recent issue of Ohio State University's *Theory Into Practice,* summarizes this changing spirit. He suggests that teachers have become—and primarily through their associations—more interested and active in the political and moral issues of the day as they have found themselves buffeted by many societal fears, tensions, and pressures. As a concomitant and result of their rising level of professionalism, teachers have also become vitally concerned about their rights and responsibilities. They are, Hopkins says, increasingly concerned with what they term the paternalism which has resulted, at least in part, from the greater bureaucratization that often accompanies school district consolidation. Within these larger school organizations, more complex and powerful problems are faced by professionals who are hindered by organizational and societal demands. And the increasing proportion of male teachers, who are the sole providers for their households, has forced salary levels to become a major concern.

The end of a previous era occurred in December of 1961, with the organizational election for the right to represent all of the teachers of the

---

* An address by Harold Webb, Executive Director, National School Boards Association, on July 13, 1965, to the National Institute on Collective Negotiations in Public Education cosponsored by Phi Delta Kappa and Rhode Island College, Providence, R. I.

New York City school system. Teachers now are proposing, through their various organizations, a more highly formalized system of communication than has existed in the past. They are advocating legislation for formal negotiation procedures, and school boards—as well as teachers, superintendents, and the public—are reassessing these implications in American education.

Prior discussion at this and other meetings has been broad, varied, and has dealt with most of the fundamental aspects of the overall question of collective negotiations. Discussion which will follow at this institute gives promise of covering those areas of question not yet touched upon.

Therefore, I shall limit my remarks rather narrowly to the topic assigned me—but will attempt to cast my discussion in terms of the implications to public education, the welfare of youngsters, and the institution of local control. If the policies of NSBA are not viewed in this light, then they are viewed in a vacuum. I make the point because too often those who question our policies seem to feel that they can be discussed without considering the implications they have for the total picture in education.

As you know, the National School Boards Association is a federation of 50 state school board associations. The membership of these 50 state associations comprises approximately 18,000 school boards—about 50 per cent of the total number of such boards in the country—but these 18,000 boards are responsible for more than 95 per cent of the public school enrollment.

Neither the state school boards associations nor NSBA exercises legal authority over the operation of local school boards. As we all know, public education is a local and state matter, and school boards operate under broad general policies established by state departments of education. Board members are agents of state government.

Therefore, when state associations or NSBA promulgate policies concerning school board operations, or on the relationships to be maintained between board members and the professional staff, these policies have no legal force. They are, rather, guidelines for local boards—which can be recast and reinterpreted by local boards to meet local conditions and local aspirations.

Given this condition, why, then, pay any attention to our policies?

The answer lies, first, in the way the policies are developed; and, second, in the nature and influence of NSBA itself. Let me clarify.

The leadership of NSBA is drawn from the individual school board members throughout 50 states who are both state and national leaders. The policies they formulate for NSBA, then, reflect both the most experienced, knowledgeable, and enlightened school board point of view on the critical issues of public education and the best practice across the country in the operation of the public schools.

Second, NSBA is the *only* national organization which represents school boards and the school board point of view. Therefore, what it has to say at the national level about good practice in the public schools must have significance for all who are concerned with public school operations.

What I have said is preface to the question of NSBA position on collective negotiations. I think it is appropriate here to comment that organizers of this conference have selected a phrase—"collective negotiations"—which reflects the interest of two teacher organizations. In labor practice, talk is of "collective bargaining"; the NEA has suggested that we consider "professional negotiation." You give us a little of each, but I assure you it makes it no more palatable to school board members. We are against "collective negotiations," and we are also against "professional bargaining," if you should call a conference on that subject in the future.

The National School Boards Association, at its 1961 convention in Philadelphia, stated its official position on collective negotiations in official definition of our *Beliefs and Policies.* This was reaffirmed in substance at the 1963 convention in Denver, in 1964 in Houston, and again this year at the Boston convention of NSBA.

These policies say:

> The retention of local and state controls depends upon the willingness of local and state boards to accept and discharge their responsibilities . . .

And part of that responsibility, as our *Beliefs and Policies* indicates, is the matter of authority:

> The authority of the board of education is established by law and this authority may not be delegated to others. Strikes, sanctions, boycotts, mandated arbitration, or mediation are improper procedures to be used by public school employees who are dissatisfied with their conditions of employment.

The sections of our policies which are also quite pertinent to our discussion are contained in Section Two, entitled "Responsibilities of Local School Boards." After a general preamble and statements of general responsibilities, the association spells out its belief in the value of written policies:

> School boards should adopt clearly defined written policies, based on a thorough understanding of the educational process. In formulating the policies they should consult individuals and groups affected by the policies, and, since changing conditions bring changing needs, should periodically review policies. They should recognize that while school boards are policy-making bodies, they properly delegate the execution of policy to employed professional administrators.

And, the NSBA *Beliefs and Policies* states:

School boards should employ professional and nonprofessional personnel with competence and personal qualifications which command community respect. Appropriate to the importance of their role in the communities, all personnel should be adequately compensated to assure their economic security and their working conditions should permit them to effectively exercise their skills and duties.

School boards should recognize the great contributions to overall planning that can come from the knowledge and experience of classroom teachers, administrators, and other professional personnel and give careful consideration to plans, suggestions, and recommendations of these professional people in the area of teaching conditions, needs, and personnel problems. In determining general policies relating to the operation of the schools, handling of personnel problems, and the general welfare of all professional personnel, each local school board should set up satisfactory procedures for communication with all professional personnel. Such procedures should be clearly stated and publicized and all professional groups and their representatives should be encouraged to present their ideas and recommendations.

School boards should also establish and use free channels of communication with all their personnel so that decisions affecting their interest and welfare may be made only after careful board consideration has been given to their views, recommendations, needs, and grievances.

School boards, subject to the requirements of applicable law, should refrain from compromise agreements based on negotiation or collective bargaining, and should not resort to mediation or arbitration, nor yield to threats of reprisal on all matters affecting local public schools, including the welfare of all personnel. They should also resist by all lawful means the enactment of laws which would compel them to surrender any part of their responsibility.

Now, let me summarize what the leadership of NSBA intends to convey in these policy statements:

1. The views and recommendations of professional staff *must* be listened to and taken into account by the school board in its deliberations. Prior to any decisions by a school board, there must be ample opportunity for discussion and exchange of views between board members and professional staff. The association's policy statements clearly recognize the right of teachers' organizations to work for the enhancement of their professional status and also their right to recommend the adoption of policies by the board of education. The concern of school boards lies in the definition of policy making which is held by these teacher organizations. A former NSBA president, Mrs. Fred Radke, expressed it in this way in a speech at our 1965 convention: "It is time for teachers to decide whether they are calling for joint *responsibility* with boards of education—or whether they are saying we have joint *concerns* with boards of education, and we want our opinions

to be heard and our counsel to be carefully considered before decisions are reached by the board. If it is the latter, school boards can give this their support." It should be stated that teachers also have responsibility in this matter of communication. There must be communication up and down within their organizations. Teacher organizations sometimes take full credit for success and shift blame for failures to the board of education.

2.   The proper channel for professional staff to approach the school board is through the superintendent of schools. Professional staff should not attempt to circumvent the superintendent in presenting positions, grievances, or other matters to board members.

3.   Unless local or state law otherwise provides, school boards may *not* enter into negotiations, collective bargaining, mediation, or arbitration. To do so would be to abdicate their legal responsibility—and boards of education above all else must operate within the framework of law.

Where we run into trouble with the above is in the impasse situation. Many teacher organizations and numerous other interested groups or individuals keep coming up with proposed new machinery to be considered in the event professional staff and boards come to loggerheads. Invariably, these proposals involve appeal to a higher authority. By law, in the state of Wisconsin, the Wisconsin Employment Relations Board is called into such situations. A similar piece of legislation now is before the governor of the state of New Jersey.

I submit to you that plans which embody these procedures are not acceptable machinery for the impasse situation.

Any provision for appeal modifies the role of participants in any effort to reach agreement. If there is an appeal process, the court of appeal should be the board of education itself. In other words, the board should be called upon only when teachers and the superintendent cannot agree.

Either professional staff must accept the ultimate decision of the board of education, or the community must vote out of office its board of education, which represents it in matters pertaining to the school operation, and vote in a new board, which presumably will respond to the views of the community and the needs of the professional staff. There are no other acceptable alternatives.

The fact is, as I know most would agree to privately even though they find it impolitic to so state publicly, once you establish a higher authority than a local board of education for resolving matters on which staff and boards are in disagreement, you will have effectively abolished the existing local board of education and established a new board.

No professional staff will feel obligated to accept its responsibility to its board of education if it knows it has recourse to another body for final decisions. Further, there is no end on the road to higher authority. If ultimate decision-making power is removed from the local board and given to the state department of education, it will not be long before a new body is looked to beyond the state department for final decisions—perhaps the governor, perhaps the U.S. Office of Education in Washington, perhaps a national commission.

Guidelines in this matter of board-superintendent-staff relationships have been drawn, not only by NSBA, but by many of the state school board associations. Workshops and seminars have been offered to local boards of education by many state school board associations. Publications on this subject have been issued by the state school board associations.

We feel it is time right now for professionals to look hard at the course they are pursuing and to ask themselves whether it is really in the best interests of youngsters and public education.

If the strength of our system of public education lies in local control—as almost all are agreed—then let us stop this nonsense of finding ways and means of destroying the very institution we profess is our greatest strength.

Let me conclude with these two thoughts:

1.   The real problem in teacher-superintendent-board relationships is adequate communication among the parties involved. If this could be solved, then the solutions proposed through collective bargaining, or professional negotiation, or what you will, are an expedient that will in the long run create more problems than they will solve.

2.   While there is no question that boards of education have a great responsibility in seeing that there is proper opportunity for two-way communication, and that communications with the board must be seriously considered, it is only part of the communication problem. Equally large are the related questions of who is communicating for professional staff, and what responsibilities do professional staff have for taking into account the realities of the local and state situation when formulating their own positions for presentation to the boards.

As we continue discussions such as these here at the institute, we must work together in good faith, honestly recognizing, as Frederick Staub has so ably pointed out, that *we*—not forces or circumstances—are making decisions for which we must hold ourselves accountable, and that our purpose is to seek better ways of accomplishing the goals of public education.

In summary, NSBA is opposed to collective bargaining and any other method of reaching compromise agreements with boards based on threat of sanction, strike, or appeal to third-party decision makers because, in the view of the most experienced and enlightened board members in the country, these approaches to the resolution of differences between boards and staff do not meet the best interests of the children and do not serve the welfare of the community.

NSBA's leaders feel that the existing machinery is adequate to meet the challenges of the times—and that all who are a part of our great system of public education must meet our responsibilities in preserving this institution.

Once we attack the essential elements of the great institutions in our society, we attack the very bedrock upon which we have built our way of life.

III-6

SCHOOL ADMINISTRATORS VIEW PROFESSIONAL NEGOTIATION*

American Association of School Administrators

In its 1965 resolution entitled "Staff Relations," AASA said this:

> We believe that teachers, school boards, and administrators are all committed to the advancement of public education and that the goals and interests of these groups are highly interrelated. We believe strongly that the development of school policies and programs and the solution of school problems can best be accomplished by these groups working in harmony and with respect for the roles of each. We believe that effective policy development involves important contributions by each group.
> We believe that evaluation in staff relations is to be welcomed. We commend careful study and the development of principles that should govern these relations and define the responsibilities of the various groups while maintaining the integrity of each. We believe that shared responsibility for policy and program development is a professional concept requiring a unique professional approach. We maintain that the superintendent of schools has a unique responsibility to provide leadership in these matters.

The philosophy of staff relations having been stated, it remains to define positions on a number of hard, practical issues related to this important concept.

Development of Personnel Policies

In 1963 the Executive Committee and staff of the American Association of School Administrators developed and published a lengthy policy statement entitled *Roles, Responsibilities, Relationships of the School Board, Superintendent, and Staff*. It contains a section which sets forth the beliefs of school superintendents concerning the development of personnel policies.

* Excerpted by permission from American Association of School Administrators, *School Administrators View Professional Negotiation* (Washington, D.C.: American Association of School Administrators, 1966), pp. 33-58. (Footnotes have been renumbered.)

The section bears restatement in the context of professional negotiation:

> We believe that teachers, school administrators, and school boards must together seek pathways yet uncharted in the area of personnel policies and practices.
>
> We believe that the superintendent has a responsibility to see that opportunities are provided for staff members—teachers, supervisors, principals, and specialists—to play appropriate roles in developing personnel policies and in maintaining professional working conditions.
>
> We believe that the superintendent has a responsibility to assist staff members—in ways satisfactory to them—in studying welfare problems, in developing proposals pertaining to staff welfare, and in presenting them to the school board for consideration and action.
>
> We believe that shared responsibility in policy development is a professional concept. It assumes a commonality of goals and interests among teachers, school boards, and administrators; and it assumes that service to children is the paramount consideration and that welfare provisions for teachers are means to that end.
>
> We believe that the right to discuss pros and cons and to participate in developing a program does not imply the right to make decisions. Although consensus should always be patiently sought and will often prevail between staff and school board, the board must retain its responsibility and legal right to make decisions.
>
> We believe that no matter how generous and benevolent arbitrary decisions may be, they have a debilitating effect. When people are involved, they not only assume responsibility for making decisions work, but each performs at a higher level of productivity.
>
> We believe that failure to find appropriate and acceptable means of involving staff members—teachers, principals, and supervisors—in developing policy that directly affects them will lead to divisiveness, tension, and conflict that will impair the schools and adversely affect the education of children.
>
> We believe that there is no one best procedure for sharing responsibility for policy development. School board members, administrators, and classroom teachers must develop policies and practices appropriate to local conditions, rather than adopt those established elsewhere.
>
> We believe that if boards of education fail to make reasonable welfare provisions for all staff members and fail to provide machinery through which grievances can be given appropriate consideration, their respective state legislatures are likely to establish appeal procedures.
>
> We believe that there is an intrinsic value in local decision making which is worth preserving to the maximum extent consistent with the obligations of citizenship in the state and nation.[1]

It is apparent that the development of personnel policies in the sixties calls for far different, and certainly more formalized, procedures than here-

---

[1] American Association of School Administrators, *Roles, Responsibilities, Relationships of the School Board, Superintendent, and Staff* (Washington, D.C.: the Association, a department of the National Education Association, 1963), pp. 12-13.

tofore have existed in most school systems throughout the nation. Professional negotiation agreements represent one approach to the matter; collective bargaining contracts, another. The wishes of the professional staff on negotiation procedures and on the content of agreements will frequently prevail. It is essential, however, that the superintendent of schools be deeply and actively involved in the development of policies which affect the staff and the school system's operation.

The Merits of Written Negotiation Agreements

One of the fundamental principles of effective school personnel administration is that policies should be in writing, widely disseminated, and, where appropriate, officially adopted by boards of education. These principles are equally pertinent in the area of collective negotiation. There are obvious advantages to be gained from putting agreements in writing: a written agreement clarifies the roles and relationships of all those involved in the negotiation process; it clearly outlines procedures to be followed; it sets out the responsibilities of the various parties; it avoids, insofar as possible, the likelihood of future misunderstanding on the part of individuals who may not have had a part in the original development of the procedure. As a result, a written negotiation agreement will greatly enhance the smooth and efficient operation of the schools.

It is estimated that apart from the states which have laws on the matter, there are approximately three hundred locally developed negotiation agreements presently in existence. It seems apparent that there are few jurisdictions in which there would be legal impediments in the way of boards of education wishing to adopt such agreements.

Sound written negotiation agreements will serve as an excellent foundation for the development of personnel policies. In view of the advantages to be gained from their adoption and the ever-mounting pressures being exerted for the development of appropriate formalized negotiation procedures, it is recommended that all school districts cooperatively develop and adopt written negotiation agreements appropriate to their own unique local circumstances.

The existence within a district of more than one employee organization claiming to represent the professional staff presents a thorny problem to boards of education and their chief school administrators. Although in the absence of a statute a board cannot be compelled to recognize one organization exclusively for the purpose of negotiation, virtually every one of the voluntary negotiation agreements currently in existence provides for the recognition of a single organization as representative of the staff. Of the current state legislation, California's law is the only one which specifically calls for proportional representation. It does so by means of five- to nine-member committees comprised of organizational representatives in proportion to the relative membership strengths of eligible employee organizations.

Exclusive negotiation rights have been slower to be recognized in public education than in other fields of employment. The concept is well grounded in both laws and regulations governing private and public employment relations. Exclusive recognition in any federal agency is granted to the employee organization which enrolls a majority of staff, and only such an organization has the right to negotiate the formulation of policies with the employing agency.

There is a danger here, however. Mathematically, if there are exclusive negotiation rights (and assuming the majority organization represents only 51 per cent of the staff) it is possible for 26 per cent of a faculty to determine policies and proposals binding to all. Schoolmen must be ever alert to the danger of what De Tocqueville once called the "tyranny of the majority."

From a practical standpoint, it makes good sense to negotiate with a single organization, providing, of course, that it can be ascertained beyond any doubt that such an organization can speak for the majority of the staff. Such designation places additional responsibility on the organization selected and hopefully would encourage a stronger and more mature approach. The rational basis for a policy of granting exclusive negotiation rights is the power of a board of education to adopt those policies which in its judgment promote the best interests of the school system and the educational program. Such a policy is desirable and legal in most jurisdictions so long as two conditions are met: (a) that the policies developed by means of negotiation with representatives of the majority organization be uniformly applicable to all staff members, regardless of membership in the organization; and (b) that the rights of all individuals and minority groups to present their views to the board of education at an open meeting be vigorously protected.

Composition of the Negotiation Unit

Education is a unique enterprise in that much of its success depends upon the closest possible working relationships among teachers, principals, administrators, and supervisors. In order to maintain this type of relationship, it is desirable that all segments of the professional staff belong to a single staff organization. Some elements in the profession would have teachers believe that administrators and supervisors are their natural enemies. Just the reverse is true. It has traditionally been the case, as it is at the present time, that administrators and supervisors are the natural allies of teachers.

The vast majority of negotiable items pertain to all professional personnel within the district. Even in the case of salaries, the majority of districts include all professional personnel within a unified structure, relating administrative-supervisory salaries to those of classroom teachers by means of ratios, percentages, or dollar differentials. All professional personnel desire and promote respectable and pleasant working conditions, satisfactory work loads, specialist assistance, instructional materials in sufficient quantity, and reasonable class size. There is, or should be, no inherent conflict of interest in all-inclusive organizations.

On the other hand, each segment of the professional staff should be able at all times to arrive at considered judgments about matters of importance free of domination or coercion from other segments. In some jurisdictions, it may be desirable to maintain independent classroom teacher and administrative-supervisory units within a single organization, each free to develop independent judgments where appropriate. Any differences or disagreements among various segments of all-inclusive organizations should be thoroughly aired and reconciled before negotiations take place.

It seems clear that a pattern of negotiation forced upon unwilling individuals or borrowed from another segment of society without regard to the unique characteristics of education will in the long run be unsatisfactory and work to the detriment of all concerned. All-inclusive organizations have operated successfully in the past and will continue to operate successfully in the future as long as all parties desire to make them operate successfully and as long as the specialized needs of units within the organizations can be met satisfactorily and independently. Local preference, based upon unique local circumstances and not upon arbitrary rules handed down from outside agencies, should determine the type of negotiation unit which most satisfactorily fills the needs of the district.

AASA maintains that local educational associations made up of teachers, supervisors, principals, and administrators working together in close harmony best serve the cause of education. Whatever the pattern of representation or organization eventually chosen, however, no teacher, supervisor, principal, or administrator should be unrepresented in the process.

Content and Timing of Negotiations

The question, "What is negotiable?" has been the subject of much controversy in educational circles. Some hold that *all* matters are negotiable; textbook selection, building construction, sequence of curriculum, and the selection of instructional materials are but a few examples. Others contend that negotiable matters should be restricted to salaries, benefits, and working conditions. Arguments can be marshaled on either side of the question. The AASA finds the reasoning for a rather broadly construed concept of negotiation most persuasive. There is a substantial difference between bargaining over wages and hours in the industrial context and negotiating over matters of common interest in the educational context. If education is truly a profession, all professional personnel have a legitimate interest in the decisions that affect their pupil clientele, the effectiveness of their own work, and the quality of the educational program.

Obviously, negotiating the selection of or the exclusion of a specific textbook for a specific course offering would be nonsensical, as would negotiating a curricular sequence or the educational materials to be purchased for third-grade social studies. However, the *process* by which these basic decisions are made can be the subject of negotiation. The principle of including in decision making those most directly responsible for carrying out the decisions is quite pertinent here. Of course, not all matters are negotiable on a district-wide level, and provision should be made for localizing policy making. Many policies can best be made at the building level, but the *way* in which these policies are made can indeed be negotiated. Further, it should be pointed out that there is a difference between negotiation and participation. Many aspects of public education are appropriate areas for teacher participation. Not all are subject to negotiation.

Professional negotiation agreements to date have tended to designate rather broadly the subjects considered appropriate for negotiation. Most agreements go far beyond what one normally envisions as "welfare" concerns. The AASA believes negotiation, in good faith, may well encompass all or some aspects of policy governing such items as—

1. Curriculum
2. Inservice education
3. Personnel policies
4. Teaching assignments
5. Transfers and promotions
6. Recruitment of teachers
7. Discharge and discipline of teachers
8. Provision of physical facilities for teachers
9. Grievance procedures
10. Recognition of the negotiating team
11. Lunch and rest periods
12. Salaries and wages
13. Welfare benefits
14. Class size
15. Leaves of absence
16. Expiration date of negotiation agreement
17. Other mutually agreed-upon matters which directly affect the quality of the educational program.

The Association believes that some items are not negotiable and that a school board may refuse to bargain about non-negotiable subjects without violating its agreement to negotiate in good faith. A school board should not negotiate any items which would violate existing state laws. It could not agree, for example, to operate a school system less than the minimum number of days required by state law; nor could it negotiate a millage rate in excess of the legal maximum; nor could it negotiate a clause in the contract permitting employees to strike in violation of state law; nor should it negotiate any item that would result in violation of the applicable code of ethics. Illustrations of other non-negotiable items include, but are not limited to, the following: the selection of legal counsel to the board of education, determination of the financial and pupil accounting system to be employed by the board, and the selection of the superintendent of schools, to mention but a few.

The timing of negotiations is important too. Year-round negotiations are expensive, time-consuming, and unnecessary. Certainly, negotiation on matters involving expenditures of district funds should be completed well before budget-making time and should be commenced early enough in the year so that "crisis sessions" do not become necessary. Policy discussions which do not involve the expenditure of funds can be carried out at other times during the year, and perhaps among personnel selected for their specialized competencies in the matters under discussion.

There are, and will be, staff organizations which do not as a matter of policy desire to negotiate on matters unrelated to the direct and personal welfare of their members. Some do not feel a readiness to discuss these matters or prefer to "leave it to those who get paid for doing it." This attitude ignores the untapped resources for improving the quality of education that lie in the professional staff.

Each local district should be encouraged to work out the best procedures possible for involving staff members in the negotiation of matters which affect the quality of education provided. Such procedures should be carefully adapted to the particular needs of the individual district.

Zipper Clause

Boards often insist, and AASA believes rightly so, upon including a "zipper" clause in the negotiation agreement. This clause in effect assures that negotiation will not be reopened for a specified period of time, such as a one- or two-year period. The inclusion of a zipper clause helps the board and administration focus teacher attention upon the actual teaching process and gives more stability to the operation of the school system. A typical zipper clause follows:

> The parties agree that all negotiable items have been discussed during the negotiations leading to this agreement, and therefore agree that the negotiations will not be reopened on any item, whether contained herein or not, during the life of this agreement.

Grievance Procedures

In its 1963 publication *Roles, Responsibilities, Relationships of the School Board, Superintendent, and Staff,* AASA listed the following as one of the superintendent's responsibilities:

> He works out with his associates, within the framework of board policy and staff organization, appropriate ways and means through which grievances can be appealed to the board when such an appeal is sought by the aggrieved and through which the grievances can be satisfactorily adjudicated with no fear or form of retaliation.[2]

A grievance may be defined as a complaint based upon an event or condition under which an employee works, allegedly caused by misinterpretation or inequitable application of an established policy. A grievance procedure should not be confused with the negotiation procedure itself. Negotiation is the process by which policies are jointly developed; a grievance procedure is one of the jointly developed policies. A grievance policy is similar to the judicial process by which the administration of legislated policies may be tested. It represents the presence of procedural due process within a school district. Grievance procedures will vary greatly from district to district due to differing local needs and conditions, but the following principles may be applied to the evaluation of any procedure:

It should be cooperatively developed and in writing.

It should be an integral part of the negotiation agreement.

It should clearly define a grievance.

It should encourage resolution of the grievance as close as possible to the point of origin but also contain a specified sequence of steps, with reasonable time limits imposed at each step.

It should provide for adjudication of grievances through regular administrative channels or through channels provided by the recognized staff organization.

It should provide for participation by an impartial third party as one of the steps in impasse resolution, with subsequent appeal to the final authority—the board of education.

It should safeguard the grievant from prejudice or retaliation as a result of the processing of the grievance.

All internal methods of resolving a grievance should be used before any external means is employed.

In every employment relationship, however enlightened and democratic the administration, grievances and dissatisfactions will arise. A well-conceived procedure for grievance adjudication which will resolve the dissatisfactions

---

[2] American Association of School Administrators, *op. cit.,* p. 10.

and redress the legitimate grievances of staff members is essential to the efficient and harmonious operation of a school district.

Mediation and Appeal Procedures

Successful negotiation results in agreement acceptable to all parties. It would be naive to suppose, however, that negotiation always leads to agreement. There will be times, despite good-faith efforts to arrive at equitable solutions to common problems, when persistent disagreements simply cannot be resolved by the parties involved in the negotiation process. Although boards of education cannot and should not give up their legal responsibility to arrive at final decisions concerning matters of policy, there are no legal barriers to seeking the advice and recommendations of impartial, knowledgeable third parties. Such a step should not be taken lightly, nor before the most painstaking work on the part of the superintendent, board, and staff to seek a satisfactory compromise. Failing this, however, there should be some recourse. The channel of resolution should be developed along with, and be an integral part of, the written negotiation agreement. In 1963, AASA published the following statement in *Roles, Responsibilities, Relationships of the School Board, Superintendent, and Staff*:

> We believe that both the board and the professional staff—teachers, principals, and other administrators—should at a time that is free from tension and controversy, develop together a plan to be used in case of persistent disagreement. In those few, highly unusual instances where major controversy threatens to disrupt the schools, an appeal to an unbiased body should be available to either the board or the teachers, or both. The function of this third party should be limited to fact finding and to advisory assistance. Its identity might vary from state to state, but it should always be an agency which has responsibility for some segment of public education in the state. Included among such organizations might be a state board of education, a state department of education, a state university, or a state public college. It should be made clear that such a study would be conducted without disruption of the schools. A report should be made to both the board of education and the staff.[3]

Effective personnel administration calls for the most expeditious possible resolution of disagreements over the development of policy. It is believed that, when all else fails, impartial mediation and appeal provisions will hasten the achievement of satisfactory agreement. It is essential, however, that such provisions be kept out of the machinery designed to resolve differences between workers and management in the framework of private business which is not well suited to solving the problems of professional personnel in a public school system.

[3] American Association of School Administrators, *op. cit.*, p. 14.

Sanctions

The National Education Association defines sanctions as follows:

> Sanctions, within the context of this statement, are defined as a means to prevent the violation of a right or responsibility. . . .
>
> As used by a professional education organization, sanctions mean censure, suspension or expulsion of a member; severence of relationship with an affiliated association or other agency; imposing of a deterrent against a board of education or other agency controlling the welfare of the schools; bringing into play forces that will enable the community to help the board or agency to realize its responsibility; or the application of one or more steps in the withholding of services. Sanctions are used only to improve educational opportunities through the elimination of conditions detrimental to effective education. The most severe types of sanctions should be applied only as a last resort where conditions are such that it is impossible for educators to give effective professional service.[4]

Types of sanctions which may be applied against a school district or a community and its official bodies include—

1. Censure through public notice including release of investigation report; articles in national and state journals; reports through various mass media of communication.

2. Notification to state departments of education of findings concerning unsatisfactory conditions.

3. Notification to certification and placement services of unsatisfactory conditions of employment for educators.

4. Warnings to members that acceptance of employment as a new teacher in the school district would be considered unethical conduct and could lead to discharge from or future refusal of membership in the national professional association.

5. Advice to members presently employed that, if their private arrangements permit, they should seek employment elsewhere.[5]

As AASA has stated:

> We believe that in those exceedingly rare situations where the professional staff believes that the school board or some other legal fiscal control body has denied reasonable requests for conferences, for study, and for presentation of welfare proposals, or has demonstrated flagrant unwillingness to provide reasonable salary contracts or other welfare provisions, the professional staff has the right to present all the facts to the public and to their professional associates in other school districts. On the other hand, where the staff obstinately holds to an un-

[4] National Commission on Professional Rights and Responsibilities, *Guidelines for Professional Sanctions.* (Revised edition, Washington, D.C.: National Education Association, 1966), p. 9.

[5] National Commission on Professional Rights and Responsibilities, *op. cit.,* p. 16.

reasonable position which disrupts or seriously impairs the operation of the schools, the school board has comparable rights and obligations.[6]

These types of sanctions have upon numerous occasions during the past few years been applied with high degrees of success in correcting educational inequities. They have been most successful when preceded by thorough investigations and applied on a unified basis by the local, state, and national associations working in concert. When applied on a responsible, professional basis, with ample warning, sanctions can be a very powerful tool for the resolution of serious educational problems.

Strikes

Teacher strikes, or the withdrawal of service, whether or not taking place in conjunction with sanctions, are generally considered illegal. There are statutes in 15 states prohibiting various types of public employees, often including teachers, from striking. There are no statutes which provide that teachers may strike. In the absence of statutory provision, the judicial view has traditionally been that public employees do not have the right to strike.

Aside from the legal implications of teacher strikes, there are moral and ethical considerations. Children should not be deprived of their education, nor should communities be deprived of their schools. Moreover, the strike, involving refusal of services to the district and the children, is usually a violation of the teacher's contract and a detraction from the ethical image of one charged with instilling in students the concept of responsibility in meeting and fulfilling obligations.

Responsible teachers' organizations should not be left without appropriate means with which to resolve intolerable situations or educational conditions, the solution of which has defied all reasonable procedures of negotiation. Such a tool exists in sanctions—a procedure worthy of a true profession. The sanction does not involve interruption of teachers' services to the students during the school year. Its impact is primarily on the civic body—board, community, or state—responsible for the intolerable conditions.

AASA endorses the proper use of sanctions by a professional organization. *It does not condone teachers' strikes under any condition.*

Negotiation agreements should not depend for their success upon power tactics on the part either of staff or of board of education. There should be no need for weapons of any sort so long as a negotiation agreement is in effect and adhered to in good faith by all parties to the agreement.

State Legislation

As previously pointed out, the pace of the enactment of state statutes governing relationships between educational employees and their governing

[6] American Association of School Administrators, *op. cit.*, p. 14.

boards is accelerating. Each succeeding legislative year will witness the introduction of legislation in scores of states. Eleven state laws are already in effect; many more will be enacted in the years immediately ahead. It is of crucial importance, therefore, to take a long and hard look at the type of legislation which is being proposed, since each law enacted will have a most profound effect, not only upon public education in the various states, but upon the basic structure of the organized teaching profession.

Legislation will, of course, vary considerably among the states. However, there are a few basic principles which should be observed in the development of any state law. To meet the unique needs of education, any law relating to board-staff relations should meet the following criteria:

It should be designed specifically for education and not seek to cover teachers under provisions in effect for all public employees.

It should provide for local determination of the negotiation unit. Every member of the professional staff in local districts should be given a voice in choosing how he wishes to be represented.

It should not mandate an election as the exclusive means of determining majority organization status. Elections should be required only in cases in which it is not possible to ascertain majority support of competing organizations by such means as verified membership lists, authorization or designation cards, dues deduction records, or signed petitions.

It should provide for mediation and appeal of procedural disputes or impasses in negotiation through educational channels, rather than through channels designed for mediating labor disputes in private employment jurisdictions.

If the unity and independence of the teaching profession, built up so painstakingly over the years, are to be preserved, laws must be developed which recognize the uniqueness of the educational enterprise and the overriding community of interest and purpose which suffuse all professional personnel engaged in the education of children and youth.

Union Affiliation

At its 1966 convention the American Association of School Administrators adopted the following resolution, entitled "Teacher-Administrator-Board Relations":

> The Association reaffirms that teaching is a profession with all of the obligations thereof. We believe that there are common goals and interests among educators—teachers, supervisors, and administrators. We further believe that the development of school policies and programs and the solution of school problems can best be accomplished by these groups working in unison and cooperatively with board members with respect for the unique role of each.

Efforts to superimpose a pattern of staff relations borrowed from another segment of society, whether through legislative fiat or staff election, will do major harm both to the education of children and to the basic unity of our profession and should be resisted vigorously. We therefore support the concept that shared responsibility for policy development and program development is a professional concept requiring a uniquely professional approach.

We believe, too, that local education associations, made up of teachers, supervisors, principals, and superintendents working together in close harmony, best serve the cause of education.

We believe—

1. Teachers of children from all walks of life should not be identified with or obligated to any one segment of the economy, but should be independently organized in order to examine more objectively the many social, political, and economic problems which face America's future citizens.

2. A school district's teachers, supervisors, principals, and superintendent should work as an educational team characterized by mutual confidence rather than be divided against each other.

3. Machinery designed to resolve differences between nonprofessional personnel and management in the framework of private business is not well suited to solving the problems of professional personnel in a public school system.

Teachers must be free, of course, to join or refrain from joining any organization of their own choosing, and this freedom should be vigorously upheld by boards of education and administrators. Moreover, strict impartiality must be observed when dealing with staff organizations at the local level. Impartiality, however, should not be construed to require equal recognition of staff organizations regardless of their relative membership strengths. Nor should it prevent members of the administrative-supervisory staff from speaking their minds concerning organization of the teaching profession. Every staff member, regardless of his position, should be perfectly free at any time to speak out on the programs and activities of organizations attempting to affect education. This is as true for organizations within the profession as it is for organizations outside. Those who believe, as AASA does, in a profession that is independent and beholden only to its members and to society as a whole, rather than to any particular segment of society, should be free to speak in support of their beliefs. To do less is an abdication of personal and professional responsibility.

THE UNIQUE POSITION OF THE
SUPERINTENDENT OF SCHOOLS

There is no position in other professions, business, or industry comparable to that of the superintendent of schools. Upon him rests final responsibility for the efficient operation of every aspect of school district operation. As stated in *Roles, Responsibilities, Relationships of the School Board, Superintendent, and Staff*:

> Ever since the third decade of the 19th century, the superintendent of schools has been a key person in the educational process. The broad outlines of the community's educational program emerge as he marshals resources, supplies information, stimulates discussion and research, resolutely faces critical problems, and judiciously weighs alternative courses of action; as he extends opportunities for staff members to acquire new insights; and as he evaluates, recommends, and initiates action.
>
> Today, the superintendent of schools occupies a complex and demanding position. He is often torn between diverse alternatives, obligations, and responsibilities.
>
> Yet, it seems clear that the professional superintendent has one allegiance that transcends all other commitments. Although he is a devoted member of his professional group and deeply concerned with the success of his associates, his allegiance to the learner supersedes all other loyalties. This commitment need not and should not place him in conflict with his colleagues. Its very nature makes him seek assiduously and vigorously to maintain environmental circumstances which his associates desire, need, and must have to work to best advantage. One of the major concerns of the superintendent always has been and always should be to help provide those conditions which enable teachers and all other staff members to achieve their professional goals.
>
> Neither does this freedom of operation by the superintendent suggest disloyalty to the school board. It is his professional judgment, wisdom, and leadership that make him valuable to the board. School trustees should never seek nor achieve subservience from the school administrator. In fact, when controversy rages most violently, his role is one of independent, judicious statesmanship governed largely by his depth of professional insights and his primary commitment to improved educational service to pupils and to basic human values.[7]

Concerning the superintendent's specific role in negotiation, two extreme positions are often voiced: (a) that he be completely bypassed and have no place in the negotiation process, and (b) that he be the chief negotiator representing only the board of education in all of its dealings with the staff. The Association does not believe that either of these positions will contribute to the long-term good of the school district or its educational program. The superintendent should play a significant role in professional negotiation, his basic obligation being to the welfare of the pupils and to leadership in the formulation of sound educational policy. He should be an independent third party in the negotiation process. He should review each proposal in light of its effect upon students and work closely with both the board and the staff

[7] American Association of School Administrators, *op. cit.*, pp. 8-9.

representatives in an attempt to reach agreement in the best interests of the educational program. His position as leader of the staff and executive of the board requires this. He, or his representative, must carry this role into formal negotiation where, in most cases, with legal advice, he will continue to serve as interpreter in difficult communications between the board and the staff. In school systems where such a position exists, he may delegate the actual negotiation to an associate or assistant superintendent or a director of personnel acting under his direct supervision. In smaller school systems where the superintendent performs all of the functions of a central office staff, he inevitably will have to assume this role himself. In no instance should the responsibility for negotiations be delegated outside the profession.

Obviously, the superintendent cannot be represented in negotiations by the local association, whether or not he is a member. Likewise, his position of independence would be undermined were he to vote in any election to determine the negotiating organization. The superintendent, whether in person or through an associate, should be an active participant in negotiations. He should exercise free and independent judgment on all educational matters, providing resource material and information to assist all parties in arriving at reasoned decisions, clarifying issues, and making proposals based upon what is best for the district and its educational program. At times, when negotiations become tense, he may rightfully assume the role of expert witness.

Patterns of negotiation inevitably vary, depending upon the size of the district, the wishes of the staff, and former relationships and modes of operation. Regardless of the pattern, however, the superintendent under no circumstances should be bypassed. Somehow, the negotiation process must recognize the uniqueness of education and the uniqueness of the superintendent's role. Anything which weakens the effectiveness of his position in the district will ultimately weaken the schools.

A TIME FOR RESPONSIBLE ACTION

New patterns of staff relationships require many changes in local school administration; old, established traditions and processes no longer suffice. It avails little to debate the desirability of these changes in relationships or to bemoan either their existence or their speed. Changes are here, and their pace will quicken rather than abate in the years ahead.

New processes and new insights into the nature and means of policy formulation are needed, not only to upgrade the professional status of teachers but also to improve the conditions under which they work, thus enhancing the quality of education. As personnel policies and administrative processes are revised and improved, much will depend upon the wisdom, care, patience, forbearance, and sound judgment of the individuals and groups of individuals involved in this evolution.

It is the firm belief of AASA that problems are better prevented than solved and that satisfactory negotiation procedures are best developed in a climate of goodwill before the need for them becomes acute. It is believed that the superintendent of schools, if he is to continue in his position of educational leadership, must assume responsibility for initiating and guiding changes in patterns of staff relationships. Written negotiation agreements which carefully delineate the roles and responsibilities of the superintendent, the board, teachers, administrative and supervisory staff, and professional organizations are essential to the smooth and efficient operation of the schools. Whether it is developed at the local level or through state legislation, it is imperative that the voice of the superintendent be heard with respect to the most desirable type of agreement or legislation.

There is still time to outgrow the more petulant concepts of negotiation, and to move toward more mature concepts of shared responsibilities.

The superintendent must contribute his professional judgment, experience, and understanding to the development of appropriate new procedures of staff negotiation. The challenge has been given; professional negotiation is the best means by which it can be met.

III-7

THE ALBERTA TEACHERS ASSOCIATION:
A VISION VINDICATED*

Arthur Kratzmann

Teachers' organizations in the United States, claims Myron Lieberman, are irrelevant in the national scene, are tragically futile in protecting the public interest and the legitimate vocational aspirations of American teachers, and are generally quite unimaginative and unproductive.[1] We may not, perhaps, accept this forthright critic's evaluation as accurate, particularly if we have vested interests in one of the national organizations. Yet if we are intellectually honest we are compelled to admit that teacher organizations in the United States fall far short of their potential, both in terms of membership welfare and with respect to service to the teaching clientele, not to mention general impact on educational progress.

How can this gap between the actual and potential be bridged? Again, it is Lieberman who has set forth the most comprehensive list of concrete recommendations and objectives. Many Americans consider them revolutionary and impractical; certainly, the proposals represent sharp departures from the present activities of the National Education Association and the American Federation of Teachers and their affiliates.

Yet if we look north of the forty-ninth parallel we find teacher organizations, particularly in Western Canada, which have incorporated into their *modus operandi* the great majority of Lieberman's recommendations. One of these, and perhaps the most progressive—the Alberta Teachers' Association—is the subject of this article. Some attempt will be made to determine a number of implications for the American scene. Of course, any cross-cultural comparisons are difficult to make; yet an analysis of the Canadian scene does suggest possibilities for the United States. If nothing else is achieved, it will become abundantly clear that Lieberman's proposals, while regarded by many

* Reprinted from *Phi Delta Kappan,* Vol. 45 (March, 1964), pp. 288-92. Arthur Kratzmann is Executive Director, Alberta School Trustees' Association, Edmonton, Alberta.
[1] See Chapter IX of Myron Lieberman, *The Future of Public Education.* (Chicago: The University of Chicago Press, 1960).

in his own country as those of a radical visionary, have long since developed beyond the level of romanticism in Western Canada.

Included both as proposals in Lieberman's *The Future of Public Education* and as achievements of the Alberta Teachers' Association are the following: competitive salaries for staff officers of the association; relatively high dues for a state organization (ATA fees begin at $48); a membership-paid staff officer ratio of 1:2,000 (ATA—1:1943); abandonment of labor affiliation (ATA early considered, but decided against, affiliation); safeguards against administrator domination (school superintendents can be associate, but not active, members); mandatory membership (a legal requirement in Alberta since 1936); a check-off system of dues collection; an enforceable code of ethics (effective since 1936); a shift of emphasis from local to state levels (ATA has strong control over local activities); increased organizational pressure on school boards (the author is well aware of ATA's pressures!); collective bargaining (again, in Alberta since the Thirties); master contracts covering a wide range of working and living conditions (developed in Alberta with the advent of collective bargaining); formal grievance channels (ATA has both internal and external channels of appeal); professional control over entry to teaching (ATA has representation on teacher education and teacher certification committees); and impact upon curricula (ATA is represented on all state curriculum committees). Many more partial achievements of Lieberman's proposals could be added. But the list is sufficiently long to characterize the Alberta Teachers' Association as an avant-garde state organization in North America.

EMERGENCE AND EARLY DEVELOPMENT OF THE ATA

The ATA, like many Canadian teachers' associations, emerged and developed rapidly at the close of the World War I period.[2] It was formed in 1918 from without the Alberta Education Association, which was a loosely-knit, diffuse organization including government officials, school administrators, teachers, and professional and lay people interested in education. The ATA, early named the Alberta Teachers' Alliance, represented a rebellion of Alberta teachers against substandard working and living conditions imposed by local school boards, and embodied a collective demand for improvement. As it emerged, in an atmosphere of sharp controversy, the organization took on rather distinctive characteristics for a Canadian association. It was for teachers only—senior administrators, labor, and the lay citizenry were excluded from its ranks; all teachers had equal membership rights and responsibilities. There were no divisions according to sex, teaching levels, subject

[2] See J. M. Paton, *The Role of Teachers' Organizations in Canadian Education* (Toronto: W.J. Gage Ltd., 1962).

specialties, and the like. And it established a comprehensive and revolution-ary platform of welfare objectives and a militant air promising their early attainment. The major influences upon the ATA, apart from the catalytic conditions in Alberta, came from abroad. The AFT in the U.S. was creating appealing headlines at the time, and the accomplishments of the British National Union of Teachers were being propagandized by immigrant British teachers. John Barnett, an Englishman, was named as first secretary of the ATA and he left an indelible imprint upon the organization after thirty years of forthright and dedicated service.

The emergence of the ATA, with its demands for adequate contracts, salaries, pensions, administrative units, and working conditions, and with its challenges to the authority of officials of the Alberta Department of Education and school boards, evoked anticipated opposition—violent opposition— from the Minister of Education and the School Trustees' Association in Alberta. It was a case of a precocious youth upsetting the homeostasis of the traditional educational decision-making family. And precocious it was—for its constitution, its legislative and policy-formation patterns, its membership expectations, its general educational goals, and its welfare objectives were so well developed as to stand the test of time for decades, with only minor amendments. Despite the violent opposition from the time-honored power structure for education, the ATA fought, without compromise, for the realization of its platform. Twenty years later, as we shall see, most of the welfare objectives had been achieved, or at least the structures had been established for their eventual attainment.

Before these achievements are analyzed, the reader should realize that the Alberta Teachers' Association developed at the provincial (state) level within a system of government for education which placed very extensive powers in the hands of provincial legislators; the ATA area of influence was and is clearly bounded by the borders of Alberta; and furthermore, the association was and is the only state agency for Alberta teachers and has not had to compete for membership with any other teachers' organization. In these respects, the Canadian and United States contexts for state associations vary markedly.

ACHIEVEMENTS OF THE ATA

One is impressed, upon studying ATA documents, with the sheer volume of time and effort devoted to teacher-welfare issues and particularly to security of tenure, salaries, and pensions. As well, the stability of stated organizational objectives is strongly in evidence; year after year, the association approached the Alberta government with identical requests for provisions for continuous contracts for teachers, stated reasons for dismissals, government-endorsed salary schedules which would recognize training and experience, pensions provided by teacher and government contributions, and improved working and living conditions. And year after year, the Alberta School Trustees' Association brought pressures upon the legislature to offset ATA demands. In all matters of salary and tenure involving lack of agreement on the part of boards and individual teachers or groups of teachers, the association sought referral of the cases to a neutral board of reference; in fact, in all of their "welfare" dealings with school boards they have shown, until recently (when the welfare tide, based upon public opinion, has tended to ebb), a willingness to abide by the rulings of a third and neutral party.

For a number of reasons, the "golden years" for the association, in terms of improved social and economic status, came in the 1935-41 period. During these years the ATA included among its welfare accomplishments legislative sanction of the following: (1) Continuous contracts, with severance only upon the mutual agreement of both parties, and the right of the teachers to appeal against dismissal to a neutral board of reference. (2) Abolition of the individual form of contract, and teacher acceptance by letter assuring the positioning of the teacher on a group salary schedule. (3) The right to bargain collectively with school boards for salaries and for living and working conditions, as well as the right, in extreme conditions, to strike. (4) The legal definition of a salary schedule, making provisions for a minimum salary and annual increments for teaching experience. (5) Increases in the statutory minimum teacher's salary for Alberta. (6) A joint teacher-school board contributory retirement plan.

Since 1941, the legal bases and internal and external machinery already established have been used to make annual gains in membership welfare. The major progress during the Forties and Fifties related to salaries and to fringe benefits included in teachers' contracts, as well as to the inauguration of an improved pension plan.

Collective bargaining procedures are singled out for brief but special attention. While the ATA resisted the efforts of labor leaders to have the association affiliate with the organized labor movement, its officials nevertheless secured an official legal interpretation of the Labor Act of Alberta that extended to teachers the full range of bargaining privileges previously granted to labor in the private sector of the Alberta economy. Such benefits, sanctioned by a clause in the province's school act or code, included collective bargaining, closed-shop procedures, a dues check-off system, the use of neutral Labor Department conciliators in times of dispute, and the use of strike action as a final bargaining weapon. In every instance the ATA itself is the bargaining unit for local teachers, advising them at each stage, assisting them closely in times of dispute, and maintaining special funds to assist them during strikes. Teachers' locals tend to be coterminous with major administrative jurisdictions for education in the province.

ORGANIZATIONAL STATUS AND RECOGNITION

Since its inception, the ATA, considering itself to be the only body competent to form and transact the opinion of those engaged in teaching in Alberta, has striven for both improved internal controls and external impact. The 1918 Executive Council of the association envisioned the day when the organization would embody all Alberta teachers and when it would obtain recognition on all committees, boards, and authorities where curricula, instructional materials, examinations, and teacher training and certification were under discussion. These goals were realized many years ago. Undoubtedly, the passage of the Teaching Profession Act of 1935, together with its 1936 amendments, ranks as the outstanding turning point in the struggle for recognition and representation by the ATA.

This legislation, which was paralleled by similar statutes in Saskatchewan in 1935, and which was to be imitated by every Canadian province in later years, has been described by Paton as "a case of plucking success from the jaws of failure, or of dire necessity proving to be the mother of invention."[3] In an effort to offset the vicious circle of low membership, inadequate funds, and ineffectual organization, and to strengthen the ATA in its teacher welfare platform during the depression years, officials of the alliance sought and secured a mandate from Alberta teachers to seek legislation affording the ATA full professional status with mandatory membership and internal controls over member action. The first of these requests was met in 1935; the membership and discipline clauses were added in 1936. These were indeed revolutionary pieces of legislation.

The Teaching Profession Act was to have a great impact upon the internal control activities of the association. In the first place, it made membership of Alberta teachers in the ATA compulsory; no teacher could any longer remain as a non-joiner. This could perhaps have resulted in severe problems of fusion of opinion, attitude, and action on the part of dissident teachers had a supplementary clause of the act not given the ATA power to devise its own disciplinary by-laws and to secure machinery to enforce them. Consequently, teachers were not only compelled to join the association, they were forced to abide by ATA-formulated policies, including those which guaranteed a controlled and unified voice for the organization and those which spelled out member-member, member-association, and member-employer reciprocal rights and privileges. A third feature of the act was of

[3] *Ibid.,* p. 44.

vital significance for the ATA's material resources: The 1936 amendments not only brought all teachers into the association, it brought adequate financing. Association fees were high and have remained high when compared with the dues of other state associations.

The Teaching Profession Act also brought two very significant changes in the ATA's relationships with external persons and agencies. In the first place, the association for the first time became the state-sanctioned voice for Alberta teachers, a feature which the ATA fully clarified in its internal by-laws. Secondly, the association, in one legislative swoop, became potentially much more powerful in terms of membership, finances, and consequent impact upon the Alberta educational front. That the school trustees fought the legislation and that the government acquiesced reluctantly suggests that many realized what statutory membership would mean in the way of the mobilization of teacher opinion and action. Here was a body of teachers dependent upon municipal and provincial funds for their salaries and conditions of work, being given the wherewithal, with legislative blessing, to grow strong enough to exert a great deal of control over their employers and conditions of employment.

A CHANGE OF EMPHASIS

During the first thirty years of its development, the ATA was first and foremost a member-welfare association; only in recent years has it redirected its emphases so that it may be described as a service or a "commonweal" organization as well, promoting the interests both of the teaching clientele and the public-at-large in its internal and external activities.[4] The shift in emphasis, most marked during the past five years, appears to have resulted from: (1) A process of goal replacement necessary to maintain the identity and cohesion of a group which had achieved most of its long-range objectives. (2) The constant appeals of the public and external Alberta agencies to shift ATA's focus from "union" to "professional" activities. (3) A readiness on the part of the membership to assume a larger responsibility, via their parent association, for on-the-job professional improvement.

Regardless of the motivation, the association now devotes large blocks of time and money to the sponsorship of small and large group meetings, conventions, seminars, and workshops, to the publication of service-oriented materials, and to the use of field consultative services related to the improvement of teaching. Having attained an adult status with respect to member

[4] These typologies of formal organizations are advanced by Peter M. Blau and W. Richard Scott in *Formal Organizations* (San Francisco: Chandler Publishing Co 1962).

ship welfare, the organization is in the adolescent state of maturity in terms of its extrinsic, public-service, or "professional" activities.

THE ATA AND THE AMERICAN SCENE

The American Federation of Teachers and the National Education Association and their respective affiliates are offering teachers of the United States two different routes to economic parity and professional stature. The former speaks of collective bargaining and coercive action to achieve welfare benefits, and has accomplished little by way of the direct promotion of general educational and instructional programs. The latter is concerned with professional negotiations, sanctions, a persuasive partnership with teaching communities, and the dissemination of materials designed to improve the teaching competence of members. There seems little chance of a reconciliation of differences, of a meeting of the ways.

What does this description of the activities of the Alberta Teachers' Association contribute to the discussion of these means of achieving an almost identical end? What it says is obviously limited by differences in societal contexts noted earlier. The ATA developed at the provincial level within a system of educational government which placed very broad powers in the hands of provincial legislators; it emerged and grew in a country which, educationally, has been more concerned with regional developments than with national trends; and it came to fruition without competition from any other professional organization. Nevertheless, the following observations, based upon ATA developments, appear to be pertinent to the American situation:

1. "Unionism" is unionism and "professionalism" is professionalism, and never the twain shall meet? Recent ATA activities would tend to discredit this American myth. Both types of activities are possible under one roof, to the advantage of both the teacher-group and the public. Any organization which ignores either welfare or service responsibilities, or which attempts to avoid similarities to the approach of other competing agencies by purely semantic emphases, is destined to fall short of its true potential.

2. The ATA proved that teachers can fight for their place in the sun, independent of the largesse of other groups. Alberta teachers achieved their welfare and service stature without reliance upon labor affiliation or the direct contributions of senior school executives, this in contrast with American counterparts.

3. Myron Lieberman has called upon teachers to shift their emphasis from local to state and national levels. If the Alberta situation has any transfer value, it would appear that, as American teachers enter the state or

federal power arena, boards of education will probably be forced to develop policies and procedures which will permit them to operate in the same sphere. One might, therefore, expect a vitalization of the state and national school board agencies.

4. In unity—in the teaching profession as elsewhere—there is strength. Following the 1935-36 legislation, the ATA became an increasingly powerful and recognized force in the Alberta power structure because, above all, it represented the entire teaching force of the province. The true potential of American teachers to influence school board and governmental decisions is probably offset by their division into two competing camps. If reconciliation or compromise is permanently offset by long-established vested interests, perhaps Lieberman's plea for a third agency may, in future years, represent the only possibility for capitalizing on the best of both existing organizations.

5. As American teacher groups become successful in formalizing collective bargaining procedures, the role of the school superintendent seems destined for close scrutiny and modification. In resolving the obvious conflict which occurs when "his" board of education—of which he is a line officer—is in open dispute with "his" teachers—of whom he is a professional colleague —he will likely become less of a decision-maker and more of an information-giver with respect to teacher welfare. At least this has been the lot of his Canadian counterpart.

6. Finally, it is suggested that the ATA, which has taken on many of the characteristics Lieberman has proposed, has, because of such actions, assumed a position of educational leadership in the province of Alberta, both for its own membership and for its clientele. It has developed successful channels of influence in the educational power structure of Alberta. While there have been instances where opposing agencies and individuals have deplored their militancy, their paternalism, and the sheer power which at times exudes from their headquarters, it cannot be denied that the ATA has achieved sound salaries, pensions, and other welfare benefits for its members and has, of late, evidenced its desire and ability for improving education through improved member service. These achievements, in my opinion, offer some vindication of the Lieberman vision.

IV

ORGANIZATIONAL ISSUES IN COLLECTIVE NEGOTIATIONS

The growth of the collective negotiations movement has caused many problems for teacher organizations. For example, should these organizations represent all certificated employees in the school district, including teachers and administrators? Or should they represent the classroom teachers only? What about the nurses, librarians, and guidance counselors? In some cases a state agency will decide which employees should be represented in negotiations; in other cases the matter will be agreed to by the parties involved. This section includes six articles which analyze some of these problems.

Regardless of the method of determination, however, teacher organizations will have some difficult problems with personnel who are represented by the organizations but are not members of them. There are also knotty problems involving persons who are members of the organizations but who cannot be represented by them for various reasons. Should these members retain the same voting rights as members represented by the organization? Should they form a separate organization to look out for their own special interests? School administrators are undoubtedly the most important group involved in these controversies; their role in teacher organizations is analyzed in Myron Lieberman's article entitled "Administrator Participation in Teacher Organizations." He also discusses whether a teacher organization can negotiate effectively when administrators are members.

Another problem accentuated by the growth of collective negotiations is organizational security. This problem arises when an organization is designated "exclusive representative" of specified groups of employees of the board of education. The organization must then represent all employees in the specified groups regardless of whether the employees are members of the organization. Under these circumstances, what are the responsibilities of the employees to the organization which represents them in negotiations? Should they be forced to join the organization? Michael H. Moskow discusses these problems in his article entitled "Teacher Organizations: An Analysis of the Issues." He distinguishes between organizational coercion to join an organization and administrator coercion to join.

One of the most highly publicized aspects of the collective negotiations movement is the intense competition between the National Education Association and the American Federation of Teachers. This competition has resulted in charges and countercharges by both organizations concerning the nature of membership in each organization. William T. Lowe approaches the controversy in a unique manner by comparing local affiliates of both organizations in terms of membership characteristics. His findings are reported in "Who Joins Which Teacher Group?"

If collective negotiations are to take place on a school district level between local teacher organizations and school boards, what role will the state organization play in the process? Frederick L. Hipp, executive secretary of the New Jersey Education Association, provides some provocative suggestions in "The Challenge to Leadership in Solving Problems of State Associations." Inasmuch as the New Jersey Education Association has been deeply involved in collective negotiations at the local level, Hipp's article reflects the author's considerable experience in working with local teacher organizations.

The article by H. A. Doherty illustrates the way in which an effective Canadian teacher organization prepares for negotiations. The author, a staff member of the Alberta Teachers' Association, makes many valuable suggestions concerning organizational preparations for negotiations.

Finally, the article by Stanley M. Elam reflects a view concerning teacher organizations that is receiving increasing attention in recent years. Merger between the NEA and AFT may not be as difficult to accomplish as is commonly thought; Elam's article explains why such a merger is not only feasible but highly desirable from certain standpoints.

IV-1

THE IMPACT OF COLLECTIVE NEGOTIATIONS
UPON TEACHER-ADMINISTRATOR RELATIONSHIPS*

Myron Lieberman

One of the important effects of collective bargaining in public education is likely to be a clarification of the relationships between teachers and school superintendents. Currently, it is customary for superintendents to belong to the local education associations which represent the teachers as employees. This has always placed superintendents in an awkward position. As the chief executive officer of the school board, a superintendent is clearly a managerial employee. Nevertheless, in most school systems he is also regarded as the spokesman for the teachers in a community. The result is that the superintendents are placed in a position where they are expected to represent both sides in matters pertaining to conditions of employment.

Some educators have contended this is as it should be. The superintendent supposedly rises above his partisanship for one or the other side to advocate what is fair for both. In practice, however, the superintendent's tenure in a particular community depends upon his pleasing the school board rather than the teachers. It does not take much imagination to realize that the teachers are gravely handicapped by this situation. The inclusion of managerial representatives in an employee organization is prohibited by law in private industry.[1] This is necessary to prevent employer domination and to insure that the representatives of the employees will in practice advance their interests instead of those of the employer.

The domination of teachers' organizations by school administrators was largely responsible for the formation in 1916 of the American Federation of Teachers, a union affiliated with the AFL-CIO. The AFT excludes superintendents and places a number of other restrictions on the inclusion of admin-

* Reprinted from Myron Lieberman, *The Future of Public Education* (Chicago: University of Chicago Press, 1959), pp. 171-77. (Footnotes have been renumbered.) Myron Lieberman is Director of Educational Research and Development, Rhode Island College.
[1] Technically, it is prohibited only if the employee organization seeks the jurisdiction of the National Labor Relations Board. However, most large employee organizations find it to their advantage to do so.

istrative personnel in its membership. However, the AFT is numerically overshadowed by the National Education Association, which has over 600,000 members. The NEA has always favored the inclusion of administrative personnel in the same organizations as classroom teachers despite the fact that some of its affiliated local education associations are restricted to classroom teachers. The NEA has taken the position that to exclude administrators from a teachers' organization would mean adopting a trade union practice which may be appropriate in industry but has no place in a profession.

The advent of collective bargaining in public education is likely to present the NEA with some very difficult questions of policy and practice. Obviously, if collective bargaining is to be prevalent in education, it becomes important whether the representatives of management—in this case, the school superintendents—are excluded from the employee organization. Certainly, it is just as important to protect the integrity of employee organizations in public as it is in private employment. It is precisely the lack of this protection that makes a mockery of trade unions in the Soviet Union. In that country, employee organizations are dominated by the government, that is, by the employer. For this reason, they are of very limited value in protecting the rights and working conditions of their members.

Authorities in the field of public personnel administration agree that when it comes to the need to protect employee organizations from employer domination, there is no valid distinction between public and private employment. The experience of organizations of postal employees in the United States bears this out. In the early 1900's, many postal employees joined AFL postal unions in order to get rid of administrator-dominated organizations. Since then, the problem has come up in scores of other organizations of public employees, and the solution has always included forbidding membership to or weakening the influence of administrators within the employee groups.

The fact that some of its own local associations exclude educational administrators is usually ignored by the NEA. Such exclusion is thought to be justified only because, in the communities affected, the school administrators did not treat the teachers kindly. The NEA has also ignored the fact that the American Association of University Professors excludes from active membership persons whose duties are half time or more administrative in character. This exclusion is even more rigid than the exclusion of school administrators from the American Federation of Teachers. Thus we have the paradox that administrators of public institutions of higher education are excluded from the organizations of professors, but the administrators of public school systems are not excluded from organizations of public school teachers. If such exclusion is necessary to protect the integrity of the AAUP as an employee organization, it would seem equally necessary in the case of organizations of public school teachers.

In defense of NEA policy, it is contended that local associations in other professions are open to all members of the profession. This is true, but it overlooks basic differences between education and these other professions. Physicians do not stand in an employer-employee relationship with one another; therefore, there is no need to exclude doctor-administrators from the local medical associations. Likewise, the practitioners in other professions are so seldom in an employer-employee relationship with each other that a policy of excluding employer-professionals would hardly make sense in a community-wide organization of professionals.

Even though most physicians are fee-takers, some are hospital administrators. It might be argued that if my point of view were sound, it would at least require the exclusion of hospital administrators from the local medical association. The fact that this is not done supposedly shows by analogy that the union point of view on administrator membership is unsound in a professional association. However, there are good reasons for not excluding medical administrators from local associations, reasons which do not apply to educational administrators.

A local medical association is not an employee organization; a local teachers' organization practically always is. A local medical association does not represent all the physicians in negotiations with a single employer, who is represented by a physician-administrator. Such a situation would call for the exclusion of the physician-administrator who negotiates conditions of employment on behalf of the employer. In other words, where an employer-employee relationship does exist between members of the medical profession, an employee organization can be organized, and it can exclude the employer-professional; but there would be no point to excluding the physician-administrator from a local medical association which does not bargain with anybody and which has no reason to do so.

In fact, where the situation confronting physicians is similar to that confronting teachers, the physicians do engage in collective bargaining. In some communities, the costs of medical services are borne largely by the health funds of unions. Because so many of their prospective patients are covered by the union's health fund, physicians who are not approved by the medical administrator of the union have no chance to practice successfully in these communities. Furthermore, the fee schedule set by the union has a strong influence on the economic position of the physicians. In these communities, therefore, the physicians must come to terms with the union in somewhat the same way that teachers must come to terms with a school board. In both cases, there is little realistic hope of professional employment other than from the one major employer.

In these comunities, where the physicians are dependent upon one employer just as are the teachers, there is a growing tendency toward collective bargaining between physicians and the unions. The physicians as a group negotiate conditions of employment, even though this is technically still a matter for individual doctors and patients to decide. What is even more interesting is the fact that more and more physicians are specifically calling for collective bargaining as the best procedure to determine fees, schedules, and other conditions of employment in such situations.

Another factor in the medical situation which lessens the need to exclude physician-administrators from the medical associations is the tight control over entry which is exercised by the medical profession. This puts the individual physician in a much stronger bargaining position than the individual teacher. Administrator domination is not a serious problem in the medical profession because the individual physician is not dependent upon a particular employer in the community. The teachers, having only one employer, and lacking any effective control over the supply of teachers, lack the power to bring the employer to reasonable terms. In short, physician-employees are in an incomparably stronger position than teacher-employees; hence administrator domination of medical associations is less likely than administrator domination of educational associations.

The problem of administrator membership in teachers' organizations involves much more than the status of school superintendents in local associations. Principals will want some organizational medium to protect their own interests. What will be the status of principals—should they be regarded as managerial employees, as another kind of teacher, as a craft union within the employee organization, or as an independent employee group? Perhaps it is a mistake to think of principals as a homogeneous class of educational employees. Note that in industry, the label "foreman" actually covers a wide range of supervisory personnel. Some have very little supervisory or managerial responsibility, others have a great deal. One must look to the occupational situation, not the label, to determine their status in an intelligent way.

Similarly, there are basic differences between the principalship of a New York City high school and that of a small rural school. In the former, the principal is a powerful administrator who supervises a school with 3,000 students and perhaps 250 teachers. The principal of a small rural school may teach most of the day, supervise as few as 3 teachers, and be a mere rubber stamp for the county superintendent of schools. A high-school departmental chairman in New York City has more administrative responsibility than many principals in small rural schools. For this reason, it is difficult to propose any inflexible dividing line between managerial personnel and other employees. As long as collective bargaining is conducted from school district to school district, there will be variations in the constituency and the framework of the teachers' organizations.

The impact of collective bargaining upon administrator membership in teachers' associations is difficult to predict. The possibilities are numerous and depend upon factors which cannot be assessed very well at this time. For example, the extent to which teachers are successful in achieving control over entry to teaching will have important repercussions in their membership policies. The more rigorous this control and the more it forces communities to compete for teachers, the less danger will exist of administrator domination of teachers' associations and the less need there will be to exclude administrators from these associations.

Although there are many possible solutions to the problem of administrator domination, the National Education Association has yet to make any constructive contribution toward a sensible solution. The NEA admits that there has been some administrator domination in the past but treats all suggestions that the problem still exists as a trade union criticism beneath the dignity of professional teachers to answer. This attitude must give way to one which is more in accord with occupational realities. Some restrictions will have to be placed upon administrator membership in the organizations which bargain on behalf of teachers. There is, of course, no reason to restrict administrator membership in professional organizations which do not have any bargaining functions.

IV-2

TEACHER ORGANIZATIONS:
AN ANALYSIS OF THE ISSUES*

Michael H. Moskow

The recent development of negotiation procedures between school boards and teacher organizations has had a strong impact on the teaching profession and on teacher organizations. Both the American Federation of Teachers and the National Education Association have developed their own concepts of negotiations, and they have made strong efforts to persuade school boards to conduct representational elections and to negotiate with the designated teacher organizations. To say that competition has been spirited here is to illustrate dramatic understatement.

Although the two organizations have been competing since 1919, the struggle gained new impetus in December, 1961, when the United Federation of Teachers, a local affiliate of the AFT, was elected bargaining agent for 44,000 New York City public school teachers. The UFT received over twice as many votes as the NEA's hastily formed contender, the Teachers Bargaining Organization. More important, though, was the fact that for the first time the labor movement gave active support, in the form of personnel and financial resources, to a local of the AFT. Shortly after the victory, the AFT joined the Industrial Union Department of the AFL-CIO, the major contributor to the UFT.

Since that time, the IUD, headed by Walter Reuther, has been deeply involved in organizing public school teachers and conducting campaigns for collective bargaining. In response to this challenge, in 1962 the NEA formed the Urban Project [which became the Urban Services Division several years later] to direct its fight against unionization. In the ensuing struggle, large sums of money have been poured into the campaign by both contenders.

* Reprinted from the *Teachers College Record,* Vol. 66, No. 5 (February, 1965), pp. 453-63. Michael H. Moskow is Research Associate Professor of Economics and Education at Temple University.

NEA BACKGROUND

The NEA has a membership of over 900,000 consisting of "classroom teachers, school administrators, college professors, college administrators, and specialists in schools, colleges, and educational agencies which are both public and private." Classroom teachers in public schools constitute over 85 per cent of the total membership. One of the major beliefs of the NEA, however, is that since education is a profession unique unto itself, membership in associations should not be limited to classroom teachers. Therefore, *all* state affiliates and most local associations accept both teachers and administrators as members.

In line with its concept of professionalism, the NEA uses the term "professional negotiation" to distinguish its efforts at bargaining from the traditional collective bargaining procedures of the labor movement. When an impasse arises, it advocates various forms of third-party intervention, most of which consist of modified types of mediation and fact-finding, requiring the bargainers to accept a decision of an impartial arbiter. At no time, however, does it advocate using state labor relations agencies or state mediation agencies since, in its opinion, disputes should always be settled through "educational channels." In extreme cases, when agreement cannot be reached, the Association may resort to sanctions ranging from publicizing unfavorable teaching conditions in a particular school district to a mass refusal to sign contracts by all teachers employed in the district.

In reality, "professional negotiation" is a generic term which the NEA uses to refer to a wide variety of different relationships between school boards and local teacher associations. For example, a local affiliate is considered to have a Level I professional negotiation agreement if the school board has made a written statement, which may be in the minutes of the board meeting, that it recognizes the association as the representative of all teachers in the district or even merely as the representative of its own members. Level II agreements consist of recognition and establishment of a negotiation procedure. If a means for settling impasses is added, the agreement is then considered Level III.

It is interesting to note that the Association classifies as professional negotiation a general school board policy statement which establishes a procedure for recognizing employee organizations, but names no specific representative of the teachers. In addition, dual and proportional systems of representation are considered professional negotiation. On the basis of this inclusive definition, it is not surprising that the NEA can claim over 346 local affiliates that engage in professional negotiation. It does not mention, however, that most of these local groups are merely recognized by the school board as the representative of their members or of all teachers in a district—

often a far different thing from the actuality of meaningful negotiations in practice.

UNION'S RISE

Nationally, the AFT has over 100,000 members, the majority concentrated in large cities. The constitution grants locals the right to determine on an individual basis whether or not administrators shall be admitted as members; but few administrators join, and they are often prohibited from holding office or even voting on motions. Thus, the Federation emphasizes that it is the only organization specifically devoted to the interests of classroom teachers.

As expected, the AFT makes no effort to distinguish its approach to teacher-board relations from traditional collective bargaining. Although it does not advocate strikes as a means of settling impasses, the 1963 national convention passed a resolution (No. 79) which recognized the right of locals to strike under certain circumstances and urged ". . . the AFL-CIO and affiliated international unions to support such strikes when they occur." This resolution is of special importance because previously there had been no official strike policy even though locals had been supported when they went on strike.

Although the AFT has been advocating collective bargaining for over 20 years, it has displayed no clear understanding of exactly what collective bargaining for teachers distinctively entails. In fact, the confusion over the AFT's definition of collective bargaining is quite similar to that exhibited by the NEA on professional negotiation. For example, although the AFT claims to have approximately 12 written agreements between school boards and teachers' unions, only four of them include terms and conditions of employment, while the others are merely recognition agreements. In addition, several agreements do not provide for exclusive recognition; and in two cases, the school boards have signed written agreements with both the NEA affiliate and the AFT local.

It is clear, then, that in reality many of the local affiliates of both organizations, while supposedly negotiating, are doing little more than making statements at open meetings of their school boards. It appears, however, that both the NEA and the AFT are aiming for a procedure whereby the school board and the teachers' organization would jointly determine the salaries and conditions of employment of the teachers. Only when this is achieved will true negotiations take place.

In terms of the effect upon school administration, no significant difference between the approaches of the NEA and the AFT seems discernible. Although there are broad ideological differences between the two organizations, the practical impact of their policies is almost identical. The school superintendent finds great difficulty in distinguishing between the NEA's "professional holiday" and the AFT's "strike." If it is often claimed that the AFT is more militant than the NEA, many local instances have been found to the contrary. When negotiations are conducted by either of the two organizations, essentially the same problems arise, and the participants assume essentially the same roles. And even the general tenor of negotiating sessions seems very similar.

Meanwhile, the battle rages between the NEA and the AFT for the power and prestige that teachers' loyalties will bring and for the dominance of one broad ideology over the other. That battle is well reflected in the recent debate in the *Record* between Carl Megel (2), representing the union, and Mrs. Marion Steet (4), spokesman for the Association.

WHO COERCES WHOM?

Megel pictures the AFT as a strong defender of teacher rights and liberties. After labeling the NEA a "company union," he then attempts to document his argument that administrator coercion is responsible for most of the NEA membership. He presents examples of teacher contracts and salary schedules which contain clauses requiring membership in educational associations. He quotes from administrator bulletins to teachers, urging them to join educational associations, and he then questions the mystique of a voluntary membership of 100 percent. After giving several other examples, he restates the AFT's position on the freedom of teachers to join organizations of their own choosing.

In explaining his criticism of administrator coercion to join educational associations, he claims that "it keeps teachers weak; it denies them an opportunity for real leadership in an educational democracy." At another point, he claims that "an intimidated teacher is a frightened teacher. A frightened teacher becomes a poor teacher, unable to teach democracy properly to sons and daughters of free Americans."

Mrs. Steet takes up this challenge and, in her usual eloquent manner, makes the best of a bad case.[1] Her central claim is *"not* to justify any coercive or conscriptory membership practices of teacher associations or teacher unions, nor to attempt to prove that there is no coercion of membership in teacher organizations anywhere in the United States." Yet she later asserts that a careful study of Mr. Megel's documents ". . . causes one to doubt seriously whether Megel has uncovered even a small coercion conspiracy against teachers." She does admit, however, that four of the bulletins which

[1] Mrs. Steet has debated with AFT representatives before my education classes at Temple University on three different occasions.—MHM

Megel presented "do say crassly that teachers are either required or expected to join specific professional organizations."

She then very cleverly puts Megel on the defensive by presenting a well-documented case that the AFT engages in coercive practices. Mrs. Steet concludes that

> It should be noted that in all his efforts to round up documentary evidence of membership coercion in professional associations, the author has not submitted a single teacher *contract* within the decade of the 1960's containing a clause requiring membership or "service fees" to any professional association.

APPEARANCE AND REALITY

Thus, although she claims that she does not try to prove that "there is no coercion of membership in teacher organizations anywhere in the United States," what she ends up doing is, first, to criticize coercion of any kind to join teacher organizations; second, to attack Megel's evidence that there is coercion to join NEA affiliates; and third, to attack the AFT for engaging in coercive practices. She leaves the reader with the impression that there is no evidence to support Megel's contention that coercion is applied to teachers to join education associations, and that if there is any coercion (which she admits is wrong), then it occurs in such a small number of cases that it is of no great concern.

Unfortunately, this approach by Mrs. Steet is somewhat misleading. She would have been on much safer ground if she had said that the NEA realized that there was administrative pressure on teachers to join educational associations in some school districts, but that [the NEA is] attempting to eliminate this practice. She could have supported this contention by showing that teachers are more active in the Association than they had been in previous years.

My own opinion is that anyone who claims that administrator coercion does not exist simply has not come in contact with classroom teachers. It is quite common for a teacher to be told by his principal or superintendent that he is expected to join the Association. Obviously, pressures of this type will rarely be overt or in written form because the practice of forcing a public employee to join an organization as a condition of employment is almost always considered illegal. This does not mean that informal pressures are any less formidable to the teacher.

Pressures will usually be similar to the type described by the Wisconsin Employment Relations Board in the following case:

> It was found that the superintendent had unlawfully assisted the local education association in obtaining recognition on the basis of signed

authorization cards checked by the school auditor, while at the same time the superintendent told the local union affiliated with the Wisconsin Federation of Teachers to petition the WERB for an election if they wished to secure representation rights.

In a later case the Board held that

> a school district, by the action of its principal in soliciting membership applications and dues and by selling tickets for the convention of the Wisconsin Education Association to the teachers employed by the school district, unlawfully assisted such organization and interfered with the right of its employees to join or refrain from joining a labor organization.

Even though most pressures will be informal, a surprisingly large number of documented cases exist. For example, if Mrs. Steet doubted Megel's contention, all she had to do was to read a letter in the November, 1964, issue of the *NEA Journal*. Addressed to the Educational Policies Commission under the date of September 10, 1964, it said,

> I am a new teacher beginning my teaching career. As a part of my orientation, I was told that I *must join* my professional organization—the NEA. I have done so. However, I have been unable to find out just what I will receive in return for my membership dues and loyalty (italics supplied).

The 1955 report of the Committee on Government Employee Organization Relations of the American Bar Association contains the report of a study conducted by the NEA in 1952. In a survey of 1,516 superintendents, over 16 per cent reported that teachers were required to join education associations.

Further evidence of teacher conscription is supplied in my own survey of 150 public school teachers from three different sections of Pennsylvania. Forty-eight per cent of the respondents said there was administrative pressure placed on them to join a teacher association.

When presented with evidence that an administrator is forcing teachers to join, Mrs. Steet's response, typical of the NEA's attitude, is that "professional teachers should and do rebel against such practices. Moreover, the NEA and its affiliates encourage and support teachers in throwing off any such tyranny."

COERCION AND UNION SHOP

Things, however, are not quite so simple. It is unreasonable to expect a teacher to rebel against his supervisor when it may mean his job; it is equally unreasonable to expect the NEA to be with him at the barricades. A bit of analysis may help.

First, for example, it is necessary to separate the problem of *administrative* pressure to join teacher organizations from *organizational* pressure to join teacher organizations. The latter refers, of course, to the union shop issue, a controversy all its own that must be separated from the former problem.

Under the union shop, the majority of employees force a minority of employees to join their organization. Instead of being unilaterally decreed by the administrator, it is a right which an organization of employees has obtained through negotiations. If the majority of employees are opposed to the organizational security provision, they then have the right to vote out the organization in a secret ballot election.

The union shop issue is basically one of "majority rights" versus "individual rights." It is often termed the "right to work" issue, but more accurately it is the question, "What is the obligation of the individual employee to the organization required to represent him in negotiations with the school board?" Although this is a question on which reasonable men disagree, Mrs. Steet assumes that the union shop can never be educationally sanctioned.

Forced membership, however, is not necessarily an evil if it is controlled by teachers. Actually, it can be argued that if teaching is ever to be truly a profession, it will be necessary for teachers themselves to control entrance to the profession. Under these circumstances, forced membership into the teachers' organization becomes only an integral aspect of professionhood. A requirement of this type is far different from coercion by administrators, which usually interferes with the effectiveness of a teachers' organization.

Failing to recognize this distinction, Mrs. Steet lumps together the union shop and administrator coercion and then argues against both as if they were the same thing. Ironically, Megel agrees with Mrs. Steet on this point. His opening sentence is, "The American Federation of Teachers maintains that teachers have the right to join professional organizations of their own choice without coercion or intimidation." In a later section of the article he restates that "The American Federation of Teachers has historically supported the right of teachers to join the organizations of their own choosing."

SISTERS UNDER THE SKIN?

Megel's views and those of the AFT are completely opposed to the attitude of the AFL-CIO. In fact, Megel's arguments are quite similar to those used by the Chamber of Commerce and the National Association of Manufacturers in their fight against the union shop. In arguing for a right-to-work law, the Chamber of Commerce states that "A right to work law guarantees that an employee will have the right to work at his job without being *forced* by anyone—the government, an employer, or a union—to join a particular union."

As the AFT grows in size and wins exclusive representational rights in other school districts, its present position on teachers' freedom to join organizations will become less tenable. Local affiliates which have won exclusive representational rights will want to strengthen their position and thus eventually obtain union shops. A step in this direction has already been taken in New York City, where the UFT has negotiated a provision that prevents an officer of any other teacher organization from representing a teacher who has a grievance. In the near future, pressure from locals will force a change in the position of the AFT on this issue.

The NEA will find itself in the same situation. In fact, leaders of its local affiliates who were victorious in elections with the AFT have already felt the need to strengthen their position as the dominant organization. The Milwaukee Teachers Education Association, which won a representational election last spring, has petitioned the Wisconsin Employment Relations Board to deny the Milwaukee Teachers Union the right to a dues check-off and to prohibit the MTU from representing teachers when they have grievances. This type of local pressure will produce a change in the NEA's national policy, and eventually the NEA will have to find some euphemism for the "union shop" and begin to advocate it for "professional" reasons.

ADMINISTRATOR DOMINATION

Unfortunately, the arguments of both Mr. Megel and Mrs. Steet are somewhat misplaced. With the advent of collective negotiations, one of the most important issues facing any group of teachers is administrator domination of teacher organizations. In order for negotiations to be effective, teachers must be represented by an organization that is primarily concerned with their own interests. If an administrator controls a teacher organization, there is no guarantee that the best interests of the teachers will be represented at the negotiating table.

The NEA is correct in saying that teachers have a great deal in common with other educators (*i.e.,* administrators and supervisory personnel) because they are working in the same field. It does not recognize, however, that a teacher organization controlled by administrators will not be as effective in meeting the distinctive needs of teachers as will be an organization that is controlled by teachers themselves.

Whenever the subject is mentioned, administrators frequently assume that a personal attack is being made, and an objective discussion of the problem becomes exceedingly difficult. On the contrary, most administrators would never think of attempting to dominate their local organizations. But the fact remains that there are instances where this practice occurs, and where the threat exists at all, the classroom teacher clearly needs protection.

Since the supervisor has the authority to act in the interest of the employer, there is no assurance, of course, that he will act entirely in the interest of the employees. In addition, because of the great difference between the job of the supervisor and those of his subordinates, their separate interests may not be served best by the same decisions. Maximum benefit for the teacher can only be obtained when leadership of his organization is devoted exclusively to his interests. Thus, when a teacher organization is controlled by administrators, the conflict of interests is most likely to produce an unjust situation for the teacher.

This conflict is illustrated vividly in the not unusual circumstances exemplified in Missouri:

> MSTA [Missouri State Teachers Association] leaders take great care to avoid actions that would result in divisions in the educational lobby. As we shall see later, in 1961, MSTA shied away from taking stands that might alienate school boards or county superintendents. Indeed it seems fair to say that a major reason Missouri has no teacher tenure or minimum salary laws is that the MSTA has not wished to alienate its school board supporters in behalf of its classroom teacher constituency by recommending such proposals to the legislature. Unity strengthens MSTA's bargaining position, but also imposes limits on its objectives(1).

There are many other cases in which the interests of the administrator and those of the teachers will conflict. Suppose, for example, that the teachers decide it is necessary to invoke sanctions against their school district. If a principal or superintendent were leading the teacher organization, it is inconceivable that he could take such an action against himself; an administrator understandably has too great a vested interest in seeing that the schools remain open and that a large number of prospective teachers apply for jobs in his jurisdiction. Comparable trouble arises when a teacher organization urges the reinstatement of a teacher fired for reasons unacceptable to his peers, but must do its urging through the same superintendent responsible for the contested dismissal.

These examples only appear farfetched. One result of collective negotiations of all types is that teacher organizations will become much more active, and under these circumstances, it is essential that the organization be controlled by the teachers. If control rests anywhere else, the negotiating power of the organization will be diluted.

A VOICE WHOLLY LOST?

Documented cases of administrator domination of teacher organizations are numerous. For example, in the 1952 yearbook of the American Association of School Administrators, results were reported of a survey on the role of the superintendent in the comprehensive local education association in his community. Out of 3,135 replies, 50 per cent of the rural superintendents and 56 per cent of the city superintendents reported that they were regular members and participated on a par with other individual members. Over 32 per cent of the rural superintendents and more than 20 per cent of the city superintendents stated that they were influential members and were consulted on the selection of officers and determination of policies.

Further evidence is supplied in the survey I conducted of 150 Pennsylvania teachers. Sixty per cent of the respondents said that their teacher associations were dominated by administrators.

Even if it is not admitted that the NEA is dominated by administrators, it must be recognized that the organization does not speak for the classroom teacher. At its 1963 convention, the Department of Classroom Teachers, which "represents" 85 per cent of the membership, voted to invoke sanctions against the state of Utah. It also voted for a resolution that would have forced segregated local and state affiliates of the NEA to admit Negro members or drop their affiliation. On the next day, the Delegate Assembly voted against both of these resolutions; consequently, they were not put into practice. In effect, even though the classroom teachers were in favor of these two resolutions, the NEA took an opposite stand.

Too, the AFT claims that although 85 per cent of the NEA's membership is classroom teachers, its Executive Committee of 11 members has only two classroom teachers; its Board of Trustees of six members has only one classroom teacher; and the 75-member Board of Directors involves only 22 classroom teachers.* To the best of my knowledge, the NEA has never denied these allegations. When questioned about the subject, NEA representatives claimed that they have no figures on the subject. Thus, there is no reason to think that the AFT's charges are inaccurate. The crucial problem, then—with which neither Mrs. Steet nor Mr. Megel really come to grips—is one of how to prevent administrators from dominating teacher organizations. An outright ban on administrator membership in teacher organizations would be one possible solution to the problem. Given present conditions, however, a more feasible solution would be to permit supervisors to join teacher organi-

* These statistics are for 1964; by 1967 the percentage of classroom teachers on the Executive Committee, the Board of Trustees, and the Board of Directors had increased substantially.

zations but with certain safeguards to prevent basic conflicts of interest. Such safeguards would exclude administrators from elective office, from important committee chairmanships, and from voting; they might even entail a provision for having administrators leave the meeting room when a controversial topic is discussed.

Some of these procedures are followed by public employees' unions recognized under President Kennedy's Executive Order No. 10988. In addition, some private employee unions have provisions to accept supervisors into membership but without eligibility to serve on the executive board or on the negotiating committee.

NEA'S MAJOR FAILURE

Mrs. Steet refers to the "substantial contribution of the professional teacher association to public education and teacher welfare." In one place, she points to the "impressive accomplishment" of the NEA, and later she even refers to the "phenomenal success" of the NEA. In talking about the rate of increase in teachers' pay, she considers the 65 per cent increase in salaries and the fact that teacher salaries are now about "16 per cent above those in industry" to be "impressive."

It is difficult for me to see how Mrs. Steet can claim such sweeping success for the NEA in improving teacher welfare when the average salary of all teachers in 1963-1964 was $5,963. Teacher salaries were 1.7 per cent above earnings for all employees in manufacturing industries, and average earnings of federal civilian employees in 1962 were 12.6 per cent above those of teachers. In 1959, earnings of all teachers ranked 14th among average earnings for 18 professions. Only social and welfare workers, librarians, clergymen, and dieticians earned less on the average than all classroom teachers in the public schools. In Mrs. Steet's own school district in Philadelphia, the *maximum* a teacher can earn with a master's degree plus 30 credit hours is $8,750.

Another indication of the NEA's failure is the success of the AFT in winning nine of the 20 representational elections held since 1961. On close examination, the victories prove to be remarkable accomplishments: Not only is the AFT generally lacking as a professional organization, but its affiliation with the labor movement is anathema to many teachers. There seems little doubt that that affiliation has seriously hampered its organizing efforts, yet many AFT leaders still view their labor connection as something close to holy and, consequently, refuse to examine its actual benefits and costs. In any case, the AFT victories can only mean that teachers are dissatisfied with the NEA.

THE UNION IMPACT?

At the 1964 NEA convention, many of the speakers discussed the challenge created by the labor movement's active interest in organizing teachers. Had the NEA been successful, it would not today be facing this particular challenge.

This challenge of the AFT has apparently produced many drastic changes in the organizational structure of the NEA. For example, the funds allocated to the NEA's Urban Project, which is responsible for teacher negotiations, have increased remarkably since 1961-1962, when only $28,000 was spent. In succeeding years, expenditures increased to $215,000, then to $389,000, and finally this year to over $440,000. In addition, the Board of Directors ". . . authorized expenditure of an additional $500,000 to be expended this year through national, state, and local action to strengthen the local affiliates" (3). Consequently, over 10 per cent of the NEA's budget is now being spent on teacher negotiations—which indicates that at least financially the Association is becoming more of a teachers' organization.

On the local level, collective negotiations have caused a similar trend. For example, in the districts where representational elections were held and eligibility to vote was determined by an impartial person, principals and other administrators have always been excluded from the unit of representation. This trend can only result in administrators being forced into a secondary role in the NEA. In fact, it could easily result in administrators withdrawing from the NEA.

As it is now organized, however, the NEA can never be an effective organization for representing teachers in negotiations with school boards. The average teacher currently pays $10 national dues, $10 state association dues, and approximately $2 local dues. This dues structure is top-heavy. Because the bulk of the funds must be expended at the local level, if the school district is too small for sufficient money to be accumulated, then possibly county or even state associations will have to direct negotiations. At present, the Urban Project has approximately 25 staff persons who have been attempting to service from Washington the local and state associations. After two years of traveling the country, the Urban Project staff is finally beginning to realize that its task is impossible. Unable to serve effectively in this way the thousands of school districts in the United States, the NEA has begun to allocate funds directly to state and local associations.

Traditionally, local education associations have been inept in improving teacher welfare. For example, in a 1959 NEA survey of the activities of local education associations, 80 per cent of the local associations reported that they sent two or fewer communications to their school board during the past year. Ninety per cent of the local associations said they received two or fewer communications from the school authorities. As expected, 75 per cent of the associations reported that they spent the majority of their time participating in social activities.

ORGANIZING FOR THE FUTURE

From all indications, it appears that this image of the local association is changing and that teachers are finally realizing that it is essential for them to form effective organizations. Obtaining funds for education involves a sophisticated power struggle, and teachers are rather late in accepting this fact.

Since teachers have no power to bargain individually similar to some college professors, the role of the teacher organization in this struggle will be crucial. Because teachers can only be protected by an effective organization, it seems probable that the teacher organization of tomorrow will be quite different from either the AFT or the NEA.

First, it will be structured to function effectively in collective negotiations. Most likely, negotiations will be conducted at the local level, but if they move upward to a county or regional level, then the county organization will control the majority of revenues and full-time personnel. State and national organizations will provide support in the form of consultants and research services; but in large school districts, the local organization will retain full control. In smaller districts, the state organization will play a more important role, and in some states, negotiations will move rapidly to the state level.

Second, the primary function of the organization will be to serve the needs of the teachers. As collective negotiations become more widespread, administrators will be pushed out of any decision-making positions in the teacher organization unless they are completely dedicated to the welfare of the teachers. A very loose affiliation will be retained with organizations of principals and superintendents.

Third, negotiated compulsory membership provisions will be widespread. Not only will teachers be required to join organizations after they have been hired, but in some cases school boards will only be able to hire teachers who are organization members.

Fourth, subject-matter organizations, like the National Council for the Social Studies, will continue to be organized on a national basis, and most original contributions in curriculum and study materials will come from national committees specifically organized for the purpose.

Fifth, each local organization that is negotiating will have at least one full-time person, and dues will have to be sufficient to pay for assistance from various specialists such as attorneys and consultants. The rapid increase in the number of full-time executive secretaries working for local teacher organizations indicates that a trend in this direction has already begun.

Finally, as the negotiating organization obtains higher salaries for teachers, its concern will begin to shift toward professional issues on which teachers can act effectively. Such problems as the management of dropouts, the preparation of students for college, and the improvement of guidance systems are illustrations. This shift to a dual orientation has already begun in New York, where the United Federation of Teachers, the exclusive bargaining agent, has expended enormous energies on the "effective schools plan" for long-range improvement of the city's public schools.

REFERENCES

1. N. A. Masters, R. H. Salisbury, T. H. Eliot, *State Politics and the Public Schools.* (New York: Knopf, 1964).

2. C. Megel, "Teacher Conscription—Basis of Association Membership?" *Teach. Coll. Rec.,* 1964, *66,* 7-17.

3. National Education Assn. *Addresses and Proceedings.* V. 102. (Washington, D.C.: The Association, 1964).

4. Marion Steet, "Professional Associations—More Than Unions," *Teach. Coll. Rec.,* 1964, *66,* 203-218.

IV-3

WHO JOINS WHICH TEACHERS' GROUP?*

William T. Lowe

The American Federation of Teachers and the National Education Association are engaged in a full-scale battle to obtain the support of public school teachers, particularly those from the large urban and suburban school districts. In some communities, local affiliates of the NEA and of the AFT are openly competing for members and are willingly and aggressively undercutting each other at every opportunity. School districts which have chapters of both groups have witnessed very heated recruitment and counter recruitment campaigns.

This article is not another in a series which tries to identify the differences in the purposes of these groups, nor is it an attempt to defend one group at the expense of the other (1, 3, 4, 5, 7, 8, 9). Rather, this is an attempt to determine whether or not there are significant differences between the teachers who join one group or the other and those who refuse to join either one.

It is believed that this question is of considerable significance. The so-called "professional" groups themselves should know whom their respective recruitment campaigns may be likely to attract. The anti-union superintendent should be interested so he will be able to "protect" his teachers and his community by refusing to hire "undesirables." The pro-union superintendent is probably just as interested in "protection." According to one national survey nearly two-thirds of the chief school officers questioned believe and strongly hope that the union will never organize the majority of the public school teachers in the United States (6). But more important, the question seems significant because there appears to be a considerable amount of stereotyped thinking which leads to prejudiced categorizing of teachers and their motives on the basis of their affiliations. The "good guys" are pictured as being very, very good; the "bad guys" are horrid.

To get a partial answer to the question of whether or not AFT, NEA,

* Reprinted from the *Teachers College Record*, Vol. 66 (April, 1965), pp. 614-19. William T. Lowe is Associate Professor of Education in the School of Education, Cornell University.

and non-affiliated teachers[1] are different from each other, a school district with both union and NEA subgroups was surveyed. The district is a rapidly growing suburban one with all of the problems of a booming pupil enrollment. Almost 800 teachers, counselors, and other nonadministrative professional personnel are employed, and nearly 18,000 pupils are registered in this system. Approximately 600 of the teachers completed a detailed questionnaire in an after-school meeting, and the data for this study have been taken from this instrument. Let it be clearly understood from the start that no claim is being made that this is a representative community. It is simply one community facing a struggle between NEA and AFT affiliates. Any generalizing on the basis of these observations is a bit dangerous.

Five hundred thirty-one of the questionnaires were usable. The responses were divided into three categories on the basis of teacher-group membership —e.g., Group A includes 55 (10 per cent of the respondents) members of the local unit of the AFT; Group B, 325 (61 per cent) members of the teachers' association affiliated with the NEA; and Group C, 151 (28 per cent) teachers who had joined neither group. Differences among these were examined on 23 variables.

SOME FINDINGS

Sex. Was sex related to membership in teachers' organizations? Were men more likely to join the AFT than were women? Were women more likely to stay out of both teachers' organizations?

Of the 531 teachers in the study, 257 were male and 272 were female. Twenty per cent of the AFT members, 60 per cent of NEA members, and 42 per cent of nonaffiliated teachers were female. Using the chi-square test with a 5 per cent level of significance,[2] it was determined that significantly more AFT members were male and that significantly fewer men than women joined the NEA. Finally, women were significantly more likely to be organized into "professional" associations than were men. Put another way, men were significantly more likely to be unorganized. If they did join a teachers' group, they were more often a member of the union than were their female counterparts.

Tenure. Was the amount of experience in present teaching assignment related to membership or nonmembership in teachers' associations? Were "settled," "secure" teachers who "know the routine" more likely to support

---

[1] AFT and NEA are used to designate the local organs of these organizations even though it is possible to belong to the local teachers' association without belonging to the National Education Association.

[2] This test was used to determine statistical significance throughout the study.

one group than the other? Were the "brash youngsters" more likely to belong to one or the other group?

The answer in this community was no. NEA and AFT members could not be distinguished on the basis of tenure in their present assignments. Length of service in the same job did seem to be associated with joining one or the other of the groups, but not with membership in one as opposed to the other. Experienced teachers in any given school in this community were, on the average, more likely to be a member of a teachers' association than inexperienced ones, but tenure in one school was not more closely associated with membership in a specific group.

I also considered the variable of total teaching experience regardless of where it occurred. The same results were uncovered; there simply was no apparent relationship between amount of experience and membership in one as opposed to the other teachers' organization. The only significant relationship was that more experienced teachers were more likely to be organized.

Proximity to assignment.   Was the location of a teacher's residence associated with his group memberships? Did being one of the "home towners" have any significance in this regard?

The answer was no. It just didn't seem to matter where one lived.

Marital status.   Being married and living with one's spouse similarly was unassociated with membership in these groups. At the same time it must be remembered that sex was significantly related to specific group membership.

Teaching level.   Elementary teachers were significantly more likely to join the NEA than they were the AFT or stay unaffiliated. An amazing 81 per cent of all the elementary teachers were associated with the NEA, whereas only 4 per cent had joined the AFT. Also, elementary teachers were more likely to be organized than teachers at other levels.

Junior high school teachers were significantly more likely to join the AFT than they were to join the NEA. In fact, nearly half (49 per cent) of the total AFT membership in this community came from the junior high group although only 19 per cent of all the teachers in the sample were from this level. Twenty-seven per cent of all junior high school teachers in the sample joined the union, whereas only 10 per cent of the whole staff did so. Also, the junior high school group were meaningfully more likely to be unorganized than were their elementary school colleagues.

The senior high school faculty did not significantly deviate from the overall percentage on the matter of AFT membership. They were, however, significantly less likely to join the NEA, and they were more likely to remain unorganized than were their colleagues.

PURPOSE AND AFFILIATIONS

Objectives. Were these three groups different on the basis of what they believed the purposes of public education ought to be? Did AFT teachers in this community believe that the primary purpose of the schools was one thing, while the NEA teachers believed it was something else?

What teachers believe is, of course, difficult to learn and to quantify. Each teacher selected from a list of 16 possible objectives for public schools the four that he thought were least important.[3] His selections defined his beliefs about educational aims.

The NEA, AFT, and nonaffiliated groups agreed on personal teaching objectives; there were no significant differences between the groups on this criterion.

Other memberships. There were no significant relationships between a teacher's membership in religious, fraternal, service, and civic organizations and his belonging or failure to belong to teachers' organizations.

There were some differences on the matter of membership in the Parent-Teachers Association. NEA members were significantly more likely to join the PTA than were either the AFT members or nonmembers. Two out of every five AFT members did not belong to the PTA, but fewer than one out of five NEA members failed to join it.

The results of the question regarding the state education association membership were as expected. Since this group is an affiliate of the NEA, it would seem to follow that fewer AFT members would support the group. Only four out of the 55 AFT supporters claimed membership in the state education association.

[3] The 16 statements of purpose from which the respondents had to choose were as follows:

    a. A fund of information about many things.
    b. Efficient use of the three r's—the basic tools for acquiring and communicating knowledge.
    c. Specialized training for placement in a specific job.
    d. A sense of right and wrong—a moral standard of behavior.
    e. A feeling for other people and the ability to live and work in harmony.
    f. An understanding of government and a sense of civic responsibility.
    g. Loyalty to America and the American way of life.
    h. Knowledge of world affairs and the interrelationship among peoples.
    i. A well-cared-for, well-developed body.
    j. An emotionally stable person—prepared for life's realities.
    k. A continuing desire for knowledge—the inquiring mind.
    l. Enjoyment of cultural activities—the finer things of life.
    m. Information and guidance for wise occupational choice.
    n. The habit of weighing facts and imaginatively applying them to the solution of problems.
    o. The homemaking and handyman skills related to family life.
    p. Management of personal finances and wise buying habits.

Finally, on this matter of membership in other groups, I wanted to see if membership in the teachers' organizations was associated with membership in the professional associations of the various academic disciplines or those concerned with the teaching of specific subjects. The teachers were asked to indicate membership in other professional associations with such examples given as the American Historical Association or the National Council of Teachers of English.

Curiously enough, the AFT members indicated a significantly larger interest and membership in this type of organization even though many of the groups like the two suggested here have a working relationship with the NEA.

JOB SATISFACTION

Morale. The final group of questions were asked to ascertain whether or not a teacher's morale or his perception of the way in which his school environment either helps or hinders him in the performance of his job was related to his membership or lack of membership in teachers' associations. Since morale, like purpose, is difficult to measure, a number of specific questions were raised: How do you rate your own morale (five classifications)? How do you rate your colleagues' morale (same five classifications)? Would you still be a teacher if you could make the decision again? If so, would you come to this community? Would you stay in this community if you could have equal opportunity elsewhere? Does your administration and your school board help, hinder, or have little effect on your teaching performance?

On the matter of self-perceived morale, the AFT teachers were more unhappy than were the NEA or the nonmember groups. On the average, they consistently and significantly said that their morale was lower. Furthermore, the AFT teachers rated the morale of their colleagues lower than did the NEA or the nonaffiliated teachers.

Significantly more AFT teachers than NEA or nonaffiliated teachers would choose some other career if they could make their vocational decisions again. Sixteen per cent of the total group took this position, whereas 31 per cent of the AFT teachers did. Significantly more AFT teachers wished they had never come to the community in which they were now teaching and wouldn't do so again if they could alter their decision. Significantly fewer NEA and nonaffiliated teachers would leave the community being studied if they had the opportunity without suffering a financial loss.

A significantly larger number of the teachers in the NEA thought their administrators were making a direct effort to help them teach than did AFT or nonaffiliated teachers. There were no significant differences between the groups on the question of whether or not the board of education was helping the instructional staff be better teachers. The interesting (and alarming) result of this question was that only approximately seven per cent of all teachers thought their board was directly trying to help them.

Parenthetically, the dissatisfactions of the teachers in this system centered on the following complaints, ranked according to frequency with the first item being most often reported:

1. Improper expectation or use of teacher time and talent. Clerical, policing, and guidance duties were most frequently criticized.

2. The low respect and esteem for teachers held by the board of education and the community.

3. The slight amount of involvement of teachers in the decision-making process, particularly in curriculum matters.

4. Failure to compete with other professions and even other school systems on salary and other economic issues.

5. Instructional problems—grouping difficulties, classes too large, and instructional aids not available.

CENTRAL QUESTIONS

In this community, then, a dissatisfied teacher was more likely to join the American Federation of Teachers than to be unaffiliated or join the NEA. Sex, teaching level, and membership in the PTA and in other professional organizations seemed to be related to membership in one or the other of the three categories used in the study. Tenure, marital status, the fact of living and teaching in the same community, membership in most community organizations, and the stated objectives for education did not reveal any significant differences among the three groups.

What do these data mean? Editorializing is extremely tempting, but as is usual in a study of this type, it is difficult to make any definite statements regarding implications. Perhaps a few questions will be permissible.

First, what does this study say regarding the stereotypes frequently held about AFT members? Some of the prejudices often heard elsewhere simply are not supported in this community. AFT members are not "brash youngsters," not "newcomers," not "foreigners." They are not the teachers with the ultraprogressive or superconservative objectives for teaching. In fact, their objectives in teaching seem to be virtually identical with those of their colleagues. They are not outsiders who drive into town from another community. They don't belong to different social, religious, or recreational groups. They do belong to the scholarly associations to a greater degree than their brethren. Furthermore, on the basis of conversation with a number of teachers in the system being surveyed and a series of interviews with the local leaders of the AFT and the NEA, I *suspect* that the NEA, AFT, and unaffiliated teachers in this community are identical in terms of their educational backgrounds, their sincere interest in children, and their initial dedication to the profession.

Second, the groups were markedly different on the basis of morale. Sex, teaching level, and PTA membership were associated with teachers' group membership, but these variables were also associated with dissatisfaction when the teacher group factor was held constant. This leads me to ask what can and should be done about teacher dissatisfaction? Why is the AFT more closely associated with poor morale? Why are junior high school teachers so much more dissatisfied than elementary school teachers? Why were so many teachers of all groups indifferent or hostile in their reaction to their board of education?

Third, why are so many teachers uncommitted? When this struggle for membership is going on, why do so many teachers refuse to belong to either group?

Finally, in the long run, is the competition between the groups good for the profession or harmful? Will better working conditions *and* a better learning situation for children develop because of this rivalry? Is either one of these outcomes really likely to occur?

We have raised more important questions than the ones we have attempted to answer. These and closely related issues are in urgent need of study if teachers are wisely to attain genuine professional status and if the educational climate of our schools is to be profitably enriched.

REFERENCES

1. Barstow, R. J., "Which Way New York City—Which Way the Profession?," *Phi Delta Kappan,* 1961, 43, pp. 118-24.

2. Johnson, M. J., *Factors Related to Teachers' Grade Level Preferences, with Particular Reference to Grades 7 and 8.* (Ithaca, New York: Junior High School Project Research Series, Cornell University, 1961).

3. Kline, C., "The Professional Pattern in Teachers' Organizations," *Teachers College Record,* 1961, 63, pp. 121-27.

4. Lieberman, M., "The Battle for New York City Teachers," *Phi Delta Kappan,* 1961, 43, pp. 2-8.

5. Megel, C. J., "The Union Pattern in Teachers' Organizations," *Teachers College Record,* 1961, 63, pp. 115-20.

6. "Most Teachers Will Not Join Unions, Administrators Believe—and Hope," *Nation's Schools,* 1962, 59, p. 5.

7. Smith, F., "The Teachers' Union *vs.* the Professional Association," *School & Society,* 1962, 90, pp. 439-40.

8. "Strikes or Sanctions," *Phi Delta Kappan,* 1962, 44, pp. 1-11.

9. "Teacher's Choice," *Economist,* 1961, 201, p. 1218.

IV-4

THE CHALLENGE TO LEADERSHIP IN SOLVING PROBLEMS OF STATE ASSOCIATIONS*

Frederick L. Hipp

As we observe the literature on education that comes across our desks and into our reading rooms, we are constantly struck by forces that were distant only a few years ago—or were not as acute in their demands for attention as they are today. Many of these forces are causing us to take a new and constant look at the total structure and functions of professional associations, top to bottom.

The phrases should be familiar to you. They include: "the angry young man," "the outside organizers of teachers," "strikes, sanctions, and picketing," "administrator domination," "integration protests"—in both the North and the South, "federal encroachment on education," "the urban executive secretary," "teacher-board negotiating," "one man, one vote," "the anti-establishment college professor," "better teacher working conditions," "school board meddling in administrative responsibilities," and what have you.

You name it and we have it. Each of these changes is banging at our doors and ringing our telephones for primary attention. The state association cannot look the other way, nor can the national or the local. We must face these challenges head-on—and with every ounce of strength and wisdom we can muster.

In a very real sense we are at war. We are in a war of survival as professional associations—and to survive we must fight every obstacle that stands in the way of the onward march of education and the profession.

You and I have fought many a battle over the years. But we have never been challenged to the extent that we are being challenged today. Hard as we may have worked in the past, either as individuals or as associations, our efforts must be redoubled manyfold.

In facing a battle or a war, the first thing a good military power does is

* This paper was presented at a conference of presidents and executive secretaries of state education associations in New York City, June 25, 1965. Frederick L. Hipp is Executive Secretary, New Jersey Education Association.

to assess its resources. The resources of our professional associations are so great that we have no cause for panic. Let's see what we have to work with.

First, we look at the NEA's annual budget. There we have more than $10,000,000. Second, we find that the annual income of state associations is more than $18,000,000. That is a total of $28,000,000 annually. This does not include the financial resources of our affiliated groups in the various disciplines of our profession. To this we could also add the budgets of thousands of local, county, and regional associations, a figure unknown to me at this time.

In addition to the financial resources at our disposal, we have trained man- and woman-power to help us along. The NEA has 134 professional employees, the NEA departments 132, state associations 442, and an estimated 100 in local and regional associations for a grand total of about 800 professional staff members. There are also at least 1,000 secretarial and clerical employees. In addition, we have something that is more valuable than money and staff. That priceless resource is the loyalty of thousands upon thousands of educators in virtually every school district in the land. The membership is approaching one million in the NEA and 1,600,000 in affiliated state associations.

It is obvious that we are not starting from scratch. The problem is to use all of these resources in the most effective ways.

This, then, requires a very close look at our associations. I am not here today to tell you how to organize or reorganize your associations, but primarily to call attention to some of the major forces which, I think, are going to cause great changes in our collective outlook, our manner of operation, our priorities, and the structure of our associations. That is, they will cause these changes if we are determined to become even stronger and meet the challenges of the day. If anyone thinks that he or his association can continue operating in the same old way, he and his association are destined for extinction.

Let us take a look at some of these tornadoes rampaging through our land:

The militant teacher. The teacher today is better educated than he has ever been. He knows more by far about his subject matter and about how a child lives and learns and grows than most of us did when we were graduated from college. The average teacher today is younger in chronological age and in teaching experience than he was only a few years ago. More teachers —and a higher percentage of our teachers—today are men. And most teachers—of both sexes—are married.

No longer do these teachers consider teaching to be a calling separate from the mainstream of American life. It is no longer some kind of monastic order that sustains its breath on early vows of dedication.

To the hundreds of thousands of young men and young women who have swelled our ranks in recent years, determination is more important than dedication.

These young people are determined to do an effective job of teaching. They identify education as a great force for social betterment. And, when needed resources or support fail to come their way, they are not content to swallow their private dreams or their personal pride. They have no intention of patiently filling the teacher's chair when they know that they are not able to teach the way they know they should. Unquestioning dedication to them is a contradiction in terms.

These young people are also determined to have their full share of America's affluence—at least as much as their friends and associates from college are finding in other degree-requiring occupations. Keeping up with the Joneses is very much a part of our American way of life. Status climbing may take a variety of forms; and you will find today's young teachers very much a part of it. They are determined to serve society and improve it through education; but they are also determined to do so at the same time they support their families and enjoy the material and cultural advantages open to most Americans.

Because of their youth, their vigor, and their determination, some of these young people are not as concerned as you and I might be about certain traditions. Some of their ideas may be quite different from yours and mine. The NEA hit it on the head in a poster which said:

> The American teacher is fashioning a new image of himself. He is becoming a respected professional determined to be involved in the creative enterprise called *the school system*. This changing image reveals the teacher as capable and eager to face the issues of the day, aware of his own sense of destiny. By his teaching he helps to shape the world of tomorrow. Decision making, self-direction, instructional innovation, civic and social leadership—these are all part of the changing face of teaching.

It is imperative that these young, vigorous, and able teachers find a place in every association where their constructive leadership can find expression. They should be welcomed to become a vital part of local, state, and national associations and encouraged with open arms.

Professional negotiation. This insistence that the circumstances of teaching be favorable and that teachers' own personal interests be advanced has led more and more teacher groups to demand formal professional negotiation agreements. Teachers want to be treated like people. They want boards of education to sit down—behind closed doors—and give teachers a voice in the determination of policy.

Paternalism and unilateral decisions on the part of boards of education are a thing of the past—and should be.

No school board has ever had complete, autonomous power to run things any way it liked. Boards don't operate in a vacuum. They hear from politicians, from parents, from the Chamber of Commerce, from the Tax-payers Association, and all kinds of other "persons of influence." What teachers expect is that they—the front-line troops, the persons most directly involved—also have their voice heard, recognized, and respected in the development of all matters of importance.

As we succeed in passing professional negotiation laws in our state legislatures and as local boards of education adopt such procedures at our request, our profession has a responsibility to provide the research and negotiating know-how to get results.

This means that our state and national associations will be very busy training people for this work.

In many instances it is necessary for us to send staff into these communities and negotiate directly with local boards of education for local associations. Where states have hundreds of local associations and hundreds of school boards, this means a tremendous increase in the field staff of state associations as we are presently organized. This leads us to another recent development.

The urban movement.   Over the past few years we have seen a remarkable increase in the number of urban executive secretaries in some of our states. Aside from the problems generated in some areas by this movement, I look upon this development as holding out the greatest hope for professional associations. Properly selected and installed, the urban executive secretary gives tremendous strength to a local association, that segment of our profession where we are the weakest. He provides continuity of leadership in a situation which typically changes its leadership every year or two. We now have an able, full-time staff in Washington where we have one point of attack; our states are similarly equipped at our second point of attack where decisions are made in state capitals affecting the profession.

We need to give every encouragement to local associations, operating at that third and very important point of attack, the local board of education. Furthermore, that is the one point where those who would change the profession to a trade attack us most vigorously and most successfully. In looking at our associations, I am convinced that, more and more, we should actually take the initiative in establishing paid talent at the local level. We should also consider how we can encourage this development financially.

Strikes and sanctions.   Looking into another poser, it is obvious that the profession has not yet made up its mind concerning strikes and sanctions. We have some pious resolutions on the books; but they fail to cover the great variety of situations that have raised their unruly heads in recent years. In practical situations where hundreds, or even thousands, of teachers in deep frustration decide not to carry out their duties, the resolutions often go unnoticed. In our willingness to praise or condemn one or the other method of direct action in cases of extreme frustration, we sometimes overlook the fact that a situation must be resolved by whatever method.

New Jersey teachers, members of professional organizations, have employed various kinds of sanctions and work stoppages on different occasions and for different reasons since the Forties. Though no one enjoys such a situation, many teachers have demonstrated great personal courage in their efforts to correct very bad situations brought about by recalcitrant boards of education or benighted communities. I am not here to praise, condemn, or criticize the use of direct action in these difficult situations. The only way I have to evaluate them is to use the only yardstick I know, namely, "Are the children better or worse off because of a teacher work stoppage?"

If I were to generalize, I would say that there have been two fundamental reasons for teacher strikes and sanctions in our state. First, the board of education was unwilling to sit down behind closed doors and carry on reasonable negotiations with teacher representatives on a matter of serious proportions. Second, a decision by a board of education or official body was based upon political motivation rather than on what is good for education.

Strikes and sanctions are not generated overnight. Their causes have been growing for years. In some communities, the pleas of teachers are ignored and their leaders treated with great disrespect by boards of education who seem to be bound by no code of ethics and no sense of responsibility for good education.

In some cases—where thousands of children have been neglected, where year after year many of the best teachers have moved away, where classes are so large and conditions are so poor that only the most superficial instruction is possible, where the schools have been used for political purposes, where every conceivable legal means has been exhausted over a period of time—it can be more professional to take direct action in an honest attempt to solve problems of long standing than to fail to act.

In addition to the criterion of the effect of work stoppages upon children, there is also the legal aspect of the situation. Should teachers participate in direct action when it is illegal to do so? Most members of our profession will answer in the negative. That is, in my experience, they will answer in the negative until they, themselves, are directly involved in a frustrating, tense situation.

When our state association is involved in a situation of this kind, we explain the law, the risks teachers will take with respect to tenure, pension rights, and salary, and let them make the decision. This explanation often discourages the use of a strike or extreme sanction. Should a local association vote in favor of direct action, however, we then support it in its action.

Legality may not be the crucial issue. The argument that an extreme sanction is legal while a strike is not, is not impressive. Both involve the withdrawal of service, and in both the children miss certain expected schooling. The extreme sanction—the resignation of teachers and blackballing of the district—even though it may be legal, can have a far more devastating effect upon children than the typical brief teacher strike. In my book any work stoppage, legal or illegal, is a strike. A strike is a sanction and an extreme sanction is a strike.

In a larger context, however, a sanction is any negative act against a board, a city council, a community, an individual, or any authority that has the responsibility for making a decision. Hence there are many kinds of sanctions that can be employed in a situation short of a work stoppage. Some of these can be more effective than a work stoppage in certain communities. The city fathers in one resort community were more concerned when their teachers voted to use billboards saying, "Jonesville, the home of the discontented teacher," than they were over a possible strike. They reacted quickly and favorably upon this billboard threat.

It is important that teachers recognize this communicative aspect of their actions. The reason they invoke a sanction is to gain attention to their cause—to develop such overwhelming public sympathy that even the most recalcitrant public official must respond. Their cause must be just and their actions appropriate.

In most of our communities the presence of a state association field man or a dozen teachers at a board meeting is enough to sound the alarm. Those communities want contented teachers and jump at the least sign of dissatisfaction. Those are the places in which we really enjoy working.

In other districts, however, it is hard to get attention. These particularly are our bigger districts, our older cities, and our fast-growing development tract suburbs. Here public interest and responsiveness is often dulled by the remoteness of most citizens from the centers of power. Communication on public issues is seldom personal but rather depends on abstract interchange through the mass media.

The bigger the area, the more competition we face from other public disagreements, disorders, and disasters, the more of a problem teachers have awakening an apathetic public. You need to bite a dog to make the news; and that is just about what teachers in some towns have had to do to get anyone to pay attention to their plight.

Indolent and neglectful boards of education, city councils, mayors, and communities are the real causes of all kinds of sanctions, including work stoppages. Honest and fair use of the professional negotiation procedure by school authorities and educators can correct such situations through reason, intelligence, and respect for personality. When boards and communities fail to live up to their responsibilities to provide good education for their children, the education profession has a responsibility to children to do everything in its power to correct the situation. If it is illegal for teachers to withhold services, it should be illegal for a community to neglect the proper education of its children.

Every state education association must face this problem sooner or later. While I suggest that we do not be hasty about voting official positions, I would hope we are giving considerable thought to such issues in advance of their occurrence.

Emergence of this problem dictates that state associations have professionals on their staffs with ability to aid in resolving situations of this kind. Tact, savvy, and guts of an able staff member can work wonders where pious resolutions have failed .

State associations dare not be caught unprepared.

The shift of power.   As we examine the structure and program of our state associations, we must seriously take note of the great forces at work that can change our functions and our activities both in kind and in degree. A high percentage of the gains that education has made in the past is due to the activity and strength of the state association. The traditional American concept that education is a state function has been responsible for this. Hence our state associations have grown in money, members, and manpower.

This may or may not be true in the future. Forces are pulling in different directions upon the state association—and I am not sure which of these forces will win. My only hope is that our collective wisdom will recognize these forces and cope with them to strengthen the total profession.

We cannot consider the possibility of strengthening local associations by adding staff on the local level without weighing how this will affect state association structure, operations, program, and strength. The fact that the negotiations we carry on now are with local school boards causes eyes to turn in that direction with more frequency. Ineffective, weak, and poorly informed boards of education are asked to do more and more. Reapportionment—"one man, one vote"—is making tremendous political changes within our states. And the great event of 1965, the Federal Elementary and Secondary Education Act, is very much in the picture. At the same time, important programs of the Economic Opportunity Act are having an impact upon local and state school systems.

The pattern that we establish within our states now in working with local associations, in helping to strengthen their leadership, and in participating in local negotiations can strengthen or weaken the state association.

"Should the state association, for example, help to finance the office and staff of a local association—or should the state association provide assistance to the local through its field service?" "Should the state association refrain from raising its own dues and encourage the raising of dues on the local level to support a stronger program there?"

With reapportionment of our state governments, we see a shift from the traditional influence of the rural areas toward the cities and suburban areas of our respective states. People in cities very often think differently from rural people on many issues.

We expect this move to very much affect our legislative program. In our state, it will be more difficult to expand the state tax program and easier to secure some personnel benefits. Mass organizations which influence large blocs of voters will have more promise of success with their lobbying activities. We expect more talk of lotteries and other forms of gambling as a way of replenishing state coffers. In each of these issues, the state association is unavoidably involved.

The total effect of reapportionment on education can be tremendous. This "one man, one vote" theory will also bring demands for reapportioning of the governing bodies of our state education associations. Again, our respective association structures will inevitably be changed as an indirect result of a decision of the United States Supreme Court.

In the long run, perhaps the most significant influence upon our associations is the tremendous increase in federal funds flowing to our local school systems. One larger school district, for example, is dealing with twelve different federal agencies. The unique principle in distributing federal funds through the anti-poverty and education acts has avoided (1) federal control and (2) distribution of funds through state agencies. Most of the money for education goes directly from Washington to the local communities. By and large, the amount is determined by the imagination and know-how, not in state offices nor in Washington, but in the local community. The function at the state level is more or less routine.

Therefore, the communications between the local community and Washington are at an increasing tempo, with some communities actually employing personnel whose sole function is to be familiar with federal education laws for the distribution of federal funds and to formulate plans to get federal money for the local community. They frequently travel from the local community to the nation's capital. Washington and the local community become more important to each other.

There is no sign that this will lessen. It will likely increase. The belated recognition on the part of our nation's power groups that more and more education has a salutary effect in solving the nation's social and civil rights problems, plus the demand by leading economists that the federal government spend more and more money to keep our economy healthy, are obvious signs that we are only on the threshhold of federal spending for education. The role of the state association is not immediately apparent as it sees this great wealth whizzing by from Washington to the local communities.

A variety of changes could take place in our association operations. The three most obvious are: (1) The local association will become increasingly important—beyond our present imagination; (2) the National Education Association will increase tremendously in importance and function as it works with the federal government more and more on financial matters; and (3) the state association will decline in relative importance as the state government ceases to be the key determinant of the welfare of the public schools.

Likewise, increased federal support for the U.S. Office of Education and our state departments of education is greatly expanding the activities of these agencies. In areas of research, public information, and curriculum improvement these governmental bodies are now serving a function that was once only provided by professional associations. I am not suggesting that we stop gathering data, publicizing facts, or holding teacher improvement conferences; but we must recognize that our activities in these areas will become less generalized and pointed more toward our specific purposes.

From this point on, one can conjecture in a variety of directions. Because of the inability to negotiate individual teacher benefit packages in 25,656 school districts in the nation, this function could be removed from the local districts and taken over by the state. In this case, the state association would have to remain very strong. It is even possible that, as the federal government increases its interest in the local school system, negotiations on key conditions of employment would be carried on in Washington for all school districts in the land. This, again, would place a premium upon the strength of the NEA.

A better way of saying it probably is that the local and the national associations must be as strong and effective in meeting their responsibilities as most states now are in meeting their legislative responsibilities. The state association need not become weaker, but the others must become stronger. It is very possible, too, that *all* must become stronger; if not stronger, then different in many respects from what they are now.

It is likely that the possible developments mentioned here will not come about overnight. However, if you and I expect to remain abreast of the situation in our respective states, we must be alert to the possibilities. It is better to have a part in determining our direction than to be buffeted hither and yon in panic by every whiff of air.

It is not important which is stronger: local, state, or national. It is essential, however, that our associations at every level be able to cope with the problems in their respective spheres of influence—and that the total profession be organized from strength, with wisdom, rather than expediency.

There are other questions that come to mind when we begin to evaluate our associations, questions which I do not have time nor wisdom to treat here. Among these are:

1. "What shall be the role of superintendent in the professional association?"

2. "What part should principals play in the negotiating process?"

3. "What services, if any, shall our associations provide to take full advantage of the anti-poverty and education acts?"

4. "Now that parochial and private pupils are getting a nip of the tax dollar, should we open and promote membership to faculties of those schools?"

5. "What should be the function of the NEA regional offices and how should they coordinate their activities with the state and local?"

6. "How shall we organize in the colleges and what services should we render on that level?"

You think of other questions as you concern yourselves with meeting the pressures and opportunities of the day.

Imagination, determination, persistence.   As I look ahead in visualizing the program of professional associations, I would say:

1. The sooner we are constitutionally united on all levels the better. We should pay one dues for local, state, and national associations. And these dues should be high enough to do a tremendous job—perhaps $10 per month for 10 months. We might even have a common name, such as the NEA, New Jersey Chapter; or similar to what we're putting on next year's membership cards, the United Teaching Profession, New Jersey Branch.

2. We will make over our constitutions to correspond with the shifting political power within our states.

3. We will place more emphasis on our obligations to the local association, on one hand, and to the NEA and Washington on the other.

4. We will be more interdependent, sharing manpower, money, and special talents with other states. This is already taking shape in the East Coast NEA region.

5. We will be in the forefront of educational research and experimentation as we place even greater emphasis upon the importance of the able teacher.

6. With education as the great healer of social ills, we shall exercise greater leadership in eradicating poverty, promoting human rights, attacking disease, crime, ignorance—even murder on our highways. These must stand out in our professional association programs.

7. We will place greater emphasis upon the importance of leadership

training for all leaders, including ourselves. New approaches to old problems are rapidly coming to the fore and we must know how to handle and make the best use of them.

8.   We will be harder hitting and more aggressive. People must see us as an *action* organization, aiming high, hustling, bustling, efficient, energetic and fast moving—always moving. We must move with courage and imagination to build teaching into the best and most respected of professions. We have the resources and the know-how to brighten the educational future for all children of our land—black, white, brown, red, tan, or yellow. With more than $28,000,000 annually, 800 trained professional staff members, 1,000 estimated clerical and secretarial workers, and 1,600,000 members of state associations, we are well on our way. We have accomplished much in the past. There are greater victories in the future.

Three characteristics stand out as essential to our future growth and success. I am sure that our profession is endowed with them. They are:

First, *imagination*. And we remember that Napoleon said, "Imagination rules the world."

Second, *courage*. About courage the third-century Roman poet Plautus wrote, "Courage in danger is half the battle."

The third is *perseverance*. Shakespeare spoke wisely when he said, "An enterprise, when fairly once begun, should not be left till all that ought is won." And Carlyle adds his wisdom in the words, "Every noble work is at first impossible."

IV-5

ORGANIZATION FOR COLLECTIVE NEGOTIATIONS*

Hugh A. Doherty

Effective aid to local teachers' associations in the conduct of collective negotiations requires a well-organized approach at the state or provincial level.
While the national association can provide much useful help, the sheer numbers of local negotiations preclude any extensive service by the national association at the local level. I would advance the thesis that the role of the
national association might well be to increase the competence of the state
associations and possibly to provide direct service to very large urban associations. I would further argue that successful collective negotiations will
be carried on at the local level to the extent, and only to the extent, that
the state associations succeed in raising the competence of local negotiators.

The Teacher Welfare Department of the Alberta Teachers' Association organizes its work in three broad classifications:

1. Field service.
2. Active negotiating on behalf of local associations.
3. Communications.

The objectives of our field service work are to provide local associations with information relative to the economic status of teachers and to
instruct the negotiating teams of these associations in the elementary skills
of collective negotiations. One staff officer is assigned full time to these functions and two others assist as far as their duties as negotiators allow. These
efforts are supplemented by a force of 25 "economic consultants" who are
practising teachers who have attended special training seminars and are
available in the evenings and on Saturdays.

Early in each school year our field service officer and economic consultants arrange to attend meetings of local associations to inform the
teachers of current economic conditions. They also attend meetings of the

* Address presented July 14, 1965, at the National Institute on Collective Nego-
tiations in Public Education, cosponsored by Phi Delta Kappa and Rhode Island
College, Providence, R.I. Hugh Doherty is Executive Assistant, Alberta Teachers'
Association, Canada.

local Economic Policy Committees to help in framing tentative proposals for presentation to the school boards. In addition, they organize training sessions for the negotiating sub-committee members of each local association. I should add that this field service is offered to locals. Whether or not they make use of it is their own decision.

To supplement this field service, a series of Area Briefing Schools are held each fall. Since the non-urban part of our province is divided into eight geographical districts, one of these schools is held in each. In addition, an Urban Salary Conference is held with its program assigned to cover the more complex problems of city associations. Our negotiating season customarily begins about the first of February. Toward the end of March, a second series of meetings occurs. The fall meetings provide an opportunity for associations to exchange information about their tentative proposals to boards and to discuss economic and other information more fully than can be done in the smaller groups. At the spring meetings, each association reports on the progress of negotiations, problems encountered, and possible useful tactics for overcoming these problems.

In addition to the types of field service mentioned above, any local association will be provided with the services of a consultant at any time it requests such service.

The Alberta Teachers' Association strongly encourages locals to attempt to complete their negotiations at the local level, but will provide the services of a negotiator at the request of any local which has reached an impasse. Two staff officers are assigned negotiation for locals as their major work and, occasionally, one of the more experienced economic consultants is assigned a dispute when an overload develops. The negotiator will then handle the dispute until its final disposition, which may progress from meetings with the board to our equivalent of the fact-finding and arbitration stages, and even to a strike vote, mediation, or a strike. This last is a most infrequent stage.

The communications aspect of our work takes in all publications which are designed to keep local associations informed of developments over the province. The most regular communication is the *Economic Bulletin,* published monthly, which provides current data from the Dominion Bureau of Statistics and other sources. It is designed to provide for locals the most up-to-date material possible for use in formulating and supporting their proposals to school boards. It also includes summaries of settlements, provincial averages, and other relevant matters. The distribution of the *Economic Bulletin* is restricted to those actually engaged in teacher welfare in each local.

During the negotiating season, a *Collective Bargaining Report* is also issued. This is published weekly and contains information supplied directly by local negotiating teams. It contains such things as teacher proposals to school boards, board counter-proposals, and settlements agreed to. Its purpose is to keep each local negotiating team informed of developments in other areas almost as soon as they happen. In general, after a development of any kind, the chairman of the local association phones his district representative immediately and passes on the information. The district representative sends a weekly summary to the Teacher Welfare Department which consolidates all such reports and issues the *Collective Bargaining Report*.

This, then, is a very brief account of how one teachers' association organizes on the provincial level for collective negotiations. We attempt continually to expand and upgrade our efforts, but the basic components of field service, active negotiating on behalf of local associations, and communications are likely to remain.

IV-6

PROSPECTS FOR AN NEA-AFT MERGER*

Stanley M. Elam

Suggest in a partisan group that education's two warring employee organizations should merge and you are likely to be hooted from the room. "Their outlook and programs are poles apart," it will be said. But this reply ignores the facts, some of which are recent developments.

Privately, leaders in both factions admit that rivalry between the American Federation of Teachers and the National Education Association must eventually end in merger or alliance. Too much money and energy are being wasted that might better be directed toward common goals, and bitterness is building up which can be exploited by the enemies of both groups for decades to come. Michael Moskow, a labor economist with the Drexel Institute, says: "Merger will definitely occur, but probably not for about five years." He notes that already some NEA and AFT affiliates have made overtures for merger at the local level.

Until recently, the rivalry between the NEA and AFT may have served some useful purpose. For example, AFT successes, particularly in New York, forced the NEA to intensify its teacher-welfare efforts [see "Organizing the Teachers" by Stanley Elam, *The Nation,* June 29, 1964]. The Urban Project, which has promoted scores of "professional negotiation" agreements between local associations and boards of education, was a direct result of the concessions and written contract that AFT Local No. 2, the United Federation of Teachers (UFT), won from New York City's reluctant board. The state-wide sanctions program, so effective in Utah and now on trial in Oklahoma (a more difficult state) is the NEA's alternative to the strike, on which AFT locals depend as a last resort. Sanctions may involve a variety of actions by the local, state and national units: boycott, publicity, political action. Usually, after lengthy investigation, a school system will be declared "one where no professional person would want to seek employment." Depending on the loyalty of teachers to their organization, it can close a school—but

* Reprinted from *The Nation,* Vol. 201 (October 18, 1965), pp. 247-49. Stanley M. Elam is editor of the *Phi Delta Kappan,* official journal of Phi Delta Kappa, the professional education fraternity.

only after teachers have met their contract obligations. Because the AFT has few effective state organizations, the NEA has been sponsoring legislation which favors state-wide professional negotiation as opposed to AFT-sponsored collective bargaining in Washington, Oregon, California, and Connecticut. An aroused NEA can eventually dominate the teacher-welfare field everywhere except in the big cities—where, however, unionism is a way of life.

The AFT, suddenly aware that its membership is not growing as rapidly as hoped,[1] decided at its 1965 convention in Los Angeles to emphasize state organization, research, and publications. The new program will involve a considerable increase in dues, making them higher than the NEA's annual $10—and that will be one more point of similarity between the two bodies.

Are there real and important differences between the AFT and NEA? AFT rank and file, for example, are accused of being less devoted to the professional aspects of teaching. Not true, says William T. Lowe of Cornell, who cites the fact that AFT members are actually more likely than NEA members to belong to professional associations (the American Historical Association, the National Council of Teachers of English), even though these groups have a working relationship with the NEA.

The most easily recognizable difference between NEA and AFT members is that a significantly higher percentage of men than women join the AFT. Related to this fact, perhaps, is a difference in morale. AFT members tend to be dissatisfied, and would choose some other career if they could make the decision again. The single salary schedule is widely accepted in teaching, and a man can hardly support a family on the average salary of less than $6,000—at least not on the level college graduates and professionals have come to believe is their due. Thus they are activists and give the AFT its reputation for impatience and militancy. They are likely to be younger teachers at the junior high and high school levels, where men tend to concentrate in the public schools. (That, incidentally, is probably why many of them join professional organizations, which are more important for high school than for grade school teachers.)

AFT members, then, are the people who prefer a rapid and more or less clean solution of salary squabbles (the strike) to a slow, cumbersome, and messy procedure (sanctions). But beyond this difference of attitude, what ideological, programmatic, and structural differences between the NEA and AFT might prevent or delay merger? Only two are usually regarded as crucial.

[1] On May 30, 1966, AFT membership was about 125,000, up 65,000 from 1961 when the UFT won exclusive bargaining rights in New York City. About half this increase has been in New York City itself. Meanwhile, the NEA has grown from 714,000 to about 986,000.

First, within a month of its formation in 1916, the AFT became affiliated with the American Federation of Labor. It now pays AFL-CIO dues and makes much of the "mutual benefits of affiliation." NEA literature emphasizes the theme that by affiliation AFT teachers lose the independence of action that is important to professionals committed to objectivity and responsible to all the public. As NEA Executive Secretary William G. Carr puts it, "American teachers must remain free and independent of entangling alliances with any one group in society."

But what entanglements actually occur? In August, 1963, the UFT was on the verge of a strike in New York City. It was generating as much political pressure as possible against Mayor Wagner and the city administration. When Harry Van Arsdale, head of the Central Labor Council, threw his complete support behind the UFT, a settlement was reached which the union found acceptable. It didn't produce much money the first year, but it got some for the second. The questionable result, so far as the UFT is concerned, was the political debt contracted, for that debt is now being called. According to the New York *World-Telegram* of April 17, the UFT as part of its annual contract proposals asked the New York City board to agree not to buy textbooks, teaching materials, or equipment transported or handled by any company with which the AFL-CIO has a dispute. If this can be done, it is not fanciful to suppose that the AFT might, as the price of AFL-CIO support, be asked to boycott a textbook critical of a position the trade unions have taken in resisting new modes of production.

In the past two years the AFT and the NEA have locked horns in a series of big-city elections to choose exclusive bargaining agents. One of the first of these occurred in Milwaukee. At the time (early 1964) it was thought that direct intervention by the AFL-CIO would help the AFT cause; hence the election was not run by the AFT but by the director of organization for the AFL-CIO's Industrial Union Department. Walter Reuther, president of the IUD, made a personal visit just three days before the election on February 12. However, the Milwaukee Teachers' Education Association (MTEA) won by a 600-vote majority out of 4,012 votes cast. The MTEA campaign stressed independence for teachers and freedom from ties with organizations outside the profession. Clearly, teachers resented the AFL-CIO "invasion," and since the Milwaukee debacle the IUD has remained in the background of bargaining elections.

The experience of the organized profession in England and Canada is instructive on this point. In both countries, the leading teachers' organizations have passed through a stage of labor affiliation. The National Teachers Union in England dropped the connection some years ago. In Canada, where teacher groups are far stronger and more experienced in collective negotiations than in the United States, none is now affiliated, although at one time

—before provincial groups became effective in themselves—they were in the national union movement. The reasons given are primarily economic: it is believed that the considerable sums once spent in affiliation fees can be used more effectively by the Canadian Teachers Federation itself.

It can be persuasively argued that should the nearly 2 million U.S. teachers band together, their economic strength would be such that the disadvantages of affiliation with organized labor would far outweigh the advantages.

A second much-discussed point of difference between the NEA and AFT concerns membership in the bargaining unit. A basic labor relations tenet is that management employees should not be in the same unit as non-supervisory employees. Accordingly, the NEA is routinely dismissed by the AFT as a "company union" because it welcomes all certificated employees—including principals, supervisors, and even superintendents—in national and state organizational units, and in most local units as well. But the picture for bargaining purposes is by no means as simple as AFT literature suggests, and the NEA-AFT difference here is more assumed than real. The fact is that in one place or another the AFT welcomes "management" people and in one place or another the NEA excludes them. Overall, the NEA seems to hold the more flexible and pragmatic position on this question—the AFT would call it equivocal—because NEA policies vary with locale, with job descriptions, and with leadership qualities of individuals.

Donald H. Wollett, a labor lawyer serving as a consultant to the NEA's Urban Project office, says that what holds a unit together is community of interest, which is not the same as identity of interest. In the printing and building trades, he points out, everyone who possesses the skill is organized, whether supervisory or not. He adds: "I would wish that in structure and membership every teachers' organization could be like the Utah Education Association. There, in an outrageous breach of faith over a year ago, Governor George Clyde refused to follow the recommendations of his own committee with respect to state aid for education. A two-day walkout by teachers resulted, and it was led by the UEA president, Moroni I. Jensen. Jensen is a high school *principal*. The teachers didn't complain about administration domination. The complaints were leveled by school boards because their administrators were dominated by *teachers*."

Wollett reminds teachers that a big advantage in having an all-inclusive bargaining unit is that some of the most effective leadership may be found in the ranks of the supervisory personnel. The UFT itself discovered this when it chose Charles Cogen for its leader in early New York City negotiations. At that time he was a department head, and ineligible to vote in the election forced by his own group.

As a matter of fact, the AFT position on administrative personnel membership is by no means as consistent as the official line suggests. According to

Wollett, the AFT wanted department heads excluded in Newark but included in Philadelphia, although Philadelphia heads had more of the duties of supervisors than did their opposite numbers in Newark.

From the foregoing it would appear that the facts do not support those who say there are two insuperable ideological barriers between the AFT and the NEA. Certainly labor affiliation is not essential to effectiveness for a national teacher organization. And the ancient difference over administrative membership in the bargaining unit is more imagined than real. It is true that the AFT won't permit superintendents to be members at any level, while the NEA will. But the NEA has learned that certain administrators cannot be accepted in the local unit when the time comes for hard bargaining. And NEA teacher groups are apparently learning how to make use of leadership skill from the administrative branches when conflict of interest is not disabling.

If within the next few years merger is seriously considered by AFT and NEA leaders, what could the AFT bring to the marriage that the NEA doesn't already have? Besides some very energetic and effective leaders, it could bring a structural change which has made the AFT more responsive to its membership than the NEA has usually been. This change is the caucus system.

At AFT conventions two very lively parties are in action, each with a well-defined program, a slate of officers, and a mechanism for presenting both to the delegates. This means that there is always an organized group in opposition to the people who run the federation, a group looking for issues on which to embarrass those in office, and offering a platform to dissidents and minorities.

Myron Lieberman, a frequent critic of both organizations, points out that there is nothing like the caucus in the NEA. In an organization of almost a million members, he says, there is no political machinery, no center around which a systematic, continuing basic policy can be developed and then brought back to the organizational machinery. If merger with the AFT should politicize the NEA, then democracy would be well served within this huge, cumbersome organization.

Speaking before a national institute on collective negotiations in public education at Rhode Island College in July, AFT President Cogen said: "Increasingly, educational commentators have proposed that the AFT and the NEA merge into one organization. We would not rule out such a possibility." He went on, of course, to say that there are fundamental points at issue between the two organizations, but we are still waiting to hear an NEA spokesman come as near as Cogen to recognizing the need for merger. Perhaps, like the U.S. Government in Vietnam, NEA leaders are waiting for military success. At that point the teachers' new-found negotiating skill can bear fruit.

V

COLLECTIVE NEGOTIATIONS AND SCHOOL ADMINISTRATION

Collective negotiations affect school administration in many different ways. For example, administrative personnel must prepare for and participate in negotiations. This requires effective communication among all levels and types of administration, so that the needs and interests of one group, such as principals, are not neglected or subordinated to the needs and interests of another group, such as central office staff personnel. In addition to the manifold problems of preparing for and negotiating written agreements, administrative personnel have major responsibility for the crucial task of administering them.

Unfortunately, the vast majority of administrative personnel are unprepared by training or experience for these roles. School personnel administration in the United States has traditionally been conceived and carried on as a relationship between school administrators and individual teachers, without reference to any collective agreement or necessity for dealing with teacher organizations. The collective negotiations movement is rapidly changing this traditional approach to school administration. The purpose of this section is to show how and why these changes in school administration are taking place.

The article by Morris E. Lasker sets forth a positive approach to collective negotiations by a lawyer who is experienced in employment relations. Coming as it does from a person who has also served on a school board and been involved as a school board consultant in collective negotiations, the article reflects the increasing acceptance of collective negotiations by forward-looking school board members.

The next article sets forth the views of Bernard E. Donovan, a superintendent thoroughly experienced in collective negotiations in New York City. Dr. Donovan's views are especially valuable since they suggest the directions and problems of collective negotiations in large urban school districts. The article by Alden H. Blankenship also emphasizes the role of the superintendent in collective negotiations. Whereas Donovan's article emphasizes the substantive issues that arise in negotiations, Blankenship emphasizes the relationships of the superintendent to the school board and to the teacher organization. He also offers some procedural suggestions to boards and superintendents becoming involved in collective negotiations.

It is not generally recognized that collective negotiations are bringing about fundamental changes in education administration at the school level. The article by Luvern L. Cunningham, as of September 1967, Dean, College of Education, Ohio State University, considers collective negotiations from the standpoint of the principal. Although the article is admittedly based upon a small sample, it seems to reflect the experience of many principals involved in collective negotiations. In any case, Dr. Cunningham raises many important questions concerning the role of the principal in the negotiations process.

One of the most important aspects of collective negotiations in public education is the increasing use of third parties to assist school boards and teacher organizations reach agreement on issues which divide them. The use of such third parties may be desirable at one or more points in the negotiations process: Neutral parties may determine whether the teachers desire representation, which organization should represent them, and may help resolve impasses in negotiations. In the long run, the greatest use of impartial third parties will probably be in grievance arbitration, i.e., in disputes over the interpretation or application of collective agreements. The article by Joseph S. Murphy, Vice-President of the American Arbitration Association (AAA), outlines the services made available by the AAA, an organization which appoints or provides arbitrators in all types of controversies requiring the assistance of impartial third parties.

Many school administrators are finding themselves seriously unprepared for collective negotiations. The article by Douglas E. Weiford describes administrative preparation for negotiations in a Wisconsin community. Although the article is devoted to public employment outside the field of education, it provides many useful suggestions for school administrators who are confronted by the problem of preparing for negotiations with teacher organizations.

V-1

SCHOOL BOARD APPROACHES TO COLLECTIVE NEGOTIATIONS*

Morris E. Lasker

During the week of March 12, 1964, five state affiliates of the American Federation of Teachers held a conference in New York to discuss organizing, collective bargaining, and union participation in school policy making. Among the literature circulated by the Federation was a one-page statement at the head of which was the picture of a pretty young lady school teacher, who sent this message to her fellow teachers:

> I am Anna Mae Vener. I teach in a New York City Elementary School, P. S. 146, in the Bronx.
> I have been teaching 7 years, and I intend to stay in teaching.
> Three years ago I was not sure that I wanted to continue my teaching career, at least in New York City. Teaching was not what I had been led to believe it would be like.
> My class was large, I had no time during the day to prepare lessons, and my teaching was continually interrupted while I attended to all sorts of non-teaching chores—distributing milk, collecting money, and keeping records.
> Thanks to collective bargaining and the UFT, things are much better now. My class is smaller, and I have a voice in deciding which class I will have each year. I have two 'free' periods a week. School aides take care of many of the extra duties which used to take up my time. I have a full, duty-free lunch period every day. The union committee meets with the principal at least once a month to straighten out school problems.
> Three years ago, my salary, with M.A. degree, was $5800. Now it is $7945, and my sick leave and pension are better, too.
> I would urge every teacher to support collective bargaining and the Federation.

* An address delivered at a meeting of the Metropolitan School Study Council on November 19, 1964, and published by the Council as *New Forces, Directions, and Trends in Board Professional Staff Relationships.* (New York: Metropolitan School Study Council, undated). Morris E. Lasker, an attorney with the New York City firm of Battle, Fowler, Stokes, and Kheel, is also a former President of the Board of Education in Chappaqua, New York.

Now, Anna Mae Vener may not be a Susan B. Anthony or a Carry Nation who will go down in history, but she certainly *is* a product of the times; and her membership in the American Federation of Teachers, along with 100,000 others, establishes that collective dealings between teachers and boards of education are here to stay in many communities. And the number of communities keeps growing. New York, or at least New York State, has now been superseded by the states of Connecticut, Washington, and Oregon, whose legislatures in recent months have enacted statutes giving teachers varying degrees of legal rights to bargain collectively or consult with their board employers on matters ranging from salary to class size and curriculum.

The new statutes are a culmination of feverish activity which has been widely reported in the press in the recent past. There is no need to review the imminence of application of "sanctions" by teachers in the entire state of Utah; or the organizational activities in Chicago, Philadelphia, Boston, Milwaukee, Rochester, White Plains, Yonkers, and New Rochelle.

These developments are unmistakable signs that we are in a period of revolution as to basic relations between teachers and boards of education. If we wish to cope successfully with the present state of affairs, we must understand the revolution and its causes. Let us examine them:

Like any fundamental change in social phenomena, the factors which have produced this change are many and varied. They evolve from history, economics, demography, current events, government attitudes. They are recent developments and we can recall them with ease.

In 1937 the United States Congress enacted the Wagner Act—the law which has often been called labor's Magna Charta. This statute established it as national policy that workers had a right to bargain with their employers on a collective basis and that employers were *obligated* to bargain collectively with the certified representatives of their employees. While the Wagner Act and its amended successor, the Taft-Hartley Act, do not apply to *intra*state commerce, the act was preceded or followed by a rash of state-enacted laws establishing the same policies. And though neither federal nor state laws apply to governmental employees—or teachers—they nevertheless fixed the national attitude. Looking back we realize that, with fixed pay rates, teachers were doing relatively well during the thirties in comparison with other Americans, and so it is no surprise that in those days teachers were indifferent to collective dealing for themselves. But the national policy was set.

By the end of the war, blue-collar workers were highly and numerously organized. Their demands for wage increases, held in abeyance during the war, added to the inflationary pressures produced in other ways by a war economy, brought big pay raises for blue-collar workers, leaving white-collar employees relatively in their wake, and the white-collar worker was not losing only relatively, but absolutely, too, as inflation lessened the value of his salary.

The post-war era has also witnessed the country's greatest population growth. It is not necessary to rehearse statistics to remind you of the great teacher shortage which we have suffered as a result of population explosion on the one hand, and the training of too few teachers during past decades on the other. Happily, from the point of view of most of us, the teacher now finds himself in a seller's market. However, while this may give him an added sense of security, it also often spurs him on to secure his future position collectively with his fellow teachers. Many a teacher feels that the time to act is now: when the community needs his services most. Population growth has stimulated collective relations in another way as well—that is, by enlarging the sheer size of school systems to a point where the classroom teacher often feels that the superintendent and board members are remote figures. This remoteness is a constant reminder to the teacher that his destiny is not within his own control, as it was in the days when everybody in the system knew the superintendent and even board members by their first names. Finally, population growth has brought many young teachers into the systems; teachers who have grown up in a time when collective handling of management-employee relations has been pretty much par for the course throughout the country.

What about current events? Under this heading the leading items are: slums and sputnik. Demands on teachers have been greatly increased, first, by the need to bring up to par the education of the undereducated child who lives in a poor area; and second, by the great pressures imposed on the national educational system in the post-sputnik era. Quite naturally, these demands have made teachers feel that their role in society is more important than ever, and this awareness, in turn, has inspired many teachers to make the world safe for the teacher once and for all. To large numbers among them a collective written agreement seems to be the most effective method of nailing down their security.

As important as any factor in making teachers receptive to the idea of collective bargaining has been a sharp change in the attitude of American government itself as to the rights of public employees. This change is found at every level of government: whether it be the passage this year of the Connecticut, Washington, and Oregon statutes granting teachers collective rights; or the promulgation of Executive Order 49 by the Mayor of New York City allowing collective bargaining rights to New York City employees; or the passage by the New York State legislature of the 1962 law mandating state-wide grievance procedures; or the issuance by President Kennedy of Executive Order 10988 authorizing a varied list of bargaining rights for federal employees. Furthermore, promulgation of these orders and statutes has coincided with a nationwide drive to organize white-collar workers, with the greatest emphasis placed on the organization of governmental employees by such unions as the American Federation of State, County, and Municipal Employees.

Upon this fertile ground, enriched by history, economics, population trends and government attitudes, have fallen the seeds of rivalry between the two major teacher organizations. They are, of course, the National Education Association on the one hand and the American Federation of Teachers on the other. In the dynamics of bargaining it has long since been clear that, when rivals face an opponent, the rivals do not join forces but strive to outbid each other *at the expense of their common opponent*. It is regrettably true that this lesson applies as fully in the field of teacher-board relations as it does in the commercial world. The result of the current rivalry is, therefore, to put added pressures on boards of education and taxpayers. This is not to say that the rivalry of the Association and the Federation may not produce healthy results; but it does mean that the results obtained may be unduly influenced by so-called "political" factors, and it also means that the process of collectivization has been dramatically accelerated.

This is no mere surmise. It is corroborated by increased militancy on the parts both of the Association and the Federation: the creation and implementation by the Association of its so-called Urban Project, and the drive for organization—supplemented by the use, if necessary, of strikes—in the case of the Federation. Nor is this small scale activity. It is big stuff. The Industrial Union Department of the AFL-CIO has offered to match Teachers' Unions' funds dollar for dollar to the tune of a one million dollar goal. *The New York Times* has reported that Charles Cogen, president of the AFT, "is planning drives in big and little cities to bring about collective bargaining contracts similar to those of New York City. The goals include Philadelphia, Boston, Detroit, Milwaukee, Newark, Yonkers, New Rochelle and the 120 school districts in Nassau and Suffolk Counties."

Now is this all bad? Not necessarily so. At least, not in the view of a number of states and of some large school systems such as, for example, New York, Milwaukee, Rochester, Yonkers, New Rochelle. In varying degrees these states and school systems have accepted the principle of collective relations with their teachers, whether merely by holding elections to certify a collective representative or by going all the way to a written agreement. Board members or administrators to whom this subject is new may very well ask why other school systems have agreed to collective relations with teachers when up to recent months no law required them to do so. There are various answers, which include:

First: A view of the legitimacy of the collective bargaining approach.

Growing numbers of legislators and public administrators are coming to believe that it is as legitimate for relations of public employees to be administered on a collective basis as it is for private employees; *provided*—and this is vital—that appropriate safeguards are applied which recognize the public employee's special responsibility to the community. Board members and school administrators are in many cases among those who share the "legitimacy view"—the view that is expressed in the Connecticut, Washington, and Oregon statutes, in President Kennedy's Executive Order, in New York State's Grievance Procedure Act, in the Wisconsin Public Employees Act, and in the Executive Order of the Mayor of New York City.

Next: A second impelling factor in the minds of many board members and administrators is the need to bring order out of existing disorder, as, for instance, where the rivalry of the Association and the Federation—sometimes complicated by the third-party rivalry of a local unaffiliated organization—becomes intense. Board members and administrators find themselves meeting with representatives of not just one group but of two or three. This state of affairs before long becomes intolerable, and the average board member or administrator, who has plenty of night work without having to double or triple it, naturally seeks relief from what may be or become a chaotic state of affairs.

Third: Sometimes it seems clear that sooner or later a collective arrangement will inevitably have to be worked out. In such instances boards of education, like many private employers, have themselves suggested the idea of a teachers' election in the hope that the more acceptable group will prevail if an election is held now, whereas an election later on would have a less "satisfactory" result.

Recent experience, then, has irrefutably demonstrated that there may be positive reasons which impel boards of education and their administrators to favor collective dealings with their teachers. To these boards collective relations make sense *in their situation*. To others, however—still by far the majority—the rigidities and limitations of authority necessarily involved are considered neither desirable nor appropriate in the educational field.

Let us examine the procedures which should be followed in either case; starting with school systems which favor the collective principle.

What should a board do if it decides that for it the time of collective arrangement has arrived? The first thing it should do is to realize that, whether the new set-up is called "collective bargaining," as the Federation terms it, or "professional negotiation," as the Association describes it, the board is moving into a new and highly technical area. In this field most administrators and policy makers—and even general school board attorneys—have had little or no experience—if for no other reason than that there simply has been very little experience anywhere in the country. This difficulty is compounded by the fact that—in contrast with *industrial* labor relations—practically no substantive law exists which governs the subject.

In order to solve the problem caused by the technicality of the subject, the lack of legal standards (where a statute does not exist—that is, almost everywhere) and the dearth of experience, various boards have brought in outside experts to help them in getting a program launched. These include legal advisers to the board and impartial experts whose job it is to recommend the arrangements under which an election should be held. The function of such experts is of substantial importance, not only in determining which professional employees should be included in a collective unit—that is, for example, whether classroom teachers only or other categories as well—but also in avoiding any accusation of board partiality toward a favored organization. Finally, in conducting an orderly and valid election, an expert —like Dr. Nathan Feinsinger, Professor of Law at the University of Wisconsin and former chairman of the Wage Stabilization Board, who assisted the City of New York; or Benjamin Wolf, a former member of the New York State Mediation Board and professor at the New York State School of Industrial and Labor Relations at Cornell, who helped out in New Rochelle— determines not only which professional employees should be included in "the unit" but what choices appear on ballots, how a winner is determined, and what the physical arrangements for holding the election and canvassing the vote should be. He is *the administrator* of the election.

The very term "certification election" may be new to many in this audience. What is its significance? Certification of a representative of the employees signifies that it is *the* agent in the dealings of teachers with the board. Certification is therefore the key purpose of elections authorized by boards which wish to protect themselves from the impossible situation of having to deal with more than one group. For some school systems who believe that the collective principle is right for them, certification has been the end of the line—at least in the sense that no formal agreement has followed. For others, certification is a prelude to the writing of an agreement which governs the relations of the board and teachers on specified subjects for a definite period of time. Undoubtedly this audience will be interested in knowing the subjects that may be included in such an agreement. No better or more complete sample can be found than the agreement between the New York City Board of Education and the United Federation of Teachers, which covers the following items in 56 printed pages: union recognition; non-discrimination; salaries; working conditions—with some 70 subheads covering such matters as teaching periods, equipment maintenance, relief from nonteaching chores, teacher programs, special teachers, lunch periods, preparation periods, class size limitation, transfers, substitute teachers, sabbatical leaves, leaves without pay, sick leave, medical expenses, vacation pay, school conferences, withdrawals of resignations, assistance in assault cases, pension and retirement programs, military service, jury duty, telephone facilities and vending machines, and school hours; program guidelines; rotation of teachers; grievance procedure; restrictions of union activities; leaves of absence for union officers; check-offs; bulletin boards; union meetings; and so on.

While the New York contract is undoubtedly the most detailed in the country, other agreements, whether with Association or Federation affiliates, tend to cover much the same ground.

By far the most important subject which any board will have to deal with in the event that it enters into a written agreement—whether with an Association or a Federation affiliate—is the extent, if any, to which disputes relating either to the negotiation process or to grievances shall be referred to some person or body outside the school system itself. In such a sensitive area, where so little experimentation has yet occurred, it is not surprising that no consensus has yet developed. Approaches to the problem vary from making no provision whatsoever for referring disputes to outsiders to provision for binding arbitration. Other shades in the spectrum include:

First: Mere fact finding—in which an outside person or agency makes determinations of fact in a disputed situation and publicizes its determinations; or

Second: Mediation—in which an outside person or agency is authorized to exercise influence or persuasion upon the parties, but not to compel a solution; or

Third: Advisory arbitration—in which a person or agency appointed by agreement of the parties has the right to hold hearings and make an award which is, however, merely advisory to the parties but not binding or obligatory upon them.

It goes without saying that a board of education which agrees that its disputes may be subjected to any of these procedures should be fully aware that, although it may not be *obliged* to follow the suggestions of fact-finders, mediators, or advisory arbitrators, it will in many instances be under strong public pressure to do so.

Since each school system has its own personality and its own history, it would be impossible in this discussion to review the items which should or should not be included in an agreement for a particular system. Suffice it to say that school systems which do enter into collective bargaining with their teachers must anticipate that they will be asked to negotiate on many, if not all, of the subjects covered by the New York City contract. Your own experience undoubtedly tells you what matters are closest to the hearts of your own teachers.

These, then, are the responsibilities which school systems entering into collective dealings have to assume and discharge. Except in a very few states no legal compulsion exists, but the increased zeal of teachers, supplemented by changes in public attitudes, is resulting in pressures which many boards feel it is appropriate to accommodate. Where this is the case, boards and administrators must be intelligent, workmanlike and impartial in discharging responsibilities to teachers, students and taxpayers alike.

It is now time to take a look at that large majority of school districts that continue to feel that collective dealings are inappropriate in the educational field, and who believe that such arrangements with teachers would not simplify their problems but, on the contrary, would complicate them.

What course of action should such boards follow in order to cope with existing pressures without being overrun by them?

The first precept is simple but nevertheless deserves reiteration: that is, the constant recognition of the professional aspirations of the teachers. These aspirations are varied and numerous, and it is safest to assume that they are *all* important. They include, of course, salaries; then, all the many items that are loosely described as "working conditions"; and finally, matters which relate to educational policy itself—the clearest example of which is the question of class size.

Next: Of equal importance to keeping abreast of teacher thinking is the development of a procedure for *regular* and *adequate* communication among teachers, administration, and board. Such consultation, if it is as effective as it should be to have any value, will prove as advantageous to the administration and the board as to the teachers. If the communication is to be meaningful, the board should see to it that the teachers who speak for their colleagues are *truly* representative both of the categories of teachers and the points of view within the system. Administrators and boards should encourage straight talk by teachers. It is of no value to a board to be led down the garden path by the smiles of yes-men only to read in the local papers that a splinter group of teachers is pushing for different and more militant objectives.

It should be the purpose of administrations and boards in such a situation to *anticipate* the problems of their staff and to *prevent* difficulties rather than to indulge in cures which are almost always more expensive in dollars and human relations. It is plain common sense that if teachers are happy with the existing situation they will not need new remedies. The best advice in any situation, therefore, is to keep your teachers happy. Obviously, this must not be at the expense of the students nor the unreasonable sacrifice of the community. But while all generalizations are risky, it nevertheless remains true that the American teacher who is convinced of the sincerity of effort of administrators, boards, and taxpayers is not likely to press demands unreasonably or at the expense of his students.

It would be presumptuous for an outsider to suggest to you a program for assuring the satisfaction of your teachers. You are the experts on this subject. If you are not, now is the time to begin to be.

We have talked about boards of education who feel that collective dealings make sense for their systems, and others who do not. One element, it seems to me, is vital in either case: that is, preserving and strengthening the position of the superintendent and his staff. These men, we should remember, are the only people in the game who can be expected truly to understand *all* of the dynamics of the situation—to understand fully both the objectives of the teachers and of the board.

So the wise board will see to it that the superintendent is in the forefront as the board's agent, whether in formal negotiations or informal situations, and the board will insure the superintendent's presence in all discussions between board members and teachers.

The wise board will also avoid the pitfall of sheer negativism. The winds abroad today cannot be blown back, and if the waves are lapping against your beach you will be no King Canute.

The more experience accrues on the subject of collective board-teacher relations, the more it indicates that basic human motivations cause and produce the same results here as in the private sector of our society; and so, sheer negativism will be no more successful than it has been in industrial relations. On the contrary, whether undertaken by individual boards or groups of a board, the negative approach may well trigger a more militant response from teachers. Some people view this year's developments as the result of such militancy.

In spite of the obvious difficulties involved in these "new forces in board-professional staff relationships," we can nevertheless look forward to the prospect of a good future.

We cannot, of course, return—in the province of education any more than in any other—to the days or attitudes of the one-room school house.

But we are presented with an exciting challenge, a challenge to teachers, administrators, board members, lawyers, and law makers—to create a new and higher standard of conduct in the solution of matters of collective and mutual concern.

Educators at every level rightly consider themselves to be professional men and women and to be involved in an activity which is central to the welfare of the community. Today teachers and boards of education alike properly ask the community to spend new billions of dollars and a higher percentage of the community's resources in pursuit of improved educational standards. The community is responsive, but on its part it asks a high sense of responsibility from all who participate in the educational process. Boards of education and teachers have before them a great opportunity: to prove that when the complexities of modern life require collective solutions, the process will not be approached with hostility and inflexibility, but with the gracious assumption that reason and good faith exist on both sides. Above all, educators must set as their undeviating standard an improved education and a better life for the students whose whole destinies they shape. If this measure is applied, the future of board-professional staff relations will be creative and fruitful, whatever the precise course that is followed.

V-2

SPEAKING FOR MANAGEMENT*

Bernard E. Donovan

I always thought the superintendent was the leader of the teachers, but I am told now that I am not. I am now the arm of management. This may be true, but I can't believe that management in a school system can be compared to management in industry.

I would like to tell you what some of us feel as the result of several years of experience with negotiations or collective bargaining or whatever you prefer to call it.

In the first place, I think we just have to decide that negotiation is here to stay—period. I'm not arguing whether negotiation is good or bad. It's here. Our problem is to live with it, not to talk about whether we'll have it or not.

Those of you who do not have it now, watch out tomorrow morning. Particularly those of you who are complacent—those of you who look in the mirror and say: "This couldn't happen to me. It happens to the other superintendent because his personnel methods are not good, but my people love me." You're going to be the first one that will get hit with collective bargaining.

I am not here to discuss from management's point of view, whether the teachers of this nation should organize in unions or in professional groups. I firmly believe that that's the teacher's business and not mine. And if the teachers in one locality choose to organize professionally and in another locality choose to organize in a union, I think that is the teacher's business. Therefore, no matter what the type of organization—and I must say with all due respect to my learned colleagues here on each end of the table that these days I can't tell them apart when they campaign—I am going to pose for you four or five problems that management faces when negotiating with the teaching profession.

First, the problem arises as to where do working conditions end and

* Bernard E. Donovan, "Speaking for Management," in "Collective Bargaining vs. Professional Negotiation," *School Management* (November, 1965), pp. 69-72. Dr. Donovan is Superintendent, New York City Schools.

where does educational policy begin. I will give you an example: What is class size? Is it a working condition, or is it a matter of educational policy? If you think it over, you will find it is a gray area. There are elements in it that have to do with a teacher's working conditions, in terms of load. But there are also elements in it that have to do with the proper number of children that can be handled for a specific type of subject under particular circumstances. Therefore, in our city, we have so far supported the stand that class size by itself is not something that we will put into an agreement, but we will put in a maximum, what we call an intolerable maximum, class size. Not an average, not a median, but an *intolerable maximum* which we believe becomes a working condition for a teacher.

Another example of this would be the rotation of teaching assignments. The demand is that teaching assignments be rotated. As far as I am concerned, speaking for management, rotation is not the type of thing that is done in education. Every English teacher can *not* teach every English class. Every English teacher can *not* teach journalism. Every English teacher can *not* teach dramatics. Every English teacher is *not* equally capable of handling the honors class. So that automatic rotation as a principle to me is not something that we could consider, unless we were to give up our desire to serve the children with the most effective type of teaching in the classroom.

Now, it is good to open up opportunities to teachers. It is good to move teachers around, to give them a chance to teach the special classes, but always knowing that you have selected a teacher for the teacher's strength and not merely for his seniority.

The second item that I think is important is *the very damaging effect on the schools of what seems to be the class struggle between the teacher and the supervisor.* To some extent, supervisors and administrators have become anathema to the classroom teachers. It is felt that the organization of teachers must be just that of classroom teachers, and that supervisors and administrators don't belong in the organization, because they are part of this managerial class. I don't believe that. I know that the AFT has criticized the NEA for a long time, for just that point—that it has had supervisors and administrators in it, along with teachers, and that they have dominated it. Well, I'm not going to enter that argument. But I don't believe that there is a division possible within a school system between the teacher and supervisor if the child is going to be taught effectively. There is bitterness in a school when that happens. In our city it got to the point where the administrators organized, and are now recognized for collective bargaining by the board of education—the heads of departments, the assistant principals, the principals, and even the assistant superintendents. (I'm the only one who is not organized at the moment. But when I get back, I'll take care of that.)

I firmly believe, on the side of management, that educational leadership is necessary. The administrator has a role to play that is important. I know about democracy in the school. I am in favor of it. I am more in favor of it than all the professors who have taught it as theory in many education courses, but have rarely seen it in practice in our schools. But democracy, too, needs leadership. And good supervisors and good administrators—who once, by the way, were classroom teachers—are needed in the schools. I don't think that we can just ignore them and make them clerks in the organization.

The third of the five things, is the negotiation process itself. The negotiation process is time-consuming. In our city we had 54 sessions between March and June lasting three or four hours each. And they were good sessions and they were on important matters. But it is time-consuming. The superintendent is supposed to be the negotiating agent for the board of education. It's a little difficult to take that much time negotiating and still operate a school system. If you are a financially independent district perhaps you can settle matters at the board level, because you raise the taxes for it. If you are in a city like New York, where you are financially dependent upon the city, you can never settle at the board level under present negotiation practices because the purse strings are in the hands of the city government and not the board of education. So it goes beyond the board of education.

Now, I would allude to one other matter in negotiation. *One of the most difficult parts of the negotiation process is cliff-hanging.* "If this doesn't work, we'll strike." "If *this* doesn't work, we'll strike,"—cliff-hanging to the last day so that you don't know whether the schools will open or not open. It pushes decisions that are important into hasty conclusions, sometimes not good for the teachers themselves. Because hasty decisions in matters of import are wrong, and cliff-hanging is not a good procedure, I must say on behalf of the union in our city that, after our past three experiences—and this is the third agreement we have concluded—we both agree that this type of negotiation cannot continue. Negotiations must be shorter, more to the point and concluded *before* we get to the cliff. I hope this will happen. I see signs of us working together better. I just hope it continues to work that way.

Now, lastly, there is *an element in here that is causing us a little difficulty and that is, "What is the right of the public in the matter of teacher negotiations?"* Here we sit and negotiate with the teachers and we come to an agreement that uses up the budget. And then the public comes to a board meeting and asks: "What about maintenance? What about text books? What about improving transportation? What about some innovative programs? Where is the money for it?" At the moment, we have to say there isn't any. Now, I'm not saying this should be blamed on the teachers, please. The blame has to be shared. Part of it is because the public itself doesn't really finance education the way it should for everything it wants out of education. But on the other hand, when the board negotiates with teachers and it is forced to use more money for salaries and working conditions than it felt it could use, then you must take that money from something else. And this is what the public is asking about.

I'll close by repeating the remark, "Negotiation is here to stay." I think in the long run that if the voice of the teacher is heard—if the voice of the teacher is admitted to the councils of administration—it will be good for the school system.

Too often we have mouthed the idea that you should consult with the faculty and then we have gaily moved on our way without doing so. Or else we call "consultation" telling them at the last minute what it is you're going to do. And that is called consultation. That is *not* consultation. That is dictatorship. So I think that if we give teachers proper voice, we will strengthen the schools after a period of some stress.

The stress will be largely for the administrators because when you have an able group of teachers, talking to you on a new level of authority, you very often feel your control slipping. It is difficult to yield a little authority. It is just as difficult for the administrator as it is for the teacher in the classroom. The autocratic teacher has a much easier job, than does the one who lets the children join in the activities of the class.

I think we have to set up a more effective negotiation process. I think that we have to remember that our first allegiance is *not* to the teachers, it is to the students. The teachers come close behind that. But students come first.

Last, I think that as the teachers' organizations mature—and maybe as we mature with them—education as we argue it will be more than salaries and working conditions. There are signs now of teachers' organizations willing to take up the other aspects of recruitment and internship and effective teaching and better schools. That is the hope of the future.

V-3

THE ROLE OF THE SUPERINTENDENT IN TEACHER NEGOTIATIONS*

Alden H. Blankenship

One of the more complex problems facing the superintendent of schools today is the identification of his proper role in the area of teacher negotiations. Can he serve effectively as the executive officer of the board of education and provide professional leadership as well as administrative direction to the staff? Is it proper for the superintendent to serve only as a fact-finder for both the board and the staff and to refuse to act as a negotiator for any party? Is the desire of some teacher organization leaders to negotiate directly with the school board and to bypass the superintendent a development that should be encouraged? These and related questions have not been answered to everyone's satisfaction.

In part, the role of the superintendent is determined by our basic philosophy of education and, in part, by the basic guidelines and principles that implement this philosophy. This assumption points up the importance of a clear statement of philosophy and an understanding of how this philosophy can be implemented.

Most educators are willing to accept the view that public education is a joint responsibility of the profession and the public. There is little argument with the view that most boards of education, most administrators, and most teachers are sincerely interested in the best possible education for children. Each has a unique contribution to make toward this common goal, and all must share the responsibility for its attainment.

The growing tendency to expect the school board to recognize formally the role of teacher organizations seems to be consistent with the basic principles of a democratic society. It follows that the superintendent expects the teachers, through their representatives, to have an opportunity to participate in the formulation of policy that affects their welfare and their role in

* Reprinted by permission from *Theory Into Practice*, (April, 1965) pp. 70-74. Alden H. Blankenship is Director of Administrative Services, Educational Research Council of Greater Cleveland.

teaching, when they are willing to accept the obligations and responsibilities of participants.

The wise board recognizes that the success of the school system is dependent to a very large extent upon the quality of the school staff. The board members' desire to obtain the views and advice of teachers before the adoption of policies by the board is consistent with the established role of the superintendent—as executive officer of the board and chief professional advisor to the board. Neither does it negate the role of the superintendent in giving professional leadership and administrative direction to the staff. Such a procedure does not mean that teachers bypass the superintendent in the process. The desired results can be accomplished if the superintendent obtains the facts, analyzes the data, summarizes the expressed opinions of the teachers, and is then prepared to make his own recommendations to the board.

At the meeting when the superintendent's recommendations are presented for action and before the board makes its decision, the representatives of the teachers should have the opportunity to speak on the topic and present any additional views to all of the board members in an orderly manner. In the final analysis, the board should be expected to accept, reject, or modify the recommendations of the superintendent.

This makes it extremely important for the superintendent to provide the facts and related data to the board. In turn, it is necessary for the superintendent and/or his representatives to consult with recognized teacher representatives on items of interest to them in ample time for them to study the facts and prepare materials that would represent their best thinking before a recommendation is made. This approach provides the professional teacher with an opportunity to play a part in shaping policies, and it also enables the school system to benefit from the special talents and abilities of the staff in improving the program.

The superintendent has an important communication role in relation to other matters affecting the staff. It is essential that the necessary facts and information be made available to staff representatives if they are to act wisely and objectively regarding the matters that affect them. In this process, the wise superintendent must recognize both the informal and the formal communications structure.

Many superintendents feel that present staff-superintendent-board relationships are so good that they need not be concerned about the development of basic policies regarding these relationships, which are clearly stated in writing and formally adopted by the board. Regardless of the excellent relationships that exist in many school systems, the establishment of written policies and procedures merits careful consideration by the superintendent and the board. If such policies and procedures are established in a climate of mutual trust and respect, they can be evaluated objectively. It is always possible for the climate to be changed—school board elections or appointments sometimes result in the selection of one or more board members whose chief interests or ambitions are not consistent with a quality education program. This is especially true when a new board member is "power-hungry," careless about public comments, or has an "ax to grind."

If written policies and procedures are developed while everyone can be objective about relationships, these policies and procedures may help to avoid some of the misunderstandings and tensions that can result from this type of change in climate. They can also furnish guidelines for new school board members and new administrators as they approach the problems related to teacher negotiations.

One important responsibility of the superintendent in the area of employee relationships is that of helping the board develop a policy that clarifies the role of employee organizations and the freedom of the individual employee to choose the organization to which he wishes to belong or not belong, as he sees fit. This is a part of the superintendent's role as a professional advisor. A related responsibility is that of helping board members to understand and respect the fact that no individual should be coerced, intimidated, or discriminated against because of membership or nonmembership in a professional organization. In the policy that is finally developed, it should be clearly understood that the superintendent, as a professional leader of the staff, should encourage employees to join the professional organizations of their own choice.

The superintendent, as executive officer of the board, should be expected to represent the board in all matters of concern to the employee organizations or to the individual member. This means that the superintendent and his personnel assistants from the administrative staff should handle the negotiations with organization representatives. Therefore, the superintendent and/or one or more of his assistants—depending on the size of the school system—need experience and training in negotiation procedures and techniques. In fact, in medium and large school systems, it seems wise for the superintendent to advise the board to send one or more able, mature younger assistants to one of the few universities offering special training in negotiation techniques. These individuals could then develop and sharpen the skills needed in negotiations; this practice could result in a continuously improved educational program for pupils and a stimulating environment for teachers.

As of February 1965, some 350 to 500 school systems were reported to have agreements with teacher organization representatives for some type of exclusive bargaining rights to negotiate for the teachers. This illustrates the need for prompt action in preparing the superintendent and/or his assistants to be effective negotiators. There is no longer time for administrators to learn negotiating techniques by the trial and error method.

Many of the more experienced superintendents have already developed some "know-how" by negotiating with the representatives of teacher organizations, of various noncertificated employee unions, and of craft unions representing maintenance employees. Nevertheless, there is still much to be learned in the area of teacher negotiations. An early lesson to be learned is that negotiations can no longer be regarded as a one-man job. Having one or more assistants present at negotiating sessions means there will be less opportunity for some important element to be overlooked or misinterpreted.

It is the practice of many superintendents to present, very early in discussions with teacher representatives, what they believe the school system can do to improve salary schedules and working conditions for the coming year. Recent experiences indicate that in situations where one teacher organization has exclusive bargaining rights the teacher representative has said, in effect: "All right, we will begin negotiations from this point and go on from there." This reaction has tended to cause some trauma when the superintendent had already suggested what was, in his best professional judgment, a very fair solution to the salary and working conditions problem. He can avoid this problem by understanding the representatives' request at the beginning of their talks.

Another reaction that has surprised some superintendents has been the fact that teacher representatives have resented a superintendent's recommendation which gave additional benefits to teachers, but which had not been negotiated. Undoubtedly, part of this reaction by the representatives comes from their desire to say to the members of the organization, "See what we were able to negotiate for you!" However, this reaction can also be attributed to their sincere belief that a discussion of proposed recommendations will result in even *better* policies, after teachers' reactions have been considered.

The superintendent is often due for a "letdown" if he expects staff members to recognize his contributions to an improved salary schedule that has been adopted by the board. The representatives of the teacher organization generally will take the credit for these improvements. This seems to be a universal practice, but the superintendent should not interpret it to mean that his role is unimportant.

After several years' experience in negotiating with both teacher organization representatives and noncertificated employee organizations, I have identified a few techniques that seem to have merit. It is desirable to request the organization representatives to present a list of the items they wish to negotiate. The superintendent and his assistants should also present a list of items that the administration wants to have considered in the negotiating sessions—e.g., flexible schedules, methods of eliminating the individual who is not producing, techniques for dealing with the unprofessional staff member, in-service professional development requirements, carelessness in speech, habits, and dress. Negotiations can proceed more effectively if an up-to-date progress report is presented at the end of each negotiating session—covering the teacher representative's requests, the superintendent's requests, and the areas in which no progress has been made.

The superintendent who respects the rights of teachers listens with care to the ideas, requests, suggestions, and desires of the staff. He presents the facts and projects the results of the teachers' requests. Then he makes a sincere and honest effort to reach a fair agreement. In this process, he tends to give the highest priority to the welfare of boys and girls, then to the welfare of the staff and to the ability of the community to meet these needs.

In his role as professional leader of the staff and as advisor to the board, the superintendent helps the staff and the board recognize the need for developing proper communication procedures which route all correspondence and inquiries from organizations through his office. If the situation indicates that some of these items should be presented to the board, the superintendent should present them along with the related facts and his recommendation, if one is indicated.

Another important role of the superintendent and his assistants who are participating in negotiations is to keep all participants aware of the legislative responsibility of the board of education. Essentially this means that in spite of the stresses and strains that may affect attitudes and emotions during negotiations, both the superintendent and the teacher representative must be objective and remember that the final legislative responsibility for policy action in the school district rests with the school board, which is also responsible for making decisions in compliance with state statutes.

In his role as professional advisor to the board, the superintendent should accept the responsibility for providing opportunities for teacher representatives to meet with the entire board at appropriate times to discuss matters related to teacher welfare and educational problems. The superintendent should be present at these sessions and probably should introduce the representatives to the board. Individual board members should maintain a policy of refusing to meet with individual staff members to discuss individual welfare problems.

The superintendent should advise the board on the development of a fair grievance procedure. This policy should clearly outline the sequential steps in the procedure, emphasizing face-to-face action to find a solution as close as possible to the origin of the problem.

There are many related areas where the role of the superintendent needs clarification. Within the next few months or years, many superintendents will face the problem of their role in relation to representatives' requests for teacher elections for exclusive bargaining rights. As the superintendent makes his decisions, he should be aware that representatives of each competing teacher organization will be extremely sensitive to any actions that might be interpreted to mean that he favors the objectives of the opposition organization. Some organization leaders feel that superintendents who have attempted to be fair and objective toward all teacher organizations have, in reality, done a disservice to the organizations. Some feel that management is overstepping its role if any action—intentional or unintentional—can be interpreted to mean that administrative authority is being used to influence teacher actions.

Regardless of individual interpretations, the superintendent may take some positive steps in his role as professional advisor to the board and as the individual responsible for providing professional leadership for the staff. These positive actions should be taken before the superintendent and board are pushed into action in an atmosphere that is not conducive to objective thinking and planning.

It is a primary responsibility of the superintendent to be familiar with the state statutes concerning teacher negotiations, exclusive bargaining rights, and board contracts with organization representatives. He should be certain that he, the board, and the staff representatives understand the best legal interpretations of these statutes. If any profession is to expect respect for law and order, it should be the profession that has so much to do with molding the attitudes and developing the understandings of tomorrow's citizens.

It seems logical for the superintendent who believes in democracy to develop procedures that provide staff members with the opportunity to share in the development of policy recommendations that affect them and their working conditions. An effective method is to establish building, area, or system advisory councils to administration. This need not be done on a teacher organization basis, but rather should provide opportunities for all professional personnel to be represented—i.e., primary, intermediate, junior high, high school, special education, vocational education, and administrative staff, as well as teacher organizations. The council organization framework should be patterned to the size of the school system. In addition, it seems only logical for the superintendent to recommend to the board that it recognize each organization as representing the members of that organization and that their leaders be informed of any proposed policies affecting them before these policies are approved. This implies that procedures should be developed to identify the members of each organization.

It is also the superintendent's responsibility to be aware of outside resources that may be helpful in providing advice, information, or assistance. One resource that is available in many situations is the board member who has had experience in negotiations. Other resources may be available through schools of education, administrators' organizations, study councils, and research organizations.

If the school district situation is such that an election to determine exclusive bargaining rights is still demanded, the superintendent, as a professional educator, should make an objective analysis of the disadvantages and dangers as well as the advantages and possible values. If it is finally determined that an election seems to be the only practical solution, the superintendent and his negotiating assistants must be well-informed about procedures and methods and make every effort to see that the board is equally well-informed. They also have a major responsibility to make every effort to see that the election results will not damage educational opportunities for the children.

As a professional leader, the superintendent and his assistants also have a significant role in helping negotiators maintain a continual awareness of the necessity of avoiding negotiated agreements which, in the long run, will downgrade the education profession. This awareness can be maintained, in part, by an agreement on what is negotiable, what is fair, and what effects the long-range results of agreements will have on the schools and the community.

If a school board approves a contract giving exclusive bargaining rights to a professional organization, the superintendent has the moral responsibility both as executive officer of the board and as professional leader of the staff to see that all phases of the agreement are correctly and efficiently administered.

Superintendents throughout the country are currently entering some perilous and unknown areas of controversy in regard to board-administrator relationships. Their success will be determined in large part by their courage, integrity, patience, and sincerity. Their skills in human relationships and administration must be augmented by ability, sound judgment, and determined leadership.

V-4

IMPLICATION OF COLLECTIVE NEGOTIATIONS
FOR THE ROLE OF THE PRINCIPAL*

Luvern L. Cunningham

Charles Perry and Wesley Wildman concluded from their recent survey of collective activity in education that (1) collective action on the part of employees in education is growing, (2) that school administration will have an increasing rather than decreasing set of responsibilities vis-a-vis collective behavior; and (3) that the ultimate impact of collective activities on school systems is not known.[1] These remarks this morning are addressed to the last of these three observations. More specifically, I am attempting to clarify the impact of collective teacher activity on the role of the principal, and to improve our understanding of how principals might respond to these new facts of their administrative lives.

In preparation for this presentation, I invited three advanced graduate students in educational administration to assist me with the collection of some data about how principals were reacting to collective activity on the part of teacher groups.[2] The content of this paper is based rather directly on the perceptions of a small number of principals, as well as others involved in collective negotiations gathered through the interview process. Interviews were conducted with principals and other administrators in Illinois, Indiana, and Michigan. The statements reported here are tentative at best and in some cases are imbedded in emotion since some of the principals interviewed were then involved in situations where teacher militancy was pronounced.

* Paper delivered at the Seminar on Professional Negotiation in Public Education cosponsored by the National Education Association and the Graduate School of Education, University of Chicago, August 3, 1966. Luvern L. Cunningham is Dean, College of Education, Ohio State University (as of September, 1967).
    [1] Charles A. Perry and Wesley A. Wildman, "A Survey of Collective Activity among Public School Teachers," *Educational Administration Quarterly,* Vol. II (Spring, 1966), pp. 150-151.
    [2] The interview team was chaired by Bernard Watson, Staff Associate, Midwest Administration Center. The other interviewers were Thomas Maguire and Richard Smock, second year fellows in a special training program supported through a grant from the National Institute of Mental Health. The team also assisted in the preparation of this paper.

The first section of this paper contains a brief report on how principals perceive the behaviors of teachers, superintendents, boards and others involved in collective activity. The second section is directed toward an analysis of the impact of collective action on the principal's role in organizational terms, and an attempt to suggest responses available to principals as they encounter collective activity in their schools. Conclusions and summation constitute the final section.

In an article appearing in the January, 1966, issue of the *Phi Delta Kappan*[3] Wildman and Perry comment that it is the school principal who stands to lose freedom when negotiations include certain areas of administrative discretion. They were referring especially to bargaining on matters of class size; the extent to which seniority is to be used as a criterion for assignment to classes, promotions, and transfers; tranfer policies in general; the distribution of teaching and nonteaching assignments; the collection of textbook rentals; and the length of the teaching day. Our interviews with principals would support those observations. In fact we encountered a climate of considerable disquiet and uneasiness among principals and suspect that these feelings extend much beyond the extremely limited number of persons with whom we talked.[4]

HOW PRINCIPALS VIEW COLLECTIVE TEACHER BEHAVIOR

During our interviews only two of the principals perceived positive outcomes from the altered principal-teacher relationships caused by the increased teacher militancy. With these two exceptions principals stated that it would be more difficult for them to supervise the instructional process in individual buildings, and that the search for power among teachers was an attempt to usurp the prerogatives of the building principal, the individual who is legally responsible for the educational program. One respondent suggested that his discretion might be so reduced that he would spend most of his time "signing papers."

In one upper middle-class suburb a high school principal noted increased difficulty in supervising staff during the period of intensive bargaining between the board of education and the teachers' organization. According to this principal, teachers were less inclined to accept administrative direction without question, the level of cooperation and the quality of teaching declined, and the staff appeared to be interested in becoming involved in the determination of building policy. Each of these developments was viewed

[3] Wesley A. Wildman and Charles A. Perry, "Group Conflict and School Organization," *Phi Delta Kappan*, Vol. XLVII (January, 1966), p. 250.

[4] Robert E. Doherty, "Documents," *Industrial and Labor Relations Review*, Vol. 19, No. 4 (July, 1966), pp. 573-595.

as a threat to his authority and autonomy as principal. And in his view restrictions on his autonomy and authority threaten the functioning of a viable educational program.

There was general agreement among administrators that the leadership of the militant teachers consisted of young, married men in secondary schools, and that many of them aspired to supervisory and administrative positions in the school system. In only one district were the leaders described as "troublemakers" or "soreheads" with "an axe to grind." Interestingly, this was one of the districts where the principal did not perceive teacher militancy as threatening to his autonomy. As a matter of fact, this principal felt that many of the teachers' demands were justified and grew out of "questionable administration" within the district.

In each of the districts visited where bargaining, striking, sanctioning, or negotiating had occurred, resulting in some cases in teacher dismissals, working conditions as well as salaries were issues. In one district working conditions were the crucial issue but in other districts salary appeared to be the central concern.

It is not difficult to understand the concern of a principal when the issues at the heart of bargaining crises are linked directly to what he perceives as his prerogatives. When more than salary was at issue teachers' demands seemed to relate directly to teacher involvement in decisions concerning class size, the number of days in the school year, the determination of the school calendar, the assignment to extra-curricular paid activities, and building grievance procedures. The bargaining process itself seemed to be the central bone of contention.

Principals were attempting to deal with these matters in a variety of ways. One had appointed a faculty committee to advise him on matters of policy and procedure, but teachers had rejected his committee and had insisted on electing their own representatives to a policy body. In another district the principal had permitted the faculty to elect a seven member grievance committee. Each teacher was entitled to one vote, and the principal and his assistant had one vote between them. The committee apparently operated smoothly until the local teachers' organizations insisted upon the right to appoint its own grievance committee. Both committees functioned for a time, but the teacher's organization group eventually replaced the faculty elected committee. The principal involved stated that the teacher organization appointed committee was very effective, and the only "radical" on the committee was "kept in check" by his teacher colleagues. The "radical" eventually withdrew from the committee and applied for a transfer to another school.

The principals' salary schedule has been linked to the teachers' salary schedule in all of the districts visited. There was usually a ratio or an index arrangement for determining salaries of principals. As a result of this arrangement, teachers, when bargaining for their own salaries, were also bargaining for principals' salaries. In one of the districts teachers had consistently refused to accept the teacher salary schedule until principals were satisfied with the administrative salary schedule! Recently, however, the teachers' organization had insisted that principals bargain independently, and one of the demands of the teacher group was that the two salary schedules be separate and distinct. Principals reacted to this demand by threatening to file unfair labor practices against the teachers' organization if it persisted in this demand. The demand was withdrawn.

Another significant result of the growth of teacher power has been changes in the patterns of communication between teachers and principals. Because principals are not included in the bargaining process, they feel uninformed about issues being negotiated. Principals have attempted to deal with this situation by probing for information from individual staff members informally. Such procedures were effective in several of the districts, and principals reported that teachers freely discussed feelings, attitudes, and pertinent issues. Several principals described the teachers who discussed these matters as being "more professional" or as representing the "more conservative professional organization." Other principals stated that their teacher informants were from the militant group, and these teachers were frequently the best teachers in the system.

It seems obvious that a new pattern of relationships is emerging. Ironically in districts where teachers had not turned in their contract, principals perceived the teachers as "being over a barrel," "having made a serious mistake," or as "being out on a limb" without significant support. These opinions were expressed despite the fact that two of the districts were facing the prospects of attempting to open schools in September without a teaching staff, and that the general area was faced with the prospect of fifteen to twenty thousand teachers refusing to sign contracts. These potential actions would affect approximately six hundred thousand pupils.

RELATIONSHIPS WITHIN THE SCHOOL ORGANIZATION

Students of organizations know that the descriptive value of an organizational chart is limited, simply because the flow of power and control is often a product of informal relationships rather than strict definitions of formal line and staff offices. Such charts have limited value, then, only if power and control, or what we might call authority, is defined in legal or formal terms.

Two Views of Authority

Seen in this way, there are two authority structures in the school; one, the formal and legal delegation of authority to an office by reason of its placement in the organization line chart; the other, the informal and extra-legal delegation of power and control to an individual above and beyond the formal limitations of his office. Thus, those officers at the top of the formal organization have more legal authority than those who follow. One thinks here of the broad discretionary powers granted a board of education or superintendent. In contrast to this formal or legal authority construct, however, is that strange and wondrous phenomenon which permits individuals like the school custodian to wield power far out of proportion to his formal office. If one has any doubts about this observation he need only read Willard Waller[5] or Bel Kaufman.[6] Indeed, it is the foolhardy administrator or teacher who does not recognize the informal extra-legal authority emanating from the basement boiler room.

The growing wave of militancy in education has added to the anachronistic quality of the organizational chart. Indeed, it may even render such descriptions useless. Informal and/or extra-legal negotiating between the board and the teaching staff is becoming a commonplace in school districts across the country; agreements are being reached; control and power arrangements are shifting between and among the hierarchical levels of the school organization.

The Bargaining Teams

From the point of view of professional negotiations, the positions of the board and the teachers are relatively clear. Each is a representative body given the task of protecting certain interests which it represents. The positions of offices at various administrative levels in relation to these negotiations is by no means clear; as our interviews revealed there is deep unrest and growing frustration among administrators who see negotiations going on around them, but rarely with them.

The actual negotiating team may consist of the board of education and/or anyone it appoints as its bargaining agent. In many cases, the board will negotiate with the teachers directly, while the superintendent acts as an "advisor" for both sides; in other instances, the superintendent is designated as the official bargaining agent for the board and is empowered to effect a contract with the staff—within pre-arranged limits agreed upon by the board. When the superintendent is a member of the bargaining team, he frequently calls upon the business manager and the assistant superintendent in charge of personnel to serve with him. In any case, it is a rare negotiating team which includes a principal or other school officer from that area we affectionately label as "middle management."

[5] Willard Waller, *Sociology of Teaching*. (New York: John Wiley & Sons, 1932), Chapter VII.
[6] Bel Kaufman, *Up the Down Staircase*. (Englewood Cliffs, New Jersey: Prentice Hall, Inc., 1964).

If the voice of the principal is weak and ineffective at the board's side of the negotiating table, it has been excluded almost without exception from the other team. Although we found that most professional negotiations agreements allow for a merging of administrative and teaching personnel as a single negotiating unit vis-a-vis the board of education, a more radical cleavage between "labor" and "management" seems to be emerging. The precedent of big city AFT contracts, along with the growing sensitivity of the NEA to charges of being a "company union," has made the position of the principal within the local organization tenuous at best. In many bargaining agreements, for example, principals, department chairmen, and guidance counselors are excluded from the employees' bargaining team.[7]

Middle Management Frustrations

Regardless of how suspicious we are of analogies which link the problems of the school with the experiences of private industry, there is a parallel too close to be ignored between the first and second line supervisors of industry and the principals and department chairmen in the schools. For years, industrial supervisors, convinced of the crucial nature of their jobs in maintaining an efficient and productive operation, have stood by helplessly as new relationships between labor and management were carved out at the bargaining table without them. Without exaggerating the analogy, we can see a similar exclusion taking place in education. About all that we can say definitively is that if the principal is to be heard, he must be heard as a member of the administrative team rather than as a spokesman for the teachers.

Perhaps the best way to describe the emerging relationship among administrators is to say that whatever working accommodations now exist will not only continue, but will tend to polarize. Thus, if a superintendent allows poor communications to exist among his staff members now, it is difficult to imagine a reversal of this condition in a period when the superintendent is under great pressure. In addition, the traditional ambivalence of the superintendent's role—professional educator versus agent of the board—is very likely to be polarized in the direction of his role as agent for the board. If such is the case, his ability to protect the interests of other administrators will be hampered seriously. Teachers' organizations have already recognized this role shift and insist that their voice is the teacher's negotiating team, rather than the superintendent. Against such polarization, the principal stands out in bold relief as the "man-in-the-middle."

The spectre of two negotiating parties, neither one of which represents the principal, reaching accord by swapping such things as work rules that have been the principal's prerogative until now is the source of increased frustration, if not panic, for the building administrator. Interviews with prin-

[7] Doherty, *op cit.*

cipals from districts now negotiating contracts revealed as much disillusion-
ment and distrust with the superintendent's role as with the teachers' organization. These principals felt that the negotiating process was basically a fight
for survival, and that the first group to suffer from agreements reached at the
negotiating table were those not directly represented there. They cited examples from big-city contracts which, if implemented, could impede seriously
the smooth functioning of the school. For example, one such contract article
allows individual teachers to expel troublesome students from their classes,
presumably leaving the principal in a position of having to place in some
class that student whom no teacher wants. Principals insist that their job
must have equal parts of authority and responsibility, and that a dimunition
in authority necessarily creates problems as the principal tries to fulfill his
responsibilities.

Many of these principals felt that if they can be calm and resolute, those
bargaining agreement articles, which they interpret as undermining their
authority now, will be stricken from future contracts. We suspect that the
optimism implicit in this attitude may be comforting, but it hardly seems
realistic. The passing of power and control from administrators to teachers,
once begun, may be expected to continue until a major realignment has
occurred in the organization of the schools.

In short, the ability of the principal to survive and flourish during and
after this transition period will depend on his capacity to respond and adapt
to new circumstances. Since genuine participation of the principal in teacher
negotiations themselves seems an unlikely prospect, it will be the individual
building principal who has kept his fences mended in the important area of
principal-staff interaction and thus has won the respect of his teachers who
will ultimately prevail. The administrator who has drawn his authority from
the nature of his office rather than from personal and professional sources,
will not survive the change in authority structure.

PERSONAL VARIATIONS AMONG PRINCIPALS

Assuming then, that teacher militancy marks a move toward a change in
the authority structure of the schools, and recognizing the complex issues
impinging on the role of the principal, we can now take a closer look at the
differences among the reactions of the "men-in-the-middle." We have also
chosen to speculate about the meaning of those differences.

Our interviews led us to conclude that, while feelings about *what* was
happening to the role of the principal were consistent, the reactions—the
ideas of what to do about it—were quite different. The differences expressed
can be explained to some extent by several theoretical formulations that
researchers have developed in the recent past. In a recent study of executive

succession Carlson identified two general types of superintendents—those who were "place bound" and those who were "career bound."[8] Applying his construct of a "place bound" and "career bound" typology to principals, it may be safe to say that a "place bound" principal, one who has come up through the ranks of one particular school system, and one who views his authority as vested almost totally in the office he occupies, may feel considerably more threatened by teacher militancy than does the "career bound" principal. The "career bound" person generally shows less identification with a particular school system, and more identification toward what he conceives as a "professional" orientation concerning his role.

Another theoretical formulation seems particularly germane to a discussion of personal variables bearing on the reactions of principals to a new power alignment in the schools. Rokeach, in his book, *The Open and Closed Mind,* defines "open" and "closed" belief systems.[9] People who possess "open" belief systems are characterized as viewing authority in terms of its cognitive correctness and consistency with reliable information about the world, while those with "closed" belief systems view authority as an absolute. Principals could be placed in the "open" category who view people positively regardless of their beliefs, who possess a rational conception of power and status, who have a cognitive "need to know" that is predominate, and who feel little need to ward off threat. Principals with closed belief systems, on the other hand, probably accept or reject teachers on the basis of how congruent teachers' personal belief systems are with theirs and whether teachers have an excessive concern for power and status. They appear to have a stronger need to ward off perceived threat, and consequently a weaker cognitive "need to know."

These are descriptions of the extremes of a continuum of belief systems; it is as unlikely that a paragon of "openness" exists as it is that the archtype of the "closed" belief system exists. Nevertheless, research does indicate the presence of people with belief systems which relate to each of these extremes, and our interviews in several states seemed to confirm the concepts.[10] Principals expressed a variety of reactions to teacher militancy and they tended to express beliefs in a manner that indicated a propensity toward one or the other end of this continuum.

For instance, one such reaction was an admission of an inability, as well

[8] Richard O. Carlson, *Executive Succession and Organizational Change.* Midwest Administration Center, University of Chicago, 1961.

[9] Milton Rokeach, *The Open and Closed Mind.* (New York: Basic Books, Inc., 1960).

[10] For an example of the use of these concepts in administrative research, see Edwin M. Bridges, "Bureaucratic Role and Socialization: The Influence of Experience on the Elementary Principal," *Educational Administration Quarterly,* Vol. I (Spring, 1965), pp. 19-28.

as little desire, to cope with any radical shift in the control structure of education. "I was appointed to run this school, and just can't accept giving away my authority to teachers. I'll get out first." This principal was accustomed to being "the boss," to being recognized as the educational leader, and to making decisions. The thought of bargaining with teachers on matters traditionally thought to be in his domain was obviously repugnant. In this case, clear indicators of a "closed" belief system were present: authority is absolute, resides in the office, and is presently being threatened.

On the other hand, a few administrators rather than responding to threat believe that contracts developed by negotiation would actually expand their role, and allow them to routinize many details that had previously been handled by the more time-consuming route of individual consideration. These principals felt that their attention could now be focused on more important concerns of educational leadership, such as community involvement in the development of educational programs, and the fostering of collegial methods of attacking educational problems in the school. They possessed considerable faith in the professional integrity and general competency of teachers. When asked if there were concern about being forced to live by written roles and procedures, they were likely to reply ". . . that teachers will be bound by the rules too," and "that a bargaining contract can only result in a more uniform handling of problems from which we will all benefit."

We have under way at the present time a healthy "national" concern in regard to the role of the principal. At the University of Chicago, Donald Erickson has been writing about the changing role of the principal for the last three or four years. In his analysis, the "instructional leader" model is archaic and must be replaced by a new role conception which defines the responsibilities of the principal in different terms. He is suggesting that the role of the principal cannot remain static in a society marked by accelerating rates of change. The role must be modified if it is to retain its vitality in today's institutional structure.[11]

In a recent paper entitled "The Principal as Administrator," Erickson described six images which principals seem to have of themselves.[12] The *first* of these is the principal as housekeeper. The housekeeper has a smooth-operating building, details are cared for, the premises are neat and clean, and he takes pride in those surroundings. This type of principal would probably not be terribly upset by teacher negotiations. The *second* is the principal as "Daddy." In this case the principal is seen as the teachers' protector: the man who stands between the teachers and the community, the person who runs interference for them and is counsel for the defense in those instances

[11] Donald A. Erickson, "Forces for Change in the Principalship," *The Elementary School Journal,* Vol. XLV (November, 1964), pp. 57-64.

[12] Donald A. Erickson, *"The Principal as Administrator." Mimeographed,* 1966.

where the school is under attack. The "Daddy" type would be shattered by collective action because his teachers would no longer have need for his protective services.

The *third* is the image of the principal as a "super-teacher," and this, Erickson believes, marks the elementary school more vividly than it does other levels of the school organization. The "super-teacher" image incorporates the expectations that the principal has been a polished, experienced, effective teacher prior to entering the principalship and that once entrenched in the role can pass on all of the secrets of his success to those with whom he must associate. The "super-teacher" image is totally incompatible with teacher militancy; he would be caught squarely in the middle of the clash between bureaucratic and collegial authority systems.

A *fourth* image is the principal as foreman. The foreman is the supervisor—the person that sees that teachers follow advice he provides or that other responsible superiors provide. The foreman's fate, like the "super-teachers' " is uncertain under conditions of collective action. He may be asked to administer policies, rules and regulations which he has had no part in formulating. Indeed, he may disagree with them in principle, and he may run the risk of being rejected by the teachers in the process.

The *fifth,* and more recent image, is that of the principal as a change agent. Here the individual is expected to keep his school abreast or in advance of current developments; he is knowledgeable about new things occurring through all of education; and he will be trying to implement or incorporate as many new ideas into his school program as he can. The success of the change-oriented principal has hinged on his ability to manipulate his administrative environment. In our judgment this type of principal will be most successful, among Erickson's types, in accommodating to collective action situations. To have been effective in achieving innovations, the change-agent principal has already developed considerable finesse in diagnosing the significant features in his work setting; he knows those variables that either inhibit or facilitate change. Collective action on the part of teachers can be accepted as another fact of administrative life and incorporated into the leadership strategies he has developed through experience.

A *sixth,* and only now emerging image, is that of the principal as systems analyst. In this case, he is seen as the person who can make genuine assessments of the level of performance of those who work in his building. He has developed some sophistication in understanding how organizations behave and he has learned how to perfect feedback mechanisms to assist him with administrative decision making. This is, of course, an advanced definition of the principal's role and few persons have so far developed the skills necessary to perform in this way. Collective action on the part of teachers would probably not threaten such a principal. As a part of his systems training, he would have acquired sufficient understanding of organizational decision behavior to incorporate teacher participation into a rational model of administrative performance.

Although these six images are in a sense observationally based conceptions, they do indicate types which all of us have seen in operation. The types are impure, obviously; but at the same time they offer us a rough rubric for assessing the impact of collective negotiation on the principalship.

CONCLUSIONS AND SUMMATION

To sum up this discussion, there are several conclusions which in our judgment seem defensible.

(1) Provisions must be made for genuine, legitimate participation of principals in the collective negotiation process.

The severe feelings of being "left out" of the negotiation process appear to us to be a serious matter. There are undoubtedly many factors which must be taken into account in the involvement of principals: the purpose of their involvement, the nature and type of their representation on bargaining teams, the precise nature of their bargaining roles, and the issues on which their participation is germane.

We suspect that superintendents by and large, as well as boards of education are not aware of the feelings of their middle managers. In the heat of battle, many ordinary communication processes break down. It may be also, that superintendents and boards deliberately keep principals out of bargaining because they want to avoid burdening them with the responsibilities of participation in negotiations. They may feel that keeping principals "informed" completes top management's obligations to principals in this aspect of a school district's total administrative function. Whatever the individual circumstances may be, the problem needs exploration.

(2) There will be an intensification of collective activity in education involving a larger number of power groups which reflect the increase in specialization of work activity within school systems.

Joseph Garbarino, an industrial specialist, predicts that in the future administrative and managerial authority will be increasingly limited in all types of organizations. The consent of the governed notion will be extended to all employer-employee relations, in public as well as private sectors.[13] "Bargaining out of decisions" will be generalized throughout and over all institutions. He argues that operation of employee relations systems will ". . . require a high degree of administrative skill and these skills will be in

[13] Joseph W. Garbarino, "The Industrial Relations System," chapter for a book soon to be published under the sponsorship of Designing Education for the Future, Edgar L. Morphet, Project Director, 1966.

short supply. Successful industrial democracy, like successful political democracy, requires that both governed and governors work at their job."[14]

Garbarino points out that we have been moving in two different directions in the development of managerial skills and techniques:

> On the one hand is the view that administration can be made into a science or technology. An organization is studied in terms of its mission and structured in a particular way. Information is generated, processed, analyzed and a formal decision making technique is used to arrive at a policy. On the other hand is the view that administration is a political process in which the implementation of a decision is at least as important as its content. This means securing the active, willing cooperation of employees functioning less as subordinates and more as colleagues. The concept of administration as a technical skill versus the concept of administration as a social or political process is epitomized by the image that the press has created of Robert McNamara as the administrative technocrat while someone like Sargent Shriver is pictured as the model of the administrative politician. Regardless of the truth or falsity of these particular images, the dichotomy they represent is real. The problem of combining these skills in one person or of organizing their cooperation in the same institution is a major challenge. The degree of its resolution will be one determinant of the success with which the employee relations system will be able to adapt to the world of 1980.[15]

In education it is safe to predict that we will have strong organizations of administrators, counselors, and other specializations in addition to teacher groups which will bargain collectively.

(3) The tension that exists currently between bureaucratic and/or legalistic authority and collegial or professional authority will be sustained and increased.

There is some discussion as to whether or not schools are pure examples of bureaucratic organizations. Probably they are not perfect examples; nevertheless they possess some of the characteristics of bureaucracy. One of these is an hierarchial authority structure; another is the presence of rules and regulations to govern operations.

Collective action on the part of teachers is partially based on an emerging sense of collegial loyalty, identity, and opportunity for the exercise of power. The two authority system, bureaucratic and collegial, must somehow coexist in the school organizations of the future. It is apparent the two interact, and that growth in collegial power may elicit certain bureaucratic responses. For example, Anderson states:

> ... once the teacher comes to accept the necessity of rules, he may attempt to modify them to his own advantage. One such attempt is the

[14] *Ibid.*, p. 35.
[15] *Ibid.*, pp. 35-36.

growth of teacher unions. However, the perception of opposition and attempts at collective bargaining only reinforce the tendency to centralize control and to standardize behavior with rules.[16]

Thus the school administrators' recourse to expressions of collegial authority is to challenge with symbols of bureaucratic authority, in this case new rules and regulations. Time does not permit a discussion of the rules enforcement—tension producing—rules enforcement syndrome which frequently occurs in organizational life.

The schools of the future may resemble our better colleges and universities; boards of control in higher education have defined carefully the province of the board, the administration, and the faculty.[17] (They have been less successful in defining the province of students, however.) Similar allocations of responsibility may have to be achieved in our public schools.

(4) Preparation programs for administrative posts in education, especially the principalship and superintendency level positions, will need to include the substantial work in superior-subordinate relationships in complex social organizations.

For the past two decades we have emphasized the development of conceptual and human skills in the training programs for the principalship and the superintendency. Technical skills have been emphasized less, although still considered significant.

Research in industry, and in education, indicates that the percentage of an organization's actual productivity that can be affected by leadership or administrative discretion is rather limited. Robert Dubin in summarizing research on the influence of supervisory behaviors on productivity reports that the difference between "good" and "bad" supervision has little effect on the output of an organization.[18] Possibly as little as ten per cent in the variation in output of a well-supervised and poorly-supervised operation in industry can be accounted for by supervision. If, through improved supervision techniques, management is able to increase by thirty per cent that part of output that can be traced to supervision, total ouput is increased only three per cent.[19]

Dubin argues that the strength of middle management resides in maintaining communication between top management and the work force—he is

[16] James G. Anderson, "Bureaucratic Rules: Bearers of Organizational Authority," *Educational Administration Quarterly,* Vol. II (Winter, 1966), p. 28.

[17] Roald F. Campbell, Luvern L. Cunningham, and Roderick F. McPhee. *The Organization and Control of American Schools.* (Columbus: Charles E. Merrill Books Inc., 1965), p. 254.

[18] Robert Dubin, George C. Homans, Floyd C. Mann, and Delbert C. Miller, *Leadership and Productivity.* (San Francisco: Chandler Publishing Company, 1965), p. 5.

[19] *Ibid.*

an essential link. Likewise the maintenance of work force discipline and order usually devolve on his shoulders. Supervisors do more than stimulate ouput and productivity. "Indeed, among all the functions of supervisors, the stimulation of individual output *may* be of middling or even minor importance."[20]

Middle management personnel in industry perform many functions some of which may be independent of one another; the performance of one function has no influence on the acceptance by subordinates of the performance of another function. On the other hand, the supervisor's performance of two functions may interact upon each other. Thus, a middle management person who shares decisions with subordinates but is technically incompetent to handle work-flow stoppages may create a reaction quite different from that toward his administrative colleague who also shares decisions but is technically skillful and competent.[21]

It may be that the limited effectiveness of contemporary supervision can be tied to the relative emphases on the perfection of human and conceptual skills in contrast to technical skills in administrator training programs. Woodward argues that technical skills represent an extensive underdeveloped dimension of managerial training in industrial and business enterprises.[22] The same may be true in education; one example is the technical area of the assessment of individual and organizational performance. The pressure for adopting performance budgeting in education may force us to return to a stronger emphasis on the refinement of technical skills.[23]

As collective teacher action becomes more pronounced, with the consequent increases in the extension of rules and regulations, obviously substantial attention must be given to that meaning for programs of administrator preparation. A new perspective, more technical and less human, may emerge as we learn more about the changing distributions of power and authority in the years ahead.

(5) Considerable research is in order on the impact of collective action on the school organization itself, its productivity, and the relationships among those who hold occupational membership there.

The consequences of collective behavior for school systems are difficult to conceptualize for study purposes. One of the reasons that more research has not been done is the simple fact of the magnitude of the task. With or without collective action or teacher militancy we are being pressed toward more and more definitive assessment of our productivity as an enterprise. National assessment efforts are currently under way through the Carnegie Corporation

[20] *Ibid.,* p. 6.
[21] *Ibid.,* p. 48.
[22] *Ibid.,* p. 11.
[23] J. Alan Thomas, "Educational Decision-Making and the School Budget," *Administrator's Notebook,* Vol. XII (December, 1963).

and the U. S. Office of Education. Thus we may need to develop highly sophisticated performance, criteria and assessment instruments.[24]

With the refinement of new assessment technologies and the acquisition of these skills by principals, principals will have a powerful new tool for institutional control. They will be able to provide superintendents and board members with extensive data which top educational management can bring to the bargaining table. These data will become a part of the bargaining exchange—if the data are positive in terms of reporting good productivity they provide top management with one set of strategies. On the other hand, if teacher performance has been shabby such data provide the board with quite another bargaining perspective.

Given refined assessment capabilities, research can be done on the impact of teacher action on the school organization. We should be able to account for those increments or decrements in production which relate to collective activities.

(6) An assessment needs to be made of which administrative skills, conceptual, human, or technical, have the highest pay off for the school principal.

The point has been made several times in this paper that the boundaries of middle level administration are being narrowed and that the future promises even further restrictions on their discretion. Certainly conceptual skills, human relations know-how, and new technical competencies will be in demand. Our argument is brief and simple: we believe considerable attention should be given to identifying the appropriate mix among the skill types in terms of what is required in the effective operation of schools.[25]

Teachers, through the assumption of new responsibilities commensurate with their new-found collegial authority, will become increasingly responsible for educational innovation and improved organization performance. They will be responding directly to the critics of the schools rather than through administrative spokesmen. There will be few "Daddy" type principals around to act as counsels for the defense. Principals therefore will need human skills but these will not make or break him as a principal. His effectiveness will hinge upon possession of a rich array of new technical competencies which are just beginning to emerge.

(7) The administrator socialization process should be explored to determine the effect of teaching experience on administrator socialization.

Lortie has described eloquently the powerful socialization processes that

[24] For an advanced treatment of the school as an instrument of production and ways and means to measure its output more definitively, see J. Alan Thomas, *The Productive School*. (New York: John Wiley & Son, [forthcoming]).

[25] Support for this position can be found in Anne E. Trask, "Principals, Teachers, and Supervision: Dilemmas and Solutions," *Administrator's Notebook,* Vol. XIII (December, 1964).

are at work within the teaching occupation.[26] Teachers, like no other occupational group, begin occupational socialization when they enter school as pupils and continue the process through their formal education, professional training, induction and experiences with the occupation. Administrator socialization on the other hand, may begin with the teaching experience for some, with professional training for others, but in either case it is in no way as shaping or determinative as teacher socialization.

The meaning of teacher collective action for the source and supply of future administrators is not known. It is, however, interesting to speculate on the question. Administrators, at all levels, may be drawn from outside of education or recruited with a minimum of classroom teaching experience, indeed, they may be drawn directly from the ranks of undergraduates. The present system of recruiting administrators from teacher ranks may prove to be dysfunctional; the socialization process for administrative responsibilities may have been inhibited by teaching experience. Obviously, this is pure conjecture and must be so labeled.

These then are seven areas of speculation or tentative conclusions about the impact of teacher collective activity on the principalship. We hope they may stimulate questions and discussion. It is clear that changes are the order of the day in the principalship; new challenges are present; and the future of the position appears to be anything but dull and uninteresting.

---

[26] Dan C. Lortie, "The Balance of Control and Autonomy in Elementary School Teaching," in Amitai Etzioni, *The Heteronomous Professions*. (New York: Free Press, forthcoming).

V-5

THE ROLE OF THE AMERICAN ARBITRATION
ASSOCIATION IN PUBLIC EDUCATION*

Joseph S. Murphy

The presence of a representative of the American Arbitration Association in a conference of this sort is certain to raise questions in the minds of school administrators, teachers, and members of school boards. The problems discussed in a national institute on collective negotiations in public education would at first glance appear somewhat removed from an organization originally founded almost forty years ago to advance the knowledge and use of commercial arbitration.

Those of you who are from the field of history would, of course, know that arbitration is not a new process. It began, I suppose, when man first threw aside his crude weapons of force and began to approach dispute settlement intelligently. For many centuries arbitration was practiced, for example, among the ancient Hebrews, the Greeks, and the Romans, wherever men sought for justice and equity away from the might of armed soldiers or the overwhelming power of the heads of state. The process was popular in the middle ages and the days of the Hanseatic League when merchants throughout Europe had no international courts yet sorely needed the resolution of their disputes by arbitration.

There is a long history of arbitration in England, and Colonial America adopted the procedure as the only means of resolving controversies unless recourse was had to a governor of a particular territory, who sometimes was quite remote and often not the judicial type. A famous sample of arbitration in Revolutionary times is the case involving a chain spread across the Hudson River to prevent the British fleet from attacking West Point. The contracting colonials disputed the amount of payment due to the master craftsmen who made the chain. All kinds of problems, such as the cost of hiring a carriage, the price of hay, and boundary disputes between individuals were resolved by

* Paper delivered on July 7, 1965, at the National Institute on Collective Negotiations in Public Education cosponsored by Phi Delta Kappa and Rhode Island College, Providence, R.I. Joseph S. Murphy is Vice President, American Arbitration Association.

arbitration, as well as boundary disputes between the United States and Canada. American history is filled with stories of commercial arbitration. Later on, labor arbitration gradually evolved through the latter part of the 19th and early 20th centuries.

Back in 1926, almost forty years ago, the American Arbitration Association was founded as an outgrowth of two other organizations. One was the New York Chamber of Commerce, which had been handling arbitration back to pre-Revolutionary days. The other was the Bar Association of the City of New York. The new independent organization was an educational organization and had no other objective than advancement of the knowledge and science of arbitration and the provision of administrative services so that the arbitration process could be developed.

The early days of the American Arbitration Association concentrated primarily on commercial and international trade arbitration. Strangely, our first case was sort of a hybrid, in a certain sense involving a professional group, for it concerned the newly formed Actors Equity. (Whether Actors Equity was a union at that time I don't know.) In the middle Thirties the Association began to get more cases involving employees and employers and a separate labor tribunal was founded in 1937.

In the early days we had a number of insurance cases, and in the last ten years there have been a tremendous number of cases involving accidents by uninsured motorists, primarily because of court congestion. In all of these cases the people who voluntarily came to arbitrate did so under the AAA primarily because they wanted speed. Sometimes they wanted privacy, and sometimes they simply believed that self-regulation is part of our American way of life. If businessmen could get together to set up arbitration tribunals with our assistance, they would be avoiding continuing government regulation of their various problems.

In 1965 the AAA will have a case load of over 10,000 cases. Roughly 6,000 are cases involving commercial matters of all kinds, including insurance cases. And 4,000 involve labor-management problems. It is almost impossible for anyone in this room to mention a type of dispute that we have not handled over the years, including who was at fault when the foundation of a million-dollar building showed cracks, which school the children of a divorced couple should attend, what the value of certain industrial diamonds was, and whether an international bridge player properly developed the use of plastic playing cards in South America. All kinds of disputes have passed through our tribunals. Almost every major construction contract in this country has an arbitration clause. County and state agencies appear in private arbitration with contractors over all aspects of construction, from excavation to the final painting of decorative parts of a door.

Our 4,000 labor cases (roughly 40 per cent of our activity) seem to make headlines, but if someone awards $10,000 for a broken arm when a man has been out of work for a year or so, or if the county hospital gets an award providing for the reconstruction of the entire air-conditioning system because of faulty installation, arbitration does not make the papers. The result is that the AAA is generally known for its labor-management arbitration.

There is a hybrid area in which we do not conduct arbitration but rather assist in the resolution of disputes by other means. It is hybrid to the AAA because arbitration itself is technically the referral of a dispute to an impartial third party who, on the basis of evidence and argument made before him, will render an award that is final and binding upon the parties. This is the basic definition of arbitration over the years, but it is not the only method of settlement of disputes through impartial agencies or impartial individuals. There are other effective methods. Obviously, the best method is direct negotiation, where people can get together and resolve their controversies themselves. Sometimes mediation will be of value, sometimes fact finding. Sometimes there are disputes for the resolution of which we merely set up discussions for the parties themselves. There is even a group in the printing industry in New York to whom our greatest service over the years is the rental of an air-conditioned room. Whatever we can do to facilitate the settlement of disputes will be done as long as it complies with the standards of ethical conduct and the policies based thereon, which the AAA has maintained over the years and upon which its reputation has been established.

One of the obvious methods of resolving certain disputes as to representation questions has been the election procedure. Back as far as twenty years ago the AAA conducted elections whenever requested. The requests of the last several years have been increasing to such volume that we have been obliged to set up an election department as a separate division within the AAA. Our election director, over the past few years, has administered hundreds of elections and has been a consultant and advisor on many others.

The AAA's role in elections is the administration of the actual election itself. It is our objective to see that when an election is held it is fair and impartial, and that the sanctity of the secret ballot as an American tradition is preserved. We have no control over events that take place before the election is brought to us to administer. We are not interested, except as students of American public life, in what bargaining unit is agreed upon. I personally, or any officer or individual within the organization, might have opinions on this or any of the problems which confront you in the educational world, but as an agency this does not interest us except to the extent that, if you have a problem in this connection, we want to be able to assist you in resolving it by whatever means you desire. We have no interest in whatever preliminary arrangements are made by you or are established by a law under which an election may be held, or are made by a moderator who was agreed upon by you to decide preliminary issues as eligibility, challenges, method, and number of polling places, etc., except insofar as these arrangements pertain to the efficient and fair conduct of an election.

In the elections we have administered we have found that many problems arise because of preliminary determinations made either by private agreement or by rulings of moderators. Three elections to which Professor Moskow referred earlier in this conference were conducted by the AAA in Rochester, Newark, and Philadelphia, and in each there was a great deal of variation, as well as considerable similarity. All three had some preliminary issues resolved by a moderator. In each instance the authority of the moderator to resolve initial problems varied. In one case his activity was considerably curtailed and he was restricted to such details as time and place of voting. In another instance he was given a blank check and determined many other questions such as eligibility, absentee voting, etc. In the third instance the moderator was given the same blank check but mediated and secured agreement on most of the problems.

The securing of agreement does not necessarily mean that the most efficiently run election will result, particularly if the agreements set up difficult and costly procedures. The matters that concern the AAA or a moderator or even judges in court are substantially as follows: We are concerned with the date, the time, the method of voting, the problem of absentee ballots, the polling places, their location, accessibility, the form of ballot (is it by machine or by paper ballot?), the problems of electioneering near booths and during polling times, and the problem of eligibility, not only with regard to groups of people but even individual eligibility. Eligibility may be concerned with such cases as that wherein a man with some alcoholic trouble went on temporary or terminal leave, transfers, etc., which can cause considerable difficulty, particularly in a large educational system. In smaller educational systems the actual personal eligibility of each one can be more readily established.

Another problem that we are concerned with is proper identification. In a small area most everyone will know everyone else. If you have 10,000 people voting, the question of identification can be a worrisome thing. I don't think any teacher would be actually dishonest in trying to vote three times, or sending someone else in to vote, but if regulations are set up by a moderator for the interested groups with respect to identification, then this method of identification, even though it poses problems, must be followed by the AAA. (In this area the AAA is prepared to give consultative advice out of its experience.) It is also true from my observation of teachers at some of these elections that even in questions so basic as identification some will have personal reasons which impel them to leave their pocketbooks at home or to go to the wrong polling place and vote a challenged ballot. Then, all of a sudden, it is disclosed to them that they should have gone to a different voting place. At great inconvenience to themselves, they immediately proceed to this place and try to vote there.

The accuracy and the accessibility of eligibility lists also cause problems. We have had excellent cooperation from boards of education and superintendents of school systems in this connection. But when an election date is set a month and a half ahead on the basis of a payroll, many changes will occur and a list provided as of that date may be considerably changed in a larger system through transfer, promotion, etc. Another problem is caused by the so-called "floating" voter. This is the transient teacher who will teach in one school one day, in another school another day, and so on. Such a teacher might not be on an eligibility list of a particular school on the day of the voting and might be at a school fifteen miles away from the one to which he or she is normally assigned. Finally, there is a question of acceptance, by everyone involved in the election, of the necessity for clearly demonstrated impartiality in the administration of the election. The Association prefers that there be properly authorized observers from interested groups present at each polling place and at the final tally. There is need for an atmosphere of fair play for all concerned so that no one is taking advantage of unusual situations. This particularly concerns electioneering if there is no law whereby electioneering can be controlled. There certainly can be and has been agreement on the type of electioneering that is legitimate for teachers individually and for observers. It is, however, a serious matter if some observer at the polling place says with mistaken zeal, "Vote for my organization." Consequently, signs, loudspeakers, big buttons, and personal consultation with somebody in a line of voters constitute something apart from our American spirit of fair play. We assume teachers have made up their minds at the time they go to a polling place and cannot be swayed by any electioneering. It is only the enthusiasm and interest of the representatives of interested groups in an election of this sort that cause difficulty. I would suggest that all who participate in any kind of election make every effort both to be and to appear absolutely fair with regard to electioneering rules during the voting period and at the polls. Bitterness and acrimony resulting from an election period may affect the relationship of a teacher with his board or with his fellow teachers or teacher organizations throughout the years to come. If any form of dishonesty occurs or unusual electioneering gimmicks are used such as hanging a ten-foot sign reading "Vote for . . . . . ." over the voting booth, a great deal of trouble and hard feelings can arise, although the chances are teachers will not be influenced in the slightest.

It must be remembered that when an election is conducted under private administration, private administration does not mean the AAA only. An election may be conducted by an individual, by a government official acting in private capacity, or through an appointment by a governmental agency. Enforcement of regulations may be difficult, although there are some state laws that will reguluate certain election problems. Privately run elections have no such laws and need agreement by all parties concerned. Public voting has a law and established regulations to control situations and to consider complaints. Complaints will be made over minor errors that can occur (not errors by the AAA, but by the voters, obviously!), and the forum for resolving whether this affects the election is a difficult one to establish. If an individual is asked to decide the effect of a ten-foot sign over a voting booth, he has almost no guidelines upon which to work. Election arbitrators fill this need and, consequently, agreement on an election arbitrator to rule on issues is desirable.

When the AAA is first requested to conduct an election, its procedure is to look first at the factual situation and ascertain that we have the agreement of all parties to the election. With this in mind, we ask if certain details of procedure will be agreed upon before we proceed, or are preliminary questions to be resolved as has been done in the past by moderators, or chairmen, or by an election arbitrator. If the latter, a waiting period is necessary, of course, until a moderator is selected and decides all the preliminary questions of appropriate units, eligibility, and the other factors involved in the election, including the mechanical details which may affect administration. When the AAA has examined the information available, the matters agreed on by the parties to the election, and the findings of the moderator, it establishes a workable procedure in consultation with all parties concerned. This procedure will take care of many tiny little items such as notices of election, notices on a bulletin board, accessibility of mail boxes in a school, etc. All of these insignificant matters may pose problems later, and it is desirable to obtain a resolution of all such issues by some kind of mediation, joint agreement, or whatever it may be.

A question was raised earlier in this conference about costs of election. We cannot give you an estimate of the cost without full information as to the type of election desired. Our procedure is to say that we will run the election at cost, depending on what the parties wish. If machines are desired, it costs more than paper ballots. If a mail ballot is requested, it is cheaper but introduces many confusing problems. Parties tell the AAA the kind of election they want and the Association tries to give them an estimate of cost. We need to know how many voting places are required, how many people are liable to be at each place, how many hours the polls are to remain open, and any unusual factors involved.

The AAA's fee is 15% to 20% over and above the expenses, which may include travel, printing, postage, payments to people who are hired and paid on an hourly basis, an election supervisor, or an agreed-upon election arbitrator who will decide any disputed questions that may arise during the course of the election. In many instances the AAA fee is negotiated.

The election arbitrator normally has a simple task. If a voter partially rubbed out a pencil mark in one box and made a mark in another, the arbitrator will decide whether this vote is valid or not. If someone has made some unusual identifying marks or preaches a little sermon over the box he thinks he is voting in and signs his name, the arbitrator determines whether or not this becomes an eligible ballot. These and similar problems have to be decided by someone. It is peculiar that we rarely secure agreement on a disputed ballot, probably because one side is always losing the vote. Nevertheless, the issue of the disputed ballot has to be resolved. Decisions may be made by the AAA, but in larger elections are often made by an election arbitrator. Quite a number of experienced election arbitrators are now available.

The question was raised in yesterday's program as to the cost of certain specific elections. Mrs. Carlson, our election director, reports the following figures for the following large elections:

City	Estimated No. of Eligible Voters	Expenses	AAA Fee
Rochester*	1,100	$1,157.75	$250.00
Newark	3,100	$4,780.86	$500.00
Philadelphia*	11,000	$3,523.54	$750.00

* Parts of the election moderator's fee are not included in the expenses here.

The expenses in these three elections were based on certain factors upon which the parties to the election agreed in advance. This agreement included the use of a moderator or mediator to decide on a number of preliminary questions, the selection of a large number of polling places, and the desire for a count immediately after the polling places were closed. It should be noted that in all of these elections no cost accounting was made of the time of the Association's executives, clerical work, etc., with certain exceptions.

It might be helpful to consider the Newark election in some detail. To begin with, two teacher organizations were contesting the right to be the exclusive representative for the entire school system of Newark. The Board of Education and the superintendent of schools and his office were not party to the agreement nor did they participate in any way in resolving the issues which arose. A representative of the board and of the superintendent was present to indicate what the school system's position was and whether or not any particular election arrangement conflicted with school policy. They were extremely cooperative with regard to providing information, lists of teachers, and general background information.

The AAA, when first contacted, was asked to appoint one of three individuals as a moderator to make preliminary rules. A hearing was set up and a discussion of all the problems with the election was held. The AAA, for educational purposes, asked permission to make a transcript of the meeting. The parties agreed but then proceeded to order a transcript for themselves. The cost of the transcript for the preliminary meeting represented a sizable part of the election expenses. Secondly, the election moderator ruled that the election should be held in neutral locations within one-half mile of each school. To secure such neutral territory a considerable amount of time and money was spent in setting up the polling places. The cooperation of the Mayor and the Fire Department enabled us to keep this cost to a somewhat reasonable figure.

One of the chief reasons for comparatively high expenses in the Newark election was that 226 ballots were challenged and of the 2,746 ballots counted on the evening of the election, each teacher organization had 1,373 votes. The M.I.T. Electronics Division advised us that the likelihood of there being a tie at 1,373 each is so infinitesimal that their computers were unable to find out and advise us how often it might happen. The 226 challenged ballots were the subject of a series of meetings in which both parties argued the validity of the ballots before the election arbitrator, who made a final decision on each one. Some of the factors which he had to consider before validating a ballot were whether or not there was compliance with the rules for identification; the actual status of a group of teachers at the time of the election; late arrival of ballots from absentee voters; the actual position of the individual at the time of the voting and at the time of the preparation of the mailing lists; etc.

Many of these problems might have been easily solved had it not been for the closeness of the election. The moderator's fee in this instance, therefore, was quite high. It included a per diem charge for the session before the election and the time spent in writing a directive resolving the problems posed to him, for the actual day of election, and for four days of hearings with respect to the 226 challenges. Were it not for the unusual expenses of this election, the arbitrator's fee, and the transcript, the cost of the Newark election would not have been proportionately different from other elections.

An unusual procedure for voting developed in the election for the Philadelphia school system. School buses were used as portable voting booths and traveled to all of the schools in the system in accordance with a prearranged schedule. The election was conducted on a day in which there were no classes, but teachers were obliged to be at the schools for the day for general administration purposes between the two semester terms.

The AAA's experience in conducting elections dates back more than twenty years and encompass a wide variety of elections of all kinds. In the labor-management field, balloting has been conducted to determine collective bargaining representatives primarily for those who may not be covered by applicable laws, for example, those in shipping companies and the Master, Mates, and Pilots Association; employees in private (and public) hospitals, universities, social agencies; and many others who seek a private non-governmental administration of their elections.

In addition, we have conducted elections to select the officers of trade associations and of officers for unions and for boards of directors of housing corporations. We have conducted votes to determine whether a union would accept or reject contracts with private companies as well as with major municipalities.

Again, the AAA has administered elections to select the school trustees of a private institution. In one instance we conducted an election to determine which minister in a church in California would be the resident clergyman for the particular church.

In conclusion, it should be brought to your attention that it is not only in connection with election activity that the AAA should be of interest to the educational world. AAA's services are mentioned in many memoranda of agreement on contracts between teacher organizations and boards of education, usually in a clause such as this:

> Any dispute arising out of the interpretation or application of this memorandum of agreement (or contract) will be settled by arbitration under the rules of the American Arbitration Association.

Other contracts involving educational groups provide for advisory arbitration in which the award is not binding but merely persuasive, though the parties usually live up to the award. The AAA is also written into contracts to provide mediators or fact finders with or without recommendations.

Arbitration involving employees often produces unusual problems because conflicts with law and civil service regulations must be considered. Classifications and grades and notes established by legitimate authority are often excluded from binding arbitration.

As the years pass by, arbitration for professional employees of public bodies will pose a difficult problem to the educational world. The American Arbitration Association, as an institution devoted to the advancement and knowledge of voluntary arbitration, is being approached daily for information, and stands ready to be of service wherever individuals from all parts of public education seek its assistance.

V-6

ORGANIZING MUNICIPAL MANAGEMENT FOR EMPLOYEE RELATIONS*

Douglas G. Weiford

Our body of knowledge on public labor relations remains meager, full of many questions and few answers. It is a field which has now emerged as a formidable and extensive problem, but in which acceptable and workable definitions of the most basic terms are not available, and in which little consistency in policy exists from city to city and from state to state.

At the outset I shall levy a blanket criticism. As a group, city officials in recent years have devoted an enormous amount of time to the development of a growing body of knowledge on municipal affairs, to techniques and procedures, to planning on the grand scale. We have moved to meet many new municipal problems with enthusiasm and dedication. But on this emerging business of what we now call Labor Relations, governmental officials thus far have done relatively little except to discuss it in sharply negative terms.

In many of the cities and counties throughout the United States, unionism of public employees is still relatively unknown. Terms like "collective bargaining," "exclusive representation," "business agent," and "deadlock" have a strange and unfamiliar ring. The manner in which many local governments establish wage and fringe benefit policies remains rather casual and largely unilateral. For example, how many times have you seen a group of employees come before the city council late in the budgetary process, stand politely before the councilmen, file their requests, enter into little discussion and no debate, and then depart. Then, sometime later, in the last-minute flurry of finishing their budgetary review, the council will make a final and unilateral decision on wages and proceed to some other, and perhaps more pressing, matter.

The steady growth of unions in the public service indicates that this casual approach to employee wage and fringe benefit matters has about run

---

* Reprinted by permission from *Minnesota Municipalities,* November, 1964. Douglas G. Weiford is City Manager, Eau Claire, Wisconsin.

its course. Whether municipal officials like it or not, it must be recognized that employee organizations are steadily demanding and winning a bigger role than ever before in influencing the official policies and practices which affect them.

Moreover, I think we can correctly assume that the future will see a continued steady growth in the number of employee organizations, in the number of people holding membership in them, and in the strength and influence which will be brought to bear on local government with respect to all matters affecting public personnel.

It is my own view that this trend, with all its inherent difficulties, is not entirely undesirable. For I believe that employee organizations and governmental management can frequently serve complementary rather than antagonistic roles in accomplishing the purposes of government.

As most of you know by now, Wisconsin has moved to the forefront in formalizing relationships between local governments and their employees. In Wisconsin we are directed by state law to give unions official recognition and to bargain with them under "good faith" conditions. If a deadlock finally results, either party to the dispute may petition the Wisconsin Employment Relations Board to institute advisory fact-finding procedures.

Among many local governmental officials this law has caused head shaking, murmurings of disaster, spirited discussion, and occasionally violent argument. But up to this point the skies have not fallen, and most objective observers would probably say that the law is working reasonably well. On one thing, though, all can reach agreement: The new Wisconsin law has radically changed the method by which local governments deal with their employees, and has required us to give critical thought to the problem of reorganizing ourselves to cope with this totally new concept of employee relationships.

There is reason to believe that various other states may follow Wisconsin's example, and if this is true, you can derive considerable profit by becoming familiar with our experiences.

Throughout my presentation I shall convey to you my general approval of the trend toward formal negotiations between governments and their employees. At the same time, however, I will take care not to give the impression that all of this will take place in a kind of remote and peaceful Never-Never Land. By its very nature, labor relations is the stuff of which conflict is made. It is exhausting and tedious. It is full of emotionalism and political hazard. At times it develops into a hard, cruel business. And implicit in the whole process are conflict and struggle between traditional procedures and the goals of the various employee organizations.

The growth of strong unions will interject into the daily routine of the public official substantial and sometimes startling changes. The financial impact is obvious. The cities that have not kept pace with advancing wages, changing working conditions, and modern personnel management will find aggressive union activity reflecting heavily on the municipal treasury. Perhaps even more important is the fact that various institutional procedures are certain to be challenged. Chief among these are the civil service system and the integrated pay plan. Indeed, the historic civil service system may be headed for a life and death struggle on the battlefield of collective bargaining.

So-called merit systems of pay increases will come under bitter attack and, because they are based principally on hard-to-defend subjective standards, will often be replaced with across-the-board increases in each collective bargaining unit. The standard types of classification and pay plans will face frequent union onslaughts; annual attacks may be anticipated on pay ranges and classifications for various positions. Individual job holders on union advice can be expected to refuse work assignments unless the duties are set forth specifically in written job specifications. Joint management-union evaluation of job classifications will become common.

The diversified nature of municipal work encourages separate union organizations. Where a number of such unions exist, they will be in competition with each other as well as with management. Each will struggle to better its position with the result that the traditional concept of "equal pay for equal work" on a government-wide basis and the maintenance of an overall system of values in the classification plan will be increasingly difficult to maintain.

Aggressive unions will sometimes win concessions which are not awarded to non-organized employees, resulting in problems of morale and the organization of additional bargaining units. Seniority rather than performance will be stressed as the principal criterion for promotion to non-supervisory positions. Disciplinary problems will be carefully watched by unions, and members will be defended by union attorneys. Union membership will be considered by the individual worker in certain classes of position as more significant and more protective than civil service status.

Local governments will be required to spend considerable portions of each year both in direct negotiations and in time-consuming preliminary preparations. Struggles during negotiating sessions will become emotional at times, requiring formal procedures to minimize personal involvements on both sides of the bargaining table. As individuals, city councilmen can expect to receive pressures from unions both prior to and during negotiations. If all else fails, it should be anticipated that unions will bring political pressures including direct appeals to the public for sympathy and support. When agreements are finally reached they will increasingly be placed in contract form to be signed by both management and labor.

Even this brief recitation makes it perfectly obvious that the road ahead is not likely to provide smooth traveling. Nevertheless the fact must be accepted that the formation of employee organizations flows from deep-seated human needs. They will continue to be formed and will grow stronger. As public officials, we must recognize this and develop the necessary attitudes and skills to cope with what lies ahead.

I submit that it is a healthy thing to be forced to *think* about our systems and procedures and types of organization. I further submit that union activity is one of the forces of change that will require local governments to undertake some basic reexamination of elementary, but neglected, matters. Let me give you an example.

A certain city in Wisconsin with which I am familiar has never bothered to adopt formal personnel procedures. Systematic recruitment procedures and training methods have never been utilized. For years it has been the policy of this city to hire its laborers and semi-skilled workers from the ranks of those who were either on relief or who were likely prospects for the relief rolls. Public employment in this city has thus been viewed as a kind of "dumping ground," and the standard of employee performance is about what you would expect under the circumstances.

When the Wisconsin Employment Relations Act was made applicable to municipal employees these refugees from the relief rolls formed a union and set about to bargain with the city council. Among other things they demanded the same scale of wages that various other cities pay. They will probably succeed in achieving this goal. In a certain symbolic sense, the chickens have come home to roost. It might be half a generation before this city will be able to equate employee productivity to the wage levels it will be called on to pay.

So I would remind you that one of the most basic rules in organizing management for employee relations is the absolute necessity to establish and maintain recruitment and selection techniques of the highest quality.

Before discussing other elements in the organization of management for employee relations, let me digress for a moment.

Perhaps we would do well to realize that employee relations is a two-way street and that employee organizations judge us even as we judge them. We, too, can organize ourselves (or fail to organize) in such a way as virtually to insure conflict and dissension.

I thought you might be interested in some complaints that unions have about us, so I asked the executive director of the Wisconsin Council of County and Municipal Employees about the pet peeves he and his field representatives encounter in dealing with local governments. His reply included these points:

Grossly apparent in the collective bargaining relationships with the public employer is the complete lack of skill on the part of many public employers in bargaining with the union. There is an art to conducting negotiations. Over 90 per cent of the public employers have not mastered the basic fundamentals of the art.

At the present time, city attorneys, district attorneys, city and county clerks, department heads, and sundry other officials are all participating in bargaining. Continuity in the bargaining process is lacking and diversity of opinion is rampant.

The public employer has a strong tendency to hold off bargaining until the final moments (budget time). A bargaining atmosphere produced by delay and procrastination is not good to say the least. Under these conditions the meetings with the union are too brief and too few. It is amazing how frustrated a union representative and the membership he represents can become whenever this happens.

Another point is the fact that a great many public employers conduct their collective bargaining sessions as if it were a formal hearing. There is nothing, in my experience at least, that surpasses an informal gathering around a table as a device to bring off a successful bargaining session.

There is a blind reluctance on the part of many public employers to accept a clause in an agreement providing for arbitration of any disputes that may arise from the agreement. It would seem to me that this is the only logical and reasonable method to use in settling unresolved disputes especially when we consider the alternatives.

Finally, there are those important elements which fall under the heading "Common Courtesy." We ask these things: Please do not indulge in personalities. Answer correspondence and petitions promptly. Keep appointments and be on time. A union representative may have traveled a great distance to handle the bargaining and the local officers may be sacrificing time and money to represent the union. Their business is just as important as yours. If the appointment is delayed or not kept, considerable money and effort are wasted and good will is impaired.

With some of these comments in mind, let me describe the negotiating procedures which we utilize in Eau Claire. These, I must hastily add, are at best experimental in nature.

A city council surely is a most unlikely negotiating agency. It is by design a cumbersome thing, subject to all of the fierce and uncertain elements of political life. During something as delicate as labor negotiations it must be expected that each councilman will attempt to keep an eye on the attendant publicity, his personal image, the next election, and the tax rate all at the same time.

There is really nothing wrong with this. A typical city council is simply not a closely knit group in the manner of a private board of directors, and no one should want it any different. But this requires that we ask ourselves an almost unanswerable question: How is it possible to organize a city council for effective employee relations? Here again we have no choice but to be pragmatic, for it is an inescapable fact that only the city council can make final decisions on financial matters. For this reason, it has been determined in Eau Claire that, difficult or not, the city council *must* perform an active role in labor negotiations.

In very large cities this may not be practical, nor will it be feasible in cities with grossly diffused managerial systems. In most council-manager cities, and in some mayor-council cities, it does, however, appear to offer possibilities.

It works like this. Beginning about two months prior to negotiations, assemble all necessary data. Study local wage rates for comparable municipal positions. Contact cities in the state of the same general size and composition, and pool information with them on wage rates and fringe benefits. Analyze the cost-of-living index. Develop this material in readable report form.

See to it that the unions file their requests at an early date. Develop the financial impact of their demands.

Submit all of this material to the city council.

Arrange for the full city council and the bargaining units to meet at least once and preferably twice in order to clarify all requests. Bargaining is not an academic process. If councilmen remain aloof and detached from the earthy process of battle, great trouble can lie ahead.

Then, once the atmosphere has been established and the demands and counter demands clearly enunciated, the process can assume more flexibility and the chief executive (either mayor or manager), along with his staff and with a few designated council representatives can proceed with subsequent meetings on a more informal basis. In such a procedure the full council must receive detailed minutes of each meeting so as to remain in close touch with developments. If negotiations bog down, the full council may then reenter the bargaining process and seek to find areas of agreement.

An air of informality is sought in all such meetings, and no business other than that of bargaining is ever scheduled. If agreements can be reached, well and good. But if all attempts fail, a final council decision is reached in late August and the details are placed in an official resolution.

The Eau Claire Board of Education follows a somewhat similar procedure in bargaining with teachers and custodial employees. It is interesting to note that the board has bargained with its employees for at least 20 years and consequently was relatively unaffected by the adoption of the new law.

As I mentioned earlier, public employee unions will sometimes bring direct political pressure if the negotiation process does not give them what they want. Partly for that reason, and partly because of the public's right to be kept informed, all bargaining sessions in Eau Claire are public and are fully reported by newspapers and other news media. Deliberations (strategy sessions) of both parties take place in executive session, but the negotiations themselves are public.

In our view, this procedure facilitates the proper conduct of democratic government and at the same time provides some degree of protection from political attack if negotiations break down.

Cities with diffused management, including independent civil service commissions, will very probably have a much more difficult task in developing an orderly labor relations procedure.

Many of our municipal organizations, for example, set the personnel director aside from the mainstream of management, so that he is neither fish nor fowl in this emerging area of labor relations. On this question I support the viewpoint that personnel administration is clearly a management function and that the concept of the independent personnel agency stands in need of reexamination.

At any rate, where managerial responsibility is scattered among a number of agencies and officials, there appears to be no alternative but to form a negotiating team representing all of the elements of management. Since such a team cannot make final decisions it can do no more than make recommendations on the matters under negotiation and hope for the best.

In this connection it seems clear that the emergence of strong unions in the public service will tend to make more urgent the need to reevaluate those governmental structures and procedures which originated primarily for the purpose of coping with problems of another era, and which now tend to make the decision-making processes of government unduly slow and cumbersome.

There are a few important questions which I shall mention and because of the press of space pass over quickly.

What are the differences between dealing with a local union and a national union? The major difference, in my view, is the broader perspective and the professional approach introduced by the business agent of the national union. Contrary to the municipal stereotype on this question, I prefer dealing with the professional as opposed to local talent.

What about the unorganized employees? We have taken no steps to include these people in the bargaining process and do not intend to do so. All citizens have the right to petition the city council and this obviously includes non-union employees. The point of difference is that the city council is not obligated to bargain with such individuals or groups, nor do they have the legal right to seek advisory fact-finding if the council refuses to accede to their demands. It is another inescapable fact, however, that the bargaining groups usually gain benefits for the unorganized workers whenever they gain something for themselves.

What about the problem of exclusive representation? Once again we must be realists. The formation of employee organizations is strictly an employee matter in which management cannot interfere. Nevertheless it is perfectly evident that the bargaining process extended to a multitude of separate bargaining units could seriously damage the effectiveness of the municipal organization. If exclusive representation is the alternative, then I favor it.

What effect is union activity likely to have on integrated pay plans? I suspect the bargaining process will probably require that at least three separate and distinct pay plans be established, one for trades and labor employees, one for the uniformed services, and one for the remaining classes.

Is there any special kind of training which should be given to department heads and other key management people to assist them in dealing more effectively with the labor relations problem? The responsibility for bargaining should not be diffused among various and sundry line officials, but should remain the responsibility of the chief executive and his staff and of the legislative body. Thus I do not consider it necessary to go beyond the routinely accepted principles of personnel administration in training the various management levels. Such training, however, must be consistently applied. Otherwise the embarrassing situation is likely to arise where the union leaders consistently exhibit a greater knowledge of the city's personnel rules and procedures than do some of the management people.

My own basic philosophy on unions in the public service centers around two points: (1) That government is obligated to grant to its own employees the right of self-organization, and (2) that the use of economic weapons by governmental workers should be prohibited.

Once these conclusions are made, others inevitably follow. If employees are to be allowed the right to form or join labor organizations, then it follows that some orderly procedure should be developed for the official recognition of such organizations. It also seems evident that an orderly procedure for negotiating with these groups must be developed within the peculiar limitations of the governmental process.

Finally, if the use of economic weapons by government employees is to be prohibited, then some kind of alternative machinery must be established to help resolve disputes. By its very nature such machinery must bring impartial third parties into the picture, but because the fixing of wages, hours, and conditions of employment is legislative in nature it is clear that all third party referees must be limited to advisory roles.

If these conclusions have any validity at all, it would appear desirable for the broad outline of the labor relations pattern to be established by state law. Home rule arguments notwithstanding, it is my belief that a state statute similar to that adopted by Wisconsin is preferable to the aimless conflict and struggle which otherwise almost surely awaits the local governments throughout the nation.

VI

STRATEGY AND TACTICS IN
COLLECTIVE NEGOTIATIONS

The articles in this section deal primarily with the process of negotiations. The first two articles discuss organizational strategy and tactics in winning representation elections against a rival organization. The first is by David Selden, Assistant to the President, American Federation of Teachers; the second analyzes election results in the Detroit and Cleveland school systems from the viewpoint of Dick Dashiell, an NEA staff member who was an active participant in these elections. Both of these articles were originally confidential publications for the use of AFT and NEA local leaders. The editors are grateful for the opportunity to publish them in their original form, so as to convey some idea of the growing intensity and sophistication of the rivalry between the NEA and the AFT.

The remaining articles deal with the strategy and tactics of negotiations rather than the strategy and tactics of winning a representation election. There is no automatic outcome to collective negotiations. Typically, the outcome depends to some extent at least upon the actions of the parties during negotiations. Although most of the articles discuss this problem from the standpoint of the teacher organization, their content is also relevant to the negotiating problems of the school administration.

The article by Donald H. Wollett sets forth a view of strategy and tactics by a leading authority on collective negotiations in both private and public employment.

The relative merits of "strikes" and "sanctions" are a matter of considerable controversy at the present time. The article by Barbara Carter describes the impact of the sanctions imposed upon the state of Oklahoma by the Oklahoma Education Association and the National Education Association in 1965.

The last article in this section lists some suggested procedures which should be observed by all parties to negotiations. These suggestions are taken from a recent publication of the U.S. Civil Service Commission for the benefit of federal administrators who must negotiate with organizations of federal employees pursuant to the provisions of President Kennedy's Executive Order 10988.

No selection of readings on strategy and tactics in negotiations would be complete without some reference to teacher strikes. Unfortunately, it was not feasible to include such references in this volume. In any case, even the recent articles on the subject do not deal adequately with the large number of teacher strikes in 1965 and 1966. A recent comparative analysis of strikes and sanctions may be found in Myron Lieberman and Michael H. Moskow, Collective Negotiations for Teachers *(Chicago, Ill.: Rand McNally, 1966), pp. 289-309.*

For an extended analysis of the issues in teacher strikes, see Myron Lieberman, "Teachers' Strikes: An Analysis of the Issues," Harvard Educational Review, 26 *(Winter, 1956), 39-70; and "Teachers' Strikes: Acceptable Strategy?"* Phi Delta Kappan, XLVI *(January, 1965), 237-40.*

VI-1

WINNING COLLECTIVE BARGAINING*

David Selden

Within a very short time collective bargaining will be the normal and established relationship between teachers and their boards of education.

Unlike most professionals, teachers are employees. They work in groups for a single employer, a board of education or a city. What could be more natural than that teachers should organize in such a way that they could negotiate an agreement covering their salaries and other terms of employment. This is the essence of collective bargaining.

However, "natural" though collective bargaining may be for teachers, the sad fact is that in most school districts the relationship between teachers and their employers is largely paternalistic—when it isn't downright oppressive. Collective bargaining is a way to break through this pattern of paternalism. It is the road to maturity for the teaching profession.

Under collective bargaining, the board of education is under obligation to reach *agreement* with the teachers' bargaining agent in regard to salaries, working conditions, fringe benefits, status, and professional standards. This agreement is embodied in a written contract, which is renegotiated each year or at the end of its effective period. It cannot be changed without mutual consent.

Beyond the Legal Frontier

The right of employees to join organizations of their own choosing, the obligation of the employer to bargain with the union representing the employees, and the right to conclude a binding collective bargaining contract is guaranteed by law for employees in private industry.

Such is not the case for teachers. Not that collective bargaining is

* Originally published under the same title in 1965 by the American Federation of Teachers, 716 N. Rush Street, Chicago, Ill. 60611. David Selden is Assistant to the President, American Federation of Teachers. In granting permission, Mr. Selden states: "The following collective bargaining guidelines for AFT locals were written in 1962 before any of the present state collective bargaining laws were passed. Some of the material is no longer applicable, and the booklet is in the process of revision."

against the law for teachers; it's not. It's just that, except in a very few states, teachers and other public employees are *excluded* from the labor relations laws.

Thus, the AFT is thrusting out beyond the legal frontier. We must develop the law as we go, either by formal state legislation, or by district-by-district agreements.

Legislation or Local Action?

AFT locals and state federations should not neglect either the state legislative or local approach to collective bargaining—but by far the greatest gains can be made through local action. The experience in New York City supports this view.

Legislation to provide for collective bargaining machinery for New York City teachers was introduced by friendly legislators in 1956. The bill never got out of committee despite strenuous efforts in each legislative session. When collective bargaining was finally won five years later, it came by action by the New York City Board of Education.

Almost all AFT locals which have won CB contracts have done so via local action: East St. Louis, Butte, Pawtucket, and others.

So, draft your model legislation, exercising caution against restrictive features. Obtain the support of your state AFL-CIO. Make use of the bill for objective publicity purposes—but don't pin your major hopes on it! We can't sit back and say, "There ought to be a law!"

Exclusive Bargaining Agent

Before you can negotiate a collective bargaining contract with your board of education you must be recognized as the exclusive bargaining agent for the teachers in your jurisdiction.

In private industry you would simply petition a labor relations board for certification as the exclusive bargaining agent. The labor board would ascertain whether or not your union really represented a majority of the employees for which you seek to bargain. If the answer is "yes," you would be certified, and your employer would be forced to bargain with you.

The labor board may use various means for verifying representative status of a union. But, in almost every case where the claim of the union is contested—either by the employer or by a rival organization—the labor board orders an election so that the employees may vote.

Furthermore, the labor board will order an election if an organization with less than majority membership asks for bargaining status and shows that it has the support of at least 30 per cent of the employees to be covered.

Surrogate Labor Relations Boards

Since you have no labor relations board to which to appeal, you will have to create a substitute. This is what we mean by developing our own law as we go.

There is nothing to prevent a board of education from turning over the problem of electing an exclusive bargaining agent to an impartial third party.

In small school districts this "surrogate labor relations board" might be a committee of citizens chosen by mutual consent of the teachers and board of education.

In most school districts, however, the wisest course will be to insist that the task of performing the duties of a labor relations board be turned over to professionals specializing in this field. There are a number of organizations which can do this sort of job—The American Arbitration Association, The Honest Ballot Association, and others. Also, many state labor boards are authorized to conduct CB votes if both the employer and the employees agree.

A board of education *can* act as its own labor board—but there are many dangers in this seemingly more direct approach. "Associationism" is the rule in most school districts. If the board of education—the employer—conducts the election, it will be difficult to prevent partiality toward the "company union" education association.

The many technical problems in establishing collective bargaining should be handled by *impartial experts*. Who should be in the bargaining unit? Should it be teachers only? Teachers and minor supervisors? Everybody? How about nonclassroom educational personnel? Substitutes? When will the election be held? How much time will be allowed for campaigning? Will all organizations have equal access to teachers' letterboxes, bulletin boards, and other means of communication? What precautions will be taken against interference by administrators?

The answers to these questions could determine the result of the election. AFT locals have nothing to fear from honest and fair CB elections—but there is a danger that we may be "counted out" in many districts unless we insist on proper procedure.

Getting Started

As we have stated, there is no law *to prevent* your board of education from conforming to the principles of collective bargaining. The problem is how to get the board to do it!

Boards of education *will* behave like employers no matter how agreeable the members may be as individuals. Some boards may agree that CB for teachers is perfectly natural, but many will not. Neither will most superintendents of schools. Boards and superintendents are more apt to regard a move toward collective bargaining as a personal affront.

The education association will immediately recognize the drive of your union toward CB as a challenge to its preferred status. The usually intimate relationship between the board, the superintendent, and the leaders of the association means that you must be ready to take them all on, if need be.

Getting started is your first and major obstacle. Your members *must* be committed to the campaign.

"Support" vs. Membership

The fact that your local's membership is less than a majority of the teachers should not deter you. There are many reasons why your local could have less than a majority in membership, but this would not prevent you from winning CB. If you are ready to accept an all-out commitment to victory, if your program represents the hopes and aspirations of the teachers, and if you keep the teachers with you at each step, *you will win.*

Votes, not just membership, determine the result in a CB election. Otherwise, the education associations with their huge "drafted" memberships would inevitably come out ahead. During the campaign, *membership* in the local should be down-played in favor of *support.* Many teachers will support you in a secret ballot election if you take actions which merit that support, but many of these same teachers will not become members until they feel it is "safe." As a matter of fact, when a teacher says "no" to an appeal to join the union you may have lost his vote because he may feel he has to be "consistent." After you have become the exclusive bargaining agent, membership recruiting is easy. Most teachers will want to belong to "the organization."

Mobilizing for Victory

Once you have decided to "go for CB" your local should regard itself as a candidate for public office—and run scared. You will need to use all the techniques of political campaigning, even if yours is a small school district.

Assess your strengths and weaknesses. Reexamine the policies of your local. In "old" locals this process may prove agonizing, indeed. Find a formula for reserving "splitting" questions for resolution by the membership *after* the election. Concentrate on the things which unite teachers.

The drive for collective bargaining must involve *mass action,* because the final result will depend on the votes of the teachers, and your board of education and superintendent of schools won't accept a CB election unless you have demonstrated a mass demand for it.

Here are some of the things you will need for effective mobilization:

1. a program of collective bargaining proposals which fulfills the hopes of the teachers;

2. effective internal organization;
3. staff;
4. money.

CB Proposals

Your proposals which become your platform or program make CB worth fighting for. Furthermore, this platform or program is what you can't get without collective bargaining.

Don't limit your CB proposals to salary improvements. Take a close look at your school system: class sizes, teacher loads, sick leave, sabbatical and other leaves, extracurricular policy, hiring policies, promotion policies, assignment of nonteaching chores, lunch hour and bus routines, administrative practices, retirement policies—everything which affects teachers.

Draw up a complete platform. Ask teachers, *members and nonmembers,* to participate in the process. Then let everybody know about it—over and over again, so that each point becomes identified with your local. Later, if the association "steals" program points, let teachers know you welcome the added support—but no "joint committees!" If your board adopts part of your platform before CB is attained, it's a feather in your local's cap, and should encourage teachers to further effort.

You can also dramatize isolated issues to win teacher support during the course of the CB campaign.

Your platform will be the means of attracting the support of nonmembers—the votes you need to win. The more commitments you can get from nonmembers, the better your chances.

Internal Organization

Your local, small or large, should secure the active participation of every member. Beware the "one-man local!"

Hold frequent meetings of your top leadership—at least once a week—to make sure that everyone has the same idea about what is being done and what should be done. Then make sure that the lines of communication between membership and leadership are open—up and down.

You can keep in communication with your members in a number of ways. During school hours the members in each school should know how to get in touch with their school representative. Meetings of the members in the school unit should be held every week to discuss the progress of the campaign. When possible, open these meetings to nonmembers too, to involve them in the campaign.

Outside of school hours, keep the telephones busy. A pyramidal telephone network should be set up so that the leadership of the local can get in touch with as many members as possible just by starting a telephone message relay at the top of the network pyramid.

Then, of course, you will have your local publications: your local's newspaper and "flyers" on special topics.

Money

You will need money—more than you think. Here are a few ideas on how to get it.

If your dues schedule is too low, raise it. Remember, you are asking your members for a *total* commitment; they know this means that they will have to give added financial support. Since you are not particularly worried about recruiting new members during the campaign, there is no reason to keep dues low as a recruitment incentive, either.

It is often possible to raise money by simply asking teachers for it—members and nonmembers. If you want an ad in the paper, or a radio or TV program, take a collection from *all* the teachers. When a nonmember gives a dollar to a union cause, he has made an investment, and a certain degree of commitment goes along with it.

Other AFT locals may also give or loan money if you ask them, and your central labor body and the rest of the labor movement will also support you if you really mean business.

Fund-raising activities should be sponsored for the money itself and also to dramatize the collective bargaining objective.

In a pinch you can *borrow* from your members. During its CB campaign the United Federation of Teachers in New York City sold $100 "CB Bonds" to its members and raised more than $15,000.

Staff

You may be beginning to realize that winning collective bargaining involves a lot of work.

You will find that you cannot rely on volunteer efforts alone. Many of the officers and members of the local will be putting in a double day: one at school and the other at union headquarters. But even this will not be sufficient to cope with the resources of the NEA-sponsored association and the school administration if they really want to make a fight of it. You will have to hire some sort of staff. With planning, this can be done at relatively little cost.

You will need a headquarters—an official office with a telephone, or several phones, and clerical service. Perhaps your central labor body has a spare room which you can use for the duration of the campaign. If not, a vacant store, or inexpensive office will suffice. You need not have *full-time* clerical service. Use a telephone answering service for calls during school hours; encourage teachers to call after school hours when the office is manned by officers. Key officers should have home phones for union business so that family phoning does not get in the way of incoming messages.

You may find it advantageous to pay some of your members to "moonlight" for the union so that you can be sure about getting out mailings, making phone calls, checking lists, supervising volunteers, and getting other jobs done on time.

You should also ask for help from your AFT National President and of your State Federation President. They can't do the job for you, but these experienced officers and their staff may be able to save you headaches and give extra manpower at times when your own resources just won't cover. *Don't* go ahead on your own, however, and expect the AFT or the state federations to bail you out. Check first to see what you can count on.

Preparing the Way

You know you are going to need platform, organization, money, and staff—but if you wait until you are all set before you begin your CB campaign you may never get started. These requirements come much easier under the urgency and pressure of the campaign than they do while you are still in the talking stage.

Once you have set up your headquarters and picked people to handle specific jobs—a telephone network coordinator, literature distribution, publicity, and fund-raising—start an educational campaign among the teachers to explain what collective bargaining means. Literature, meetings, advertising, public relations; use every possible means to show that CB means orderly personnel relationships and true professional status.

Avoid any premature challenge to your board of education, superintendent, or local education association. Accent the positive: CB is the *normal* way to handle teacher-superintendent-board of education relationships. Show how other professionals have benefited from collective bargaining: newspapermen, musicians, actors, engineers, and others. Stress the democratic nature of collective bargaining.

Building a Program

Start building your program at once. Some of the key parts of your program, such as the salary demands, require careful pre-study by your union leadership. Most of the program, however, should come from the teachers themselves—members and nonmembers. Here's how to do it.

1. Mimeo a *tentative* first draft. Include salary increases, fringe benefits, improvements in sick leave, sabbaticals, maternity leave, class sizes, teacher loads and programs, payment for extracurricular activities—any practice or policy where there is room for improvement.

2. Distribute copies to every teacher, with the explanation that you are building your program for "this year," and that you want their help.

3. Attach a tear-off suggestion blank and invite teachers to list additional points, make suggestions about the points listed, and offer comments about the program in general. Stress the confidential, anonymous nature of the replies. Provide a definite method of getting the suggestions back to you. What you want is *participation*.

4. Collate the returns and prepare a "final" list. Don't worry about the length of the list: the longer the better. If the suggestion is good for the teachers, include it.

5. Now send out the list again for a "vote" by the teachers. The more "official" you can make this vote, the better. The best method is to attach a petition form to the list and get teachers to sign that they support the program. Your union representatives in each school can circulate copies of the program with the attached petition blanks. If teachers won't sign their names to a petition, conduct a secret ballot vote. Voting by schools, conducted by your building representative is the best procedure, but a mailed ballot can always be used if you cannot arrange for school voting.

6. If you use a mail ballot, however, couple it with a telephone campaign to "get out the vote." Also, use a "referendum committee" to conduct the balloting, so that the results are less subject to challenge.

If you handle this part of your campaign properly you should accomplish the following:

1. You have a CB program which appeals to the teachers.

2. You have generated a degree of commitment to your program by nonmembers.

3. You have inspired confidence by your adherence to democratic procedure.

4. You have gained the initiative.

Presenting Your Program

Now the time has come to make contact with your board of education.

Your activities thus far have been limited to building internal strength and arousing teacher support. You have a comprehensive program and you have publicized it. To maintain your initiative you must take action to achieve the program. The next step is to send the list of program points—all of them—to the board and *ask for negotiations*.

Note that you do not ask the board to *adopt* the program. What you want is *negotiations*. This is important, because either way you're pretty sure to get a negative response, and it is much better that refusal to negotiate—undemocratic procedure—be the issue than any specific program point.

The board may be able to advance many reasons for not acceding to a specific salary or other demand, but to refuse "to talk" with you puts the board on the defensive. The only *valid* excuse for not negotiating with you is that the board does not accept your representative status, and this will point up the need for a collective bargaining election.

Here is what may happen to your request for negotiations:

1. Your request is ignored.
2. Your request is "taken under advisement."
3. Your request is attacked or ridiculed.
4. Your request is referred to the superintendent.

If the board directs you to talk with the superintendent, you should comply. Since the *board* has referred you to the superintendent, you should make clear that he is thus acting as the board's agent in meeting with you. Such would not be the case if you were to go to the superintendent first.

Incidentally, here is a point where the AFT approach differs importantly from that of the NEA. The NEA rejects collective bargaining as a labor technique, but does accept "professional negotiation." This doesn't seem to be merely more NEA semantics. The NEA wants teachers to take their problems to the superintendent and let *him* do the negotiating with the board.

The AFT objective in collective bargaining is to conclude a written contract between the representative of the teachers and their employer, the board of education. We understand, however, that the board does have the right to choose someone to represent it, just as do the teachers.

So, meet with your superintendent. The chances are that *he* will also want to "take your program under advisement," and you will find yourself in much the same position as though the board had begun the stalling in the first place.

There is also a good possibility that the superintendent will call you to a joint meeting with the association. Your response should be a firm and clear *no*. It's hard enough to negotiate with the superintendent without having to negotiate with the association as well! Make this clear without alienating teacher support. Don't attack the association; welcome the support of individual association members and even the association itself—but make it clear that you cannot enter into three-way negotiations.

The Authorization Petition

So far, the spotlight has been on your program, rather than collective bargaining per se. In pedagogical terms, you have been motivating the teachers, and if you have done the job well, collective bargaining should now be a felt need.

You are now ready for your first formal move for collective bargaining: the "authorization petition." Here we follow the procedure of the labor board for private industry. Labor boards require an organization seeking bargaining agent status to submit proof that it has the *support* of at least 30 per cent of the employees in the proposed collective bargaining unit.

Even if you have more than 30 per cent of the teachers in membership, use the authorization petition to gain the support of nonmembers. Don't stop your petition when you have received 30 per cent. Make sure all teachers are asked to sign the petition.

You may want to consult an attorney specializing in labor law—but since yours is not a "legal" problem in the strict sense, you should not lean too heavily on legal counsel.

The statement on the petition should read something like the following:

PETITION
TO THE BOARD OF EDUCATION OF CENTRAL DISTRICT #9
MIDDLE COUNTY, PENNSYLVANIA

WE THE UNDERSIGNED teachers and other nonsupervisory educational employees of Central School District #9, Middle County, Pennsylvania hereby authorize the Middle County Federation of Teachers to represent us for the purpose of collective bargaining, and we do hereby petition the Board of Education of said school district to direct that an election for the purpose of determining an exclusive bargaining agent for teachers and other nonsupervisory employees in said school district be held by an impartial agency, such agency to be selected by agreement among the interested parties.

DATE	SIGNATURE	ADDRESS

Instead of a petition, authorization cards may be used. The petition form is preferred, however, because it is easier to get teachers to sign when they know that they are not alone. Start off the petition by getting the signatures of the union members first; then go to the most sympathetic nonmembers. Leave the "tough nuts" until last. A strong "selling point" is the fact that you are petitioning for an *election,* in which everyone will have a chance to *vote* by secret ballot.

The authorization petition may be a high hurdle, but it is essential. Signing a petition doesn't rate high on any militancy scale, but it still may be above the level to which many teachers are willing to go. Signing often represents a personal act of independence against a paternalistic employer.

Your appeal in overcoming reluctance to disturb the status quo rests on strong moral grounds as well as self-interest. The right to petition is guaranteed by the United States Constitution and state constitutions. This very right to petition for a collective bargaining election has been guaranteed by the Wagner Act to all workers in private industry. Why should a teacher have less rights than a carpenter, factory worker, musician or actor?

If, in spite of your efforts to persuade teachers to sign the petition, you have a difficult time achieving the normal 30 per cent, this doesn't *necessarily* mean that you can't win the CB election if and when it is held, but it does mean that you should find out why teachers won't sign. If it's fear of administrative or public disapproval, this influence will operate with much less force in a secret ballot vote than in signing one's name to a public petition. It is, therefore, still possible to win the election despite the hard time with the petition.

However, if the reason for the reluctance of teachers to sign your petition is that they just don't like the union, it becomes obvious that you must do much more educating and self-evaluation before you proceed.

Special Problems in Connection with the Petition

The authorization petition is a key point in your whole collective bargaining campaign.

For one thing, your petition defines your idea of the proper bargaining unit. The "bargaining unit" is *not the union* doing the bargaining; it is *the employees* for whom the bargaining agent bargains. You should seek to define the unit so that it includes the largest number of school employees among whom you can win an election.

The ultimate determination of which employees are in and which employees are out of the bargaining unit should be made by the surrogate labor relations board chosen to conduct the election. However, the action of the union will have a strong bearing on this determination.

The petition campaign itself presents the school administration with problems, because it solidifies your support. The superintendent will almost certainly interpret the circulation of the petition as a cloud on his horizon. He may wait to see what develops, but as your campaign gets rolling you can expect him to take preventive action.

The pattern of opposition from superintendents which seems to be developing in localities where AFT locals have begun CB campaigns is a turn to more active company unionism. The NEA's American Association of School Administrators, the dominant force within the NEA, at its spring 1963 convention, boldly advocated closer cooperation with local education associations as the best way to handle teacher drives for collective bargaining status. This "union-busting" pattern ties in with the NEA scheme for "professional negotiation."

A campaign for collective bargaining by Denver teachers was temporarily stymied by the superintendent in the fall of 1962 by using the "professional negotiation" gambit. When the union petition campaign began to gather steam, the local "company union" education association and superintendent entered into an agreement for "professional negotiation" which was subsequently pushed through the school board. When put on paper, "professional negotiation" turn out to be a typical "sweetheart contract" or "employee representation" plan similar to the type favored by antiunion employers 30-40 years ago.

The way to stop this sort of "run-around-left-end" is to make certain that you have solid teacher support *before* you launch your petition campaign. The private deal between the superintendent and the association must be exposed as antiunion and antidemocratic, and both teacher and public opposition should be speedily and forcefully organized.

Getting the Board to Schedule the Election

As we have pointed out, you can't go to court and force your board of education to schedule your collective bargaining election, even though you have followed the petition procedure specified for such elections in private industry. In this respect the labor laws, by excluding teachers and other public employees, make them "second class citizens." Your success in getting past this obstacle depends on (1) teachers' support, and (2) public support.

So far, we have stressed techniques for winning teacher support, because unless you are successful in this effort you can't win the election if and when it is scheduled. Also, the fact that teachers want and demand collective bargaining rights is your most important asset in winning public support.

The public will respect teachers when the teachers show that they respect themselves. When you assert your belief that you are entitled to the same rights as other employees, many people will accept this principle at face value. However, you cannot safely rely on teacher strength alone to swing public support your way. If the board of education decides to make a fight of it, the board will appeal to the public to back its stand. Therefore, your best strategy is to get there *first*.

Labor Support

AFT locals have a source of public support which is not available to the associations. This is the labor movement. Even here, however, you can't take support for granted. Although the idea that teachers should bargain collectively with their boards of education has been widely accepted by most labor leaders, some still have lingering attitudes which place teachers on a pedestal to be admired, but kept away from the practical realities of union functioning.

Thus, it is extremely important that your local be thoroughly integrated in the local and state AFL-CIO bodies. Be sure your full quota of delegates attends all meetings. You should choose delegates who can make friends among the representatives of other unions without getting tangled up in the intraorganizational politics which, as in all democratic institutions, is usually present. Serve on committees. Support the special projects of your central and state labor bodies, even though you may think these do not directly concern you. After all, your struggle for CB rights does not *directly* concern other unions either. Union solidarity is an *ideal* which can be achieved only if you work at it.

In addition to the obvious and minimal cooperation with other unions mentioned above, more direct action should be taken. Private conferences should be held with key union leaders to explain what you are doing and what you expect from them in the way of support. *Don't expect them to do the job for you!* Don't become a dependent ward of the labor movement! You must act in your own behalf; then you can demand and get the support of other unions.

Supporting action from organized labor can take many forms, and you will have to decide what will best serve your interests. Most local union newspapers will publish articles explaining your point of view if you submit them. Most local unions will permit a teacher speaker to appear at a membership or executive board meeting. If you want public statements from union leaders, care should be taken not to give the impression that "the unions are trying to take over the schools."

Your AFL-CIO affiliation is an important source of strength, but don't make this your *only* weapon in your battle for public support.

Public Relations

When we think of public support, most of us think of the magic term "public relations." The image we have is a flow of publicity based on press releases, in which we "tell the public our story"—usually in manifestos of a few thousand well-chosen words. This glamorous sort of public relations is important, but it's only a small part of a really effective public relations program. Furthermore, in most localities the local press is apt to be somewhat less than sympathetic to your drive for CB rights, and most editors will prefer to write their own editorials, even if they are sympathetic to your cause.

Guidelines for developing good press relations are available from the AFT national office and these will be very helpful. The general rule to keep in mind, however, is that good press publicity results from *doing good things*. "Actions speak louder than words" is a good maxim. It could be rewritten, however, as, "Take the right *actions* and the right *words* will follow."

It isn't necessary to "pussyfoot" about your demand for collective bargaining. If you are apologetic or defensive, the public is apt to get the idea that something is wrong with what you are doing. Instead, show that your demands are in the best interests of the schools and the children. This is another reason why your list of bargaining demands should be much more than a program for salary increases and fringe benefits.

Good teaching conditions make good learning conditions. A demand for smaller classes is a demand for more individualized instruction for the children. A sick leave program is a plan for making it possible for sick teachers to stay out of the classroom. A duty-free lunch hour demand, in addition to being a campaign for "the right to eat," is also a way to conserve teacher energies for the professional teaching service for which teachers are employed.

You can dramatize your demands for improved working conditions by exposing the ways in which present school conditions deprive children of educational opportunity. Again: action is better than words. A survey; a "case study"; a photograph; a petition; a public meeting; a banquet or luncheon; research—each of these things are *actions* which create news which is much less vulnerable to distortion than unsupported public statements and opinion.

Parent and Civic Leaders

Winning the battle for public support—over the opposition of your school board, if necessary—is the key to winning the larger battle for collective bargaining. Even more important than publicity is the more basic sort of public relations with parent and civic groups.

As in winning labor support, conferences should be held with key community leaders. Simple, direct explanations of what you are trying to do, coupled with offers of cooperation on projects of mutual interest can do a lot toward smoothing the way for firm support. You can be sure your employer, the board of education and the superintendent, will not neglect this important job; you must make certain that the teachers' point of view is also presented.

One very useful tool in building public support is a "citizens council for better schools." Perhaps your community already has such a council. If so, become an active member. If there is no "better schools committee" in your locality, you can set one up. The wisest course is to induce a parents' group or civic association to take the lead in the formation of the committee. If the committee is merely a creature of the union, its effectiveness will be seriously curtailed.

If you cannot set up a permanent better schools committee, you may be able to get up a list of prominent citizens who endorse the "right to vote" in a collective bargaining election for teachers. The endorsement list serves the dual purpose of getting the board to act favorably on your petition and giving teachers confidence that collective bargaining is "all right." Note that the endorsers are backing the "right to vote"—not your local union per se. If you assemble a list of endorsements of your local, you can expect your opposition to prepare a similar list for *its* side. Thus, the contest becomes a sort of public popularity poll, instead of concentrating on getting CB rights established.

This is not the place to give a complete discussion of public relations techniques. Check with the AFT national office about how to handle your special problems.

One important observation should be made, however. Some AFT local leaders have felt that public relations efforts are a waste of time, since in any public showdown between teachers and their board of education, the latter has all the high cards. This is essentially a defeatist attitude; an excuse for inactivity. You can win the battle for public support if you work at it. Furthermore, you don't have to muster overwhelming or even majority public support to be effective.

If you can demonstrate that a *significant segment* of the public supports your views, your board will be restrained from outright opposition to your campaign, in most cases, and your chances of moving your board to positive action are immeasurably improved.

Kit of Tools for Action

So far, all the techniques which we have discussed for getting your board of education to recognize your CB petition fall under the heading of "persuasion." If these methods are properly carried out, your chances for success are excellent.

Furthermore, as more and more AFT locals, and public employees generally, achieve collective bargaining status, the necessity for using more direct methods becomes less likely. Nevertheless, if you are looking for ultimate answers to the question of what can be done if your board of education does not respond to all your "peaceful" efforts, the following suggestions may be your "tools of action."

I. *Campaigns to win public support:*
  A. *Motorcades*—A motorcade is a parade of cars, decorated with appropriate signs and displays, to call public attention to your problem.
  B. *Mass picketing* of board of education headquarters. The famous "walks" by Chicago teachers are a variation of this technique. The purpose of such mass picketing is to turn the pressure of public opinion against the board. Timing, however, is very important in attempting this procedure.
  C. *"Honor picketing"* of schools in the morning before school begins. This type of protest action brings the problem into the local community, stirring up grass roots public support, rather than the more generalized support resulting from headquarters picketing.
  D. *Public petition campaigns.* The advantage of this action is that it can be kept rolling over a period of weeks or months, generating mounting pressures, if successful.
  E. *Mass meetings.* These provide a forum for "sounding off" in a public

way against unreasonable action by your board of education. Its success is in some relation to the attendance. For this reason, effort must be made to get out the membership.

II. *Direct Action:*

    A. *Electing favorable school board*—in districts where school boards are elected, resolution of controversy can be attained by active participation in campaigns to elect board members favoring collective bargaining and supporting democratic school procedures. Candidates for the board of education should always be polled to determine their attitudes on vital school issues, including collective bargaining. It must be understood that favorable candidates can be elected only as a result of an active, vigorous campaign.

    B. *Mass sick leaves and slow downs*—These forms of direct action have built-in self-defeating defects which make them difficult—if not dangerous—to use. By their use, the union may be placed in a dubious moral position, and they can actually be a demonstration of weakness.

    C. *Stoppage of extra curricular activities*—This involves the cessation of those activities which are extraneous to the fundamental school program. Those extra curricular activities which you choose to boycott should be chosen with care so as not to lose valuable public support.

    D. *Withholding contracts*—In areas where individual contracts are issued, contracts may be assigned to the president of the local to strengthen his hand in the negotiations. This step should be taken with utmost caution and it would be wise to consult the AFT office before so doing. Use of any of these devices requires extreme caution to prevent the loss of valuable public support.

III. *Work Stoppage*

If you are considering strike action, you must be reasonably certain of carrying the action through to its successful conclusion. If you have that much strength, you ought to be able to get your CB election *without* a strike except in the most extreme circumstances.

Carrying out successful strike action is a complex problem and should not be given the once-over-lightly treatment. Your ability to conduct a successful work stoppage can be a powerful "enforcer" which enhances the probability of success of less drastic activities, but there is a vast difference between the *ability* to strike and the actual *use* of the weapon. There is probably nothing worse, from a tactical standpoint, than *talking* strike without being willing or able to back up your words if your bluff is called.

Having exhausted all of the aforementioned tools of action, and after consultation with the AFT National Office, in accordance with the AFT convention action, work stoppage may be your final alternative. It must be remembered at all times that the American Federation of Teachers has long maintained that CB is the avenue by which teachers can resolve their griev-ances and eliminate the need for a strike. Therefore, the public must be kept aware of the fact that CB is the ultimate aim.

Winning the Election

There is no surefire method for inducing your board of education to grant your petition for a CB election, of course. Nevertheless, with persis-tence, hard work, and wise leadership, your chances of success in this venture are good—and even if you do not achieve success right away, your local will be greatly strengthened as a result of your efforts.

Your campaign to win the CB election is really an extension of the cam-paign to get the election scheduled. If you have followed along thus far, you have established the solid base from which the winning vote total will result. The period of actual electioneering is usually relatively short—a month or even less.

Winning the election is a problem of politics, and the usual "rules" apply: (1) mobilize your supporters, (2) sharpen your publicity, (3) contact your voters.

One caution should be noted; very few elections are won by attacking your opponent. You should concentrate on getting the teachers to vote *for* you, rather than *against* your opponent. This point reemphasizes the impor-tance of your *program*. Furthermore, when you attack the "other organiza-tion" you may cause nominal members of the group to rally in support of their membership in the organization.

The emphasis in the election campaign should be that the *vote* does not affect membership. No one has to be a *member* of the AFT to vote for you —and voting for the AFT does not necessarily mean that teachers will *have to join* the AFT if you win. This concept flows from the long AFT campaign against forced membership in administrator-dominated NEA-affiliated associations.

In any political campaign, nothing beats the personal appeal. Every union member must be a campaigner. Every teacher must be contacted by personal call or by telephone. In the final days of the campaign, chief reli-ance should be placed on a massive telephone campaign. Every voter should get a phone call.

School lunchtime meetings are good campaign forums.

You must supply most of the ingenuity and energy. No one can do it for you. THE MAIN IDEA IS TO LEAVE NOTHING TO CHANCE. KEEP EVERYBODY WORKING RIGHT UP TO THE DEADLINE.

VI-2

LESSONS FROM DETROIT AND CLEVELAND*

Dick Dashiell

When considering the elections in Detroit and Cleveland—or in any other city which involves the American Federation of Teachers (AFT)—it is essential that you understand that the American Federation of Teachers is a "front" in the drive by organized labor to take over the teaching profession in the United States.

This drive is generated by the fact that the number of blue-collar workers in the labor force has been, and is, dropping steadily; and the number of white-collar workers has been, and is, rising steadily. Naturally, the American Federation of Labor and Congress of Industrial Organizations (AFL-CIO) *must* enroll more white-collar workers in order just to stand still, not to mention grow, insofar as its membership is concerned. It feels that if it can enlist teachers, its task of organizing technicians, clerks, secretaries, draftsmen, stenographers, government employees, and millions of other white-collar workers will be made very much easier.

Spearheading labor's drive to capture the loyalty, and dues money, of teachers is the Industrial Union Department of the AFL-CIO, commonly called the IUD. Walter Reuther, president of the United Automobile Workers and vice-president of the AFL-CIO, is president of the IUD. Mr. Reuther told the AFT convention three years ago that one million teachers would be unionized.

The IUD executive director is Jack Conway, former administrative assistant to Mr. Reuther in the UAW and acknowledged to be one of the most brilliant men in the labor movement. Its director of organization is Nicholas Zonarich, who has worked on the staffs of a number of industrial unions. In fact, he is a former president of one of them, the Aluminum Workers of America. Heading up the drive to organize teachers is Franz Daniel, a former

---

* This is a case study of two elections to determine which teachers' organization would win exclusive representation rights, prepared for presentation at the NEA Conference on Professional Negotiation, September 10, 1964, in Chicago. Dick Dashiell is a Professional Assistant, Urban Services Division, NEA.

organizer for the Amalgamated Clothing Workers and of the AFL-CIO itself. He is shrewd, capable, and energetic.

These men form an intelligent, hard-working, hard-hitting leadership. Do not—I repeat, do *not*—underestimate them.

The Industrial Union Department consists chiefly of men and women in mass production industries: auto workers, electricians, steelworkers, oil workers, rubber workers, and the like. Their unions made up the vast bulk of the CIO before it merged in 1955 with the American Federation of Labor to form the AFL-CIO.

I will refer later to specific examples, in Detroit and Cleveland, of the strategy and tactics of the trade union approach to teachers. Suffice it to say at this point that not a single, solitary affiliate of the teachers' federation asks a board of education for an election to determine which organization shall represent teachers unless the request has been approved by IUD headquarters in Washington, D. C. Or is it in Detroit?

I do want you to keep in mind throughout this discussion of the Detroit and Cleveland situations, just what, and just whom, the profession in Detroit and Cleveland was fighting.

What did we learn in Detroit and Cleveland?

I guess the first thing we learned—or at least the first thing *I* learned— was to stock up on dexedrine to stay awake and on Sominex to put me to sleep. An elephant's hide, I found, was also most helpful.

Seriously, though, the elections proved once again that you can't make a silk purse out of a swine's ear. Or beat the Yankees with a sandlot ball club.

What I am saying is, Detroit and Cleveland proved that, to win an election, a professional association must establish a record of achievement.

1. It must have a vigorous program.

2. It must have an active leadership.

3. It must have an organizational structure with responsibilities assigned in well-defined areas, and provision for a free exchange of ideas.

4. It must have good communications with the teachers.

5. It must have good relations with the public.

6. It must have a hard-hitting membership recruitment program, particularly in the high schools and, more particularly, among men in the high schools.

7. It must identify problems that are bothering teachers.

8. It must encourage the more alert, creative, and active members to assume tasks of real responsibility in the association. These include teachers new to the profession.

9. It must be ready to move into an election contest quickly and effectively.

10. It must cooperate with its state association, and with the NEA.

11. It must have a strong staff. This means, primarily, that it should have a capable, full-time, salaried executive secretary, with competent secretarial and clerical help.

12. It must understand that the real "shakers" and "movers" in labor's drive to organize teachers are the chieftains of the AFL-CIO Industrial Union Department.

13. It must understand the strategy and tactics of the IUD.

Basically, those are the things that a local professional association must have, and must do, and must understand, if it is to win a representation election in a contest with the union.

Now, as you know, the Detroit Education Association and the Cleveland Education Association lost their elections—the DEA on May 11, 1964, and the CEA exactly four weeks later, on June 8.

The DEA received 3,848 votes to 5,739 for the Detroit Federation of Teachers, which polled 59.9 per cent of the vote. The CEA received 2,026 votes to 2,701 for the Cleveland Teachers Union, which polled 57.1 per cent of the CEA-CTU vote, and 55.2 per cent of the total vote. (Unlike Detroit, Cleveland teachers were permitted to vote for neither contending party, and 162 of them did.) Both unions polled a majority of the total number of teachers.

Both the DEA and the CEA possessed several of the ingredients I have just outlined for a successful professional group. The Detroit association, for instance, had a good, full-time executive secretary, although he had not been on the job long enough to get the organization under a full head of steam by the date of the election. And the Cleveland association had accomplished many vital goals in behalf of the city's teachers.

But neither of them possessed enough of the essential qualities to pull through victory.

When I say that a professional association must establish a record of achievement, I mean also that the record should be common knowledge among teachers. This was not true in either Detroit or Cleveland. I will bet you even odds that when the election campaign began not more than one per cent of the teachers in either city could tell you two things that the professional association had done for them in the last three years.

It is a fact that the Detroit and Cleveland Education Associations, for at least one year, and probably longer, had been the most effective organizations representing the public school teachers. Their effectiveness can be well documented. But did most of the teachers know it? I say no.

They would have been even more at a loss to tell you what the state association or the NEA had accomplished. We found, for instance, that many teachers in Detroit gave the teachers' union credit for obtaining state tenure. The fact is that it was the Michigan Education Association which was responsible for obtaining enough names on a petition to force the legislature to consider the tenure measure. And the NEA backed that up with potent lobbying so that tenure is now mandatory throughout the state of Michigan.

Important as it is for a local association to establish a good record, the Detroit and Cleveland experiences showed that even more important is a program of action. What does the association propose to do about teacher transfers? What is its policy on extracurricular duties? Is it making a study of tax sources which may prove to the board of education that salaries can be raised without bankrupting the school district—or of the needs of members and potential members without causing the president of the taxpayers' alliance to go out and shoot himself? The association *must* be responsive.

Teachers are people, and like other people they don't care as much about what the association has done for them in the past as they do about what it's doing for them now and is going to do for them in the future. They're grateful for the coffee you brought them, but when are you going to put a little sugar in it?

Most teachers, even in highly ingrown areas like Detroit and Cleveland, and even those teachers from union homes, really want to be considered professionals. They are looking for the same status and recognition as all other teachers. They *want* to belong to professional associations *if* they can feel that something active and constructive is going on in these associations. But in too many cases nothing is going on, so they turn to the union or become susceptible to union appeals.

To carry out a strong program, there must be vigorous leadership on the part of the elected officers. This, frankly, was lacking in the two cities we are discussing today. At least it had been lacking until the threat of an election galvanized the officers into action. Frankly, the elections were good therapy—like an electric shock applied to the seat of the pants. At least some of the old ladies kicked off their tennis shoes, and the old young men took off their shawls.

Even militant leadership, however, can be shackled by a structure that resembles either a busy gnat or a beached whale. Quite candidly, when I first went into Detroit—more than a year before the election—I was appalled by the proliferation of committees and the lack of operational guidelines for them. Committee members either were stumbling over one another or were carefully avoiding one another. Neither there nor in Cleveland did there appear to be any real channel of communication between one committee and another.

Incidentally, in Detroit, one-third of the committee chairmen were appointed by the president of the DEA, one-third were appointed by the Board of Directors, and one-third were elected by the Congress, composed of 300 or so chapter chairmen. (As a sidelight, the Civil Rights Committee had no Negro on it despite the fact that approximately one-fourth of Detroit teachers are Negro.)

Neither in Detroit nor in Cleveland was there really a good flow of information from the membership. Too many building representatives—or chapter chairmen, as they are called in Detroit—felt "left out" . . . or were lazy . . . or did not sympathize with the aims and objectives of the association . . . or wanted to be the star ball-carrier instead of the blocking back . . . or liked the title but not the toil . . . or were feuding with the officers or fellow teachers or both over real or imagined slights, past or present. Some of them refused to distribute material we circulated during the election campaign in their buildings. Too many were the only individuals in their buildings who would take the job and felt imposed upon. Maybe new approaches to the selection of BR's should be studied.

One of the real pillars of the Detroit association structure was the District Directors—known as DD's. The DD's—one to each district in the system—are teachers who are paid to keep in close contact with the membership in their districts' schools, find out what's "bugging" them, arrange appearances in their districts of officers and others who can explain the association's program, and, in general, take the temperature and feel the pulse of DEA people. They report to the executive secretary.

This leads us into the subject of communications with the teachers, both members and nonmembers. The best communication in the world is face-to-face. This goes without saying and everybody who has ever heard of Adam and Eve should know it.

Even so, it's easier said than done—particularly by building representatives who must do the talking in a large city such as Detroit or Cleveland. It's amazing that so many persons who make their living by the spoken word—by teaching—hesitate to speak up for the professional association for which they have accepted positions of responsibility.

Both Detroit and Cleveland have attractive monthly publications. But they are confined to the membership and are sent to the buildings. Their other material—flyers, brochures, pamphlets, and so forth—were about specific topics, such as insurance, retirement, and so on. Many were promotional.

The chief trouble with the written material in both cities was that they didn't reach all the teachers, and nothing was sent into their homes.

Detroit and Cleveland illustrated that it is absolutely essential—I'll say it again, absolutely essential—that any association that may face an election in either the near or distant future—and that's just about every urban association in the country—should have the home mailing address of every member of the professional staff. And also their telephone numbers. (I'll explain why in a minute.) Otherwise it will have to do what the DEA and CEA people did when an election was called—run around like chickens with their heads cut off frantically trying to obtain the addresses from the Board of Education, or the school buildings, or the city directory, or the phone book, or somewhere. In short, the DEA and CEA were caught with their addresses down.

I won't go into the "do's" and "don'ts" of communications. You can get plenty of help in that field from the National School Public Relations Association (NSPRA). But I do want to say that I believe the associations in both Detroit and Cleveland would have been in better shape if they had paid someone *who had no other duties with the association* to handle their publications. This is not meant as criticism of the people who did supervise the writing and editing of materials. On the whole, they did a commendable job. But they were restricted by the press of their other duties with the association and by the lack of time.

It might be well for urban associations to consider hiring a professional newspaperman who needs the money, and who can be trusted, to edit their publications. You can throw some association newspapers and newsletters up to the ceiling and read all the news in them before they hit the floor.

The topic of communications with the teaching staff is often lumped with public relations. But although they are similar in many respects, they are different in others. It's like mixing apples and oranges. A professional association president or executive secretary may be a jim-dandy in getting his message across to teachers, but a complete and utter flop when it comes to reaching the public. I think that, to a degree, that was true in Detroit and Cleveland.

Again, I don't intend to talk about public relations methods. However, the Detroit and Cleveland campaigns taught one thing about public relations and the local association: *Don't hide your light under a bushel.* Don't think it is unprofessional to boast of your accomplishments, or to let the newspapers and radio and television stations know what you are doing or what you plan to do. The managing editor of one of the daily papers in Detroit told a group of us, "For Pete's sake, let us know what's going on in your association. The union always let's us know what's up. The DEA doesn't. Give us your propaganda. What's wrong with propaganda? It might be news. We're in the news business. So we like it."

In Cleveland, we met with the editorial writers of both papers—and of course with the education writers. Well, they didn't give us editorial support during the election, but I'm convinced that what we had to tell them of the professional association vis-a-vis the teachers' union will stand us in good stead some day—perhaps when the next election rolls around, as roll it will.

A good program of public relations will help you reach teachers that you miss in association publications. It helps to keep members who might think of dropping out of the association, it helps to gain new members, and it helps to win votes at the polls.

The two elections we have been discussing proved that the weakest support for the professional association came from the male teachers in the secondary schools. I don't think any proof was needed, and I don't think the situation in Detroit and Cleveland was different from that in nearly every other city. But it was brought home forcefully by the campaigns—like a pot of dynamite on the kitchen stove.

Now there have been several thousand explanations—pedagogical, sociological, psychological, logical, and illogical—of just why the professional association has a tough time recruiting the male secondary teacher, but I think if you rolled them all up into a five-letter word it would spell *image,* which goes back to the business of accomplishment, movement, program, structure, communications. Whatever the reason, the Detroit and Cleveland campaigns demonstrated that enlisting men teachers on the side of the association is crucial. This is true not only because they are making up a larger and larger percentage of the teaching staff as time goes on, but they are more influential, and they are more active than most of the women teachers. Many women teachers have home duties which prevent them from participating in association work in so full a measure as the men.

Arousing the sympathies of men teachers really means recruiting men teachers into the association. By and large, I believe, the man teacher is more committed to his organization than is the woman teacher. He is less likely to switch. Put another way, he is more likely to remain loyal to his group when he votes in a representation election. That was certainly true in Detroit and Cleveland.

To enlist teachers, men or women—and, indeed, to win elections—the association must know what concerns them most professionally. Is it class size? Instructional materials? Salaries? More time to teach? Discipline? Tenure?

In Detroit, *no* one had *ever* asked the teachers what troubled them most until the DEA polled them by telephone during the election campaign. Their big problems were, in the order of frequency mentioned: class size, relief from nonteaching duties, salaries, more and better instructional materials, transfers, administrative cooperation, and fringe benefits. No one in the DEA office from the president on down would have guessed that those problems bothered the teachers in that order. Incidentally, the Detroit Federation of Teachers got the "smarts" and used the same issues during the campaign— *after* the DEA had publicized them in its campaign newspaper.

Despite what was learned through telephone polling in Detroit, one of the basic problems that the profession faces as it competes with the union is the lack of motivational research to determine the factors that most appeal to the urban teachers. The state associations could be of great assistance here, among other areas. Are we going into these fights without knowing what we should do to win, and how we should do it? Does the material we disseminate *really* stir the teacher and affect his motivational impulses?

Frankly, I don't know. But if the profession had a good motivational research program, we *might* be astonished to learn what the urban teacher really wants. We may be so astonished, in fact, that the purposes and program of a local association may have to be completely redirected, and the high goals and high hopes of our state and national organizations may have to be completely reevaluated.

Here's a good place where the Detroit and Cleveland associations could have used the talents of their more enthusiastic, committed members—particularly the younger teachers. If there had been an adequate system of interaction between the teachers, members or otherwise, and the association leadership via perceptive members who were assigned the job of finding out what their colleagues were thinking, it could have saved much time, thought, and energy during the campaigns.

There is a great danger in urban associations, as in state associations, that an "old guard" may retain power over long periods of time, freezing out younger potential leaders and, at the same time, maintain its control principally to advance its own status locally, state-wide, and nationally.

Because new teachers have little or no background regarding their roles in professional life outside the classroom, the entire burden of orienting them falls on a few leaders. Many associations—such as those we're talking about —have ceased this "ABC" training. Yet no method of "educating" potential teachers has been found. Colleges do not prepare the teacher to be a citizen of his profession. Little is being done to build in him an understanding of professional organizations, and the advantages and necessities of professional philosophy over a philosophy that is largely—sometimes solely—committed to wages, hours, and working conditions.

This draws us into the topic of the types of teachers who work in urban school systems. I hate to shatter illusions, but my observations in Detroit and Cleveland—as well as in other urban communities, but particularly in the two at issue—are that we may have duped ourselves into believing that *all* urban teachers are qualified professional practitioners with sincere interests in teaching as a profession.

There are many loyal, hard-working, thick-or-thin association members who are real professionals. But I see three broad patterns of teachers which have developed in urban areas. There is the truly dedicated, somewhat aging, spinsterish professional—single or married, female or male—who came to our cities many years ago when they were pleasant places, the prestige places, in which to teach. That teacher is now lost in the educational, social, and economic upheavals taking place in the cities, particularly in the so-called "central cities."

This teacher has traditionally supported the professional associations. Yet when it comes to a fight that requires determination and evangelism, that teacher is missing and must be presumed dead.

Then there is the young militant teacher who has come into a community where conditions make effective teaching almost impossible. Salaries and teaching conditions are such that it would take a revolution to change things. On top of that, he sees his college mates—many of whom are in less socially responsible positions—buying a second TV set and a new bag of golf clubs while he worries about shoes for baby. He feels that revolutions aren't either caused or won by professional associations but by professional revolutionaries. And he identifies the latter with the trade union movement.

Last, there is a small group of generally incompetent teachers who can't find employment in districts where applicants are numerous. So they find their way to cities, many of which are so desperate for teachers they'll hire anybody whom a state certifies as being a teacher and a doctor certifies as being alive.

This group is more interested in holding a job than anything else, and so when it comes to the professional associations they just don't give a damn. They tend more towards the union type of organization because it emphasizes welfare benefits and job security.

Any discussion of Detroit and Cleveland must necessarily concern itself with the three prototypes of teachers I have sketched. They are *fundamental* to understanding the situations there. This includes the hard task of getting teachers involved in the professional association.

Getting teachers to participate in association activities not only benefits the organization in its day-to-day tasks, it also creates a reservoir of manpower and womanpower upon which to call in a campaign. Persons who had association roles to play were of invaluable assistance during the two campaigns we're talking about.

They helped mightily by working for the DEA and the CEA in short campaigns. And by short, I mean short—s-h-o-r-t: a few weeks in Detroit, one week in Cleveland. That is all the time the boards of education allowed between the time they called for elections and the date of the elections. They manned the mailing rooms, they monitored union speakers, they operated the telephones.

This is not a treatise on campaign techniques, on whether to run four eight-column ads or eight four-column ads, or how many TV and radio spots to buy, or the most effective way of using volunteers, or which union charges should be answered and which should not be. Lessons regarding techniques of campaigning were learned in Detroit and Cleveland. Many of them, but by no means all, because each city is unique, can be applied to elections that will be held in other cities. But campaign strategy and tactics are merely the frosting on the cake. If the batter in the cake is mixed properly, you don't have to worry too much about how it will taste, frosting or no frosting.

But I do want to point out that the single most effective campaign operation in Detroit and Cleveland was polling teachers by telephone. Initially, there were a number of objections voiced to this in each city—and loud ones. But in Detroit more than 8,000 of the 9,600 teachers were reached by the telephone brigade. As I mentioned earlier, that was how the campaign team discovered just how important certain issues were to the teachers there.

In Cleveland, in just one week, 2,400 of the 5,200 teachers were contacted by phone. These teachers were asked how they were going to vote in the election. Out of the 280 buildings represented, the teachers in only one voted significantly differently from the way they said they would vote.

The lesson here is: You *can* assess how teachers will vote in a representation election through the use of telephone polling. (This held true in the Milwaukee election in February, 1964, as well.)

Another "plus" for the local associations during the campaign was the cooperation of the state organizations. In Detroit, the Michigan Education Association assigned eight of its staff men to work in the city throughout the campaign. The campaign manager, in fact, was an MEA staffer—George Brown, director of public relations. The MEA executive secretary, Dale Kennedy, was in and out frequently. All these people were indispensable in setting up meetings in the school buildings to get the DEA message across. Their advice and their expertise in various fields were invaluable.

In the Cleveland campaign, the Ohio Education Association sent six of its top people to work in the campaign full-time. And full-time meant 16, 18, and 20 hours a day, full speed.

The point is that the Detroit association had established a working relationship with the Michigan association, and the CEA had done the same with the OEA. The basis for full cooperation during a campaign had been set.

There were faults and cracks in these bases, as I'm sure the local and state groups would all concede. But there was none of the "hands-off" attitude on the part of the local or the state groups in the Detroit and Cleveland situations that seems to exist in certain other cities and states—and which, frankly, makes my hair assume a perpendicular stance.

Detroit and Cleveland didn't want Lansing and Columbus to blow up. And Lansing and Columbus didn't particularly care to see Detroit slide into the river and Cleveland disappear into the lake. They needed each other. State associations *cannot* ignore the existence of urban association problems and the presence of unions in urban centers.

What I've just said about the relationship of the two city associations with their state groups can also be said about their relationship with the NEA. The same is true of the MEA-NEA and OEA-NEA partnerships during the campaign. My friends, it *has* to be that way, throughout the country. If we don't swim together, we'll surely sink alone, one by one by one by one.

Incidentally, Detroit illustrated the great potential for membership that lies in urban areas. Nearly one-half of the state's nonmembership potential is in that city.

I've been talking about how, from lessons learned in Detroit and Cleveland, urban associations can remain strong or become strong, as the case may be. I want to add one more thing before I get into the unionism section of this presentation. That is this: A strong urban association should have a full-time executive secretary. The executive secretary should have many qualities and should perform many duties which I won't go into now because I'm not making a speech about executive secretaries. I simply want to emphasize the necessity of having such a person in an urban association—particularly an urban association threatened by the trade union movement. I feel that one of the strengths of the Detroit Education Association, and one reason it suffered only a defeat and not a disaster, was that a full-time man was in the executive secretary's chair. And I feel one reason the Cleveland Education Association received fewer votes than the union was that its executive secretary was serving in only a part-time capacity. The CEA has since hired a full-time man for the job.

An executive secretary should have enough secretarial and clerical help so that he won't have to spend time licking stamps, cranking a machine, or watering petunias. And, of course, he needs an adequate budget. The budget should be tailored to the needs of the association, not the other way around. We found that out in Detroit and Cleveland too!

Several things happened in Detroit and Cleveland that were quite revealing as to how the union operates. In Detroit, the Federation attacked the NEA and DEA in almost equal proportions, but its venom was reserved for the NEA. This was an effort to divide and conquer by exploiting the unawareness of many teachers concerning NEA services. It also fired at the MEA in another attempt at dissension. There were attempts to put the Detroit association on the defensive because it was affiliated with the national and state associations. You can be certain that technique will be used in other states.

The Detroit Federation borrowed the services of a member of the public relations staff of the United Auto Workers to edit its newspaper. I understand he quit in disgust. But the fact that the teachers' union went to the UAW for help was interesting, if not exactly astonishing.

The Federation paper took pains to print the address of our "hideaway" office that served as a campaign headquarters and of which only three or four DEA people, outside of the campaign team, were aware.

The fact that the opposition has a pretty good intelligence system was illustrated again in Cleveland. One of the people on our team phoned a hotel to see if the AFT's director of organization was registered there. He told only two or three association persons about the call. But a member of the AFT staff kidded him about it later and told him "we know everything you do."

Most revealing about the Cleveland affair was the fact that the Cleveland AFL-CIO apparently knew that the Cleveland Education Association was not ready for an election and so it made a deal, seemingly, with the president of the Board of Education, who actually runs the seven-member board. The apparent deal was that if the board held a surprise, quickie election before the end of the school year the Cleveland AFL-CIO would support the board president in the next year's mayoralty campaign. The board president confirmed this in a conversation with an OEA staff member. Furthermore, the resolution by which the board set up the election was written in the office of the president of the Cleveland Teachers Union. The union president so stated himself. Union propaganda had been prepared and was ready for distribution in the school buildings the day following passage of the resolution.

Politics also had been a determining factor in the Detroit election. The Board of Education there had resisted appeals and demonstrations and strike threats by the union for a sole bargaining election until the state attorney general issued an opinion that school boards could negotiate and bargain with organizations acting as exclusive agents for teachers. Can there be any doubt that the attorney general, who is elected to office, issued an opinion upon the request of union leaders?

Both in Detroit and Cleveland, the teachers' unions avoided issues that were most hurtful to them. They didn't talk about the many real problems of education which the state associations and the NEA can help local educators solve. Instead they created the impression that teachers should vote for the teachers' union because the teachers' union is part of the AFL-CIO and therefore can somehow hammer out a deal with the board of education better than the professional association. That was baloney, but a lot of teachers ate it.

They talked about the so-called "contract" between the United Federation of Teachers in New York City and the Board of Education there. They said it meant pressed duck for dinner and two Cadillacs for every teacher in the New York City school system. They didn't talk about their contracts elsewhere or even say where these contracts were.

They talked about how they would get salaries raised, but they didn't mention that higher pay for teachers means broadening the tax base or increasing sales taxes, which the union movement has fought time after time in place after place.

They kept the ball in the association's court. And I must say they did a good job of it. Some of their propaganda was so blatant and misleading it was insulting to those who knew the score. It was like serving pabulum to a queen. But the trouble was that there were many teachers who didn't know the score. They were starving, and the pabulum tasted good.

The unions are experienced hands at making sound appear to be substance and fury resemble finesse.

In that connection I want to read to you excerpts from a news story which the *Detroit Free Press* published the day after the election. It should be pasted up in every office of every urban association—and state association—in the United States. It was written by Gene Roberts who, by the way, was coauthor of the widely-read book, *The Censors and the Schools.* Its headline was: "Story of DFT's Success: Image of Dynamic Action." Here, in part, is what the *Free Press* story said:

> The DFT drew heavily from the city's nearly 3,000 nonaffiliated teachers to beat the Detroit Education Association and become bargaining agent with the school system.
>
> It was a question of images. [Speaking of images, the first time I walked into the office of the Detroit Education Association was in 1963. The first thing that struck my sight was a 1958 calendar.]
>
> In talking to *Free Press* pollsters Monday, teachers at Southeastern High School used words like "dynamic" and "militant" to describe the AFL-CIO union.
>
> The DEA was viewed as the more conservative of the two organizations. It campaigned with talk of professionalism rather than unionism and prided itself upon cooperation—rather than militance—with school administrators.
>
> "I don't belong to either the DFT or the DEA," said Dan Brown, a first-year teacher at Southeastern. "But I voted for the DFT. It seems dynamic" ...
>
> Teachers have been impressed for years with the "action" given them by the union ...
>
> Paul Garbe has been teaching for seven years and has "supported the DFT all along."
>
> "We are a more militant organization," he said. "We aren't afraid to say specifically what we are for." ...
>
> For more than a year, the DFT has made major news, creating the image of an organization on the move. ...
>
> In contrast, the DEA appeared on the defensive, reacting rather than acting.

That story hit the nail smack on the head. It explains why the DFT has grown from 15 members when it began in 1931 to 5,100 members when this news story was written. And why the DEA dropped from 5,537 members in its peak year of 1954-55 to 3,886 members in 1963-64, a loss of 1,651 members. This represents a decline of almost 30 per cent in the total membership.

A few final words. Don't depend upon a board of education to set up ground rules for an election that are fair to the professional association. It will often play one organization against another until a choice has to be made—under its rules.

In Detroit, the election procedures were so stringent—or should I say silly?—that department heads who taught four or five classes a day were not allowed to vote. So the DEA was penalized because a substantial part of its membership was disenfranchised. Even the Wisconsin Employment Relations Board (WERB), which conducted the election in Milwaukee under a state law that is patterned after the labor-management relations philosophy of a conflict of interest between management and employee, was not that tough on administrators. In Milwaukee, vice principals who carried more than 50 per cent of a normal teaching load could vote.

Let me tell you something else the Detroit Board of Education pulled. It stipulated that each teacher representative must be either an active teacher or a teacher on leave of absence. That ruled out the DEA's full-time executive secretary because he had moved to his job from outside the Detroit school system. It did not rule out the full-time president of the teachers' federation, however, because she was a teacher on leave. Furthermore, the board hired an expert, an experiencd personnel man, to negotiate with the teachers' representatives. So what you see there is a pro representing the board against amateurs representing teachers.

Now one more word—a final, final word. I trust that you state association people who live in states where there are laws that prevent school boards from negotiating or bargaining exclusively with a teachers' organization don't think that "it can't happen to me." It can. State AFL-CIO's are working to see that it can.

Their lobbyists are busy in the legislatures to get the laws changed, or in the offices of attorneys general pleading for opinions that say the laws do permit such bargaining. And their lawyers are preparing court cases challenging the laws. Don't forget what Nick Zonarich of the IUD told the 1964 AFT convention in Chicago. Talking about teachers, he shouted: "We are ready to put on the greatest organizing campaign ever seen to organize the unorganized."

And he said the IUD was ready to match the AFT dollar for dollar to "expand the union and establish collective bargaining."

VI-3

THE STRATEGY OF NEGOTIATION*

Donald H. Wollett

This paper is addressed to persons who are interested in education, not only for others but also for themselves. I shall try to approach my topic in that spirit and I hope others will do so also. I make this comment because some of the things I am about to say may be provocative. Such a reaction is calculated on my part, because I hope to generate questions concerned with an intense, practical exploration of the strategy of negotiations. Unless we state the problems correctly, we cannot ask the right questions or find the right answers.

My topic is "The Strategy of Negotiation." Before we discuss a strategy, we have to identify what it is we are talking about. I think it is important to put strategy into a proper setting. Therefore, I want to spend some time discussing a strategy for *what* I am trying to do. My point of departure is Resolution 15, adopted by the NEA Representative Assembly in Detroit a little over a year ago. This resolution deals with professional negotiation and, among other things, says that what we want is a method whereby teachers, through their professional associations, can "participate" with boards of education in determining policies of common concern, including salaries and other conditions of professional service. The text of that resolution was reaffirmed in Seattle just last July with one change—the word "determination" was stricken and the word "formulation" was substituted therefor. The first problem is to identify as exactly as we can the type of participation with boards of education which Resolution 15 contemplates.

TYPES OF PARTICIPATION

There are three basic types. The first one is this: The teachers' association presents its proposals on salary levels and transfer policy, sick leave,

* Adapted from a paper delivered at the NEA Conference on Professional Negotiation in Chicago, September 10, 1964. Donald H. Wollett is a partner in the New York Law firm of Kaye, Scholer, Fierman, Hays, and Handler.

preparation time, and other matters to the school board, or perhaps a school board committee, with the superintendent present; two or three questions may be asked and answered, or maybe there won't be any questions. The meeting is then closed with an exchange of mutual pleasantries and polite expressions of gratitude and esteem. Shortly thereafter the school board takes action which bears no resemblance to what the teachers proposed. That's one process.

The second one is as follows: The teachers' association again presents proposals and supports them with data and argument. The school board or its representatives discuss these proposals, their wisdom, their feasibility; advise the teachers' representatives of the reasons why they are probably not presently acceptable. But the board gives solemn and polite assurances that the proposals will be thoughtfully considered; subsequently, the board takes about the action it had in mind all the time, usually without advance notice or further discussion, and the teachers' association grumbles but acquiesces. That's the second kind of procedure.

Then there is the third one where the teachers' association presents proposals, again supported by argument, evidence, data. This is followed by an exchange of specific counter-proposals made by board representatives and by counter-counter proposals from the teachers' association. Through this process of give and take, areas of disagreement are narrowed and finally eliminated, and the teachers' association and the board reach a bilateral agreement on the matters which were but no longer are at issue. Or, alternatively—and this may happen, despite many meetings and good faith and earnest efforts to reconcile differences—areas of disagreement remain, the parties come to an impasse with neither willing to make an additional concession.

Which of these three types of procedure is contemplated by the term "professional negotiation"?

Surely not the first one. The dictionary tells us that to negotiate is to confer with a view to coming to terms. Resolution 15 states that the process we're interested in is one for reaching "mutually satisfactory agreements." This language was reaffirmed in Seattle verbatim. The procedure of merely making proposals or expressing points of view does not look toward nor will it accomplish any kind of an agreement on anything. Therefore it cannot be the kind of teacher participation referred to in Resolution 15.

To use the descriptive label of F.J.C. Seymour, assistant executive secretary of the Alberta Teachers Association, this process is the "white cane" approach, which is predicated upon the notion that the school board, overcome with sympathy for the plight of its underprivileged teachers, will put something in the cup. Such a procedure has about as much to do with the process of negotiation as bullfighting has to do with agriculture.

How about the second type? This procedure, which has some dignity because it gives the teachers' association some status and because the school board is willing to discuss the teachers' proposals and may even give them some weight, comes closer to negotiation; but it falls far short of the mark because it terminates in a unilateral decision in which the teachers acquiesce but to which they do not agree. Acquiescence, giving-in, is not agreement, and it certainly is not mutually satisfactory agreement. To refer to Mr. Seymour again, I think he would describe this as "organized supplication." The American Federation of Teachers would call it, as it has, "collective begging." Whatever it is, it is not negotiation, because it does not produce an agreement to which both parties subscribe.

The conclusion I reach is obvious: The third type of procedure is the only one which conforms to the generally understood meaning of the term "negotiate," and the spirit of Resolution 15.

I will tell a story which illustrates the point. I am indebted to Edgar Benton, a member of the Denver Board of Education. As you know, we have a professional negotiation agreement in Denver. It has been working pretty well. A year ago the Denver Classroom Teachers Association and the Denver Board of Education were engaged in protracted negotiations, primarily over salaries, which at one point became dangerously close to an impasse, if indeed they didn't reach that point. During the course of these negotiations, in which Edgar Benton, of course, was involved, he and Palmer Burch, president of the Board, had some conflict over the nature of the process. Finally Mr. Benton said to Mr. Burch, "The trouble with you is that you don't understand the difference between unilateral action and bilateral action." Mr. Burch said: "Yes I do. Let me illustrate the difference. You know I am a building manager. I manage several buildings. Let's suppose that I want to close the service entrance to a building at six o'clock at night, whereas previously it has been closed at eight o'clock at night. I don't want that extra two hours in there. Now suppose I don't consult any of the tenants in the building. I just make the change from an eight p.m. closing to a six p.m. closing. That's unilateral action. But suppose, before I make this change, I consult every tenant in the building. Then, although an overwhelming majority tell me that they don't want the change made, I do it anyhow. That's bilateral action."

Of course neither action is bilateral. Both are unilateral and neither involves the process of negotiation.

NEGOTIATION AND COLLECTIVE BARGAINING

Now I want to turn to another question which, in a sense, is a digression. But I think it is important because it has produced confusion in our ranks, and perhaps some mischief. That question is: Is there a difference between negotiating and bargaining? I suggest that if we look to things and not to labels, to substance and not to form, the honest answer is "No."

Some of us are wary of the word "bargaining" because it's widely used by the American Federation of Teachers. May I say I think this is a false fear. Bargaining is not peculiar to the vocabulary of trade unionists. It is a perfectly respectable word, widely used by men of affairs to describe the process that makes the marketplace work and which permits our government to function. Those of you who have been involved in legislative activity know how important the process of negotiating or bargaining is to the enactment of legislation.

Nor should the word bargaining be repellent to us simply because it is preceded by the word "collective." Collective bargaining as distinguished from just plain bargaining simply refers to a process whereby a group of many sellers bind together for the purpose of negotiating the terms and conditions under which they will provide service to a single buyer. Semantics aside, I put to you this question, and I hope it will generate some discussion. Is this definition of collective bargaining very different from the procedure or the process we envision when we talk of professional negotiation? And would one be guilty of heresy if he said that professional negotiation is a sophisticated and specially developed species of collective bargaining, tailored to fit the unusual needs, requirements, and responsibilities of a particular type of highly skilled and highly educated public employee, a teacher?

MULTIPLE vs. SINGLE ORGANIZATION NEGOTIATION

I now turn to another question which bears on the negotiation process. I regard it as fundamental, and I think we need to be clear on this too before we talk about strategy. This question has vexed us: Should the teacher organization which has majority support be the sole participant in the professional negotiation process? If it is true, as it is, that negotiations look toward mutually acceptable agreements on policy matters, is it not clear that the answer to this question must be "Yes"? Several teacher organizations can present proposals (Procedure One), or participate in discussions (Procedure Two), but how can more than one negotiate a mutually satisfactory agreement? How can this be done in practical terms? There can be only one policy in a school district governing such matters as salary, salary increments, or transfers. If Organization A has one proposal, Organization B another, and Organization C a third, how, looking at the realities of that situation, can agreement on a single policy, which is what is needed, ever be reached?

You may argue that this difficulty can be surmounted by having a teachers' negotiating committee consisting of equal or proportionate membership from several teacher organizations. This is a plausible a priori argument. The trouble is that it flies in the face of the evidence, at least the evidence with which I am familiar. Such committees are torn with interorganizational rivalries and are unable to function on an effectual, unified basis. The result is that a school board involved in such a multilateral procedure will ultimately take the only practical course open to it. It will make a unilateral decision and take unilateral action without paying much attention to any of the organizations.

If a realistic analysis of the negotiation process demonstrates, as I think it does, that only one organization can effectively participate in it, which organization should it be? The answer is found in the well-accepted political principle of majority rule.

NEGOTIATION STRATEGY

Now let's talk about strategy. At the outset I want to distinguish between strategy and tactics. (Incidentally, the terms strategy and tactics are war words. They come from the lexicon of the military.) *Strategy* refers to a plan of action. It is the science and art of the effective use of strength to attain an objective. *Tactics* refer to the plays and moves to be made while actually engaged in combat with the adversary. In your negotiations, if you are bargaining, you are in a room; there are people on the other side of that table; tactics refer to moves or responses you make vis-a-vis the adversary. Those are tactics, whereas strategy has to do with the plan you have when you go into that room.

Let me illustrate this by looking at collective bargaining for a minute. I use the United Automobile Workers' current bargaining with the Big Three automotive manufacturers as the example. At a sticky point in the negotiations, Reuther said that our prime target is Chrysler. The Chrysler contract expires at 10 a.m. Wednesday, and the other contracts with Ford and GM will be extended beyond that time. Now this reflects a strategy, and the strategy is very simple. The reason why UAW picked out Chrysler and pressed first on that firm was on the theory that Chrysler is in the process, with relatively new management, of recapturing its former position in the market. Chrysler lost ground steadily for fifteen years. Now it has reversed things. Thus Chrysler is the manufacturer least willing to take a strike while its competitors continue to produce. Chrysler was most vulnerable to pressure; therefore the pressure was put on there first, with results which apparently were quite good from UAW's point of view. The strategy, having been successful in establishing a pattern at Chrysler, then is to pick off Ford and GM successively.

EXAMPLE OF TACTICS

As an example of tactics in collective bargaining, I'll draw on a rather homely illustration. The company and the union had been bargaining for some weeks over a multiplicity of issues and finally they had come to the point where the only issue that was not firmly resolved, and this is often the case, was money. They were about 12¢ apart, as I remember. Then they went into a series of around-the-clock sessions, which is the fashion in this business. It is a kind of war of attrition—put everybody in an uncomfortable room, don't feed them, keep them on hard seats, and see who can last longer. They went around the clock one night and finally got the difference narrowed down to about 8¢. They went to about ten o'clock the next evening and got it down to about 5¢ and then they stuck there. It went on and on; no move. It got to be about four o'clock in the morning and the international representative for the union, who was their chief negotiator, a man in his 70's who didn't look very strong, a dried-up little fellow with sallow complexion, complained that the smoke was strangling him. At about four o'clock he went into a coughing fit and couldn't speak. His face became red, he was gasping for breath, and finally he left the table and just managed to make it to the couch in the corner of the room. He would come up into a sitting position about every thirty seconds and go back into another of his violent coughing fits; you could hear it all over the room. This went on and on and on. This was the background for talking about that nickel that was still blocking agreement. Finally, after about thirty minutes of this noise from the couch, the chief negotiator for the company in whose office this was taking place stood up and threw his pencil down and said, "My God, give him the nickel and get him out of here before he dies"; whereupon the guy got up and felt swell. That's a tactic.

ELEMENTS IN DEVELOPING STRATEGY

I'll talk of strategy during the time I have left, not of tactics, because tactics are techniques and, for the highly skilled, a kind of artistry. Such things as tactics cannot be learned by talking, listening, or reading. You have to do it to learn.

Moreover, I am not going to undertake to construct a model strategy for professional negotiation because that's not realistic. There is no one strategy that will fit all situations. If you are involved in professional negotiation, you must build your strategy, tailored to fit the dimensions of your situation. In order to do this you need to know the answers to a lot of questions. Let me mention, illustratively, some of the facts you need to know in order to build a strategy which fits your negotiations. Is the superintendent secure in his job or is he insecure? What of each school board member? To whom is he politically indebted? Who influences him? How much does he know about teachers and teaching? And how much does he really care? What are the labor market conditions? Has the superintendent had trouble recruiting? Has he had trouble holding good teachers? What are the attitudes of the community? Are the citizens indifferent about their educational system, concerned about it, upset with it, pleased with it, or just smug about it? Are they sympathetic with teachers or are they the reverse? And what about the press? This is public business—professional negotiation. What about the press, the monitors of negotiation? Are they going to be favorable or unfavorable?

A BLUEPRINT FOR STRATEGY

What I will do is to give you a kind of blueprint which sketches the essential supporting and abutting beams upon which you may build a particular strategy of negotiation. These, I think, are fundamental. These are the foundations of the strategy. They are not the strategy itself.

The essentials as I see them are as follows: *First*—and it sounds very simple, and it is simple, but it's important—is *state of mind*. You must be convinced that you have as legitimate a place at the bargaining table as the board and the superintendent. Believe me, if you aren't convinced of that, *they* won't be convinced, and you will be crippled throughout the entire procedure by a disabling psychology of inferiority. You will feel that you are there by sufferance rather than by right. You will be at a disadvantage all the way through. I would hope that somehow we could agree that when a teacher association or its spokesman addresses a board of education, whether it is a public meeting or a negotiating session, it would be considered grossly unprofessional to start out by saying to the board, "Mr. Chairman, Members of the Board, and Superintendent, we are so grateful, so grateful, that you are permitting us to speak to you." What should be said is: "It's about time that you people looked for some intelligent advice on your problems." That's the kind of attitude to have.

Second. Don't permit the board or superintendent to subvert by legalisms the state of mind that you have as much right in that room as they do. The rights of school boards are not divine and the prerogatives of superintendents are not sacrosanct. It is true that the law vests ultimate authority and responsibility for school management in school boards. But it is also true in fact, although not in form, that the complexity of contemporary educational problems frequently causes school boards to delegate to the superintendent and his staff the effective decision-making authority on many important policy matters. If a school board legally can de facto share its authority with the superintendent, it can de facto share it with the teachers' association. Nor do I see any insurmountable legal obstacle, certainly in the overwhelmingly majority of states, to a school board's officially acknowledging an arrangement whereby it declares, as a matter of board policy, that (a) it will negotiate with the teachers' association in a good faith effort to reach mutually satisfactory agreements on the formulation of policy; and (b) it will reduce those agreements to a written document, signed and executed by the board and/or the superintendent and the teachers' association and embodied in an official board resolution. In most instances, if a school board will not agree to this, it is not because it can't, but because it doesn't want to.

Third. Formulate your proposals carefully, realistically, and concretely before you approach the bargaining table. There are three fundamental steps that you have to take in order to do this: First, *know the facts.* This is a big job. Probably what the local association needs to do is to create a committee on teacher welfare or teacher economics. The name is not important; the function is. To get the pertinent data, you need the help of the state association, you need the help of salary consultants, and so on. This is a job for hard work; it's a job for experts; it's a job that needs to be done carefully and thoughtfully, because your whole case in the money area is going to depend on the extent to which you know these facts. If you don't know them, you are going to be so badly crippled in negotiations that you will be an easy mark if someone wants to make you an easy mark. It would be gilding the lily for me to tell you what kind of facts I am talking about. You are experts; there are many salary consultants here; you know more about the kind of economic data that are pertinent than I do. You know the importance of comparative wage and fringe data in the labor market where your district recruits, of consumer price index figures, of turnover statistics, of comparative wage and fringe data for other employed professionals, e.g., engineers, in the labor market area serviced by colleges and universities from which your school district recruits. Speaking of turnover statistics, at what level of experience and preparation do teachers resign? How many resigned in the last five years? Why did they resign? Where did they go? Why did they go where they went—more money, better fringes, or what? How many substandard teachers, e.g., those with credit shortages, have been hired in the district? How many specialty billets have been filled by nonspecialty teachers?

You also need to know the data pertinent to your district's fiscal picture. If it is a fiscally dependent district, is additional revenue likely to come into the hands of the city council? If it is a fiscally independent district, has it exhausted its power to increase millage levies without a referendum or legislative authority? If it has not, how much power does it have left? How do tax levies in your district compare with tax levies in surrounding districts? What is the effective buying income of the citizens in your district?

One caveat. It is important to have an awareness and understanding of school financing in the district because it may have a bearing on the strategy you develop. However, it does not follow that you should scale down or discard a justifiable demand or proposal simply because the school board is hard-pressed for money. It is not the job of the local teachers' association to find the money to meet reasonable and just demands. That responsibility belongs to the board. Leave it there. The bargain that is finally struck—remember at this point you are making proposals—the bargain that is finally struck, and the agreement that is finally reached, will adequately reflect competing pressures on the board's budget. You should anticipate these pressures but you should not succumb to them unless and until you have to.

The second thing you need to know is what your members want. Remember it is what they want, not what you want, that counts. What are the areas of teacher discontent? What do they want in salaries? What can they make a reasonable and just case for? How do they want it spread? Do they want it across the board or index or what? How about transfer policies, promotions, fringe benefits, teaching conditions, class size, preparation time, teacher aides, duty-free lunches? It is important to have the members participate in the formulation of the proposals that you make to the school board when you initiate the negotiation process. *But I want to enter another caveat here.* Your members may want the moon; don't get trapped into promising it to them. Inform them of the problems, talk to them about the fiscal realities of the school district, let them know this so they have some understanding of the difficulties of your job. Educate them to the fact that negotiations, like politics, is the art of the possible. There are no magicians in this business. Transmit to them your firm determination to press with vigor the proposals that are finally formulated, but do not be Pollyannaish or sanguine about the prospect of success. Be realistic, but don't overbuild the expectations of your members in terms of what you are going to deliver out of professional negotiation, because if you do they will remain dissatisfied at the end of the line no matter how skillful a job you do.

Finally, with respect to formulating proposals, out of this process of education, of educating your members—and they are educating you too —you should acquire a sufficiently well-informed judgment as to what they want and expect that when negotiations enter the final stage you will know what to trade and what to hold onto, as well as how far you can compromise on a given proposal without incurring strong membership dissatisfaction and perhaps revolution or defection.

THE STRUCTURE OF NEGOTIATION

I want now to talk about the structure of negotiation. This is my fourth major point.

1. Insist on full freedom to select those persons who represent the teachers' association in negotiations. Recently, a board of education adopted a policy which limited the teachers' spokesmen to persons presently employed in the district or on leave of absence. Don't go for this. That's a strategy designed to weaken the strength of teacher representation. It limits the participants to the boss and the employees and gives you a bad psychology in the negotiating room. In a large district, furthermore, the board will probably hire a full-time, experienced negotiator, hoping to set up a negotiation context in which a full-time pro is pitted against part-time amateurs. Don't buy it. Furthermore, the advantage of introducing experts and consultants into the negotiation, an advantage which will usually be with you, will be lost.

2. Insist that the representatives of the school board include persons who have effective decision-making authority in respect to the matters being negotiated. Meaningful negotiations cannot be conducted with lower echelon members of the administrative staff who serve only as conduits to the persons who have real authority. If you fall into this trap in negotiations, more likely than not you will simply be giving the other side two bites at your position.

3. All negotiations should take place in executive session so that the negotiators are able to be frank and open and are free of the compulsion to posture for the press. Effective negotiations cannot be conducted in a goldfish bowl. Finally, under this heading, the negotiating team for the teachers' association should consist of not less than three nor more than five persons selected so as to reflect a cross section of the membership.

A chairman should be designated and he should be given complete control over who says what and who responds to what questions. Unless the chairman of the negotiating committee is given this control, the representatives of the school board may whipsaw the committee and impair its bargaining position. Skillful negotiators for the other side, if you've got this bull session kind of negotiating committee with nobody in control on your side of the table, may shoot a question here and a question there and get ill-considered answers; and soon they will have the members of the committee in complete confusion as to what they want or what their position really is. I have seen this happen many times. Skillful people can really exploit that kind of situation.

PROCEDURE OF NEGOTIATION

My next major heading has to do with the procedure of negotiations. I am not dogmatic about the time factor. My judgment is that a reasonable time schedule would call for the initiation of negotiations at least ninety days in advance of the time when final action on the budget must occur. It depends really on the complexity of the problems that you foresee.

Secondly, reduce your proposals to writing and present them to the board's negotiating committee at the first meeting. Don't circulate them in advance. If you circulate your proposals in advance, you will simply give the representatives of the board an opportunity to get ready and put you on the defensive at the outset.

Another point. Formulate and explain your proposals, which should be specific, in the most precise terms possible. If you want a grievance procedure, for example, present a complete and finished document as an asking proposal. Bargaining then proceeds from your proposal, not from theirs. This is better than bargaining from a general set of principles, where both sides essentially start from scratch. If you want something—your members want it—you think it's right—ask for it. To pursue the example, if your members want a grievance procedure which protects them against arbitrary and capricious supervision and guarantees them, as a final step, a full and fair hearing by a disinterested third party, lay it on the line in exactly those terms. Don't play with it. Put it out there on the table, why you want it and exactly what it is. Remember that your objective is to get an agreement; that's where this all ends up, we always hope, and a meaningful agreement is built on specifics, not generalities.

Next, don't expect too much at the first meeting. Be content to explain what you want and why you want it. This is as much as you can realistically expect to accomplish. Negotiation is a slow process and many an advantage has been lost by impatience and anxiety. Keep to the issues raised by your proposals and insist that the other side also keep to those issues. Don't break off the first meeting until there has been agreement as to the time and place of the next meeting, or at least try to get such agreement.

Next, when you have come in with a whole series of proposals, hold fast to the full package of your proposals until you get firm and specific counter-proposals from the board representatives. This is fundamental. It is essential that you avoid wearing your heart on your sleeve in these negotiations, even though you may think that members of the school board are wonderful guys (and they may well be wonderful guys). But be careful that in an effort to show your reasonableness and your under-standing of the other side's problems you do not reveal, inadvertently, what you are willing to give up and where you are willing to compromise, until you get offers from the other side. By so doing, in advance of firm counter-offers from the board representatives, you are as a practical matter making concessions without getting anything at all in return.

Do not permit negotiations to be fragmented into issue-by-issue bargain-ing. By bargaining on a multiplicity of issues, i.e., many things at the same time on a package basis, you maintain flexibility in your position and retain your ability to give only if you can also take. Study committees may be necessary where there are questions of fact in dispute or where there are particularly complex problems which require technical analysis. Study com-mittees are a sound and sensible procedure in these instances, but their func-tion is to study, not to negotiate.

If the representatives of the board make a closing offer, they may identify it as their final offer, which it may or may not be; they may identify it as such as a ploy. You don't know. But if they make a closing offer which requires you to give up some things that you think are pretty near and dear to the hearts of your members, and to compromise on others of the same sort, and you are not pretty sure of what choices your membership would want you to make, you will have to make some difficult judgments. It is perfectly proper to break off negotiations and say in response to the representatives of the board, "I am going to take this to my house of delegates for their advice." Diffuse responsibility in that situation. If you have a good house of delegates or even if you don't have a good house, it's your house and you're stuck with it. Use it.

There are two more points in this blueprint. When an agreement is reached—and it will be reached finally in the bargaining room, around the negotiating table—when it's reached, you are not going to have a com-plete agreement worked out in final form, obviously. You reach an agree-ment, a settlement, in that room, after all that work, travail, and so on, and when that happens, it's desirable to get a memorandum of under-standing executed by representatives of both sides at that time, before you leave that meeting, which covers all matters settled in as clear a fashion as you can manage.

Why now? I had an experience not so long ago. We did negotiate something for a local teachers' association and we got a memorandum signed. I insisted on that. But it wasn't quite as clear as I would have liked and I let it go in that form because I had been reading a lot of NEA literature about the identity of interests in professional negotiation—that school board people are different from other management people, that a superin-tendent is different, that he is not like the chief executive officer of a corporation. This superintendent turned out not to be very different, because once we all got out of the pressure cooker, so to speak, he began to have second thoughts. Some of the language was a little ambiguous. I knew this, but he and I had talked off the record and I thought we understood each other; we did then. He began to have second thoughts; he was out of the pressure chamber. All of us are likely to have second thoughts after the fact, and most of those second thoughts will be wishful as to what was really agreed to. Then we start to shade the deal a little bit; it isn't a matter of double-dealing; I am not suggesting that. It is just a human reaction. The first thing you know you've got a hot dispute as to what was decided, what was agreed to. This is what happened in the situation I refer to, and it made a lot of mischief.

Finally, when you reach an agreement across the bargaining table, you are committed to it. This is a good thing; you've got to be committed to it. You've got to be committed to stand by it, to support it, and to sell it to your members. Anything short of this is bad faith on your part. So, obviously, you must accept that kind of responsibility, but make its finality, so far as the teacher association is concerned, contingent upon membership ratification so that you've got final membership participation. You started out with them and they participated in formulating the proposals. It ends up with them. That's where it ought to end up. But your responsibility as a negotiator is to sell the agreement. Do not be defensive. Do not apologize because you didn't get more; brag because you got so much.

And insist upon a bilaterally executed written document of some sort. I don't much care what it's called, but a written document which embodies all the terms that you have agreed upon. The significance of this is enormous. The document may be full of legal infirmities. It may not be worth much as far as its enforceability at law is concerned, but it is a specific, physical end-product which will have great moral value in terms of the compliance of both parties with the agreement during its life. Furthermore, it is psychologically significant for your members to be able to see, to feel, what came out of this process in which they participated at the beginning and in which they participated at the end.

CONCLUSION

I have outlined here a blueprint for a strategy of professional negotiation grounded on the premise that it is essentially—I don't say entirely—an adversary process.

Some of you are doubtless offended by this premise because of your conviction that those who serve public education, whether as school board members, superintendents, or classroom teachers, have an identity of interest which makes differences superficial and which permits their resolution simply by improving communications and understanding.

To those of you who hold this view, let me say this: The word "negotiate" assumes areas of conflict, as well as identity, of interest—between buyers and sellers, conservative legislators and liberal ones, trade unions and manufacturers. And it is the process whereby these conflicts are reconciled—whereby goods and services are bought and sold, legislation enacted, and industrial peace maintained.

Do these conflicts of interest somehow disappear when professional persons negotiate? Suppose, for example, a dentist's fee is challenged and he chooses to negotiate rather than litigate. Is there conflict between negotiators? Of course. Is the conflict removed because one of the negotiators is a professional? No.

This analogy to the type of negotiations in which we are interested today is not exact because two of the three parties to our negotiations, the teachers and the superintendent, are members of the same profession. Does this different circumstance wipe conflicts of interest from the negotiating table?

Abstractly, the answer might be affirmative. The teacher is a human being who aspires to a better house, a better car, a better share of the good things in this affluent society. He is also a professional, a man who, like the doctor, dentist, lawyer, or architect, has some degree of selfless interest in the welfare of his clientele and some degree of special competence to determine how the welfare of that clientele may best be served.

The superintendent is a member of the same profession as the teachers. By hypothesis, he shares with his teachers their interest in optimum educational conditions and pupil welfare. He knows that these interests cannot be served unless high quality teachers can be attracted and retained. Therefore, ideally, he shares the aspirations of his teachers for material well-being and their commitment to the improvement of the educational program. Thus, the argument runs, he is a colleague, not an adversary. Let me say that this is ideally true and in many respects it is doubtless true in fact. However, it is not the whole story. There is a basic difference between the superintendent and the teacher on one hand and other professionals, such as doctors, lawyers, architects, dentists. The latter are entrepreneurs; the former are employees. In this fact lies the seeds of some conflict.

This is so because the superintendent has a range of responsibilities, pressures, problems, and insecurities *as an employee* which are not shared by his teachers *as employees* and, I may say, vice versa.

The superintendent's job is not protected by a tenure system; indeed, he may not even enjoy the protection of a multi-year contract. The superintendent is responsible to the school board and through it to the community for every playground injury, every parental complaint, every waste of money. He is expected to solve de facto segregation but maintain the integrity of the neighborhood school principle. He is expected to lay emphasis on the three "R's" but enrich the curriculum, encourage experimentation in teaching methodology but curtail progressivism and radical innovation, stimulate the imagination of the exceptional child but keep the library books respectably middle class, meet the needs of the disadvantaged child but protect him from the stigma of special treatment, cut out the frills but run a top-drawer interscholastic athletic program. He is expeced to hire and keep first-rate teachers but keep them in line and out of unseemly controversy, to run a top quality overall program but keep costs pared to the bone. He is expected to assuage the taxpayers' claque, toady to the women's clubs, keep on good terms with the AFL-CIO, maintain the support of the Chamber of Commerce, and keep out of politics but placate politicians. He is, at once, an educational expert, a top executive, a business manager, a personnel director, a technician in school finance, a public relations man, and a master of legerdemain. And he is also, more often than not, a very nervous man.

Most of the pressures on the school board to which the superintendent, by virtue of his job, must be sensitive are generated by the lay community and are not, therefore, of a professional nature. They are not grounded on the special competence to which a teacher rightfully lays claim, nor are they motivated by the selfless interest in the improvement of education which is the hallmark of this profession. Yet the realities of the superintendent's situation may compel him to respond to a wide range of these lay pressures. To the extent that this is true, the superintendent in practical terms tends to become alienated from his profession. His identification with the profession is diluted by his need to keep peace with the school board and the community.

Let me give some examples of the conflict between lay pressures and professional pressures in which the superintendent may be caught. A local teachers' association makes a proposal for a change in transfer policy. It will antagonize the Urban League and the school board, and superintendents don't want to do that. Or the teachers' proposal to raise salaries will conflict with the "hold the line" demands of the taxpayers' league and jeopardize the upcoming bond referendum. The association's proposal to hire teacher aides will use up the money allocated to adult education at the request of the Central Labor Council; its proposal for preparation time cannot be accepted unless the demand of the Community Council on Education for an experimental program for exceptional children is sacrificed. These are examples of conflict between lay pressures, generated by the community, and professional pressures generated by the teachers. The superintendent is caught in this conflict and his job as chief executive officer may in a given case compel him, realistically, to respond to the lay pressure rather than to the professional pressure.

There are other conflicts which simply inhere in the fact that the superintendent is the chief executive officer of the district and that the teachers, in hierarchic terms, are lower-level employees. For example, it is reasonable for the superintendent to insist upon unfettered power to designate his subordinates, his supervisors, and his principals; but it is equally reasonable for members of his teaching staff to aspire to those jobs for prestige and for money reasons. Many of those teachers may feel, sometimes not without cause, that the superintendent promotes on the basis of favoritism rather than merit; or that he uses his power as a disciplinary device, by rewarding docile and compliant teachers and punishing independent ones. Therefore the teachers through their association may want an open-bidding procedure on promotions with specified criteria, the application of which is subject to review by a third person who is not a party in interest. The superintendent is not likely to be receptive to this idea.

Here, then, are conflicts between the problems and responsibilities of superintendents and the aspirations and needs of teachers which compel the conclusion that professional negotiation, if it is to have real meaning, if it is to fulfill its promise as the vehicle whereby teachers acquire on-the-job dignity and assert as much influence over local school policy and its administration as other groups in the community, must be viewed as a process for reconciling the differences among school boards, superintendents, and teachers which in fact exist.

I am not suggesting that school boards, superintendents, and teachers are necessarily adversaries, but I don't think they are necessarily allies either. I think the truth is that they are both. There are conflicts with respect to some matters and alliances with respect to others, and the role of professional negotiation is to bridge or accommodate the differences which do exist.

What I am arguing for is realism in our conception of the setting and function of professional negotiation—for recognition of the fact that school policy is often shaped and formed by the nonprofessional voice, that some superintendents have "industrialized" rather than "professionalized" their teachers through clock-conscious personnel policies and over-regimentation, and that the way to true professionalism in education is to create a countervailing force of organized teachers which will make its weight felt —and felt heavily—in school policy and school administration.

Superintendents and school boards view the professional negotiation program with apprehension. It augurs ill, they say, because it threatens to subvert orderly principles of line-and-staff management where authority and responsibility are commensurate and because it threatens to create another set of pressures for them to contend with—another interest which must be taken into account in the process of reconciliation and compromise which underlies almost all important managerial decisions in public enterprise.

However, I predict that the day will come when superintendents and school boards (where the latter are genuinely interested in quality education) will welcome the professional negotiation program. This day will come when the program has become strong enough to teach the lesson that the cause of quality education is served where professional pressures are powerful enough to equalize lay pressures in the making of school policy and where teachers have acquired dignity and independence in performing their function as the heart of the public school system.

When this day comes we will in fact have achieved the professional unity which today is our aspiration. Until then, we will have to structure a strategy of professional negotiation built upon a different premise.

VI-4

THE TEACHERS GIVE OKLAHOMA A LESSON*

Barbara Carter

Ferman Phillips, executive director of the Oklahoma Education Association, looked worried. "It's so new," he said, with a low whistle, almost to himself. He was speaking of "sanctions," the latest weapon developed by the National Education Association as an alternative to teachers' strikes. The NEA is the mammoth professional organization of nearly a million teachers, principals, and school superintendents, and Phillips' organization, the OEA, is its state affiliate. On May 11, at the OEA's request, the NEA had declared sanctions against Oklahoma.

The term "sanctions," as used by the NEA in its guidelines for local and state affiliates, is kept purposely vague. It can mean anything from public censure to the withdrawal of teachers' services. "The most severe type of sanctions," the NEA's guidelines warn, "should be invoked only as a last resort." For as an NEA *Defense Bulletin* is careful to point out, sanctions are "sometimes dangerous."

The use of sanctions was approved at the NEA's 1962 convention, and since then they have been invoked by state and local affiliates from Waterbury, Connecticut, to Little Lake, California, more than a dozen times, with varying degrees of success and sternness. Only once before, however, had the NEA declared sanctions against an entire state. That was in May, 1964, when it publicly censured Utah for failing to raise its educational standards (and teachers' salaries). The NEA then declared it "unethical conduct" for any teacher outside the state to seek a contract there, threatened to expel members who did, and informed teaching institutions and accrediting agencies of its actions. The sanctions were not lifted until this March, after Utah had added nearly $25 million to its biennial education budget.

The NEA was first called into Oklahoma last November, after four OEA-sponsored petitions to provide more money for education had failed to pass in the general election. The OEA asked its parent organization to

* Reprinted from *The Reporter,* September 9, 1965, pp. 34–37. Copyright 1965 by The Reporter Magazine Company. Barbara Carter is a free-lance writer.

make an investigation of school problems, and a month later the NEA declared Oklahoma's educational system to be "subminimal ... in almost every area." Salaries, of course, were part of the trouble—the average teacher's salary in Oklahoma is more than $1,000 below the national average of $6,325—but only part of it. There had been no state-wide general tax increase in Oklahoma since 1937, and its school system, struggling against rising postwar enrollments and increased operating costs, had by 1963, according to the NEA, reached a "critical plane." In that year, the state raised its education budget by ten per cent, the biggest increase up to that time. It fell far short of the need, however, and the governor vetoed a bill to raise teachers' salaries. This March the OEA declared sanctions against the state and asked the NEA to follow suit in May. Two weeks before, on April 27, the voters had turned down a one-cent increase in the two per cent sales tax.

The NEA was to come down much harder on Oklahoma than it had on Utah. For one thing, the channels of communication among Oklahoma's teachers were more difficult to organize. Oklahoma has some 1,100 school districts, Utah only forty. Merely keeping out-of-state teachers from coming in, moreover, would not prove significant. Oklahoma can attract little more than ten per cent of its teachers from outside the state as it is. But the situation in Oklahoma may well have seemed tailor-made for the NEA, encouraged by its success in Utah, to improve on its sanction techniques. At least it appeared eager to do so. It has made a concentrated effort to inform the nation's major corporations and banks of Oklahoma's education deficiencies. For the first time, it set up five "relocation centers" to assist teachers who might want to find teaching positions outside the state and provided an emergency fund for them to draw on if needed. It is too soon to say just how much damage these tactics will or can actually do, but if the angry reaction of Oklahoma's political leaders is any indication, the sanctions already seem to be hurting.

THE GOVERNOR BURNS

"I don't want to talk about sanctions," Governor Henry Bellmon told a press conference on July 7, "except to say they are a paper tiger." He had just signed a new education bill, passed as an emergency measure a few days before, that added $28.7 million to Oklahoma's biennial budget for "common" schools and vocational education. The 25 per cent increase it represented was by far the greatest in Oklahoma's history. "Sanctions have had no real effect on education in Oklahoma," the governor continued, "except to thoroughly disgrace the state in the eyes of other states and in terms of potential citizens and potential investments. We've done as good a job as we know how. I don't want to hear any more about sanctions in Oklahoma," he said. "I believe the NEA has destroyed whatever confidence people had in it. Sanctions have not lessened our supply of teachers, and have had no influence on the legislators. They were going to pass the bill in any event."

Called a "political accident" in Oklahoma, Henry Bellmon is the first Republican governor the state has ever had. His election in 1962 was the result of a split in the Democratic Party, and at present Bellmon is serving the third of a four-year term from which he cannot succeed himself. Having campaigned, like many governors before him, on a "no new taxes" platform, he has done his best to keep his promise. One of his first acts in office was to veto the bill increasing teachers' salaries passed by the Democratic legislature. One of his latest was to campaign vigorously against the sales tax increase put before the voters this April. He supported Goldwater, of course, but even if he hadn't he would be considered a good conservative—like many Oklahoma Democrats. "If this state were above the Mason-Dixon Line," a local newscaster observed, "it would be right-wing Republican." As it was, Goldwater got 44 per cent of the vote.

"What do you think brought on the sanctions?" the governor was asked. "Rivalry between the NEA and the AFT," he replied without hesitation. It is an answer frequently given in Oklahoma. Yet the AFL-CIO's American Federation of Teachers has made few inroads in the state. Its three small chapters lost whatever momentum they might have had among the teachers when the AFL-CIO came out against the sales tax increase the teachers were supporting. Nationally, however, as a representative of the NEA was willing to concede, "perhaps 50 per cent" of the NEA's new militancy can be attributed to union rivalry. But, it should be remembered, it was the NEA's state affiliate that asked it to come in, not the other way around.

Not many state officials referred to the NEA's report on the "subminimal conditions" in Oklahoma's schools, and if they did bring it up voluntarily, it was usually to dismiss it because the NEA's team of investigators had spent "only a few days" in the state. A "bunch of outsiders," they were. "Not official," the governor said, in dismissing the venerable NEA as "a sort of nebulous thing."

Yet the NEA's report was based largely on an investigation conducted last year at the governor's own request by a Committee of One Hundred whose chairman was an Oklahoma superintendent of schools and president of the American Association of School Administrators. The NEA was quoting from the committee's report when it pointed out that 78 per cent of Oklahoma's high schools have fewer than 200 pupils and only 12 per cent of these small schools are accredited; that only an average of half a book a year is provided for each pupil in elementary school libraries; that many elementary teachers have 30 to 40 children crowded in their classrooms; and that nine out of ten high school students have no opportunity for vocational education other than in agriculture and office work. The NEA was also quoting this report when it ticked off the state's shortcomings in regard to special classes for handicapped children.

The NEA's investigating team on its own gathered some additional details of sorry performance: science textbooks published in the 1940's and world maps printed in 1938; antiquated buildings in which students and teachers wore overcoats during the winter classes and others with classes held in the hallways; a science laboratory with no running water and only one cylinder of gas allotted for the year; a school with one pint of disinfectant for the year; and another whose annual outbreak of infectious hepatitis could be traced to its drinking fountains.

Finally, of course, there was the matter of salaries. In 1964, when the governor requested the committee to look into the schools, Oklahoma ranked thirty-third among the states in terms of the average salary paid its instructional staff. Within a year it had dropped to thirty-seventh place. During that time, the national average for instructors' salaries went up by four per cent; in Oklahoma, the average increase amounted to 0.2 per cent.

Governor Bellmon does not feel any responsibility for the fact that sanctions have been invoked. "It has nothing to do with me particularly," he said. Couldn't it be said, for instance, that his veto of a 1963 bill to increase teachers' salaries by $1,000 over a six-year period had some relation to the current trouble? No, the governor didn't see what that had to do with it. "Our problem is to accelerate new industry in the state," he said. The salary-increase bill was "just one of those little public relations things the legislature does from time to time."

The governor, for his part, had offered a plan called "Operation Giant Stride." He unveiled it last December, calling two state-wide teachers' meetings for the occasion. With the help of visual aids, he explained how his plan would give teachers an $800 raise over the next two years; it would also raise the minimum wage for all public employees, add hundreds of miles to the highway program, straighten out the worst curves and provide more highway patrolmen, and strengthen the state's public and mental health services. "It sounds as if we're talking about an impossible goal," the governor concluded, "but we're not! And the miraculous part," he informed his audience, "is that we can have all the funds for 'Operation Giant Stride' as we need them and ... without strangling Oklahoma's growth by raising taxes." One local editor dismissed the plan as "visionary." It not only would have required the Democratic legislature's approval and a special election in which the voters would agree to placing the "full faith and

credit" of the state behind a $500-million highway bond issue (to be re-
paid from tolls); it also envisaged the further consolidation of reluctant
school districts and the shuffling of money from local school accounts to state
accounts and back again. In the end, the plan died in a committee of the
Democratic-controlled legislature.

GRINDING THE MILLS

The legislature, for its part, feels that with its new education bill it
has now done all it can. "Just tell me this," Lonnie Abbott, chairman of
the lower house's education committee and a teacher himself, asked Ferman
Phillips of the OEA a few days after the new bill had been passed. "Don't
you think we've done the best we could?" "Yes, but it's not enough," Phillips
replied. "We've spent our entire surplus over the next two years, to tell the
truth," Abbott said. Although the new bill will raise teachers' salaries an
average of $500 over the next two years, they will still fall short by $500 of
the present national average.

"I know it's not enough," Speaker of the House J. D. McCarty told
me. The easily aroused speaker had risen in the house shortly after the bill
was passed to attack the NEA as a bunch of "hypocritical psychos," and to
call its executive director a "nincompoop." Claiming that the NEA was only
using Oklahoma as a "whipping boy," he offered a resolution demanding
that the OEA request the NEA to lift its sanctions. It won unanimous approval. In addition to the new education bill, the legislature has also submitted a constitutional amendment to the people, to be voted on September
14, that would permit localities to raise their tax limit for schools by ten
mills. It could mean $28 million to $30 million more a year for schools,
if it passes and if every district raises its rates. It was one of the OEA petitions offered the voters last November; it lost only because it did not get a
majority of all votes cast in the election. It did win a majority of those
voting on it.

"Even if the millage amendment passes," McCarty said, "it's still not
enough. We'll need additional funds. Two years from now, we'll certainly
need more money."

Why hadn't the legislature, with its four-to-one Democratic control,
passed a sales tax increase itself, instead of handing the decision over to
the electorate? "We didn't have the votes," McCarty explained. "We
couldn't get the three-fourths necessary to override the governor's veto."
He pulled a sheaf of papers from his desk to show the straw votes which
had been taken and which consistently fell short by seven. He had campaigned widely for the sales tax in the April election, flying about the state
urging the people to vote "Yes," and when they turned it down by 293,000

to 171,000, whatever hopes he entertained of running for governor in the next election went with it.

Why didn't the legislature raise the state income tax? "We did," said McCarty, speaking for the House. "But our bill died in the Senate." This time, apparently, it wasn't the threat of the governor's veto that prevented action. "The electorate had just turned down the sales tax increase when we got the bill," Clem McSpadden, president pro tempore of the Senate, and a popular rodeo announcer, explained. He felt no need to elaborate.

"You can't say any one man is responsible for the situation in Oklahoma," said Richard Morgan, the NEA's representative most closely associated with the recent events in the state. He was all for the sanctions, of course, and spoke enthusiastically of the nationwide response to the relocation centers. "We wrote to 6,000 local associations in the 36 states that pay higher average teachers' salaries than Oklahoma," Morgan said, "and asked them to list vacancies for which Oklahoma teachers might apply. We got responses from 3,000 of them." By July, more than 9,500 positions had been reported "from Burlington, Vermont, across the country, as proof of our solidarity. Some who had no vacancies asked if there was anything else they could do. We told them about the emergency fund. The first contribution, $1,000, came from the state teachers' association of Utah." There was an "ambivalence" about the relocation centers, Morgan admitted. "It sounds as if we want to strip the state of teachers. We are trying to keep others out, but we need our soldiers here. We feel we should provide a service, though, for those who want to leave." How many actually relocated will not be known till fall.

Morgan was also enthusiastic about the "terrific splash-over" effect that sanctions have on neighboring states. "Texas teachers credit Oklahoma for their raise," he said, "and after Utah, Idaho teachers asked us to make an investigation, but before sanctions could be applied, the legislature made a 42 per cent increase in state aid and passed a three per cent sales tax. This is so much more powerful than strikes." Morgan told me of the NEA's plan to send formal letters "to the nation's hundred largest corporations and 50 banks," telling them that the NEA had declared sanctions against the state, and why. "The devastating part is that the longer sanctions go on, the more business is affected. And Oklahoma is dying to get new industry and investment capital."

How serious the economic effect of the NEA's latest maneuver will prove to be is an open question, but certainly it has added a new and disturbing dimension to the protest activities of teachers, one whose effect could continue long after sanctions or strikes are over. Governor Bellmon was most disturbed about this aspect of sanctions. "The NEA comes in and gives our state a black eye," and he continued, "Tulsa almost lost a new Borg-

Warner plant that will employ 500 people now and 1,500 five to ten years from now." Several mutual funds, he said, had dropped Oklahoma utility bonds. And he mentioned an atomic accelerator plant for which Oklahoma was competing.

Senator McSpadden had more to add about the atomic accelerator plant. Two committees from Oklahoma City and Tulsa, he said, had gone to the AEC and "The first question they asked them was, 'What about those sanctions?' Then they asked about the water power." Scientists want good schools for their children, and McSpadden estimated that the plant, wherever the AEC decides to locate it, will employ some 2,000 physicists.

McCarty was particularly aware of the local businessmen's concern over sanctions. Among the letters he had received praising his attack on the NEA was one, for example, from the Enid Chamber of Commerce, another from the Ford Motor Distributing Company in Oklahoma City. "Since we are competitive with Texas for industrial installations," the Oklahoma Gas and Electric Company wrote, sanctions are "a particularly unfortunate development."

The OEA can only guess at the effect that continued sanctions might have on the September vote to increase the millage rate. "These are fairly stubborn people," a local editor pointed out. "They won't be browbeaten by what they consider a bunch of outsiders." The news director of a TV station agreed. "If the sanctions continue," he said, "they'll arouse the stubbornness and intransigence of a people already intransigent enough about paying more taxes."

On August 11, the OEA's board of directors took up the matter of continued sanctions. Its executive committee recommended that it ask the NEA to lift them in part—to close the relocation centers and to remove the ban on out-of-state teachers. The board unanimously accepted the first recommendation (the centers had already closed at the beginning of summer) and rejected the second. Most likely the NEA will follow suit. On September 14, the voters will again take their turn to speak. But even if they pass the amendment to raise the millage rate, it won't be enough, as McCarty admitted. Two years from now, the state will need still more money for its education.

[Miss Carter has added the following sequel to her *Reporter* article, based on events which occurred subsequent to publication of the above— *The Editors*.]

As it turned out, Oklahoma voted two to one to raise their millage rates, and the sanctions were promptly lifted. Moreover, some 75 of the thousand-odd school districts were able to meet the September deadline for holding elections to take advantage of the new amendment, and the larger cities among them, such as Tulsa and Midwest City, either took the maximum allowed, or close to it. The sanctions had other effects as well. Classroom teachers now compose 60 per cent of the membership on the OEA's board of directors (whereas before the struggle began they were a decided minority), and, according to Richard Morgan of the NEA, the AFT has lost what members it had in Midwest City, its largest unit, numbering some 250 teachers, to the OEA.

Since then, sanctions have been applied locally in a number of cases from Knoxville, Tennessee, to Springfield, Massachusetts. The only statewide affair has been in Kentucky, where, without declaring sanctions, the teachers held a one-day "professional holiday," on February 4, 1966, to force the legislature to appropriate more than it had planned for education. Sanctions, apparently, are a theme which the NEA and its local affiliates can play in infinite variation.

VI-5

CONSULTATION AND NEGOTIATION TECHNIQUES*

United States Civil Service Commission

INTRODUCTION

Executive Order 10988 provides for "consultation" when an employee organization has been given formal recognition and for "negotiation" where exclusive recognition has been granted.

The purpose of consultation is to obtain the views of the employee organization on a current basis as new policies are being established or as employees express dissatisfaction with existing policy or its implementation. The purpose of negotiation is similar, except that negotiation further implies an effort to reach agreements which can be recorded in writing in the form of memoranda of agreement or understanding. Negotiation is normally undertaken at periodic intervals at which times the parties attempt to work out agreements governing their relationships over a specified length of time.[1]

The processes of consultation are less elaborate and are already familiar to most agencies. Therefore, the suggestions of technique which follow are primarily directed toward the handling of negotiating sessions leading to the execution of an original or supplementary agreement in a situation where an employee organization has been granted exclusive recognition. To the extent they are found appropriate, these techniques may also be applied to processes of consultation.

These guides are primarily intended for Federal establishments which have not previously negotiated agreements. The techniques suggested center around preparation and conduct of the negotiating conference, and not the substantive provisions of the agreement. Likewise, they do not touch on many of the special problems involved in those negotiations which include the establishment of hourly wages.

Negotiation is generally recognized to be an art rather than a science. It is essentially a democratic process of communication and a joint effort

* Reprinted from U.S. Civil Service Commission, *Employee Management Cooperation in the Federal Service,* Personnel Methods Series No. 15 (Washington, D.C.: Government Printing Office, 1962), 6.01-6.08.

[1] Once a policy has been established under either the processes of consultation or negotiation it is of course not necessary to consult on operating decisions.

to develop policies relating to the problems of a specific work situation. Therefore, no hard and fast rules of procedure can be provided with a guarantee of success. The suggestions which follow should be regarded simply as ideas upon which to build procedures appropriate to local needs.

PREPARING FOR NEGOTIATIONS

The success of productive negotiation can be directly related to the thoroughness of advance preparation. Ordinarily the personnel management organizations will be assigned the principal responsibility for coordinating the preparation. However, since the process of preparation is important both as an educative and an administrative procedure it is important to draw the key managers concerned with the negotiations into the preparations at an early stage. These managers can contribute much of the background from which effective negotiating decisions are made at the same time they are acquiring the understanding essential to administration of the agreement.

Selecting the Negotiating Committee

One of the earliest steps to consider in preparation is the selection of management's negotiating committee. Once selected this committee can serve as a continuing focal point for management's integrated approach to relations with the employee organization.

The size of the negotiating committee usually depends upon the size of the establishment and the variety of functions within it. Normally the membership is designed to provide representation of top management, the personnel office, and the managers of the principal operating divisions concerned. Considerations of manageability versus breadth of representation can serve to determine the effective size.

In addition to the principal members it is often helpful to designate alternate members of the committee. If the alternates participate fully in the joint work of the committee they are well prepared to fill in as committee members, as well as to do spade work in preparing for negotiations and to serve on employee-management working committees. The use of alternates in this way also greatly minimizes the difficulties of setting schedules for negotiating conferences.

The Role of Spokesman and Committee Members

The work of the negotiating committee may be expedited substantially by designating a single spokesman for the committee. Such a spokesman serves the need for a chairman or group leader in conducting the internal business of the committee. The use of the single spokesman also seems to provide for greater efficiency, continuity, and effectiveness of the presentation of management's position at the negotiating table.

When a single spokesman is used the role of the remaining committee members is still important. It is their responsibility to participate fully in developing management's position in preliminary planning sessions and later in caucuses, and to provide information from their areas of specialization as required in the course of the conference. In addition to their duties during the period just before and during the negotiating conferences,[2] these committee members should have continuing responsibility for observing operations under the agreement and contributing to the long range program for improving effectiveness of relations.

In selecting a spokesman, consideration should be given to his qualities of persuasiveness, patience, skill in clear and direct communication, and familiarity with the organization and the negotiating procedure. He must be respected by the employees and have the reputation of fairness. He must have full authority to represent management. At the outset of the employee-management negotiation relationships, when the prospective members of the negotiating committee are relatively inexperienced, the basic qualities suggested above may weigh more heavily in selection of a spokesman than the actual length of prior negotiating experience.

Anticipating the Issues

In order to prepare intelligently for negotiation it is obviously desirable to have some advance idea of the issues which are of interest to the employees. In many negotiating situations it is customary for the parties to exchange letters outlining their proposals for negotiation. While this practice has obvious advantages it may also have disadvantages if it results in undue restriction on the free introduction of matters for discussion or if it leads to submission of unduly extensive lists of requests for "strategic" purposes. The latter practice needlessly complicates preparation and consumes time in negotiation.

In the interest of informality and expediency, some establishments abide by a practice in which the party requesting a conference indicates in its letter the general areas it wishes to discuss.[3] Additional information on

---

[2] The word "conference" is used here to refer to meetings scheduled periodically (perhaps annually) for purposes of negotiation. The separate meetings which may make up any one conference will be referred to as "sessions."

[3] Following is an example of such a provision (where the agency has authority to set pay rates):

SEC. 2.6 Each calendar year one conference may be held to consider revising the rates of pay and one conference may be held to consider revising the provisions of other Supplementary Agreements. Additional conferences may be held if required under the provision of paragraph 1.5. The Project Manager or the Council may notify the other in writing that a conference is desired. Except for revisions of rates of pay the notice shall state the nature of the revisions desired. The notice shall be acknowledged within ten days and the conference shall be convened within sixty days of the date of the notice.

issues that can be expected to arise is indicated by items of known interest carrying over from previous sessions. Review of recent grievances is an additional source of information on potential areas of concern for negotiation.[4] Supervisors and staff specialists should be asked to advise of issues which they see arising which bear on possible areas of negotiation.

In addition to examining various sources of potential issues it is well to review the workings of previously negotiated solutions to other issues. This may possibly reveal a need of further negotiation on those issues or it may indicate possible patterns of solution to related issues.

Clarifying Latitude for Negotiation

As soon as the probable areas of negotiation have been identified it is essential to investigate the latitude available for negotiation in these areas and to clarify requirements for approval. These questions must, of course, be answered within the total regulatory and policy framework in which the agency operates. Sections 6, 7, and 8 of the Executive Order provide basic requirements relating to these questions. In addition to such specific limitations as are created by laws and regulations, it is well to bear in mind the more general limitation expressed by the President that the public interest must be the paramount consideration in arriving at any policy decision through the process of consultation or negotiation.

Assembling Factual Data

After identifying probable issues and clarifying negotiating authority, it is necessary to collect and assemble factual data available on each issue. The more facts that can be assembled in advance with regard to each issue and its potential solution, the simpler and less emotional will be the subsequent negotiation.

In addition to analysis of internal sources of data it may sometimes be advisable to study the personnel practices of other agencies and private employers in the area. This is especially true with regard to wages when these are set under agency wage board procedures. It is less essential in other areas. Since cooperative contacts with other employers can be one of the most valuable assets available in any negotiating situation, the greatest skill and tact that can be brought to bear is warranted in every instance. Carefully planned interview procedures should be utilized, combined with a willingness

---

[4] While grievances are not themselves the subject of negotiations, they may provide important information on possible problems in policy or relationships which can be settled by written agreement or mutual understanding. Management should avoid allowing negotiations to dwell on individual grievances which should be handled by other machinery.

to reciprocate in sharing information. Cooperating employers must be assured of confidential treatment to whatever degree requested.

Some agencies have found it possible to make use of joint employee-management committees as part of their fact-finding procedure. Where utilized, the size of such committees is best held to a minimum and complete arrangements should be agreed upon in advance both with the employee representatives and the employers to be consulted.

In addition to obtaining straight factual data it is helpful to negotiation to understand the background of any outside practices which are studied as precedents. In other words, it is helpful to understand why certain practices have been adopted elsewhere in order to determine if they are appropriate for adoption in the Government's operation. Employers will often cooperate in furnishing such explanation in addition to providing copies of their employee agreements.

Preparation of Materials

Having obtained factual background material, the normal procedure involves the making of staff analyses, the assembly of duplicated materials for preliminary use by management's negotiating committee, and the duplicating of those materials which are for joint examination at the negotiating table.

Materials to be used by the negotiating committee can be assembled in the order of probable consideration in the form of notebooks for the committee members. Included in the notebooks would be statements outlining the issues, accompanied by narrative or statistical explanations and, as appropriate, recommendations for committee consideration. Other items of information pertaining to the local establishment which may be found useful might include factual data on current staffing, current schedules of wages, copies of the existing agreement and the previous conference minutes, cost analyses, and the like. Items of external information such as explanations of trends in comparable industrial activities may also be included.

Attention should be given to including only essential data in the notebooks and to arranging it for most efficient use. The material will be of greatest value if it is developed jointly by the negotiators and the personnel staff out of the experience of successive negotiations.

A variety of worksheets may be found useful, both for preliminary study meetings and for use by both committees during the conference. "Worksheets" are forms prepared for recording the immediate information essential to the negotiation of any issue. The basic need in any such worksheet is to set forth statements of present practice with adjacent space provided for recording management's position, the subsequent proposals of both parties, comments on the proposals, and the final agreements on each provision.

Preliminary Meetings of the Negotiating Committee

Prior to the holding of preliminary meetings of the full management negotiating committee it may be found expedient to have subcommittee meetings on the issues of interest to the respective divisions of the organization. A subcommittee may be composed, for example, of the negotiating committee member representing a division and a representative of the personnel staff. A subcommittee may make preliminary analyses of factual data and develop recommendations for consideration by the whole committee.

One or more meetings of the full negotiating committee is generally an essential prelude to every negotiating conference. The objective of these meetings, which should include participation by the principal managers and the representatives of the staff offices concerned, is to review anticipated issues, review operating practices and policies, determine management's objectives, prepare tentative and alternative positions, and establish tentative procedures and orders of business. This is the heart of the preparation process and involves the education of the staff in the problems of personnel management and the coordination of operations under the agreement, as well as actual preparation for negotiation.

At this time, the full committee should analyze each of the anticipated issues to determine its cost, workability, and the apparent relative importance of the issues to the employees.

Where negotiations are closely related to parallel negotiations in non-governmental agencies, the committee will want to weigh the possible impact of each issue on the industrial practice of the area. Each request should also be considered for its long range effects within the establishment and its effect on nonunit employees, that is, employees not members of the unit represented at the negotiating conference.

The committee should then agree on the limits of its position, its counter proposals, and its reasoning on every issue. Having given this kind of consideration to the issues of interest to the employees, the committee should agree on its own objectives, their priority, the wording of provisions, and possible alternative wording.

Discussion with Top Management

An essential part of this phase of preparation is discussion between the chairman or spokesman of the committee and the head of the establishment, if he is not a member of the negotiating committee. Once the committee has agreed on the factors mentioned above, the spokesman can outline for the top executive the expected course of negotiation and the committee's recommendations for settlement. The head of the establishment would be expected to indicate any matters of special concern to himself and to higher agency levels. Top management should be kept informed during the course of negotiation to assure adequate policy guidance consistent with a workable delegation of authority to the spokesman.

Planning the Conference Arrangements

During the preliminary meeting the negotiating committee can agree on physical arrangements and scheduling for the conference, subject to later confirmation with the employees' committee. The negotiating sessions are usually held on the agency's premises. While there may be some advantage to a more neutral location, there is also less convenience for access to administrative records, consultation with staff specialists, use of recording and duplicating facilities, etc.

To minimize fatigue and create conditions conducive to constructive negotiation, attention should be given to providing adequate and comfortable table space and seating. Individual rooms should be provided for caucuses; that is, the separate meetings of the committees for consultation during the negotiations. A system can be established for handling telephone calls to minimize interruptions. Stenographic services probably will be wanted for verbatim recording of agreements, although for the official conference record a condensed report may be preferred to encourage free discussion and minimize speech making.

There are differing points of view on timing and length of sessions. (The frequency and duration of conferences will, of course, depend on local needs. An annual conference to consider revisions of supplementary agreements might be expected to take from one to three days. An initial conference to establish a basic agreement might require considerably longer or might possibly be spread over a nonconsecutive series of negotiating sessions.) For conferences expected to last several days, a reasonable schedule of meetings of about 5-6 hours a day, interspersed with recesses as necessary, seems to provide ample discussion periods without causing fatigue and with opportunity to handle some accumulation of other business. Ideally, the sessions should be scheduled so as to maintain the continuity of discussion without becoming burdensome.

It probably will be desirable to adopt a policy on the attendance of employees at the negotiating sessions. Although employees are frequently excluded from industrial negotiations, at least some Federal establishments have adopted the practice of notifying employees and permitting them to attend as observers on annual leave. A policy of permitting employees to attend does not necessarily mean they are encouraged to attend since it may be found that the presence of numbers of observers tends to lessen the air of informality and direct expression and to slow down the processes of negotiation.

Final Steps in Preparation

Although arbitration of issues under negotiation is not permitted under section 15 of the Executive order, other means of settling impasses may be used such as mediation or fact finding.[5] Where mediation has by agreement been made a part of an agency's negotiating procedure, it becomes another factor for preparation. Some establishments have provided in their agreements for standing panels from which mediators can be selected if needed. Where this practice is used, a part of regular conference planning is the review of the current status of membership of the mediation panel and the taking of necessary action to investigate and agree on the acceptability of potential members of the panel.

A final step in conference preparation is the provision of any special materials needed by the spokesman. This may include items such as an agenda, lists of the current memberships of any labor-management boards or committees previously established, current data on employment, program plans, work load data, and current information about the composition and attitudes of the employees' negotiating committee.

CONDUCT OF THE NEGOTIATING CONFERENCE

Opening the Conference

While practice in some negotiating situations is to designate a conference chairman, apparently equal success is attained by allowing the two spokesmen to conduct the meeting by mutual accord.

As the host, management's committee spokesman should take the lead in making introductions and setting an informal, congenial tone for the conference. It may be appropriate to ask management's top executive to extend a welcome and offer informal observations on current aspects of the agency's program. The employee representatives' spokesman may wish to make general observations on matters of current interest to his group.

Opening remarks can be followed by agreeing on methods of procedure, including the facilities available, the timing of sessions, the use of spokesmen, and the kind of conference record desired.

Although the processes involved in the granting of recognition to the employee organization will have been taken care of prior to the convening

[5] The report of the President's Task Force on Employee-Management Cooperation clearly shows the intent that the agencies and employee organizations make every effort to resolve any differences between them wherever possible without third party intervention. The report states: "Impasses in negotiation between Government officials and employee organizations granted exclusive recognition should be solved by means other than arbitration. Methods for helping to bring about settlements should be devised and agreed to on an agency by agency basis."

of any conference for actual negotiation, it may be desirable at this point in the conference to review and clarify for the record the status of employee representation. This will assure a mutual understanding and a documentation in the conference record of the authority and responsibility of the employee's negotiating committee to speak for all members of the employee unit concerned.

Outlining the Issues

After completing the preliminaries and agreeing on an informal set of rules of procedure, the issues for discussion should be outlined even though this may have been done in a preliminary fashion by correspondence. If the employees have requested the conference, their spokesman may be asked at this time to discuss and amplify the requests being presented with explanations of background and purpose. While further issues may arise during the course of the conference and the parties may agree to consider them, it is well to have all known issues laid on the table in the opening session.

Following a period for questions and answers, the management committee spokesman may wish to ask for a recess to study the requests. Unless the issues are unusually simple, clear cut, and well-anticipated, the conference activities up to this point will probably have taken up the opening session. Normally, management's spokesman should request a caucus in any such instance which requires a response to major issues.

While requests received in the opening session will very seldom be completely unforeseen, if such an issue is introduced management may have to delay consideration of this issue while necessary information is gathered. It may even be necessary to defer such an issue to subsequent negotiations if the time available does not permit the thorough study which is normally prerequisite to negotiation of any important item.

Use of Caucus to Prepare Responses

The purpose of the caucus at appropriate times during the conference is to study the issues then under discussion, to provide time for staff consultation, to examine the provisions of other agreements, to fix management's position, and to study and prepare the language of specific provisions. If the chief management executive occasionally "sits in" on caucuses it will enable him to keep abreast of negotiations and offer policy guidance if necessary. Key management officials who are not a part of the negotiating committee may also be asked to participate in the caucus to express their views and ensure their understanding.

Thus, the responses which management gives to employee proposals should be the product of joint effort in caucus by the negotiating committee, the staff, the managers, and top management. However, it is usually the spokesman's individual responsibility to sense the trend of negotiation, to determine timing, and to state the official response to the employees' proposals.

Elements to Consider in Responding

It is well to retain a flexibility in the sequence of handling issues, in preference to following a rigid agenda. A useful technique is to approach some of the less controversial issues early in negotiation to establish a climate of agreement.

, Since agreement does not always come easily it is customary to retain some element of concession in reserve. This is in keeping with the purpose of negotiation which is to explore, from originally divergent positions, the possible areas of agreement. Caution may suggest the making of offers on specific issues subject to ability to reach agreement on the whole "package." Management also should not hesitate to present proposals calculated to help achieve its own objectives in the process of reacting to employee proposals.

Maintaining Cooperative Relationships

In the process of working towards agreement there are principles or unwritten rules of cooperation which should be observed. A basic principle, of course, is that each party must adopt an attitude of flexibility, and cannot stand on a "take it or leave it" position. Each side shares the responsibility to understand the other's problems and to make an honest attempt to find acceptable solutions.

A major part of the success of negotiation involves doing everything that can be done to maintain clear channels of communication. This includes listening very carefully to expressions of employee points of view and responding to questions in simple and straightforward fashion. Frankness and sincerity are greatly preferable to subtlety and oratory. Care should be taken not to raise false hopes unintentionally and on the other hand not to indicate a position as being a final offer unless it is exactly that.

Federal establishments which have engaged in negotiation for some time have found it possible to conduct all of their relationships with employee groups with complete dignity and decorum even when sharp differences of opinion have existed between them. The consistent maintenance of this kind of negotiating relationship comes from the efforts of each side to operate completely in good faith and to avoid questioning the good faith of the other.

While the spokesmen are responsible for keeping the discussion moving in orderly and productive fashion towards agreement, ample time should still be allowed for full consideration on both sides of the table. Management will want to bear in mind that the employees' spokesman sometimes needs time to reconcile differing views within the employee groups represented. Time must be allowed for adjustment of expectations and internal communication.

Avoiding Apparent Impasses

By skillful use of the techniques of negotiation it should be possible in the majority of cases to find a way around apparent impasses. It is helpful occasionally to review progress and take note of areas of agreement. In those areas where the parties are still some distance apart it may help to go back and review the facts. A recess at such a time may help to temper views, bring in more information, and discover new approaches.

In some situations, if unable to agree immediately to the changes being proposed, the parties may be able to agree on trial arrangements or periods of further observation of operations under the status quo. Another possibility is that agreement can be reached to introduce the desired changes by stages, giving the party granting the concession more time to adjust to the workings of the new situation.

If the cause of disagreement lies in differing interpretation of the facts it may be possible to set up a joint fact-finding committee to study the situation in the field. Such a subcommittee would not customarily be responsible for reaching agreement on the issues, but each member would report the facts as he saw them to his negotiating committee for consideration at a later negotiating conference.

Subcommittees of this kind can also be used where much preliminary work and discussion must be done which is not economically done in conference of the whole committee. Again the function of the working committee would not be to reach agreement but to separately report the results of discussion to the respective negotiating committees for decision.

Inability of the parties to reach agreement on difficult items at any given negotiating conference should not be regarded as complete failure since many important changes can only be brought about after repeated consideration in successive negotiating conferences. Both parties must be prepared to accept the fact that even after earnest efforts to reach agreement the conclusion of negotiation may see proposals from either or both sides left unaccomplished.[6]

[6] The Task Force report cautions that the object of negotiations is to produce agreement by diligent, serious, and brief exchange of information and views. It goes on to caution that, if negotiation ceases to be productive, higher officials have no alternative but to cut off discussion and proceed with the public business. The experience of some establishments which have engaged in negotiations does not suggest that this will be a serious problem. After a brief period of experience it would be expected that the negotiators from both sides would acquire the skill and judgment to sense the point when further efforts at negotiation would not be productive and would in fact be harmful to future relationships.

Recording Agreement on Issues Discussed

As agreement is reached on each issue it is well to agree at once to the wording of the provision and record it verbatim in the conference record for later incorporation in the written agreement. This should help to assure common understanding of the parties' intent as well as to save time in drafting the agreement.

In drafting the wording of each provision care should be taken to use simple and direct language. Since the success of the agreement depends on common understanding and the faith each party has in the other, there is no need for the verbal technicalities of a legal document. By the same token it is not necessary to incorporate the smallest details of the joint relationship into the agreement. A comprehensive cataloging of tightly worded provisions is no substitute for faith and sincerity in employee-management relations.

At the conclusion of agreement on all major issues the spokesmen should go back and recheck any items passed over initially to ensure they have been taken care of. Management's spokesman may wish to make a final reading of the provisions agreed to.

It is then customary for the members of the committees to sign the agreement. This can be done by use of a signature page to save time in waiting for typing of the agreement. The spokesman should review with the committees any need for review and approval at higher levels of management and the parties should agree on the effective date of the agreement following its approval.[7]

POST-CONFERENCE ACTIVITIES

Upon final approval of the agreement, appropriate steps should be taken to publish and distribute the agreement to all employees and supervisors affected, and to interpret its results to staff offices concerned in its administration.

It may be profitable at this point to bring management's negotiating committee together for a critique of the entire process. Need for changes in preparation may be apparent at this time and can be agreed upon in advance of the next negotiation. The committee can also agree on steps needed to implement the agreement and for exchange of experience and data with other organizations.

If preparations for negotiation have been extensive, it is possible that an analysis of the staff time and resources involved will suggest alternative

[7] Section 7 of the Executive Order provides that any basic or initial agreement entered into with an employee organization as the exclusive representative of employees in a unit must be approved by the head of the agency or an official designated by him.

procedures without reducing effectiveness. The value of the time spent should not be overlooked, however. The process of preparation and discussion has an instructional and coordinative value for management officials that may not have been fully realized prior to beginning negotiations.

Once having been through the experience of a negotiating conference, the participants can look forward to future meetings with more assurance. Procedural matters that may have been problems the first time around may not be matters of concern in future sessions. Although procedures are important, the pay-off, of course, is the development of cooperative relationships between employee groups and management.

The techniques discussed in this paper are intended to help management officials meet the new challenges of negotiating conferences. The approach taken by these officials to negotiations must, of course, conform to agency instructions on this subject, and it should reflect what will work best in the local situation. Techniques should be kept simple and flexible; they must be subordinate to purpose—and the main purpose is to build more effective employee-management relations.

Appendix I

CHECKLIST OF ITEMS FOR CONSIDERATION IN THE PREPARATION AND CONDUCT OF NEGOTIATING CONFERENCES

The following list contains some suggested items for consideration in preparing for and conducting the negotiating conference:

What should be the size and composition of management's negotiating committee?

Should a single spokesman be designated?

What are the expected issues of negotiation?

Are previously negotiated procedures operating satisfactorily?

What new negotiating proposals are needed to accomplish management's objectives?

What is the latitude for negotiation on the issues which are expected to arise?

What procedure of approval is required?

What kind of data is needed?

In what form can data best be presented?

  (a) To the negotiating committee?
  (b) To the employees' representatives?

Should notebooks be prepared for the negotiators?

Should work sheets be used to record proposals and agreements?

What preliminary meetings are necessary?

Who should attend preliminary meetings?
Where should the negotiating conference be held?
What should be the schedule for conference sessions?
What provisions should be made for recording the conference?
What is to be the policy on employee attendance at the conference?
What provision should be made regarding mediation?
Are special materials needed by the spokesman?
Who will represent management on special committees?
What will be the tentative order of handling issues?
What are the plans regarding use of caucuses?
What will be the format of written agreements?
What will be the effective dates and duration of agreements?
What arrangements should be made for publishing the agreement?

Have the members of management's committee been advised of the following necessary considerations?

(a) The provisions of sections 6 and 7 of Executive Order 10988 which deal with areas of discretion and policy, the effects of laws and regulations, and the rights reserved to management.

(b) The provisions of section 7 of the Executive Order which concerns the right of an agency to take whatever action may be necessary to carry out the mission of the agency in situations of emergency.

(c) The effect which any agreements will have on other employees of the establishment who are not subject to the negotiated agreement.

(d) The importance of preserving the merit system.

(e) The need to make agreements which are in the public interest, which contribute to the goals of the agency, and which will promote better employee cooperation and therefore result in a better work force and a better work product.

VII

SPECIAL ISSUES IN
COLLECTIVE NEGOTIATIONS

There are many issues in collective negotiations. Periodical material in this area, almost non-existent in the Fifties, now fills several columns of the Education Index, *and much of it deals with issues on which there is clearly no consensus as yet. The editors have been extremely selective in this section, presenting only four articles. Of course, one reason for this is the fact that previous sections also dealt with issues; those discussed in this section were not so easily categorized as those in previous sections.*

In the first article, Donald L. Conrad, Associate Secretary of the NEA's Professional Rights and Responsibilities Commission, presents a cogent analysis of the relations between professionalism and collective negotiations. Among other things, Conrad effectively critizes the view that collective action is incompatible with professionalism. He clarifies the troublesome question of supervisory membership in negotiating units, and also discusses creative forms of negotiation being developed outside of education. Conrad's article also shows why it is necessary to reject the view that the strike is an obligatory feature of bargaining.

In the next article, Wesley A. Wildman and Charles R. Perry express their concern that collective negotiations is institutionalizing and perhaps even creating conflict with results that may be deleterious to education. While tentative, their conclusions should alert educators to some of the unanticipated and possibly undesirable effects of collective negotiations.

Impasse procedures are looming larger and larger on the negotiations horizon. Fundamentally, the problem is how to ensure continuity of education as an essential public service while simultaneously ensuring that the needs and counsel of appropriate parties are accorded adequate attention in setting conditions of educational employment. The article by Morris Slavney analyzes in some detail the practical problems inherent in resolving this dilemma. As Chairman of the Wisconsin Employment Relations Board, Slavney has been deeply involved in resolving impasses in public employment, including public education.

Finally, Charles S. Benson of the University of California, Berkeley, has undertaken a very difficult assignment especially for this volume: an analysis of the impact of collective negotiations on the principle of seniority. Surprisingly enough, Benson asserts that collective negotiations will weaken reliance upon seniority in making educational assignments. This would be a much different outcome than is commonly anticipated, yet the author's impressive record clearly demonstrates that his observations deserve careful consideration. Benson has written or edited several books, including The Economics of Public Education *(Boston: Houghton Mifflin, 1962), probably the most outstanding book on the subject published in the United States.*

VII-1

COLLECTIVE NEGOTIATIONS
AND PROFESSIONALISM*

Donald L. Conrad

In considering the applicability of traditional collective bargaining to the public school environment, a variety of important factors must be examined. My task will be to consider the educator apart from (as much as this is possible) other significant features in this environment. Insofar as negotiation is concerned, the teacher must be thought of as possessing three identities. Public school teachers are *employees*. They are *public* employees. And they are *professional* public employees. Federal legislation—most particularly the Wagner Act and the Taft-Hartley Act—has described appropriate procedures to be used by employees and employee organizations as they jointly participate in certain kinds of decision making in the private work place. Dating back to the early days of the Tennessee Valley Authority and formalized more recently by presidential executive order, collective bargaining principles (without ever mentioning the word bargain) have been applied successfully to employee-management relations in federal service and to some extent in state and municipal employment. There is little tradition to lean upon in examining the place of the teacher in negotiation relationships; however, there is a body of experience that can be analyzed in studying employed professionals in both the private and public sectors of the economy. We will want to search out the effect of forms of joint participation on the objectives expressed by professional organizations and on the methods used by professions to achieve these objectives.

PROFESSIONAL ROLE DEFINED

The classical view of professionhood, though frequently verbalized, expresses an unrealistic model of the organized professions in the United States

* Paper presented on July 8, 1965, at the National Institute on Collective Negotiations in Public Education cosponsored by Phi Delta Kappa and Rhode Island College, Providence, R.I. Donald L. Conrad is Associate Secretary, NEA Commission on Professional Rights and Responsibilities.

today. Though certain common qualities can be recognized among the major professional occupations, the environment that we are examining is characterized by a great deal of variation. Not only are occupational differences generally differences of degree, but even within a particular professional occupation (medicine, law, engineering) the variation among professional roles played is quite wide. Still more confusing to the comfortable absolutist is the realization that the modern professional person may play out in a given day a whole series of occupational roles—from manager at one point to managed the next, from supervisor to supervised, artisan to expert, and from fee-taking professional to salaried employee.

All the professions include fee takers, as well as the salaried; they include the so-called free professional, as well as the employed professional; and some will function in voluntary societies, while others utilize a variety of "closed shop" or subtly coercive forms of compulsory membership.[1]

Though many traditional stereotypes fail to meaningfully define the professional role, there are some landmarks that can be located and described. Professor Barber, writing in *The Profesessions in America*,[2] said:

Professional behavior may be defined in terms of four essential attributes: a high degree of generalized and systematic knowledge; primary orientation to the community interest rather than to individual self-interest; a high degree of self-control of behavior through codes of ethics internalized in the process of work socialization and through voluntary associations organized and operated by the work specialists themselves; and a system of rewards (monetary and honorary) that is primarily a set of symbols of work achievement and thus ends in themselves, not means to some end of individual self-interest.

In defining the professional, the Taft-Hartley Bill used language like: original, creative, intellectual, varied, and not standardized. Others would stress that professional work is unique and not interchangeable, that the value of the work cannot be measured[3] (you must pay the man, not the job), and that the work demands a high degree of discretion and judgment and is a vital service to the community. The literature abounds with such terms as: expertise, altruism, colleague control, autonomy, and trust relationship.

The difficulty (if not the impossibility) of the layman's evaluating the quality of professional expertness appears to be a particularly central characteristic. As a result of this, the client has little choice but to put himself in the hands of the practitioner. The necessary buyer trust is contrasted sharply with the more familiar *caveat emptor*. Actions that tend to interfere with

[1] Mancur Olson, Jr., *The Logic of Collective Action* (Cambridge, Mass.: Harvard University Press, 1965).
[2] Bernard Barber, "Some Problems in the Sociology of the Profession," in K. S. Lynn, *The Professions in America*. (Boston, Mass.: Houghton-Mifflin Co., 1965).
[3] David W. Belcher, *Wage and Salary Administration*. (Englewood Cliffs, N.J.. Prentice-Hall, Inc., 1962).

the trust relationship tend also to limit severely any gains that might have accrued from the application of professional skill. The professional is obligated to exercise no less care in the client interest than in dealing with his own affairs. He must not only generally behave in an honest and upright manner; just as important, he must be believed to be scrupulous by clients, colleagues, and by the public. The professional practitioner is no special kind of paragon, but his code of ethics demands behavior from him that will generally support a trust relationship. A flagrant disregard for the mandates of the code could result in professional discipline from one's colleagues.

As employers—both private and public—seek to utilize the services of professionals, some interesting accommodations can be observed. Experience indicates that professional expertness cannot be tapped to full advantage in the usual vertical, hierarchical institutional organization. The unbending superordinate-subordinate structure is quite incompatible with the familiar professional horizontal peer structure. The supervision of professionals by laymen, or even by remote professionals, is regarded as an intrusion into employee autonomy and is resisted at every turn. The more successful managers and agency heads have seen the need to break away from the more traditional organization framework and are freely experimenting with new approaches. The experimental models all have in common: the organization of professionals in the work place as they are organized in societies and associations as free professionals outside of the work place; minimal interference or restriction in decision making in areas of professional expertness; and the use of internal, departmental colleague controls in place of the more rigid vertical supervision. In this setting, the prime role of administration is one of providing overall direction and coordination with the primary goals of the total enterprise.

The services of the physician, the lawyer, the teacher, the scientist, the engineer, the architect, the dentist, the accountant, the journalist, and the psychologist—to mention some—have never been more valued and valuable than they are today. Accommodation and variation are the key themes. In some cases the professional services go through a kind of selective modification, and in others variation occurs in the work environment. Both have shown themselves capable of change without damage to their basic operational requirements. Though the professions vary greatly (as do individual professionals) in terms of any absolute standard of professionhood, the qualities of colleague control and freedom to apply expertness are absolutely essential.

CREATIVE NEGOTIATION

Just as some would adopt unrealistic stereotypes of an absolute and unmodified professional, others would apply this same thinking approach to collective negotiation or collective bargaining. Some would insist that the negotiatory relationship must mean an adversary struggle, much name calling, a kind of count-down atmosphere, and an aggressive economic warfare between the manager and the managed. The mass media tend to focus our attention on the drama and sham of bargaining, of the strike and lockout, of the apparently unrestricted profit seeking of the major unions and associations in both private and public employment. But public attention has been called to observe the "freak relationship" rather than the much less spectacular day-to-day relationships in our economy that are producing growing stability and increasing productivity. In the science of economics, negotiation has shown that it can be applied to a great variety of work environments with successful results and that it is not only a means for the reconciliation of differences between employer and employee but also a valuable method of advancing common objectives. For optimal results in agreement reaching, collective bargaining techniques must be freely adaptable as the work environment changes and as the techniques are introduced into wholly new and different environments.

In the private sector of the economy, where we see negotiation most fully utilized, the following important changes are being instituted:[4]

1. Much greater use of continuous negotiation rather than deadline bargaining.

2. Joint desire to seek answers to the needs of the industry and the needs of the organized employees through research and expert investigation, rather than through "out-of-this-world" demands, subterfuge, and a double set of books.

3. A mature and mutual realization that each is important to the other. The new manager doesn't see the employee organization as a threat to his management but as an irreplaceable asset.

4. Employees and unions are more disposed to agonize over peaceable solutions to a bargaining impasse rather than taking the "easy way" to the strike. They see this not only as mutually advantageous, but also essential (not just incidentally) in the public interest.

Resulting from Presidential Executive Order 10988, the federal government has introduced an additional set of innovations of interest to all professionals and particularly of interest to educator professionals.[5] Some of these social inventions will undergo further modification, while it is certain that others will be included into our general concepts of the body of col-

---

[4] James J. Healy, Ed., *Creative Collective Bargaining*. (Englewood Cliffs, N.J.: Prentice-Hall, Inc., 1965).

[5] U.S. Department of Labor, Report of the President's Task Force on Employee-Management Relations in the Federal Service, *A Policy for Employee-Management Cooperation in the Federal Service*. (Washington, D.C.: Government Printing Office, 1961).

lective negotiation. The accommodations to collective bargaining in public service that appear particularly pertinent are:

1. Supervisory membership is permitted in employee organizations. In Hart's discussion of this,[6] he states that in government service all employees are covered by the same work rules, leave systems, salary schedules, pension plans, and job security provisions. It is felt by many that this kind of identity tends to minimize the dividing line between the two categories of personnel, a line that is normally accentuated in the private sector. However, it is also widely recognized in federal service that a failure to restrict management personnel participation can produce harmful effects in the employee organization.

2. The agency head cannot be bound by arbitration decisions made in conjunction with contract administration. It is likely that many school boards will insist on the same kind of discretion. Theoretically, it is felt that the agency head will seldom refuse to accept the decision reached in arbitration —to do so would threaten the integrity of the whole machinery and institute a rebirth of eyeball-to-eyeball power displays in every dispute.

3. The recognition of minority organizations and individuals and a provision for lesser than negotiation relationships. The irrevocable Constitutional right to petition the government requires this kind of creative variation. Any individual employee has the right to present a grievance, and certain minority organizations have a right to persuasively present their views for consideration. It should be stressed, though, that exclusive bargaining rights can be obtained at the request of the majority organization.

The creative forms that negotiation has incorporated in recent years makes it a more adaptable instrument in the environments that utilize its techniques. It also permits a reasonable assumption that it can be adapted to new employment environments in the coming years with greater growth in its versatility and with benefit to the new environment.

PROFESSIONAL EDUCATORS NEGOTIATE

The local control of public schools presents at least one asset in terms of professional negotiation. It would appear that we are going to be able to observe the life cycle of a very large number of experimental animals. Each of the half-dozen or more states that has legislated in this area has incorporated many novel features. And in states with an absence of legislative formula, individual school districts are experimenting with still greater diversity.

What criteria should we advance in answer to the question, "Can pro-

[6] Wilson R. Hart, *Collective Bargaining in the Federal Service.* (New York: Harper & Brothers, 1961).

fessional educators negotiate with boards of education without loss or weakening of essential professionalization?" The usual criteria that are suggested in a general employment environment are: (1) strong community of interest; (2) common skills; (3) shared working conditions, supervision, and physical location; and (4) similarity of authority structure.

These must be supplemented with regard to the special demands of the professional environment. We would have to additionally ask: (1) Does the negotiation relationship limit the freedom of the professional to make decisions in the client's interest? (2) Does it distort the specialized expertness that the professional brings to his work? (3) Is bargaining incompatible with serving the public good—does it mean a selfish serving of collective egotism?

I feel that we can safely reject the assertion that the strike is an obligatory feature of collective bargaining. Other power alternatives are being utilized in federal service and in public schools to give us reason to believe that this means of resolving impasse, or more frequently this means of reserved deterrence, need be resorted to in only the most refractory circumstances and as a last resort.

Other critics of professional negotiation insist that the bargaining relationship is a union weapon and therefore incompatible with professionalism.[7] Without entering into the controversy of the ethical propriety of professionals joining unions affiliated with the AFL-CIO versus joining organizations of a clearly independent nature,[8] let it be stated that negotiation is a social invention that resides in the public domain. It is an ancient and noble technique for agreement-reaching used in diplomatic circles, in legislative activity, and of course widely in the marketplace.

Not only have teachers at all levels shown a marked reluctance to become involved in meaningful collective action,[9] many would take the position that collective action is patently unprofessional. Implied in this position is an unstated approval of individual bargaining but a rejection of collective negotiations. This opinion is just plain irrational. An individual can be a vegetarian, but an individual as an individual can not be a professional. He becomes a professional as he joins with others of similar disposition to form a collectivity that asserts: control over admission to practice, the direction of pre-professional education, and jurisdiction in the expulsion of the unscrupulous. A profession cannot hope to meet its role demands unless it is prepared, through strong internal organization and through public sanction, to assure the control of the profession over whom it shall count as a colleague.

[7] P. L. Alger, N. A. Christensen, and S. P. Olmsted, *Ethical Problems in Engineering.* (New York: John Wiley and Sons, Inc., 1965).

[8] Office of Professional Development and Welfare, *Guidelines for Professional Negotiation.* (Washington, D.C.: National Education Association, 1965).

[9] Myron Lieberman, *Education as a Profession.* (Englewood Cliffs, N.J.: Prentice-Hall, Inc., 1956).

Many educators are disturbed about solutions growing out of a bargaining relationship because this method of solution-seeking is so different from what might be the more familiar scientific method. To think of negotiating a person's body temperature, the distance to the moon, or the amount of mineral in a soil analysis is just ludicrous. But problems that the education profession faces cannot all be approached in a coldly scientific manner. We don't have objective answers to questions like: What is a teacher worth? How long should the school day be? What text supplements should be chosen? How much tax load should people properly assume? Questions of this sort require the utilization of the democratic processes of involvement and participation by those who can contribute meaningfully, and of accommodation and compromise with the purpose of discovering a consensus that can be successfully implemented.

Educators can enter into employment negotiation relationships without danger to their professional status. Negotiatory associations should properly be understood as a neutral operational feature in the functioning of employed professionals. To negotiate or not to negotiate is the wrong question. The question that must be asked and answered is, "How can negotiation techniques be best utilized to improve public education?"

VII-2

GROUP CONFLICT AND SCHOOL ORGANIZATION*

Wesley A. Wildman and Charles R. Perry

Increasing teacher unrest in our society is manifested through "collective bargaining," "professional negotiation," and other forms of group action. In many instances the concepts and procedures being employed as militancy spreads have as their underlying rationale and purpose an accommodation of *group conflict* within an organization. By group conflict we mean those situations in which large numbers of persons in an organization may share perceived deprivations, frustrations, or dissatisfactions and develop consensus on issues in opposition to consensus on another level in the hierarchy. The phenomenon we are witnessing thus raises in immediate and acute fashion the question of the appropriateness or inevitability of essentially *collective, adversary forms of interaction* for the relationships between boards, administrations, and teachers. As a preliminary inquiry into this complex issue of far-reaching significance for public education, this article will (1) examine briefly the assumptions underlying the practice of collective negotiations in industry and note the advantages and disadvantages which can accompany such collective relationships, (2) discuss the viewpoints of the two major organizations vying for teacher allegiance as to the appropriateness for the schools of collective, adversary procedures based on assumptions of conflict, and, (3) indicate some of the major conflict issues around which collective negotiation relationships in the schools have centered to date.

I. CONFLICT AND COLLECTIVE RELATIONSHIPS

Theory and research in educational administration have not hitherto been much concerned with problems of *institutionalized or formalized group conflict* within the school organization. There has been little necessity to date for educators to make reference to or draw guidance from what is known of

* Reprinted from the January, 1966, issue of the *Phi Delta Kappan*. Wesley A. Wildman is Director of the Study of Collective Action by Public School Teachers at the University of Chicago, and Charles R. Perry is Assistant Professor of Industry, Wharton School of Finance and Industry, University of Pennsylvania.

group conflict in industry. The currently dominant, broadly social-psychological "individual needs *and* organizational goals" approach[1] to the problems of administration in the school has centered attention almost exclusively on role and personality conflict;[2] the essential foci of conflict for this approach have been within the individual himself, between the individuals within the organization, or, most importantly, between organizational role demands and expectations, on the one hand, and individual personality needs and demands on the other. Recently, the conflict potential of the "bureaucracy *vs.* professional employee" dilemma has had increasing attention,[3] usually as a special case of the broad concept of "organization *vs.* individual" conflict. Generally, "conflict," as traditionally perceived and researched in the school organization, has not been viewed as likely to lead to collective action among the teaching staff in support of a consensus in opposition to the judgment of a board or administration.

The practical collective accommodation and institutionalization of group conflict as reflected by industrial union-management relationships in this country has been studied extensively and boasts an enormous literature.[4] It is now quite clear that the theory and practice of collective bargaining are based, first, on the assumption of significant and continuing conflict between the managers and the managed in any enterprise, and second, on the corollary assumption that there will be a strong, identifiable community of interest and consensus within the employee group with regard to large numbers of

[1] J. W. Getzels, "A Psycho-sociological Framework for the Study of Administration," *Harvard Educational Review*, Fall, 1952, pp. 235-46; J .W. Getzels and Egon G. Guba, "Social Behavior and the Administrative Process," *The School Review*, Winter, 1957, pp. 423-41; Egon G. Guba, "Research in Internal Administration—What Do We Know?" in R. F. Campbell and J. M. Lipham (eds.), *Administrative Theory as a Guide to Action* (Chicago: Midwest Administration Center, University of Chicago, 1960), Chap. 7.

[2] See, for example, J. W. Getzels and E. G. Guba, "The Structure of Roles and Role Conflict in the Teaching Situation," *Journal of Educational Sociology*, September, 1955, pp. 30-40; Getzels and Guba, "Role, Role Conflict, and Effectiveness," *American Sociological Review*, April, 1954, pp. 164-75; and findings reported in J. W. Getzels, J. M. Lipham, and R. F. Campbell, *Administration as a Social Process: Theory, Research, and Practice* (forthcoming).

[3] Roald F. Campbell, Luvern L. Cunningham, and Roderick F. McPhee, *The Organization and Control of American Schools* (Columbus, O.: Charles E. Merrill Books, 1965), especially Chap. 9; and W. W. Charters, Jr., "An Approach to the Formal Organization of the School," in National Society for the Study of Education, *Behavioral Science and Educational Administration* (Sixty-third Yearbook, Part II) (Chicago: University of Chicago Press, 1964), p. 260.

[4] See, for instance, Neil W. Chamberlain, *Labor* (New York: McGraw Hill, 1965); Charles O. Gregory, *Labor and the Law* (2nd revised edition) (New York: Norton, 1958); Sumner H. Slichter, James J. Healy, and Robert E. Livernash, *The Impact of Collective Bargaining on Management* (Washington, D.C.: The Brookings Institution, 1960); and R. E. Walton and R. B. McKersie, *Behavioral Theory of Labor Negotiations* (New York: McGraw Hill, 1965).

items and areas of judgment on which there will be conflict with the managing authority.

Collective bargaining as it is practiced in industry, and at least in some school systems, is essentially a power relationship and a process of power accommodation. The essence of bargaining is compromise and concession-making on matters over which there is conflict between the parties involved in the bargaining. The avowed theoretical purpose and practical effect of collective bargaining is to grant to employee organizations an increased measure of control over the decision-making processes of management. While some problem-solving may take place in negotiations, true, mature collective bargaining in either industry or school systems is much more than an elaborate structure of communications or a new, formal procedure for the mutually satisfactory resolution of problems in the organization.

The salient implementing features of formal collective employee-employer relationships consist of machinery for determination of bargaining units and majority representative, exclusive representative status, union shop, dues checkoff, right to bargain and sign an enforceable agreement, grievance procedures, binding arbitration, the strike, etc.[5] Providing any significant number of these key elements of bargaining to an employee organization constitutes an effective grant of power to that organization to wield in the collective relationship, and results in the institutionalization of the conflict presumed to exist by the assumptions we have mentioned which underlie the concept of bargaining. Extension of any or all of these key elements of private sector collective bargaining to teachers or other public employees may be and is being made by state legislation, municipal ordinance, or voluntary adoption (depending, of course, on the local legal picture) by a board of education or other public employing agency.

As is now widely accepted in this country after nearly thirty years of experience with formal, legislatively supported collective bargaining, collective bargaining can allow legitimate, and in some instances, necessary power to be acquired by an employee organization to wield in a hopefully responsible fashion for a wide variety of purposes. Moreover, the rules embodied in the collective agreement can provide equal and uniform treatment for all, and the impartial adjudication of grievances can afford protection from arbitrariness and discrimination. However, when attempting to assess the appropriateness of bargaining to education we must recognize and be aware of the disutilities which *can* accompany the introduction of adversary procedures into a work organization.

First, it is important to note that the establishment of a formal collective employee-employer relationship sets in motion certain processes which may

---

[5] For an explanation of these key elements, see Wesley A. Wildman, "Legal Aspects of Teacher Collective Action," *Theory into Practice,* April, 1965, pp. 55-60.

convert the basic underlying assumptions concerning conflict and consensus on conflict into self-confirming hypotheses. For instance, once the bargaining relationship has been established, the employee organization, as a political entity, and its leadership, may develop a vested interest in seeking out and maintaining conflict situations. Similarly, for instance, the dynamics of the collective employee-employer relationship may demand that a superintendent who has traditionally been on the teachers' side in the battle for higher salaries in his district must of necessity, for purposes of giving the union a function at the bargaining table, at least appear to oppose the teachers' demands for higher salaries.

Formal collective relationships in a school system may come to have a number of aspects which some persons, depending on perspective and context, might consider disadvantages. For example, they may ask whether, in establishing collective negotiations in schools, it is necessary or desirable to:

Assume and then put into practice an important and meaningful cleavage between, on the one hand, all of the "rank and file" professional teaching staff in a school and, on the other hand, all of those in administrative or supervisory positions; or,

Impose the comprehensive, mandatory, and universally applicable set of rules which constitutes the well-developed collective bargaining contract upon group relationships in a school system with the effect of reducing or destroying what may be, in some instances, a desirable degree of flexibility and the ability to deal with uniqueness; or,

Establish an employee organization which can become a political entity with its own imperatives for existence and survival which may in some instances be separate from the interests of the rank and file membership; or,

Run the risk of a gross imbalance in the power relationships between various constituencies in a community with the consequent misallocation of the educational resources of that community; or,

Embrace a process which can put a premium on disingenuousness and power with a resultant distortion of rationality, which should be the heart of education; or,

Support the growth of a pyramidal hierarchical structure which can itself, parallel to the work organization, subordinate the individual to its imperatives and ignore proper minority interests.

II. CONFLICT IN THE SCHOOL: TEACHER ORGANIZATION VIEWPOINTS AND APPROACHES

The two major organizations vying for teacher allegiance in this country have somewhat differing views regarding the applicability to the schools of adversary procedures based on the assumption of conflict of interest.

The National Education Association and many of its state affiliates manifest a deep-seated analytical or philosophical ambivalence and uncertainty regarding the applicability to schools of the basic assumptions of conflict and power which form in essence the theoretical and practical underpinning of collective bargaining. The NEA is not so sure about the inevitable inherency, nature, and depth of conflict in the schools, is somewhat uncomfortable using the idea of power and opposed interests to discuss the relationship of one segment of the educational fraternity vis-a-vis another, and is instinctively wary of collective bargaining as a suitable method for structuring the leader-led relationship within a school system. Being more specific about the uncertainties and variety of positions being taken by the NEA and its affiliates with regard to these questions, one can distinguish at least three somewhat differing orientations and their practical consequences:

1. It is the view of some NEA state affiliates which have given thoughtful consideration to the question that adversary procedures which employ any significant number of the key elements of industrial bargaining and which assume the existence of conflict are not appropriate for most school systems. Under this view, the well-ordered school system with a sophisticated superintendent and a reasonable board does not manifest significant degrees of conflict; having all of the facts on the table to be discussed in an atmosphere of free communication among all concerned will result in consensus, agreement, and problem-solving to the mutual benefit or advantage of all concerned, without the necessity for compromise, concession-making, or conflict. Proponents of this position maintain that to make essentially adversary procedures available to school systems in any given state by legislation will result in the use of the procedures out of competitive necessity in many instances where unwarranted; the procedures, it is held, will then tend to become self-confirming in practice, that is, will result in the creation of unnecessary and dysfunctional conflict between administrators and teachers. The adoption of adversary procedures and the threat of the use of power may be necessary, in this view, only occasionally in districts with pathologically unreasonable or intractable administrations and boards. State legislation, if any, should be limited to requiring boards and administrators to communicate on an ongoing basis with teacher groups, and should leave wide leeway for flexibility and experimentation regarding the forms and procedures of interaction to be utilized by individual school districts as they respond to their own unique sets of circumstances. In sum, this position alleges that problem-solving and consensus within the united profession and general amicability in relations with boards of education is much more frequently the reality of modern school life than conflict and compromise between and among teacher groups, boards, and administrations. Legislation recently

passed in California[6] is most typically reflective of this general orientation toward the question of conflict in the schools and the appropriateness of adversary procedures as a means of relating teacher groups to boards and administrations.

2. A less mild orientation is that typified by the Connecticut Education Association, which, while still speaking of the united profession, common interests, and the promotion of cooperation, and eschewing the rhetoric of conflict and power, yet supports passage of legislation considerably more rigorous and detailed than that now controlling the State of California. The Connecticut statute,[7] while refusing the right to teachers to strike, and while leaving it to groups of teachers and administrators in any given school system to decide for themselves whether they will be included in a common unit or in separate negotiating units, nonetheless establishes procedures which may become essentially adversary in nature and which involve in their implementation at least some of the assumptions regarding the probability of significant conflict between different groups within the school organization.

3. A third recognizable stance within the NEA family—one, perhaps, not of willing espousal but of adaptation to circumstances—is illustrated by the ability of the Wisconsin Education Association to utilize and compete successfully under the law in that state[8] which provides most of the salient features of industrial collective bargaining to the public sector, including school districts. Experience in Milwaukee and other towns of Wisconsin has indicated that while the NEA affiliate in that state may be reluctant to do so, it is evidently able, when circumstances demand, to adapt the organization's philosophy to a structure demanding what is essentially industry-type bargaining.

The position of the American Federation of Teachers is more uniform and homogeneous and somewhat easier to characterize. The AFT accepts as a given the existence of significant conflict in the schools, declares the need of teachers for power to wield in that conflict, and sees collective bargaining on the industrial model as the appropriate means for gaining the power and handling the conflict. The AFT is in full support of the Wisconsin and Michigan type of legislation which makes available to teachers most of the key elements of bargaining as practiced in industry.

Casting in bold relief and underscoring these varying philosophic orientations is the significant, practical difference of opinion between the organizations on the question of whether administrative personnel should be included in or excluded from the local teacher negotiating unit.

[6] California Legislature, *Assembly Bill No. 1474* (passed, 1965).
[7] Connecticut Legislature, *Public Act No. 298* (passed, 1965).
[8] Wisconsin, *Statutes,* Section 111.70.

The AFT's position is clear—the exclusion of administrative personnel from classroom teacher organizations and bargaining units is preferred. This position is based on what may be termed the private industry or conflict-of-interest model of supervisor-supervised relationships. The supervisor who bears the responsibility for carrying out the programs, policies, and decisions of the organization is empowered to dispense rewards and apply sanctions, i.e., hire, rate, discipline, and discharge. It is basically this power over rewards, and the status differences it implies, which provide the basis for a conflict of interest between supervised and supervisor. This conflict of interest can be characterized as a type of discontinuity in the organization—a gap in the structure.

Practically speaking, this conflict implies unwillingness on the part of labor organizations to include supervisors within their membership, as this would make the conflict of interest an intraorganizational problem. It also implies that management is reluctant to see supervisors included in a broader bargaining unit lest membership in such a unit lessen the willingness or ability of supervisors to distribute rewards and exercise sanctions in the interests of maximum progress toward organizational goals. Finally, the supervisors themselves may find inclusion to be disadvantageous due largely to their probable minority status.

The NEA's position is not as definitive, although in general it is fair to say that the organization and most of its affiliates favor inclusion of administrators in the local unit for negotiating purposes. The recent NEA-supported negotiations bill in the State of Washington[9] provides only for all-inclusive negotiating units. In Connecticut, however, a modified approach to this question appears in the recently passed teacher bargaining bill of that state.

The NEA's predominant position can be said to reflect the public service or identity-of-interest model. Public employees, particularly teachers, are judged to share with their superiors an identification with the service performed and this identification, it is suggested, forms the basis for a common interest between supervised and supervisor which overrides any differences between them. Furthermore, it is questioned whether the supervisor in a public agency enjoys the same powers, or power of the same magnitude, over subordinates as does the supervisor in private industry. Competitive examinations, possibly civil service, and the existence of due process protections may effectively deprive the superior of control over most rewards and sanctions. To the extent that the supervisor is subject to the same procedures and systems in deriving his rewards, status differences implied by dual reward systems in industry, i.e., hourly as opposed to salary compensation, can be expected to be lessened. It is also contended that common reward systems

[9] Washington Legislature, *House Bill No. 154* (passed, 1965).

in most of public employment produce a sense of common "fate" within the organization which reinforces the common commitment to service goals and produces a far greater degree of uniformity in perceptions than is true in private industry.

III. CONFLICT ISSUES IN NEGOTIATIONS

It is impossible to generalize as to the nature, depth, or inherency of conflict in schools which might have potential for producing consensus and collective action among teachers on a widespread basis. Many factors unique to the school as an organization may make the potential for formalized conflict minimal (e.g., the mores, or "culture," of the school organization, the nature of recruitment, board behavior and styles of administrative leadership, possibility of "professional satisfactions" inherent in the nature of work [high autonomy, low visibility in the classroom, etc.] outweighing deprivations suffered as an "employee" within a bureaucracy, etc.).

However, stimulation for research and guidance for the administrator may result from considering the nature of issues which fieldwork[10] discloses have become subjects of consensus among teaching staffs to be put into opposition to the judgments of boards of education or school administrations in the framework of collective negotiation relationships. While a significant portion of observed conflict can be traced to poor administrative practices or poor individual judgment, much of it represents conflict which stems from differing responsibilities and the varied perceptions produced by dissimilar circumstances and positions in the organization. The instances of conflict which fall in this latter category are cases in which there has appeared to be latitude for differences of opinion between teachers as a group and school administrators, school boards and/or the community at large; they do not involve questions which are clearly subject to rational, empirical determination; rather, these are problems which seem to require the weighing of alternative benefits and costs, and decisions based on value judgments, not facts alone.

Our summary of issues is not intended to be exhaustive or all-inclusive but illustrative only of the most important problems emerging with frequency on the current teacher negotiating scene; no judgment is made or implied as to the pervasiveness in school systems generally in this country of conflict represented by these issues.

[10] Fieldwork on the impact of teacher negotiations on school systems is being done as a part of the Study on Collective Action by Public School Teachers being conducted at the University of Chicago with funds provided by the U.S. Office of Education. Negotiating issues discussed herein have been derived from investigations made to date as part of this project.

Overall Support Levels

A basic policy decision in public education concerns the total financial support level for the individual school system, and it is not at all difficult to find any number of examples of conflict between teachers as a group and the community-at-large over the support of education. Conflict along this dimension may or may not be reflected in a local negotiation relationship. Familiar cases in which the conflict did not necessarily take place in the context of local negotiations over teacher salaries would include, at the state level, the imposition of national sanctions against Utah in 1964 and Oklahoma in 1965, and, at the local level, the walkout of teachers in Louisville, Kentucky, in November, 1964, when voters for the fourth time in nine years rejected a school tax referendum. On the other hand, an example of a situation in which conflict over total support levels took place as part of a local bargaining relationship can be found in the New York City negotiations.

One might expect that the board of education and the school superintendent would in some instances be aligned with the teacher group in any conflict with the community over total support levels, and, indeed, this is often the case. However, despite an identity of interest on the broad question of total support levels, conflict can arise between the teacher group and the board over short-run decisions concerning maximization of resources. The question in one case was, simply: Should a fiscally dependent school system submit a budget request which reflects all the true needs of that system, or should its request reflect a realistic estimate of the financial resources available from the superior political unit? The essence of the conflict centered on the location of fiscal restraints, i.e., the teacher group maintained that the board should shift the burden of such restraint to city officials rather than exercising it themselves.

This type of conflict is by no means restricted to fiscally dependent systems. The parallel issue as it arose in a fiscally independent system centered on whether the school board should tax up to its legal limit in a specific year or whether it should endeavor to maintain a margin of safety in establishing its tax rate for that year. This situation raises, in turn, questions as to the necessity for teacher groups to live with or abide by informal promises made by school boards (to facilitate passage of school tax referenda), to be satisfied with a given tax rate for some specified period. In a number of systems, teacher groups have displayed unwillingness to respect such long-term commitments and have shown a much shorter time horizon in their judgments regarding expenditure levels than have school boards or school superintendents. Whether a dollar spent today is worth more or less than a dollar spent in the future may often be a matter of judgment on which people disagree, depending on differing values and despite agreement on the essential relevant facts.

The Allocation of Funds

Just as the citizen attempts to balance claims on his income in deciding on a school tax referendum, and as the state legislature or city council attempts to balance off claims (including support for education) on its resources, so the board of education must allocate its total resources among competing claims. It is this area which has proved to be a major source of potential conflict between teachers and school boards and school superintendents.

Given acceptance of "quality education" as the goal to be achieved in the allocation of available funds within the educational enterprise, it is still possible for different parties to reach different and conflicting judgments as to how this goal can best be achieved. In various negotiating relationships, teacher salaries have been suggested (in some cases successfully) as having prior claim on existing funds over the following other items in the educational budget: 1) additional textbooks, 2) building maintenance, 3) adult education, 4) kindergartens, 5) increased special education, 6) number of assistant principals.

There appears to be room for difference of opinion within any given system as to whether more satisfied teachers will produce higher quality education in the classroom than will more textbooks or better maintained facilities. Similarly, there is evidently no universally accepted rule as to the percentage of a district's resources which should go to special education or to adult education in the interests of a balanced program and/or good community relations.

Distribution of Salary Dollars

Even though consensus has been achieved on the proportion of total resources to be devoted to staff compensation, significant differences of opinion have still arisen among the board, the superintendent, and the teachers as to how such funds should be spent. Are the interests of quality education better served by more highly paid teachers, or by more staff to reduce class sizes? Should salaries be increased at the bottom of the schedule to facilitate recruiting as opposed to increases at the top as a means of rewarding and retaining long-service teachers?

Only one step removed from these questions is that of the appropriate level of administrator-teacher salary differentials. To what extent do high differentials discourage the appearance or retention of long-service "professional" classroom teachers whose greatest skills and interests rest in teaching, in favor of a high rate of movement into administration?

Still in the area of salary schedules, conflict has arisen between teachers and an administration as to the types of academic training which should be recognized and the extent of recognition. To what extent should a salary schedule recognize small additional increments of advanced academic work? Does the addition of a "B.A. plus 15 and an M.A. plus 15" column to a schedule contribute enough, through added long-run incentive to further course work, to compensate for the short-run administrative costs involved in determining placement on the schedule? How liberal should the regulations be regarding acceptable credit for such a schedule?

The distribution of the total salary package has raised some significant strategy problems for boards, superintendents, and teacher organizations. In negotiations, the superintendent and board may have to undertake the "defense" of those outside the teacher group in the struggle for salary dollars. At the same time, the teacher group itself must achieve consensus within the group as to the relative rewards due the various segments of it. Any attempt to adjust differentials within a salary schedule has inherent potential for intraorganizational conflict.

These are all areas in which teachers as a group have had different viewpoints from boards of education who must allocate funds and staff schools, and school superintendents who must administer salary schedules. The kinds of viewpoints which teachers have expressed through their local organizations on these issues, as well as on the question of the allocation of funds within the budget as a whole, have led some participants in negotiating relationships to identify the phenomenon they term "professional selfishness." Conflict with the administration over the desire of teachers to gain in the salary area at the expense of nonteacher claims on funds, however, may in reality stem from legitimate differences of opinion as to the best means of attaining a mutually accepted goal.

Other Policy Decisions

Thus far our analysis of the substance of conflict has been limited to essentially financial issues. A review of developments in negotiation relationships, however, reveals a number of conflict questions which are not directly financial but involve the establishment of procedures and standards for certain crucial decisions or actions within the system. Among these issues can be included the following:

1. What is an optimal or reasonable maximum class size for various schools within the system?

2. To what extent should seniority be used as a criterion in such decisions as assignment of classes, promotions, and transfers?

3. To what extent should teachers enjoy a right to request and receive a transfer based on stated objective criteria? What weight should be given to factors such as length of service in the school, length of service in the system, travel time to current assignment, and other personal factors?

4. If teachers enjoy a right to transfer, what provisions should be made to enable the superintendent to achieve some balance in the staffing of

schools? Should a superintendent enjoy the counter right to transfer teachers? Should extra compensation ("battle pay") be given to induce teachers to stay in, or transfer to, "difficult schools"?

5. To what extent should teaching assignments (e.g., more, as opposed to fewer, "difficult" classes) and nonteaching assignments be strictly rotated as a matter of equity within the teacher group, as opposed to being distributed in accordance with a principal's judgment of relative ability or contribution to the overall school program?

6. Who should be responsible for the collection of textbook rentals from students? Is it a job for the teacher or for the administrative staff?

7. To what extent should the length of the teaching day be clearly defined and limited? To what extent should the frequency and length of after-school faculty meetings be limited on a system-wide basis?

On issues such as these, teachers' views on what is right or just have conflicted with the desires of the administration to exercise fully its responsibility to staff the schools, assign teachers and students, and, in general, administer the educational enterprise. Where the teachers' views are accepted, wholly or in part, and regulations are established in these areas, administrative flexibility and discretion are lost at some level in the system.

For the most part, it is the school principal who loses freedom to exercise his judgment in these areas. His discretion is curbed by the teacher group and the party responsible for negotiations on the board side of a relationship, who jointly establish standards for such administrative decisions. An arbitration case[11] arising out of the duty-free lunch provisions of the UFT-New York City Board of Education agreement clearly demonstrates this phenomenon. A principal decided to use two teachers instead of the single teacher normally called upon to supervise lunchroom aides, in recognition of the size of the cafeteria and the magnitude of discipline problems. The second teacher assigned to supervise the aides filed a grievance against this assignment and was upheld by an arbitrator, who stated his belief that the board was obligated at least to try the use of only one supervising teacher in the absence of any evidence of an increased enrollment or an exceptional disciplinary problem at the school. Similarly, provisions of the first NYC agreement which specified the distribution of teacher time freed by the employment of teacher aides removed this decision from the hands of the principals of individual schools where it had resided prior to 1962.

In these cases, the bargaining relationship has to some extent substituted centralized decision-making for decentralized decision-making on the management side. The school principals have lost some significant discretion in

[11] See text of "Arbitration Award in the Matter of the Arbitration Between United Federation of Teachers and Board of Education of the City of New York" (Arthur Stark, arbitrator), in Bureau of National Affairs, *Government Employee Relations Report,* No. 96, July 12, 1965, *Text* (Grievance Arb. -35).

this process, and there is evidence from a number of systems that they not only resent this loss but are considering and actually undertaking organization as a means of securing a stronger voice in such centralized decision-making, if not to check and reverse the trend itself. The experience of private industry has shown that some centralization is almost inevitable as a result of collective negotiations, particularly in the early stages of a relationship. Involvement of all levels of management in bargaining decisions is time-consuming, and the problem of achieving internal consensus on all decisions is difficult if not impossible.

Individual Teacher Judgment

In negotiations in some systems, teachers have manifested a desire to gain authority over decisions involving individual teacher judgment vis-a-vis the judgment and/or responsibilities of those who are their immediate superiors. Ratings, discipline, and dismissals are the most obvious types of decisions which have been the subject of conflict.

The use of teacher time represents another area in which conflict has arisen between a teacher and those who supervise him. What constitutes a legitimate use of the teachers' preparation period? Are departmental conferences a legitimate required use of such a period? Is a conference with the principal on the placement program an appropriate use of such a period? Does a teacher have a right to walk out of an after-school faculty meeting after the expiration of the time set for such meetings in the bylaws of the board? Is that teacher justified in filing a grievance when the principal calls her in after school the following day to inform her of what transpired in the meeting after she left? Can a teacher be required to escort children to a public bus stop and supervise them until they are picked up, after school has been dismissed? Can a teacher be required to escort children to lunch rooms if such escort duty infringes on her duty-free lunch period? Should a teacher be required to relieve a teacher aide and assume responsibility for her class during a fire drill if the drill occurs during her preparation period? If so, should she receive compensatory free time? These are all issues which have been raised seriously by teachers and supported by teacher groups in negotiating relationships. To many they may appear trivial, but they obviously were not so in the minds of the teachers affected nor to the administrators whose judgments were challenged.

IV. CONCLUDING OBSERVATIONS

There is little hard evidence on the question of whether collective bargaining or formal professional negotiation is either inevitable or desirable on a widespread basis in American education.

It is impossible to judge the extent to which conflict between teachers and school administrations over issues we have seen emerging in already existing negotiating relationships is inherent or "necessary" in a majority of school systems in this country, and whether or not such conflict as exists has the potential for becoming sharply focused and providing an incentive for collective action. Because few such issues have arisen to date in formal relationships, we know little of the extent to which professional "curricular-methodological" questions have a conflict-producing potential or will be appropriate for consideration in the context of negotiating or bargaining activity.

We need more analyses of specific collective negotiation relationships between boards and teacher groups which weigh both the utilities and disutilities that must inhere in every such relationship. We need them to guide us in making a judgment as to what the impact of collective bargaining and all it implies will be on the school system conceived as an institution of client-centered professionals offering services to a public constituency.

Where negotiating relationships are to become the order of the day in school systems, the uniqueness of the school as a work organization would seem to caution against immediate, uncritical acceptance of the managerial vs. "rank-and-file" dichotomy typical of industrial bargaining. More experience in this country with both separate and merged units, and study of foreign experiences where administrative personnel lead the profession in bargaining relationships, will provide a better basis than we have at present for determining whether the potential for conflict between teachers and administrators can be resolved in merged units as an intra-organizational problem, or whether separation is indicated.

VII-3

IMPASSE PROCEDURES IN PUBLIC EDUCATION*

Morris Slavney

We shall assume that an impasse exists between a local school board and a teachers' organization which has either been established or has been recognized as the exclusive representative of teaching personnel in the employ of that school board, and that said impasse exists over the terms and conditions of the employment of said teachers for the coming school term. There are various procedures which may be utilized in efforts to resolve the impasse.

MEDIATION

Mediation is the process where a neutral, with the consent of the parties, attempts to reconcile or conciliate the differences between them, usually in joint or individual sessions with the parties. It is a direct extension and part of the collective bargaining process, since any settlement reached in mediation must be one mutually agreed upon by the parties.

Who Shall Mediate? Wherever possible, mediation should be performed by a trained and qualified mediator. The technique of mediation is not a science, but an art. Mediators can, however, become proficient in the art of mediation and thereby have a greater chance of obtaining a mutually satisfactory settlement of the issues in dispute. The experienced mediator recognizes that the responsibility for the resolution of the impasse rests on the parties and so reminds them, continually if need be, of that duty. While the mediator may offer suggestions for settlement, he has no power of compulsion. At the same time, he can, and probably will, exercise his art of persuasion. While there are often fair and honorable citizens in the community who would proffer their services as mediators, I would not encourage their use in that function. Although such citizens may be well-meaning and sin-

* Paper delivered July 12, 1965, at the National Institute on Collective Negotiations in Public Education cosponsored by Phi Delta Kappa and Rhode Island College, Providence, R. I. Morris Slavney is Chairman, Wisconsin Employment Relations Board.

cere, they may nevertheless adversely affect the collective bargaining process not only in the present impasse, but in future negotiations. The private citizen in mediation adds a "c" (for citizen) to the term, which then becomes "medication." Parties in collective bargaining should be neither drugged nor salved into a settlement.

How Shall Mediation Be Initiated?   A requirement that mediation may be initiated only at the *joint* request of the parties could effectively preclude mediation of a dispute. It has been our experience that the request for the services of a mediator usually emanates from the employe organization. This is natural in view of the fact that the employe organization is usually the party seeking to change present employment conditions. It is just as natural for the employer not to initiate mediation; to do so might indicate that the employer would change his bargaining position. Thus it is apparent that a joint request would not ordinarily be forthcoming. If a mediation agency is established by local law or resolution, a provision therein permitting that agency to initiate mediation on its own motion is desirable. Such a procedure is frequently practical in situations wherein both parties feel that for them to initiate mediation might indicate a willingness to retreat from a previously established position. In any event, both parties must agree to accept mediation, no matter how it is initiated.

Authority of Representatives.   Mediation can be effective only if the representatives of the parties participating in mediation can effectively engage in negotiations. Such representatives, therefore, must have authority to make commitments on behalf of those whom they represent or to effectively recommend such commitments. The representatives need not necessarily be cloaked with final authority, for the terms of agreement should be approved by the teachers involved, and by the members of the school board. I would encourage both the teacher organization and the school board to appoint negotiating committees from their respective memberships as their representatives at the bargaining table.

The Arena of Mediation.   Mediation should not be considered a spectator sport. Because of past practice in conducting school business, it has been difficult for school boards to realize that mediation, in order to be effective, cannot be conducted in public. If the mediation session is open to the public, the representatives at the bargaining table will be reluctant, or might refuse, to divulge their true positions and motivations. Mediation in a fish bowl will drown the effectiveness of the mediator.

Mediation is most effective in executive session with the parties, either jointly or apart. Such a practice does not result in denying the public of the

right to know, since the school board involved should announce the terms
of any tentative agreement reached and should conduct a public hearing
thereon prior to formalizing its offer or position in the matter.

FACT FINDING

Fact finding is a procedure whereby an individual or a panel (the latter
consisting of at least one neutral person) conducts a formal hearing wherein
representatives of the teacher organization and the school board are given
the opportunity to present evidence material to the impasse and negotiations,
to make arguments with regard thereto, and to file briefs in support of their
positions. The fact finder or panel thereafter issues a formal document, setting forth recommendations for the settlement of the impasse. These recommendations are advisory in nature and not final and binding upon any of
the parties.

How Fact Finding Should Be Initiated. The ordinance or resolution
which establishes fact finding should also establish the requirements for its
initiation. Fact finding should only be initiated upon the filing of a formal
petition setting forth the circumstances involved. The statute should also contain the conditions under which fact finding can be initiated, and one of
these conditions should be the existence of an impasse between the parties
after a *reasonable period of negotiation.* The fact finding procedure should
not be set in motion until such time as the parties have made every effort
through negotiation to resolve their impasse.

The agency responsible for the appointment of the fact finder should be
a neutral agency and should have the power to make an investigation, either
by way of an informal investigation, or through a formal hearing, to determine whether the conditions for fact finding exist. The experience of the
Wisconsin Employment Relations Board in initiating fact finding proceedings has disclosed that the informal investigation procedure is more advantageous in all respects. Such procedure permits the opportunity for possible
mediation where no mediation had previously been conducted. The parties
are more apt to be candid concerning the matters in dispute in an informal
procedure than one which involves a formal hearing and the taking of testimony under oath. The appointing agency should appoint the fact finder only
after the results of the informal investigation have been reviewed and after
it is apparent that the parties are *impassioned* in their impasse.

Who Shall Act as the Fact Finder? Fact finding has not as yet become
a profession, and therefore there are no professional fact finders as such.
However, fact finding is akin to arbitration. In the latter, the award issued

by the arbitrator is final and binding, while in the former, the recommendations, or award, of the fact finder are merely advisory in nature. There are
a number of professors through the country who are proficient and active
in arbitration. We have used some of them in our fact finding cases. Since
their primary profession is teaching, they are apt to be familiar with the
teaching profession and the various problems and policies faced by school
administrators. No doubt most of them are cognizant of the problems and
aspirations of teachers generally. We also have appointed other professional
arbitrators as fact finders, as well as a former State Supreme Court Justice
who has participated in two fact finding cases involving teachers.

How the Fact Finder Should Be Selected. The agency making the
investigation to determine whether the conditions for fact finding exist may
be given the sole discretion to appoint the fact finder. However, I see no
objection in the parties selecting a fact finder from a panel of names submitted by the agency, by alternately striking individuals until one has been
selected. The latter procedure might result in making the fact finder's recommendation more acceptable to the parties than if they did not participate in
the selection of the fact finder.

Who Should Pay the Fact Finder? Wisconsin law obligates the parties
to share in the cost of the fact finding proceeding—that is to say, the cost
incurred after the WERB has named the fact finder. This usually involves a
per diem charge for days of hearing and time spent in the preparation of the
award, as well as the charges by the court reporter for transcribing and preparing a transcript of the formal fact finding hearing. The primary consideration in determining that charges should be shared by the parties and not
by the public is that fact finding is likely to be abused if its costs are not assessed upon the parties. Free fact finding would encourage the parties to proceed to fact finding and thereby tend to discourage their efforts to resolve
their dispute through collective bargaining.

The Fact Finding Hearing. The hearing before the fact finder should
be formal and should be public. The fact finder should limit the parties to the
presentation of only material issues and arguments. The fact finder should
be given authority to issue subpoenas, to place witnesses under oath and also
to exercise the means whereby he can conduct a fair and impartial hearing.
He should also be permitted to schedule and adjourn the hearing. It is advisable to permit the fact finder to attempt to resolve the impasse through
informal means and to encourage the parties in that regard. The fact finder
should be permitted to offer his services as a mediator, even during the
course of the hearing, where he sees a possibility of resolving the impasse

without any formal recommendations. In this regard, the fact finder should be permitted to go into executive sessions with the parties either singly or jointly. However, as in mediation, the fact finder should only mediate when both parties agree that he may act in that capacity.

The Fact Finder's Award.   The fact finder should issue his recommendations for the resolution of the dispute as expeditiously as possible. I would recommend that, prior to the close of the hearing, the fact finder obtain the consent of the parties to release a copy of the recommendations to the local press in order that his recommendations be made public. My reason is that the real effectiveness of a fact finder's recommendations is the public reaction thereto. Public interest is paramount in disputes between public employe organizations and their employers. Full public disclosure of the fact finder's recommendations may encourage the public to voice their opinion in the matter. This does not mean to say that the public voice will support the fact finder's recommendations. Most likely, there will be a divergence of opinion concerning the merits of these recommendations. At least the parties to the dispute will have to weigh the sentiments expressed by the public in effectuating the recommendations.

The fact finding procedure should require both parties to indicate in writing, within a reasonable time after the issuance of the recommendations, their acceptance, in whole or in part, or their rejection thereof. Wisconsin statutes contain no such requirement at the present time. We have found in some cases that the governing body has taken no action, either formally or informally, after receiving the fact finder's recommendations and has thus avoided the moral duty to commit itself. Failure to act, one way or the other, upon recommendations weakens the collective bargaining relationship.

FINAL AND BINDING ARBITRATION

The third voluntary process for the resolution of an impasse is final and binding arbitration. Such a procedure could be established by ordinance, resolution, or by voluntary agreement by the parties. The comments previously made with regard to fact finding can be applied to arbitration with the exception that the award issued by the arbitrator is final and binding upon the parties. I would discourage the utilization of final and binding arbitration to resolve an impasse in collective bargaining, primarily for the reason that the parties are deprived of their responsibility to reach a final determination of their dispute. A requirement for compulsory arbitration in public employment would probably set forth criteria which the arbitrators must consider and follow in rendering an award, and these criteria might very well hamper an arbitrator in rendering his award.

Wisconsin has had a law providing for compulsory arbitration in privately owned public utilities. A Supreme Court decision held that the law was not applicable to utilities whose business affects interstate commerce. For a number of years prior to the Supreme Court decision so holding, there was considerable use made of this law. The law itself establishes criteria to be considered by arbitrators and permits judicial review of the awards made by arbitrators.

Our experience under the public utility law was that weak organizations utilized compulsory arbitration and that strong organizations utilized their strength at the bargaining table. Furthermore, there is a serious question as to whether a school board, or any other municipal body, can constitutionally delegate its power to an arbitrator to establish the salaries and conditions of employment for its employes.

SANCTIONS AND STRIKES

Thus far, I have discussed procedures involving a neutral agency established to provide the means whereby disputes arising in collective negotiations may be resolved without sanctions, strikes, lockouts and concomitants thereof, and without any threats to resort to such drastic action. I have assumed that such activities, or threats thereof, cannot be accepted as a procedure provided by a neutral agency for the resolution of an impasse in public employment. However, if strikes and lockouts in public employment are specifically prohibited by law, there should be some quid pro quo for depriving employes of the right to use these pressure tactics. The Wisconsin public employe labor relations law recognizes this problem. Although it prohibits strikes, it also protects the rights of public employes to engage, or not to engage, in concerted activity and provides procedures to guarantee these rights. Wisconsin law also has established procedures for the peaceful resolution of disputes.

CONCLUSION

From participation in the various cases involving public employes, including teachers, processed by the WERB, I have observed that the parties seem to have a greater concern for impasse procedures than they do for bargaining techniques and procedures. While teacher organizations have existed for many years and have represented their membership to their school boards, the relationship between teacher organization and public employer has been that of second cousin. The concept of collective bargaining has finally reached the area of public employment, and the relationships between employe organizations and public employers are changing. The parties, in living with each other, discuss their mutual problems and argue, bargain and negotiate with each other in an attempt to reach a mutually satisfactory settlement of their domestic quarrel. We in Wisconsin believe that our public employe law, the first comprehensive state law affecting public employes and employers, has advanced the concept of collective bargaining in public employment, and has also led the way in establishing the rights of public employes, public employers, and the public generally.

It is gratifying that so many persons in the field of education, both in administration and in teaching, are seeking to learn more about collective negotiations. Labor relations, no matter how called, is not a static science, but a code of conduct which changes continually. Therefore, the administrators of labor relations laws affecting teachers must continue to seek knowledge about the problems, goals, and aspirations of the teaching profession, of school administrators, of school boards, and of the public itself.

on-the-job training and career advancement.) What does this have to do with the teachers' stake in the rule of seniority? It is the rule of seniority that passes increases in the starting (or hiring) wage along to the mass of teachers already in the employ of the district. If, for example, districts raised the salary offered to newly trained, inexperienced teachers and did not make corresponding adjustments in the pay of their presently employed persons, then the salaries of young teachers would gradually creep up on those of the older ones, and the boards would have rendered inoperative that very seniority system in which they themselves have an important stake. The function of the rule of seniority in raising the pay of teachers is especially important when teachers lack the means of negotiating with boards, and this has been their situation in the past.

So far I have been talking about matters of salary and, hence, about relations between teachers and boards of education. Other things than pay are important to teachers: assignment to a particular school, choice of which students within the school one will teach, and a host of matters dealing with choice of classroom, materials, extra duties, etc. For these matters, teachers commonly deal not with school boards but with school administrators. For past decades teachers have been witnessing the professionalization of the art of administration and the gradual aggrandizement of power in the hands of a growing cadre of school chiefs. Lacking a means to establish ground rules for making assignments and granting perquisites (and a grievance machinery for their effective enforcement), teachers naturally turned to the rule of seniority as their best defense against administrative favoritism. Though teachers could not check the growing power of their bosses, they could use seniority to keep authoritarianism within such bounds as one could live with.

What opinions can one hold about the role of seniority in the local education services? I think the answer depends in part on whether one accepts the monolithic definition of the teacher as reflecting the true state of the art of education. If teachers fall within the economist's category of homogeneous labor, then the use of the rule of seniority in making teacher assignments can have little negative effect on the learnings of pupils. Hence, if its use is favorable with respect to teacher morale, we would have to say that the net effect of its use is positive (in terms of educational productivity). If it is true that a "teacher is a teacher, etc.," then we must further resign ourselves to classroom service having a low ceiling in pay, as compared with other college-based occupations. Though boards may accept the practice of paying the experienced teacher twice the salary of the inexperienced, it comes hard to pay the senior teacher three to five times what the beginning person gets when one holds that the work performance of the two is approximately equal. Yet, it is just these kinds of differentials that are required if the advances in the ceilings of teachers' salaries are to be commensurate with those characteristic of other professional fields.

Even if one accepts the monolithic definition of "teacher," however, there is still one distressing feature of the present arrangement for adjusting salaries, namely, that teachers in seeking to advance their economic status ally themselves with the perpetuation of the shocking inequalities of educational opportunity so characteristic of our society. The secular rise in beginning salaries of teachers finds its life-force in local competition for teachers' services. By the rule of seniority, teachers parlay these gains into increases for all teachers. But clearly, rich local districts enter the competition with vastly greater resources than do the poor districts. Rich districts expectedly pay higher salaries than the poor ones—indeed, their function in American education is to set standards, including standards of remuneration—and these higher salaries reinforce other natural advantages to divert an undue proportion of highly qualified teachers to serve children of rich parents, children who enter school with environmental advantages toward learning.[3] One need not belabor the point.

I would myself go further and question whether the monolithic definition of "teacher" is any longer appropriate in American education. I feel that specialization of teachers in the schools can now be clearly delineated and that those specialities that rest upon extraordinary skill or training should draw an unusually high monetary reward, in order that salary differentials play their customary role of directing people toward those places in an enterprise where their particular skills can be most completely used. Also, there is the parallel feeling that assignment of teachers to particular groups of students on the basis of seniority *can* be assumed to have deleterious effects on learning of pupils.

Behind these feelings stand two fundamental changes that are occurring in our schools. The first is the process of placing subjects at lower and lower pupil ages. Naturally, this process can be difficult for older teachers. If it is decided to teach calculus in high school, the older math teachers may not be as fresh on the subject, not as able, that is, to deal with the questions that bright students raise, as newly hired teachers are, unless, of course, the older teacher has been willing to do a bit of work in the subject.

The second is the decision of our society to raise its expectations about what socially and economically disadvantaged children can learn. To teach children, especially younger children from slum neighborhoods, appears to call for various special, and sometimes new, competencies on the part of the teacher. It is hard to believe that all teachers have these competencies in indifferent measure. The pressure to demonstrate progress is great, even to

---

[3] On the other hand, it is often poor districts that establish standards in tax rates for education. In their propangandizing for higher pay, teachers in rich districts can thus point to the low level of "effort" their town is making.

the extent of the federal government's calling for quantitative measures of change in pupil achievement. Unless the local public schools are flexible enough in staffing assignments to get the right teachers assigned to the right tasks, it is likely that high priority educational tasks will increasingly be assigned to private bodies or to public agencies new to education—in either case, to groups free of the rigidity of staffing patterns in school districts.

It is thus fortunate that collective negotiations have appeared on the scene. In a number of states, teachers organizations, AFT or NEA, have sufficient power to negotiate effectively with school boards about salaries. They do not need any longer to be the passive recipients of those salary advances that blind market forces give them. They need not any longer be handmaidens of inequality of opportunity.

Similarly, teachers have the power to negotiate about the procedures for determining assignments and perquisites. They no longer need to hold to the rule of seniority as the answer to administrative favoritism. My impression is that teachers have exploited the first opportunity more fully than the second. It should be possible, however, for teachers to investigate what questions are to be decided by seniority and what are not. For example, assignment to a school might be regulated by senority and assignment within the school by agreed-upon and mutually supervised demonstrations of prowess. Other sophisticated unions and professional associations have managed to bring off this kind of thing.

Departures from simple rules of thumb, of which assignment by seniority is only one example, lead inexorably to the facing of complex questions. E.g., what differentation of tasks are appropriate; what different salary rates should be accorded to the different tasks; what precise measures of competence are to be used in making specialized work assignments. Complexity openly faced, nonetheless, is a characteristic of high productivity organizations. A favorable sign in education is this: Even in the early years of the practice of collective negotiations, teachers unions and associations have shown a willingness to negotiate about an unusually broad range of questions, far exceeding conventional concepts of employer welfare.

If teachers' organizations come to recognize the complexity of educational processes, it is, finally, entirely appropriate that they play a role in determining how persons shall gain the competence to fill new, specialized assignments and, in particular, that they should assume responsibility for on-the-job training of teachers in school systems. Financing of on-the-job training schemes should itself be a negotiable matter. Educational inovation, about which we hear so much, could as a result become more teacher-oriented or less of a thing that is imposed by administrator's mandate. School systems could thus become what they have always ideally been supposed, enclaves in which both pupils and teachers seek to engage in a continuous process of learning.

BIBLIOGRAPHY

The following bibliography includes only materials which are readily accessible to interested parties. It does not include mimeographed or other material not readily available from publishers or organizations. A more detailed bibliography which includes such materials may be found in Myron Lieberman and Michael M. Moskow, *Collective Negotiations for Teachers.* (Chicago: Rand McNally, 1966), pp. 431-46.

American Association of School Administrators. *School District Organization.* Washington, D.C.: American Association of School Administrators, 1962.
———. *Roles, Responsibilities, Relationships of the School Board, Superintendent, and Staff.* Washington, D.C.: American Association of School Administrators, 1963.
Anderson, Arvid. "Labor Relations in the Public Service," *Wisconsin Law Review* (July, 1961).
American Bar Association, Labor Relations Section, Committee on the Law of Government Employee Relations. *Proceedings.* Chicago: American Bar Association, issued annually.
American Federation of Teachers. *Collective Bargaining Contracts.* Chicago: American Federation of Teachers, 1962.
———. *Constitution.* Chicago: American Federation of Teachers, issued annually.
———. *Convention Proceedings of the AFT Annual Convention.* Chicago: American Federation of Teachers, issued annually.
———. Executive Council. *Recommended Collective Bargaining Election Procedures.* Chicago: American Federation of Teachers, September 4, 1964.
———. *Organizing the Teaching Profession.* A Report Prepared by the Committee on Educational Reconstruction. Glencoe, Ill.: The Free Press, 1955.
American Teacher Magazine. Chicago: American Federation of Teachers, issued bi-monthly.
———. *A Sample Study of Coercion by School Administrators in America.* Chicago: American Federation of Teachers, undated.
Alberta Teachers Association. "Submissions of the Alberta Teachers' Association to the Special Committee of the Legislative Assembly on Collective Bargaining Between School Trustees and Teachers," Special Issue, *ATA Magazine,* 45 (October, 1964).
Allen, Donna. *Fringe Benefits: Wages or Social Obligations?* Ithaca, N.Y.: Cornell University Press, 1964.

Bailey, Stephen K. *Schoolmen and Politics.* Syracuse, N.Y.: Syracuse University Press, 1963.

Bakke, E. Wight. *Mutual Survival: The Goal of Unions and Management.* Yale University Labor and Management Center Series. New York: Harper and Row, 1947.

———. "Why Workers Join Unions," *Personnel,* XXII, No. 1 (1945), 37-56.

Banbrick, James J. "White Collar Unionization," *Personnel Administrator* (March-April, 1964), 1-7, 31.

Barbash, Jack. *The Practice of Unionism.* New York: Harper and Brothers, 1956.

Barstow, Robbins. "Which Way New York City—Which Way the Profession?" *Phi Delta Kappan,* 43 (December, 1961), 122-27.

Batchelder, R. D. "Are Teachers Workers?" *New Republic,* 154 (February 19, 1966), 7. Discussion, 154 (March 12, 1966), 36.

———. "Unionism Under Attack: NEA Versus AFT," *Times (London) Educational Supplement,* 2647 (February 11, 1966), 396.

Beal, Edwin, and Wickersham, Edward. *The Practice of Collective Bargaining.* Homewood, Ill.: Richard D. Irwin, 1963.

Belasco, James A. "Resolving Dispute over Contract Terms in the State Public Service: An Analysis," *Labor Law Journal,* XVI (September, 1965), 533-44.

———. "The American Association of University Professors as a Private Dispute Settlement Agency," *Industrial and Labor Relations Review,* 18 (July, 1965), 535-53.

Benson, Charles S. *The Cheerful Prospect.* Boston: Houghton Mifflin, 1965.

———. *The Economics of Public Education.* Boston: Houghton Mifflin, 1961.

———. (Ed.) *Perspectives on the Economics of Education.* Boston: Houghton Mifflin, 1963.

Berger, Harriet F. "The Grievance Process in the Philadelphia Public Service," *Industrial and Labor Relations Review,* XIII (July, 1960), 568-80.

Beruke, M. R. "Strike at St. John's: Why the Professors Picket," *Nation,* 202 (February 14, 1966), 172-74.

Betchkal, J. "N.E.A. and Teacher Unions Bicker and Battle for Recognition," *Nation's Schools,* LXXIV (August, 1964), 35-41.

Blanke, V. E. "Teachers in Search of Power," *The Educational Forum,* 30 (January, 1966) 231-38. Same, *American School Board Journal,* 151 (November, 1965), 7-9.

Bloom, Gordon F., and Northrup, Herbert R. *Economics of Labor Relations.* Homewood, Ill.: Richard D. Irwin, 1965.

Bloomberg, Warner, Jr., and Sunshine, Morris. *Suburban Power Structures and Public Education.* Syracuse, N. Y.: Syracuse University Press, 1963.

Blum, Albert A. *Management and the White-Collar Union.* Research Study 63. New York: American Management Association, 1964.

Brown, G. W. "Teacher Power Techniques," *American School Board Journal,* 152 (February, 1966), 11-13.

Brown, R. S. "Representation of Economic Interests," *AAUP Bulletin,* LI (September, 1965), 374-77.

Buder, L. "The Teachers Revolt," *Phi Delta Kappan,* XLIII (June, 1962), 370-76.

Burkhead, Jesse. *Public School Finance: Economics and Politics.* Syracuse, N.Y.: Syracuse University Press, 1963.

———. *State and Local Taxes for Public Education.* Syracuse, N.Y.: Syracuse University Press, 1963.

Byrd, Stephen F. *Strategy in Labor Relations.* Complete Management Library Volume XV. Waterford, Conn.: Prentice-Hall, 1963.

Cahill, Robert S., and Hencley, Stephen P. (Eds.) *The Politics of Education.* Danville, Ill.: Interstate Printers and Publishers, 1964.

Campbell, R. F., Cunningham, Luvern L., and McPhee, Roderick F. *The Organization and Control of American Schools.* Columbus, Ohio: Charles E. Merrill, 1965.

Carr, William G. "Breakthrough in the Use of Sanctions," in National Education Association, *Addresses and Proceedings,* Vol. 103. Washington, D.C.: National Education Association, 1965, 19-21.

————. "Principal's Role in Professional Negotiation," *Bulletin of the National Association of Secondary-School Principals,* 50 (April, 1966), 45-56. Excerpts, *New York State Education,* 53 (April, 1966), 24-25; *NEA Journal,* 55 (May, 1966), 45-46.

————. *Report of the Executive Secretary.* Washington, D.C.: National Education Association, issued annually.

Carr-Saunders, A. M., and Wilson, P. A. *The Professions.* Oxford: The Clarendon Press, 1933.

Case, Harry L. *Personnel Policy in a Public Agency: The TVA Experience.* New York: Harper and Brothers, 1955.

Chamberlain, Neil W. *The Labor Sector.* New York: McGraw-Hill Book Company, 1965.

————, and Kuhn, J. W. 2nd Ed. *Collective Bargaining.* New York: McGraw-Hill Book Company, 1965.

Cherry, Howard L. "Negotiations Between Boards and Teacher Organizations," *American School Board Journal,* CXLVI (March, 1963), 7-9.

Cohodes, Aaron. "How New York's Gross Lives and Learns with Unions," *Nation's Schools,* LXXIV (November, 1964), 46-49.

"Comments and Reactions of Five Local Association Case Studies: A Symposium," *NEA Journal,* 54 (December, 1965), 33-40.

Cook, Alice H. "Union Structure in Municipal Collective Bargaining," *Monthly Labor Review,* LXXIX (June, 1966), 606-608.

Corwin, Ronald G. *A Sociology of Education.* New York: Appleton-Century-Crofts, 1965.

————. "Militant Professionalism, Initiative and Compliance in Public Education," *Sociology of Education,* 38, No. 4, 310-30.

Cron, Theodore O. "Inside the Teachers Union," *American School and University* (November, 1963), 42-46.

Davy, Harold W. *Contemporary Collective Bargaining.* Englewood Cliffs, N. J.: Prentice-Hall, 1959.

Diesing, Paul. "Bargaining Strategy and Union-Management Relationships," *Journal of Conflict Resolution,* V (December, 1961), 369-78.

Doherty, Robert E. "Attitudes Towards Labor: When Blue-Collar Children Become Teachers," *The School Review,* LXXI, No. 1, 87-96.

————. "Determination of Bargaining Units and Election Procedures in Public School Teacher Representation Elections," *Industrial and Labor Relations Review,* XIX (July, 1966), 573-95.

Donovan, B. E., Anderson, A., Cogen, C., and Wolpert, A. W. "Collective Bargaining vs. Professional Negotiations," *School Management,* 9 (November, 1965), 68-75.

Doolan, Richard J. *Attitudes of White-Collar Workers Toward Unionization.* Bureau of Industrial Relations, Bulletin 27. Ann Arbor: University of Michigan, 1959.

Douglas, Ann. "The Peaceful Settlement of Industrial and Intergroup Disputes," *Journal of Conflict Resolution,* I (1957), 69-81.

————. *Industrial Peacemaking.* New York: Columbia University Press, 1962.

Duncanson, D. "School Board-Staff Relations," *The Teachers College Journal,* 37 (December, 1965), 101.

Dunlop, John T., and Healy, James J. *Collective Bargaining.* Homewood, Ill.: Richard D. Irwin, 1953.

Dykes, Archie R. *School Board and Superintendent: Their Effective Working Relationships.* Danville, Ill.: Interstate Printers and Publishers, 1965.

Educational Policies Commission. *The Public Interest in How Teachers Organize.* Washington, D.C.: National Education Association, 1964.

Elam, Stanley M. "NEA-AFT Merger—and Related Matters," *Phi Delta Kappan,* 47 (February, 1966), 285-86.

————. "Rift Without Differences," *The Nation,* October 18, 1965, 247-49.

————. "Union or Guild," *The Nation,* June 29, 1964, 651-53.

Eliot, Thomas H., Masters, Nicholas A., and Salisbury, Robert H. *State Politics and the Public Schools.* New York: Alfred A. Knopf, 1964.

Epstein, Benjamin. *The Principal's Role in Collective Negotiations Between Teachers and School Boards.* Washington, D.C.: National Association of Secondary-School Principals, 1965.

Evans, J. C., Jr. "Utah Teachers Pin Hope on New Strategy," *Phi Delta Kappan,* XLVI (September, 1964), 16.

Exton, Elaine. "NSBA Opposes Teachers' Strikes and Sanctions," *American School Board Journal,* CXLVI (June, 1963), 41, 44-46.

————. "Teacher Groups Challenge Lay School Board Control," *American School Board Journal,* CXLVII (August, 1963), 28-29.

————. "Pros and Cons of Sanctions Invoked by Utah's Public School Teachers," *American School Board Journal,* CXLVII (July, 1963), 35-37.

Follett, Mary Parker. *Dynamic Administration.* New York: Harper and Brothers, undated.

Foshay, Arthur W. (Ed.) *The Rand McNally Handbook of Education.* Chicago, Rand McNally, 1963.

Frankel, S. J., and Pratt, R. C. *Municipal Labour Relations in Canada.* Montreal: Canadian Federation of Mayors and Municipalities, 1954.

Garber, L. O. "How To Free Superintendents from Negotiation Hazards," *Nation's Schools,* 77 (March, 1966), 139.

————. *The Yearbook of School Law.* Danville, Ill.: Interstate Printers and Publishers, issued annually.

Godine, Morton R. *The Labor Problem in the Public Service.* Cambridge, Mass.: Harvard University Press, 1951.

Goff, Patrick. "The Social Status of Teachers," *Journal of Educational Sociology,* XXXVI, No. 1 (September, 1962), 20-26.

Goldhammer, Keith. *The School Board.* New York: Center for Applied Research in Education, 1964.

Government Employee Relations Report. Washington, D.C.: Bureau of National Affairs, issued weekly.

Gregory, C. O. *Labor and the Law.* New York: W. W. Norton, 1961.

Griffiths, Daniel E., Clark, David L., Wynn, D. Richard, and Iannaccone, Laurence. *Organizing Schools for Effective Education.* Danville, Ill.: Interstate Printers and Publishers, 1961.

Gross, Calvin. "Ways To Deal with the New Teacher Militancy," *Phi Delta Kappan,* XLVI, No. 4 (December, 1964), 147-51.

Gross, Neal. *Who Runs Our Schools?* New York: John Wiley and Sons, 1958.

————, and Herriott, Robert E. *Staff Leadership in Public Schools.* New York: John Wiley and Sons, 1965.

————, Mason, Ward, and McEachern, Alexander. *Explorations in Role Analysis.* New York: John Wiley and Sons, 1958.

Harbison, Frederick H., and Coleman, John R. *Goals and Strategy in Collective Bargaining.* New York: Harper and Brothers, 1951.

Harris, Ben M. *Supervisory Behavior in Education.* Englewood Cliffs, N.J.: Prentice-Hall, 1963.

Hart, Wilson R. *Collective Bargaining in the Federal Civil Service.* New York: Harper and Brothers, 1961.

————. "The U.S. Civil Service Learns To Live with Executive Order 10988: An Interim Appraisal," *Industrial and Labor Relations Review,* 17, No. 2 (January, 1964), 203-20.

————. "The Impasse in Labor Relations in the Federal Civil Service," *Industrial and Labor Relations Review,* 19 (January, 1966), 175-91.

Hazelton, Paul. "Education and Politics," *Saturday Review* (June 15, 1963), 62-63, 81-83.

Healy, James J. (Ed.) *Creative Collective Bargaining: Today's Challenge to Labor-Management Relations.* Englewood Cliffs, N.J.: Prentice-Hall, 1965.

Hechinger, F. M. "The Story Behind the Strike," *Saturday Review,* May 5, 1962, 54-56.

Herman, Edward E. "Bargaining by Civil Servants in Canada," *Monthly Labor Review,* LXXXIX (June, 1966), 603-606.

Hopkins, J. "Review of Events in Professional Negotiations," *Theory into Practice,* IV (April, 1965), 1-4.

Ingerman, Sidney. "Employed Graduate Students Organize at Berkeley," *Industrial Relations,* 5, No. 1 (October, 1965), 141-50.

Johnson, R. A., and Hill, Walter A. "Management's Dilemma—The Professional Employee," *California Management Review,* V (Spring, 1963), 37-46.

Kassalow, Everett M. "Prospects for White-Collar Union Growth," *Industrial Relations,* 5 (October, 1965), 37-47.

Kaufman, Jacob J. "Compulsory Arbitration: Other Perspectives," *Industrial and Labor Relations Review,* 18 (July, 1965), 588-90.

Kennan, R. B. "Sanctions Are Effective," *NEA Journal,* 54 (November, 1965), 68.

Kerr, Clark. *Labor and Management in Industrial Society.* New York: Doubleday, 1964.

Kershaw, Joseph A., and McKean, Ronald N. *Teacher Shortages and Salary Schedules.* New York: McGraw-Hill Book Company, 1962.

Kimball, Solon T., and McClellan, James E., Jr. *Education and the New America.* New York: Random House, Inc., 1962.

Kimbrough, Ralph B. *Political Power and Educational Decision-Making.* Chicago: Rand McNally, 1964.

Klaus, Ida. *Collective Bargaining Will Help Staff Morale.* New York: Society for the Experimental Study of Education, Yearbook, 1963.

————. "Collective Bargaining by Government Employees," *Proceedings,* Twelfth Annual Conference on Labor, New York University, 21, 1959.

————. "Labor Relations in the Public Service: Exploration and Experiment," *Syracuse Law Review,* 183, 1959.

Kuhn, James W. *Bargaining in Grievance Settlement.* New York: Columbia University Press, 1961.

Labor Law Course. Chicago, Ill.: Commerce Clearing House, Inc., 1965.

Leiserson, William A. *American Trade Union Democracy.* New York: Columbia University Press, 1959.

Levin, Noel Arnold. *Successful Labor Relations.* New York: Fairchild Publications, 1963.

Lieberman, Myron. *Education as a Profession.* Englewood Cliffs, N.J.: Prentice-Hall, 1956.

————. "Teachers Choose a Union," *The Nation,* 193, No. 19, 443-47.

————. "Teachers' Strikes: An Analysis of the Issues," *Harvard Educational Review,* 26 (Winter, 1956), 39-70.

————. *The Future of Public Education.* Chicago: University of Chicago Press, 1960.

————. "Influences of Teachers' Organization upon American Education," in Nelson B. Henry (Ed.), *Social Forces Influencing American Education.* Chicago: National Society for the Study of Education, 1961, 182-202.

————. "Battle for New York City's Teachers," *Phi Delta Kappan,* XLIII (October, 1961), 2-8.

————. "Teachers' Strikes: Acceptable Strategy?" *Phi Delta Kappan,* XLVI (January, 1965), 237-40.

————. "Teachers on the March," *The Nation,* February 1, 1965, 107-10.

————. "Who Speaks for Teachers?" *Saturday Review,* June 19, 1965, 64-66.

————, and Moskow, Michael. *Collective Negotiations for Teachers: An Approach to School Administration.* Chicago: Rand McNally, 1966.

MacDonald, Lois. *Leadership Dynamics and the Trade Union Leader.* New York: New York University Press, 1959.

Macy, John W., Jr. "The Federal Employee-Management Cooperation Program," *Industrial and Labor Relations Review,* XIX (July, 1966), 549-61.

Martin, T. D., *et al.* "Compulsory Membership in Teachers Associations? A Symposium," *Phi Delta Kappan,* 33 (September, 1951), 56-64.

Maxwell, James A. *Financing State and Local Governments.* Washington, D.C.: The Brookings Institution, 1965.

McKersie, Robert B., Perry, Charles R., and Walton, Richard E., "Intraorganizational Bargaining in Labor Negotiations," *Journal of Conflict Resolution,* IX (December, 1965), 463-81.

Megel, Carl J. "Teacher Conscription—Basis of Association Membership?" *Teachers College Record,* LXVI, No. 1 (October, 1964), 7-17.

Millis, Harry A., and Brown, Emily C. *From the Wagner Act to Taft-Hartley.* Chicago: University of Chicago Press, 1950.

Mills, C. Wright. *White Collar.* New York: Oxford University Press, 1951.

Miner, Jerry. *Social and Economic Factors in Spending for Public Education.* Syracuse, N.Y.: Syracuse University Press, 1963.

Moffitt, J. C. "Sanctions Do What?" *American School Board Journal,* CXLIX (September, 1964), 25-26.

Moskow, Michael H. "Collective Bargaining for Public School Teachers," *Labor Law Journal,* XV, No. 12 (December, 1964), 787-94.

———. "Collective Bargaining for Public School Teachers," *Monthly Labor Review,* LXXXVII, No. 11 (November, 1964), 1297-98.

———. "Recent Legislation Affecting Collective Negotiations for Teachers," *Phi Delta Kappan,* XLVII, No. 3 (November, 1965), 136-41.

———. "Representation Among Teachers," *Monthly Labor Review,* LXVI (July, 1966), 728-32.

———. *Teachers and Unions: The Applicability of Collective Bargaining to Public Education.* Philadelphia, Pa.: Industrial Research Unit, University of Pennsylvania, 1966.

National Education Association. *Addresses and Proceedings.* Washington, D.C.: National Education Association, published annually.

———. *NEA Handbook.* Washington, D.C.: National Education Association, published annually.

———. Commission on Professional Rights and Responsibilities. *Guidelines for Professional Sanctions.* Washington, D.C.: National Education Association, November, 1963.

———. A Report of an Investigation. *Oklahoma: A State-wide Study of Conditions Detrimental to an Effective Public Educational Program.* Washington, D.C.: National Education Association, February, 1965.

———. A Report of an Investigation. *Utah: A State-wide Study of School Conditions.* Washington, D.C.: National Education Association, March, 1964.

———. A Report of an Investigation. *Waterbury, Connecticut: A Study of the Inhibiting Effect of Political Control on the Quality of Education.* Washington, D.C.: National Education Association, May, 1963.

———. Department of Classroom Teachers. *Classroom Teachers Speak on Professional Negotiations.* Washington, D.C.: National Education Association, 1963.

———. Office of Professional Development and Welfare. *Professional Negotiation: Selected Statements of School Board, Administrator, Teacher Relationships.* Washington, D.C.: National Education Association, 1965.

———. *Guidelines for Professional Negotiation.* Washington, D.C.: National Education Association, 1965.

———. Salary Consultant Service. *The Use of Index Ratios To Determine Salary and Salary Schedules of Supervisory and Administrative Personnel.* Washington, D.C.: National Education Association, Salary Consultant Service, undated.

National Labor Relations Board. *Annual Report for the Fiscal Year.* Washington, D.C.: Government Printing Office, issued annually.

National School Boards Association. *Report on State Survey on Board-Administrator-Teacher Relations.* Chicago, Ill.: National School Boards Association, April 24, 1964.

———. *Convention Proceedings.* Evanston, Ill.: National School Boards Association, published annually.

"NEA Removes Sanctions Against Oklahoma; More Bargaining Elections, Strikes Expected." *American School and University,* 38 (November, 1965), 24.

"Negotiating with Teachers," *School Management,* IX (May, 1965), 81-87.

"New Targets for Teachers' Union," *U.S. News and World Report,* 60 (June 31, 1966), 80.

Nolte, M. C. "Is the Board an Employer Under a State's Labor Relations Law?" *American School Board Journal,* 151 (September, 1965), 9-10. Same, *Education Digest,* 31 (January, 1966), 34-35.

———. "Teacher Militancy May Be Counter-Pressure," *American School Board Journal,* CLI (October, 1965), 7-8.

———. "Teachers Seek Greater Independence Through Legislative Channels," *American School Board Journal,* 152 (March, 1966), 7-9.

Northrup, Herbert R. *Boulwarism.* Ann Arbor: Bureau of Industrial Relations, University of Michigan, 1964.

———, and Bloom, Gordon F. *Government and Labor.* Homewood, Ill.: Richard D. Irwin, 1963.

Oakes, R. C. "Should Teachers Strike? An Unanswered Question," *Journal of Educational Sociology,* XXXIII (March, 1960), 339-44.

Olson, Mancur, Jr. *The Logic of Collective Action.* Cambridge, Mass.: Harvard University Press, 1965.

Perry, C. R. "School Board-Staff Negotiations," *Teachers College Journal,* 37 (December, 1965), 103-109.

Phelps, Orme W. "Compulsory Arbitration: Some Perspectives," *Industrial and Labor Relations Review,* 18 (October, 1964), 81-91.

President's Task Force on Employee-Management Relations in the Federal Service. *A Policy for Employee-Management Cooperation in the Federal Service.* Washington, D.C.: Government Printing Office, 1961.

"Professional Sanctions; Teacher Opinion Poll," *NEA Journal,* 54 (November, 1965), 68.

Radke, Mrs. Fred A. "Real Significance of Collective Bargaining for Teachers," *Labor Law Journal,* 15 (December, 1964), 795-801.

Ray, W. "Membership in the National Union of Teachers," *British Journal of Industrial Relations,* 2 (July, 1964), 189-208.

Report of the Special Committee on Collective Bargaining Between School Trustees and Teachers, Sessional Paper No. 85, 1965. Edmonton, Alberta: Alberta Legislative Assembly, 1965.

Report on Salary Negotiations Machinery for Teachers. Washington, D.C.: World Confederation of Organizations of the Teaching Profession, 1960.

"Representation of Economic Interests," *AAUP Bulletin,* LII (June, 1966), 229-34.

Research Division, National Education Association. *Economic Status of Teachers.* Washington, D.C.: National Education Association, published annually.

———. *Estimates of School Statistics.* Washington, D.C.: National Education Association, published annually.

———. "Fiscal Authority of School Boards," *Research Bulletin.* Washington, D.C.: National Education Association, April, 1950.

———. *The American Public School Teacher, 1960-61.* Washington, D.C.: National Education Association, 1964.

———. *Local Associations, Organization, Practices, and Programs, 1958-59.* Washington, D.C.: National Education Association, 1960.

———. *Personnel Administration in Urban School Districts, 1961-62.* Washington, D.C.: National Education Association, 1963.

———. *Professional Negotiation with School Boards: A Legal Analysis and Review.* Washington, D.C.: National Education Association, 1965.

———. *Teacher Supply and Demand in Public Schools.* Washington, D.C.: National Education Association, published annually.

Rice, A. H. "NEA Assigns Administrators to Second Class Membership," *Nation's Schools,* LXXVI (September, 1965), 38.

————."Teacher Unrest Has Damaged School Public Relations," *Nation's Schools,* LXXV (March, 1965), 46-47.

Rich, J. M. "Civil Disobedience and Teacher Strikes," *Phi Delta Kappan,* XLV (December, 1963), 151-54.

Roach, S. P. "Collective Bargaining," *School Management,* 10 (March, 1966), 66.

Rock, Eli. "Practical Labor Relations in the Public Service," *Public Personnel Review,* 18 (April, 1957), 71-80.

————. "Research on Municipal Collective Bargaining," *Monthly Labor Review,* LXXXIX (June, 1966), 615-16.

Ross, Arthur M., and Hartman, Paul T. *Changing Patterns of Industrial Conflict.* New York & London: John Wiley and Sons, 1960.

Sayles, Leonard R., and Strauss, George. *The Local Union.* New York: Harper and Row, 1953.

Scanlon, John. "Strikes, Sanctions, and the Schools," *Saturday Review* (October, 1963), 51-55.

Schnaufer, Pete. "Response from the AFT," *Monthly Labor Review,* LXXXIX (June, 1966), 620-21.

————. *The Uses of Teacher Power.* Chicago: American Federation of Teachers, March, 1966.

Schneider, B. V. H. "Collective Bargaining and the Federal Civil Service," *Industrial Relations,* III, No. 3 (May, 1964), 97-120.

Seitz, C. Reynolds. "School Boards and Teachers Unions," *American School Board Journal,* CXXVI (August, 1960), 11-13.

————. "Rights of Public School Teachers To Engage in Collective Bargaining and Other Concerted Activities," *1963 Yearbook of School Law.* Danville, Ill.: Interstate Printers and Publishers, 1963, 204-222.

Selden, David. "Class Size and the New York Contract," *Phi Delta Kappan,* XLVI (March, 1964), 283-87.

————. "Why the AFT Maintains Its AFL-CIO Affiliation," *Phi Delta Kappan,* XLVII (February, 1966), 298-300. Same, *Education Digest,* 31 (April, 1966), 19-21.

Selekman, Benjamin, M. *Labor Relations and Human Relations.* New York: McGraw-Hill Book Company, 1947.

Shenton, David G. "Compulsory Arbitration in the Public Service," *Labor Law Journal,* XVII (March, 1966), 138-47.

Shoben, E. J. "When Teachers Strike," *Teachers College Record,* LXV (November, 1963), 164-67.

Simon, Kenneth A., and Fullam, Marie G. *Projections of Educational Statistics to 1973-74.* U.S. Department of Health, Education, and Welfare Circular No. 754. Washington, D.C.: Government Printing Office, 1964.

Slichter, Sumner, H., Healy, James J., and Livernash, Robert E. *The Impact of Collective Bargaining on Management.* Washington, D.C.: The Brookings Institution, 1960.

Smith, Russell A., and Burns, Robert K. "Unionization of White-Collar Employees: Extent, Potential and Implications," Reprint Series No. 110, Reprinted from *The Journal of Business of the University of Chicago,* XXXVI, No. 2 (April, 1963), Industrial Relations Center, University of Chicago.

Solberg, James G. "Response from a School Board Member," *Monthly Labor Review,* LXXXIX (June, 1966), 622-23.

Spero, Sterling D. *Government as Employer.* New York: Remsen Press, 1948.

Stahl, Glenn O. *Public Personnel Administration.* 5th Ed. New York: Harper and Row, 1962.

Steet, Marion L. "Professional Associations—More Than Unions," *Teachers College Record,* LXVI, No. 3 (December, 1964), 203-18.

Steffensen, James P. *Teachers Negotiate with Their School Boards.* USOE Bulletin No. 40. Washington, D.C.: Government Printing Office, 1964.

Stevens, Carl M. "Is Compulsory Arbitration Compatible with Bargaining?" *Industrial Relations,* V (February, 1966), 38-52.

Stiles, Lindley J. "Ideas from Abroad for Winning Teacher Loyalty," *Phi Delta Kappan,* XLV (March, 1964), 278-82.

Stinnett, T. M. "Professional Negotiation, Collective Bargaining, Sanctions, and Strikes," *Bulletin of the National Association of Secondary-School Principals,* XLVII (April, 1964), 93-105.

———, and Huggett, Albert J. *Professional Problems of Teachers.* New York: Macmillan Company, 1963.

———, Kleinmann, Jack, and Ware, Martha. *Professional Negotiation in Public Education.* New York: Macmillan Company, 1966.

Story, H. W. "Collective Bargaining with Teachers Under Wisconsin Law," *Theory into Practice,* IV (April, 1965), 61-65.

———. "Collective Bargaining Under Wisconsin Law," *Teachers College Journal,* 37 (December, 1965), 110-15.

Strauss, George. "Professionalism and Occupational Associations," *Personnel Administrator,* 9 (March-April, 1964), 17-23, 31; 9 (May-June, 1964).

———. "Professionalism and Occupational Associations," *Industrial Relations,* II, No. 3 (May, 1963), 7-31.

Stumpf, W. A. "New World of Educational Administration: Teacher Militancy," *American School Board Journal,* 152 (February, 1966), 10.

Tannenbaum, Arnold S., and Kahn, Robert K. *Participation in Union Locals.* Evanston, Ill.: Row, Peterson, 1958.

Taylor, George W. *Government Regulation of Industrial Relations.* New York: Prentice-Hall, 1948.

———, and Pierson, Frank C. (Eds.) *New Concepts in Wage Determination.* New York: McGraw-Hill Book Company, 1957.

"Teacher Opinion Poll: All Inclusive v. Restricted Local Associations," *NEA Journal,* 54 (December, 1965), 58.

"Teacher Opinion Poll: Professional Sanctions," *NEA Journal,* 54 (November, 1965), 68.

Turnbaugh, R. C. "How To Set Teacher Negotiation Policy," *Nation's Schools,* 77 (March, 1966), 134+.

Turnbull, John G. "The Management Prerogative Issues," *Personnel* (September, 1962), 106-24.

"Union Activity in Public Employment," *Columbia Law Review,* LV (March, 1955), 343-66.

U.S. Civil Service Commission, *Employee Management Cooperation in the Federal Service.* Personnel Methods Series No. 15. Washington, D.C.: Government Printing Office, 1962.

U.S. Department of Health, Education, and Welfare, Office of Education. *Digest of Educational Statistics*. Washington, D.C.: Government Printing Office, issued annually.

U.S. Department of Labor, Bureau of Labor Statistics. *Work Stoppages Involving Teachers, 1940-62*. Washington, D.C.: Government Printing Office, November, 1963.

————. *Glossary of Current Industrial Relations and Wage Terms*. Bulletin 1438. Washington, D.C.: Government Printing Office, 1963.

Unruh, A. "Negotiations and the Role of the Superintendent," *Educational Forum*, XXIX (January, 1965), 165-69.

Vosloo, William B. *Collective Bargaining in the United States Federal Civil Service*. Chicago, Ill.: Public Personnel Association, 1966.

Walton, Richard E. *The Impact of the Professional Engineering Union*. Boston: Division of Research, Graduate School of Business Administration, Harvard University, 1961.

————, and McKersie, Robert B. *A Behavioral Theory of Labor Negotiations*. New York: McGraw-Hill Book Company, 1965.

Warner, Kenneth O. *Management Relations with Organized Public Employees*. Chicago, Ill.: Public Personnel Association, 1963.

Washington Education Association. *Guidelines for Professional Negotiation*. Seattle: Washington Education Association, 1965.

Weisenfeld, Allan. "Collective Bargaining by Public Employees," *Monthly Labor Review*, LXXXIX (June, 1966), 610-12.

————. "Public Employees—First or Second Class Citizens," *Labor Law Journal*, XVI (November, 1965), 685-704.

Wesley, Edgar B. *NEA: The First Hundred Years*. New York: Harper and Brothers, 1957.

"WERB Decision Highlights," *Wisconsin Journal of Education*, 98 (October, 1965), 16-17.

West, Allan M. "The NEA Tackles Urban Problems," *Phi Delta Kappan*, XLVI (March, 1964), 293-96.

————. "What Is the Professional Services Campaign?" *NEA Journal*, 55 (February, 1966), 27-28.

White, Alpheus L. *Local School Boards: Organization and Practices*. U.S. Office of Education, U.S. Department of Health, Education, and Welfare. Washington, D.C.: Government Printing Office, 1962.

Wildman, Wesley A. "Collective Action by Public School Teachers," *Industrial and Labor Relations Review*, XVIII, No. 1 (October, 1964), 3-19.

————. "Conflict Issues in Negotiations," *Monthly Labor Review*, LXXXIX (June, 1966), 617-20.

————. "Implications of Teacher Bargaining for School Administration," *Phi Delta Kappan*, XLVI, No. 4 (December, 1964), 152-58.

Wollett, Donald H. *Professional Negotiations: What Is This Thing?* Washington, D.C.: National Education Association, 1964. (Mimeographed)

Wolpert, Arnold W. "Response from the NEA," *Monthly Labor Review*, LXXXIX (June, 1966), 621-22.

Wyatt, R. A., and Thornberry, R. "Viewpoints on Negotiations Vary," *Teachers College Journal*, 37 (December, 1965), 102+.

Ziskind, David. *One Thousand Strikes of Government Employees*. New York: Columbia University Press, 1940.

NAME INDEX

SUBJECT INDEX

A.A.A., *See:* American Arbitration Association

A.A.S.A., *See:* American Association of School Administrators

A.A.U.P., *See:* American Association of University Professors

A.B.A., *See:* American Bar Association

Academic freedom, 33, 38, 41, 43
  See also: American Association of University Professors

Academic institutions:
  creativity in, 54
  mediocrity in, 54

Accreditation, school, 71

Adult education, 15

Administration, 10
  and collective negotiations, 275–330
  dynamic, 442

Administrative:
  authority, 308–9
  domination, 241–42
  domination of medical associations, 232
  inefficiency, 41
  training programs, 64

Administrators, viii, 36
  benevolent methods of, 62
  conflict with teachers, 79, 288
  in hospitals, 63
  separate negotiation units in Connecticut, 119–21
  supervision of professional employees, 54

Advisory arbitration, 92, 105, 283, 322, 409
  See also: Arbitration, Arbitrators, Mediation, Fact-finding

A.F.L., *See:* American Federation of Labor

A.F.L.–C.I.O., *See:* American Federation of Labor–Congress of Industrial Organizations

A.F.S.C.M.E., *See:* American Federation of State, County, and Municipal Employees

A.F.T., *See:* American Federation of Teachers

Agreements, 26
  See also: Written agreements

Alberta, 129, 139
  collective negotiation statute, 133
  economic seminar, 141
  strikes in, 138

Alberta School Trustees Association, 144, 222

Alberta Teachers' Association (ATA), viii, 133, 219–26, 266–68, 430
  achievements of, 221–23
  history of, 220–21
  influence of, 226
  policy on unionism, 225

A.M.A., *See:* American Medical Association

American Arbitration Association (AAA), 118, 191, 335
  activities in Connecticut, 118–20
  case load, 315
  election procedures, 316–22
  role in collective negotiations, 314–22
  role in public education, ix

American Association of School Administrators (AASA), 144, 187, 243, 383, 439
  policy on arbitration, 211

Labor movement, 152
Labor negotiations, *See:* Negotiating strategy and tactics
Landrum-Griffith Act, 111
Leadership dynamics, 444
Leaflets, 169
Legal aspects of teacher collective action, *See:* Collective negotiation, legal aspects
League of Women Voters, 78, 100
Legislation on collective negotiations:
in Canada, 129, 132
mandatory, 29
permissive, 29
See also: Collective negotiation statutes
Legislators, attitudes of, 81
Length of school day, 423
Little Lake, California, 159
Lobbyist, 27, 30, 31, 69, 70
AFL–CIO, 76
Chamber of Commerce, 76
Illinois, 75
Illinois Education Association, 76
Michigan Education Association, 75–6
Missouri, 75
Missouri State Teachers Association, 76
National Education Association, 76
teacher organizations, 70
teacher unions, 78
Local autonomy, 12
Local education associations, *See:* American Federation of Teachers, National Education Association, Teacher organizations, and names of specific organizations
Local government employees, number of, 6
Los Angeles, California, 97, 270
Louisville, Kentucky, 15
Lunchroom employees, 107

Majority representative, 87
in public schools, 89
Majority rights, 240
Majority rule, 19
Managerial inefficiency, 41
Managerial prerogatives, 8, 91, 448

Management, speaking for, 287–90
Manchester, Connecticut, 114
Manitoba, Canada, 129
collective negotiation statute, 134
Market place, restraints, 15
Massachusetts, 70
collective negotiation statute, 103
Mediation, 92, 112, 164, 283, 426–28
authority of representative, 427
Connecticut statute, 117
how initiated, 427
intra-union, 21
who should mediate, 426–27
Wisconsin, 104
Membership lists, 163
Membership standards, *See:* American Association of University Professors
Membership in teacher organizations, *See:* Teacher organizations
Merger, prospects for, 269–73
Meriden, Connecticut, 96, 114
Merit pay, 325
Michigan, 5, 57, 70, 72–84, 186, 298
Attorney General, 90
fiscal matters, 80
Labor Mediation Board, 70, 123–27
Public Employment Relations Act, 123
State Legislature, 75
teacher strike in, 126
unfair labor practice charges, 127
unity in state legislature, 79
Michigan collective negotiation statute, vii, 103, 123–27
Cease and Desist Orders, 124
decertification elections, 124
enforcement of, 125
fact-finding under, 125
lack of experience under, 126
mediation under, 125
run-off elections, 124
strikes under, 125
unfair labor practices, 124–25
Michigan Education Association, 125, 168, 359
Michigan Federation of Labor, 78
Michigan Federation of Teachers, 77, 125
Militancy, 33, 256
Militant professionalism, 51

#70·7230

Printed in U.S.A.